Historical Dialectology in the Digital Age

HISTORICAL DIALECTOLOGY IN THE DIGITAL AGE

Edited by Rhona Alcorn, Joanna Kopaczyk,
Bettelou Los and Benjamin Molineaux

EDINBURGH
University Press

Edinburgh University Press is one of the leading university presses in the UK. We publish academic books and journals in our selected subject areas across the humanities and social sciences, combining cutting-edge scholarship with high editorial and production values to produce academic works of lasting importance. For more information visit our website: edinburghuniversitypress.com

© editorial matter and organisation Rhona Alcorn, Joanna Kopaczyk, Bettelou Los and Benjamin Molineaux, 2019, 2020
© the chapters their several authors, 2019, 2020

Edinburgh University Press Ltd
The Tun – Holyrood Road,
12(2f) Jackson's Entry,
Edinburgh EH8 8PJ

First published in hardback by Edinburgh University Press 2019

Typeset in Ehrhardt MT Pro by
Servis Filmsetting Ltd, Stockport, Cheshire

A CIP record for this book is available from the British Library

ISBN 978 1 4744 3053 1 (hardback)
ISBN 978 1 4744 3054 8 (paperback)
ISBN 978 1 4744 3055 5 (webready PDF)
ISBN 978 1 4744 3056 2 (epub)

The right of Rhona Alcorn, Joanna Kopaczyk, Bettelou Los and Benjamin Molineaux to be identified as the editors of this work has been asserted in accordance with the Copyright, Designs and Patents Act 1988, and the Copyright and Related Rights Regulations 2003 (SI No. 2498).

Contents

List of Figures and Tables	vii
Notes on Editors	xi
Notes on Contributors	xiii
Preface	xvi
Acknowledgements	xvii

1 Historical Dialectology and the Angus McIntosh Legacy   1
   Rhona Alcorn, Joanna Kopaczyk, Bettelou Los and Benjamin Molineaux

Part I Creating and Mining Digital Resources

2 A Parsed Linguistic Atlas of Early Middle English   19
   Robert Truswell, Rhona Alcorn, James Donaldson and Joel Wallenberg
3 Approaching Transition Scots from a Micro-perspective: The
   Dunfermline Corpus, 1573–1723   39
   Klaus Hofmann
4 Early Spelling Evidence for Scots L-vocalisation: A Corpus-based
   Approach   61
   *Benjamin Molineaux, Joanna Kopaczyk, Warren Maguire, Rhona Alcorn,
   Vasilis Karaiskos and Bettelou Los*

Part II Segmental Histories

5 Old and Middle English Spellings for OE *hw-*, with Special Reference
   to the 'qu-' Type: In Celebration of LAEME, (e)LALME, LAOS and
   CoNE   91
   Margaret Laing and Roger Lass

6	The Development of Old English *ǣ*: Middle English Spelling Evidence *Gjertrud F. Stenbrenden*	113
7	The Development of Old English *eo/ēo* and the Systematicity of Middle English Spelling *Merja Stenroos*	133
8	Examining the Evidence for Phonemic Affricates: Middle English /t͡ʃ/, /d͡ʒ/ or [t-ʃ], [d-ʒ]? *Donka Minkova*	156

Part III Placing Features in Context

9	The Predictability of {S} Abbreviation in Older Scots Manuscripts According to Stem-final *Littera* *Daisy Smith*	187
10	An East Anglian Poem in a London Manuscript? The Date and Dialect of *The Court of Love* in Cambridge, Trinity College, MS R.3.19 *Ad Putter*	212
11	'He was a good hammer, was he': Gender as Marker for South-Western Dialects of English. A Corpus-based Study from a Diachronic Perspective *Trinidad Guzmán-González*	244

Index 266

List of Figures and Tables

Figures

2.1 An example of a full sentence token in PPCHE format, represented as a tree diagram — 21
2.2 Material from the PPCHE (in blue) is complemented by material from PLAEME (in red) — 26
2.3 Competing expressions of sentential negation in Middle English. Vertical lines indicate the PLAEME window. The dashed lines represent lowess regression lines taking only PPCHE data into account. The solid lines are based on both PPCHE and PLAEME data — 30
2.4 Competition between recipient–theme ditransitives with and without *to* in Middle and Early Modern English. The vertical lines indicate the PLAEME window. The dashed curve represents the fit from the Probability Multiplication Model adopted by Bacovcin (2017). The solid line represents the fit from the same model to PPCHE, PCMEP and PLAEME data combined — 32
2.5 Use of *wh*-forms in argument-gap headed relative clauses in Middle and Early Modern English. Vertical lines indicate the PLAEME window. The dashed and solid lowess regression lines (PPCHE data only and PPCHE + PLAEME data combined) are virtually identical — 35
3.1 Town clerks and assistant scribes in the Dunfermline court and council records — 48
3.2 Anglicisation in the *Dunfermline Corpus* (relative frequencies) — 52
3.3 Distribution of past suffix variants in the *Dunfermline Corpus* — 55
3.4 Distribution of past suffix variants according to stem-final segment, pre-war group (D, E, E') — 56
3.5 Distribution of past suffix variants according to stem-final segment, post-war group (H, H') — 56

4.1	The diachronic development of V6 (Aitken 1977; Aitken and Macafee 2002; Macafee 2003) and its enrichment by members of V19 set due to LV	65
4.2	The diachronic development of V12 (Aitken 1977; Aitken and Macafee 2002; Macafee 2003) and its enrichment by members of V17 set due to LV	66
4.3	The diachronic development of V13 (Aitken 1977; Aitken and Macafee 2002; Macafee 2003) and its enrichment by members of V18 set due to LV	66
4.4	Relative proportions of <l>-less and <l>-ful spellings by morphemes presenting <l>-less spellings, with a total number of attestations for each morpheme	75
4.5	Distribution of <l>-ful and <l>-less spellings in words with <l>-less forms attested in the FITS Corpus, by decade. The black line represents a density plot for the temporal distribution of the overall number of words in the entire corpus	76
4.6	Regional distribution of <l>-less spellings in view of regional coverage in the corpus: <l>-less spellings in LV contexts are given in red, with exact counts in black. The overall density of words by location is given in blue	77
4.7	Attested spellings with and without <l>, by phonological environment	78
4.8	Comparison of tokens for morphemes with <l>-less forms attested and not attested in pre-coronal contexts	79
4.9	Back-spellings: Germanic vocabulary with an unetymological <l>	81
4.10	Proportions of unetymological <l> in Germanic roots	81
4.11	Romance morphemes with <l>-less and <l>-ful spellings	83
7.1	The counties where texts with <eo> type spellings are localised in LALME (map outline: Abigail Brady)	142
7.2	Proportions of <eo> and <e> type spellings of Old English *eo/ēo* words in those texts in which <eo> type spellings appear, arranged according to county	142
7.3	Proportions of <eo> and <e> type spellings of Old English *eo/ēo* words (not including SHE) in those texts in which <eo> type spellings appear, arranged according to county	143
7.4	The distribution of <eo> type spellings in texts localised in the nine South-West Midland counties (average of proportional figures per text)	144
7.5	The distribution of <eo> type spellings per half-century (average of proportional figures per text)	145
7.6	Proportions of <eo> and <e> type spellings of Old English *eo/ēo* words in those individual texts in which <eo> type spellings appear, arranged according to (approximate) quarter-century	145
7.7	Proportions of <eo> and <e> type spellings of Old English *eo/ēo* words (not including SHE) in those texts in which <eo> type spellings appear, arranged according to (approximate) quarter-century	146
7.8	Proportions of <eo> and <e> type spellings of Old English *eo/ēo* words	

	in those texts in which <eo> type spellings appear: comparing the individual texts	147
8.1	The early ME septenary line	166
9.1	<(com)moditʃ> *commodities*. LAOS text 36: liferent from Dirleton, East Lothian. May 1447. (Source: Edinburgh University Centre for Research Collections (CRC))	189
9.2	Extract from LAOS text 36: liferent from Dirleton, East Lothian. May 1447. (Source: Edinburgh University Centre for Research Collections (CRC))	192
9.3	Illustration of palaeographic forms of the {S} abbreviation over time (Johnson and Jenkinson 1915: 63)	193
9.4	The likelihood of npl {S} token to be realised as <ʃ> over the period 1380–1500 (shading represents 95% confidence interval)	203
9.5	The likelihood of {S} being realised as <ʃ> over the geographical area represented by LAOS: black dots represent locations of individual texts, red shading represents a higher likelihood of <ʃ>, blue shading represents a lower likelihood of <ʃ>	203
9.6	The percentage of {S} tokens belonging to each 'type' category realised as <ʃ> (tokens from texts with no type specified excluded)	204
9.7	The percentage of {S} tokens realised as <ʃ> following each SFL	206
9.8	The path of a pen-stroke for stem-final <dʃ> and <nis>	208
10.1	eLALME dot map for <o> spellings in MAN, CAN, BEGAN	228
10.2	eLALME dot map for <e> spellings in LIKE, RICH, SHINE	231
10.3	eLALME dot map for <e> spellings in FIRE, DID, MIND	232
10.4	eLALME dot map for spellings of MIGHT indicating loss of fricative	234

Tables

3.1	Occurrence of English variants in the *Dunfermline Corpus* (raw frequencies)	51
3.2	Distribution of past suffix variants in the *Dunfermline Corpus*	54
4.1	Aitken's (1977) outline of V6, V12 and V13	69
4.2	Aitken's (1981) outline of V6, V12 and V13	70
4.3	Potential LV contexts in the FITS database	74
4.4	FITS morphemes by grapho-phonological context fitting the LV environments	78
4.5	Back-spelling environments by phonological context	80
4.6	Romance items in the LAOS Corpus by grapho-phonological context fitting the LV environments	82
4.7	Back-spellings: Romance vocabulary with an unetymological <l>	83
4.8	Potential contexts for back-spellings (sample words with stressed V6, V12 and V13) in Romance vocabulary	84
6.1	Incidence of <æ> for OE ǣ in LAEME sources dated after 1200	116
6.2	Early vowel-shift spellings for OE ǣ (LAEME, SMED)	123
6.3	LAEME spellings for OE ǣ^1 and OE ǣ^2, by area and date	127

6.4	LAEME spellings for OE $\bar{æ}^1$ and OE $\bar{æ}^2$, by county	128
6.5	LAEME <e> spellings for OE $\bar{æ}^1$ in early sources (before AD 1200)	129
6.6	Incidence of <ai/ay>, <æi>, <ei> for OE $\bar{æ}^1$ and OE $\bar{æ}^2$ in LAEME	130
7.1	Spelling units used for the vowel element in the twenty-seven questionnaire items: number of texts and tokens and distribution in terms of items	140
7.2	The texts with the highest proportion of <eo> type spellings	148
8.1	Texts frequencies of consonants in General British: percentages of consonants among all phonemes and among consonants only (adapted from Cruttenden 2014: 235). Total all consonants: 60.6 per cent	158
8.2	Frequencies of word-final consonants in English (percentages from Muthmann 1999: 404). Total all word-final consonants: 84.92 per cent	159
8.3	Frequencies of word-initial consonants in English (percentages from Hayes 2011)	159
8.4	Duration of PDE contour segments vs. bisegmental sequences in ms (from Minkova 2016)	170
8.5	Pre-affricates to affricates in Middle English (from Old English [c])	179
9.1	The frequency of different orthographic forms of {S} attested in LAOS	192
9.2	The structure of the dataset extracted from LAOS	194
9.3	The original categories of the SFL variable, and the frequency with which they occur in the dataset. Items below the dotted line were omitted due to low frequency	197
9.4	Frequency of text types attested in LAOS	199
9.5	Reduced typology of LAOS texts	200
9.6	Summary of a generalised additive model (GAM) of the likelihood of npl {S} abbreviation. $R^2 = 0.72$; deviance explained = 68%; n = 10,886	202
9.7	AIC scores for the full GAM model and nested models (a larger difference in AIC indicates more model improvement contributed by an IV)	205
9.8	Illustrations of SFL from LAOS manuscripts in word-final position and preceding {S}. (Sources: Scotland's Places (Historic Environment Scotland 2017); Edinburgh University CRC)	207
10.1	Authorial versus scribal forms	238
11.1	UARs and nouns in the corpus	252

Editors

Rhona Alcorn is a research fellow at the University of Edinburgh. Her research interests include the linguistics and language of Middle English and Older Scots and the structure of non-standard spelling systems. She is one of the compilers of the online *Corpus of Narrative Etymologies from Proto-Old English to Early Middle English* (2013) and currently (co-)leads several RCUK-funded projects, each based in the Angus McIntosh Centre for Historical Linguistics, of which she is Deputy Director. She teaches Middle English and the linguistic history of Scots and is the reviser of Richard Hogg's *Old English Syntax* (Edinburgh University Press 2013). Since September 2017 Rhona has been CEO and Editor-in-Chief of Scottish Language Dictionaries Ltd.

Joanna Kopaczyk is Lecturer in English Language and Linguistics at the University of Glasgow. She is a historical linguist with an interest in corpus methods, formulaic language, the history of Scots and historical multilingualism. She is author of *The Legal Language of Scottish Burghs* (Oxford University Press 2013) and co-edited *Binomials in the History of English* (with Hans Sauer, Cambridge University Press 2017) and *Communities of Practice in the History of English* (with Andreas H. Jucker, John Benjamins 2013).

Bettelou Los is Forbes Professor of English Language at the University of Edinburgh. Her publications include *The Rise of the To-Infinitive* (Oxford University Press 2005) and *A Historical Syntax of English* (Edinburgh University Press); with Ans van Kemenade, *The Handbook of the History of English* (Blackwell 2006); with Anneli Meurman-Solin and María José López-Couso, *Information Structure and Syntactic Change in the History of English* (Oxford University Press 2012). She co-authored *Morphosyntactic Change: A Comparative Study of Particles and Prefixes* (Cambridge University Press 2012). Her research interests are diachronic syntax, the history of English, and the role of information structure in syntactic change.

Benjamin Molineaux is a Leverhulme Early Career Fellow at the Angus McIntosh Centre for Historical Linguistics, the University of Edinburgh. His interests are in synchronic and diachronic phonology and morphology, with special emphasis on stress systems. He has published on these topics as applied to the history of English, Scots and Mapudungun (a language of Chile and Argentina). As one of the compilers of the From Inglis To Scots (FITS) database he has applied corpus methods to mapping the earliest sound-to-spelling correspondences in the history of Scots (1380–500). He is currently using the same methods to explore the 400-year history of Mapudungun, as part of the Corpus of Historical Mapudungun. He holds a doctorate from the University of Oxford.

Contributors

James Donaldson is a PhD student in Linguistics and English Language at the University of Edinburgh. He is currently working on anaphora and ellipsis. As a research assistant for the PLAEME project (A Parsed Linguistic Atlas of Early Middle English), he was responsible for correcting the automatic parsing of most of its texts (see Chapter 2, this volume, for details).

Trinidad Guzmán-González is Associate Professor in the Department of Modern Philology at the University of León (Spain) where she teaches History and Varieties of English. Her research focuses on historical English phonology and morphology, and also on the elaboration and analysis of lexical databases in specialised registers, and on anglicisms. She is the current Vice-President of the Institute for Medieval Studies of the University of León; she has chaired the Spanish Society for Mediaeval English Language and Literature, and has co-edited the society's journal.

Klaus Hofmann is a pre-doctoral assistant and doctoral candidate in English and American Studies at the University of Vienna. His research interests include historical phonology, language variation and change, and the study of late medieval manuscripts in Scots, English and German. His doctoral project is concerned with the relationship between word prosody and language rhythm in the history of English.

Vasilis Karaiskos is a research associate at the School of Informatics, University of Edinburgh. He is currently responsible for the digital aspects of the From Inglis to Scots (FITS) Project at the Angus McIntosh Centre for Historical Linguistics. He has previously contributed as a programmer in the production of other historical corpora (LAEME, eLALME, LAOS) at the University of Edinburgh. He is currently interested in finding useful ways to visualise the multiple layers of analysis of historical corpora.

Margaret Laing is a historical linguist and dialectologist whose academic career was at the University of Edinburgh, where she remains an Honorary Fellow. She has published extensively on medieval English including an important series of papers with Roger Lass. She is compiler of the online Linguistic Atlas of Early Middle English and a major contributor to the electronic version of A Linguistic Atlas of Late Mediaeval English and the Corpus of Narrative Etymologies from Proto-Old English to Early Middle English.

Roger Lass is a historical linguist specialising in earlier English and the relation of historical linguistics to philosophy of science. He taught at Indiana and Edinburgh and was Professor of Linguistics at the University of Cape Town 1982–2002. He edited and contributed two chapters to *The Cambridge History of the English Language* (III) and was Principal Investigator for the Corpus of Narrative Etymologies (CoNE). He has co-written a number of major papers with Margaret Laing since 2003, and is an Honorary Fellow of the University of Edinburgh.

Warren Maguire is a senior lecturer in English Language at the University of Edinburgh. He specialises in research on the synchronic and diachronic phonology of dialects of English and Scots (especially those of North-East England, southern Scotland and Ulster), and has been involved in the construction of several corpora of regional dialects of English (South-West Tyrone English, Tyneside English, and the dialect of the Holy Island of Lindisfarne). He has published papers on topics such as phonological merger, nineteenth-century dialectology, quantification of dialect similarity, Pre-R Dentalisation in English and Scots, and the linguistic situation, past and present, in Lowland Scotland. With colleagues at the University of Edinburgh, he is currently working on the From Inglis To Scots Corpus, a major project to unravel the phonological development of Older Scots.

Donka Minkova is a Distinguished Research Professor at UCLA, working on English historical phonology, metre, dialectology and syntax. Her publications include *The History of Final Vowels in English*; *English Words: History and Structure*; *Alliteration and Sound Change in Early English*; *A Historical Phonology of English*; and the edited volumes *Studies in the History of the English Language: A Millennial Perspective*; *Chaucer and the Challenges of Medievalism*; *Phonological Weakness in English. From Old to Present-Day English*; and *Empirical and Analytical Advances in the Study of English Language Change*.

Ad Putter is Professor of Medieval English Literature at the University of Bristol. He has written extensively on English and European literature of the Middle Ages. His books include *Sir Gawain and the Green Knight and French Arthurian Romance* (Oxford University Press 1996) and *Studies in the Metre of Alliterative Verse* (Medium Aevum 2007). He has also edited, with Elizabeth Archibald, *The Cambridge Companion to the Arthurian Legend* (Cambridge University Press 2009) and, with Myra Stokes, the Penguin edition of *The Works of the Gawain Poet* (Penguin 2014).

Daisy Smith is a doctoral candidate at the University of Edinburgh. Since 2014, she has held a studentship which is part of the From Inglis to Scots Project at the Angus McIntosh Centre for Historical Linguistics. Her research interests include variation in Middle English and Older Scots spelling systems, the phonological development and orthographic representation of unstressed vowels and the use of abbreviation in medieval manuscripts. She has presented her research on these topics at several international conferences and workshops. Her doctoral thesis focuses on the orthographic variation of inflectional morphemes in Older Scots legal texts. Specifically, she uses advanced statistical methods (generalised additive modelling) to investigate factors that affect the likelihood of orthographic inflection forms.

Gjertrud F. Stenbrenden is Associate Professor of English Language at the University of Oslo, Norway. She has published the monograph *Long-Vowel Shifts in English, c.1050–1700. Evidence from Spelling* (Cambridge University Press 2016). She teaches a variety of courses, including English phonetics and intonation, accents of English in the British Isles, Old and Middle English, and methods in language research. Her research interests are phonetics and phonology (modern and historical), dialectology, and language change and diachronic linguistics in general.

Merja Stenroos is Professor of English Linguistics at the Department of Cultural Studies and Languages, University of Stavanger, Norway. She has published mainly on aspects of Middle English language, in particular dialectology, orthography and morphology, and she was co-editor of *Language Contact and Development in the North Sea Area* (with Martti Mäkinen and Inge Særheim). She is one of the main compilers of the Middle English Grammar Corpus (MEG-C) and A Corpus of Middle English Local Documents (MELD).

Robert Truswell is Lecturer in Linguistics and English Language at the University of Edinburgh and Adjunct Professor in Linguistics at the University of Ottawa. He works on syntax, semantics, historical linguistics and language evolution. He is the author of *Events, Phrases, and Questions* (Oxford University Press 2011) and editor of *Syntax and its Limits* (Oxford University Press 2014) and *Micro-change and Macro-change in Diachronic Syntax* (Oxford University Press 2017). He also took the lead in development of the Parsed Linguistic Atlas of Early Middle English.

Joel Wallenberg is Lecturer in Linguistics at Newcastle University. His research focuses on the theory of language change, and how the spread of linguistic variants is affected both by properties of individual speakers and the structure of populations. He is also interested in general mechanisms of social learning, how these relate to the learning of linguistic variation, and cross-species comparisons in social learning.

Preface

This volume was born of the enthusiasm and hard work of the participants and organisers at the First Angus McIntosh Centre Symposium on the topic of Historical Dialectology held at the University of Edinburgh on the 9th and 10th June 2016. This important event promoted the Angus McIntosh Centre for Historical Linguistics (AMC) as a new centre for the study of historical language variation and language change at Edinburgh. The Symposium, and indeed this volume, was also intended to emphasise that the AMC inherits the outlook, experience and resources developed at the Institute for Historical Dialectology, its predecessor, while expanding its remit to new historical periods and language families.

Our aim as editors was to provide a lasting record of some of the key work presented at the Symposium, alongside two additional contributions that help to give a broader overview of digital methods as applied to linguistic variation across historical texts. In its outlook, the book can trace its intellectual roots to Laing and Williamson (*Speaking in our Tongues*, 1994), a compilation of the proceedings from the Colloquium on Medieval Dialectology and Related Disciplines held in Edinburgh in 1992. This seminal event in the history of the field aimed specifically to promote interdisciplinary studies and wider *intra*disciplinary collaboration, a goal we also embrace. This new work also follows on – informally – from a series of Peter Lang volumes (Dossena and Lass 2004, 2009),[1] which in turn represent a selection of the papers given at the 2003 and 2007 iterations of the International Conference on English Historical Dialectology, held at the University of Bergamo. Nearly ten years since the last publication, the present volume provides an updated view into the state of the art for the discipline, incorporating both digital and traditional methods.

---

[1] See Dossena and Lass (eds) (2004). *Methods and Data in English Historical Dialectology*, Bern: Peter Lang; and Dossena and Lass (eds) (2009). *Studies in English and European Historical Dialectology*, Bern: Peter Lang.

Acknowledgements

The editors of this volume would like to thank a number of people who have facilitated and greatly improved the contents of the current volume. First of all, we would like to thank all the participants at the First AMC Symposium – and especially those who contributed to this book. Secondly, we express our gratitude and admiration towards our fantastic and very dilligent team of external reviewers: María José Carrillo-Linares, Nynke de Haas, Patrick Honeybone, Sandra Jansen, Marcin Krygier, Merja Kytö, Robert McColl Millar, Caroline Macafee, Beatrice Santorini, Jeremy Smith, Jacob Thaisen, Jerzy Wełna and Keith Williamson. We are also indebted to the AMC Director, Heinz Giegerich, for his unfailing support We would also like to thank the wonderful team at Edinburgh University Press: Laura Williamson, Ian Strachan and Geraldine Lyons, as well as the anonymous reviewer of the entire typescript.

Historical Dialectology and the Angus McIntosh Legacy

Rhona Alcorn, Joanna Kopaczyk, Bettelou Los and
Benjamin Molineaux

1. Introduction

In its broadest terms, historical dialectology might be defined as the study of diachronic, diatopic and social variation in the historical record of languages. Insofar as it is historical it deals with time: the varieties spoken at particular points in history and the transitions between these points. Insofar as it is a study of dialects, it deals with variation across geographical and social space, broadly understood. The granularity with which we may observe the variants themselves, as well as their distribution across these key dimensions, is constrained by the quality, quantity and dispersion of the data itself, as well as our knowledge of the extralinguistic context to which they belong.

Given this remit, historical dialectology is intrinsically multidisciplinary. While at its core it sits at the crossroads of historical linguistics and dialectology, the questions it addresses are informed by sociolinguistics, history, palaeography, stylistics, critical theory, statistics, theoretical linguistics, corpus linguistics and a number of other (sub)disciplines. This volume brings together these manifold aspects of the discipline taking the ideas first developed by Angus McIntosh in the Middle English Dialect project and applying them – via powerful new digital tools – to varieties of English and Scots. This perspective complements a more prevalent outlook on historical dialects where the researchers do not reach further down the timeline than the twentieth century (for an overview of dialectology as a field today, see Boberg, Nerbonne and Watt 2018). At that time, linguistic theory and fieldwork methods, for instance a *dialect questionnaire*, developed in parallel with and inspired the production of dictionaries and atlases which reflected linguistic diversity within the living memory of today's language users or their immediate ancestors. In the present book, historical dialectology is understood as the endeavour to make sense of language variation in the first extant textual material, surviving in limited quantities and accidental coverage. The authors' focus is on a small set of closely related linguistic varieties spoken in the medieval and Early Modern periods in the British Isles; nevertheless, they sketch out a number of key methods which may be fruitfully employed in probing the historical dialectology of other linguistic families and time periods.

The breadth of the discipline's lens contrasts somewhat with the limitations inherent in capturing historical dialect data. The body of texts available for a given dialect of the past is usually both small and static, expanding only very rarely by chance discoveries of new texts. Where progress in historical dialectology can be made is by continuing to investigate and transcribe the extant material as accurately as possible, and, by digitising it, making it available to the wider scholarly community to expand the knowledge base, which can then be input to systematic enquiries, using a variety of methods, both traditional and gleaned from other disciplines. Work in historical dialectology entails the application of new analytical tools to old problems and data: the refining and annotating of datasets; the comparison and cross-referencing of available texts; the questioning of assumptions via new extralinguistic information; and the extrapolation of analyses based on data from better documented periods and locations.

Our objects of study – the dialects of particular historical communities – have dynamic boundaries, delineated both positively and negatively, that is by the forms that are present and those that are missing from a given an area, group or time. Therefore, for a particular form to be taken as a diagnostic for one variety or another, or for one text to be fitted into a particular dialect, we must take into account the traits of a large array of potential dialects. It is with these unavoidable aspects of the historical dialectology programme as a backdrop – the need to cross-check particular features across large amounts of data from different sources, places and times, and to be able to evaluate competing analyses – that digital methods have quickly become essential to the discipline.

Digitally cataloguing, cross-referencing and visualising linguistic features over extralinguistic dimensions – rather than relying on memory and analogue processing – allows the researcher to take a step back from the intricacies of the data collection and management itself and, with this fresh view, provide a more nuanced and powerful analysis. Furthermore, this digital approach gives greater traceability to claims, as well as allowing findings to be replicated and more thoroughly scrutinised. In what follows we provide a brief overview of the history of the discipline and its methods, both analogue and digital, and outline the contents of the book.

2. The methodological history of historical dialectology

The development of historical dialectology as a discipline owes much to the Amsterdam, Edinburgh and Glasgow 'schools' of historical dialectology and the major linguistic atlases produced by their proponents, i.e. those of Old French (Dees, van Reenen and de Vries 1980; Dees et al. 1987), Middle Dutch (van Reenen and Mulder 1993), late Middle English (a Linguistic Atlas of Late Mediaeval English (LALME), began 1952), early Middle English (a Linguistic Atlas of Early Middle English (LAEME), began 1987) and Older Scots (a Linguistic Atlas of Older Scots (LAOS), began 1987), produced in Edinburgh (see further Benskin 1981; Milroy 1992; Laing and Williamson 1994: 7–8, 9–10; Williamson 2012). Here we focus on a few of the milestones – arguably the cornerstones – in the evolution of the field's methodologies.

1. *The principle of diagnostic feature sets*: We can see this basic idea embodied already in the earliest attempts at a comprehensive survey of English historical dialects, e.g. those of Oakden (1930) and Moore, Meech and Whitehall (1935). The principle involves the identification of a set of distinctive features of historical written samples of known provenance for the purpose of compiling regional linguistic profiles. Since these early studies, feature sets have grown considerably in size: compare Moore, Meech and Whitehall, with just eleven test items (some of them composite) employed for linguistic comparison, to that of LALME with 280. Test items have also become increasingly elaborate and better differentiated: although most LALME items have a phonological underpinning (e.g. item 175 HOLY, item 218 SIX), others tap into the morphology (e.g. item 59 PRES 3SG, item 63 WEAK PPL), morphosyntax (e.g. item 4 SHE, item 8 THEM), orthography (e.g. item 1 THE, item 54 MIGHT) and lexis (e.g. item 10 SUCH, item 108 CHURCH) of late Middle English. With these larger, more linguistically diverse, sets of test items have come more finely grained dialectal analyses: whereas Moore, Meech and Whitehall differentiate ten regional varieties of Middle English (ME), LALME reveals that these ten idealisations are actually part of a rich dialect continuum.
2. *Understanding scribal practice*: The last half-century has witnessed a shift from authorial language to scribal language as the object of linguistic enquiry. This is entirely thanks to an insight expressed in McIntosh (1973: 92) about copying procedures. McIntosh recognised three types of copying scribe: the *literatim* copyist (type A, rare – at least in late ME); the comprehensive translator (type B, common); and the partial translator (type C, also common). This tripartite typology now allows us to distinguish, on the one hand, type A and type B copyists, each a producer of linguistically homogeneous output (albeit type A attests to the language of its exemplar, type B to the language of its scribe) and, on the other, type C copyists, whose output is linguistically mixed.[1] McIntosh's insight has thus extended the historical dialectologist's quarry from a small set of mostly documentary originals to the much larger set of literary copies.
3. *The fit-technique*: Prior to the fit-technique there was no scientific way to place a written sample on a dialect map on the basis of its linguistic features alone. The technique, another of Angus McIntosh's gifts to the discipline, is so named for its ability to 'fit' an unprovenanced, linguistically homogeneous, sample within a dialect continuum by reference to a matrix of previously localised features (LALME vol.1, §2.3; Benskin 1991). The technique was initially a manual exercise, employing tracing paper, pencil and layers of cross-hatching to indicate areas in which an attested feature does not belong. Once fitted within a continuum, the sample itself then becomes an intrinsic

---

[1] Depending on the degree of mixing, type C copies may also include significant stretches of linguistically homogeneous material suitable for dialectal analysis (Laing 2004; Laing and Williamson 2004).

part of the matrix, refining and possibly even multiplying the diagnostic points of reference for the 'fitting' of other contemporaneous samples.

4. *Surveys by tagging*: Although the number of test items in the LALME survey was unprecedented, the selection of these items was settled before the survey began and there was no mechanism for extending or refining the questionnaire once things were underway.[2] In a hugely successful effort to enrich our knowledge of the complexities of medieval dialect continua, compilers of LAEME and LAOS (both published initially online in 2007 as beta versions) adopted a tag-based method of data collection. This involved tagging each token of every word (and many component morphemes as well) in a diplomatically transcribed corpus of samples of early ME and Older Scots, respectively, in order to indicate the token's lexical and/or grammatical affiliation. The resulting tagged corpora are available online, where they can be freely consulted to determine which words (and which morphemes) are attested in which samples, in what numbers and in what forms. Since the majority of samples in these corpora can be associated with a particular time and place (whether from extralinguistic evidence or by fitting), so too can be their attested forms.

The developments in historical dialectology, as in any other discipline, have been enabled and propelled by technological and methodological advances: from pen and tracing paper to electronic datasets with robust search capabilities. The focus on historical dialects of English and Scots in this volume highlights the methodological continuities as well as innovations in the context of pre-1700 dialectal diversity in the British Isles.

3. The digital turn in historical dialectology: A state of the art

3.1 Data collection

Any data collection for historical dialectology requires a careful transposition of the material from the original medium into one that is more easily accessible for analysis. For the medieval period especially, this entails manually transcribing the manuscripts, a major undertaking which still presents a technological and methodological challenge. Optical character recognition (OCR), which has been successfully employed and constantly improved for digitising printed texts, has not yet rendered reliable enough results for handwriting, especially for medieval and Early Modern cursive hands. There are ongoing attempts at creating software which could automatically transcribe handwritten text (Dantas Bezerra et al. 2017; see e.g. the HistDoc project in Switzerland, Fischer et al. 2012, or the most recent Transkribus tool developed at the University of Innsbruck as part of the Recognition and Enrichment of Archival

---

[2] LALME's 'Southern Appendix' consists of a set of items which were not surveyed systematically: instead only notable (i.e. unexpected) forms were recorded and only for the Southern area of the survey.

Documents (READ) project (https://read.transkribus.eu/; Toselli et al. 2017)) that could revolutionise the creation of machine-readable repositories of textual material with historical dialectal interest. Large quantities of such archive material have never been edited and survive in manuscript format only. Digital technology has obviously improved access to the materials, as increasing amounts of manuscripts, accessible so far only on site in archives and libraries, are being scanned and placed online. This technological revolution enables scholars to produce electronic corpora of local materials with more ease. One can also rely on edited and printed versions of historical manuscripts for digitisation where available, which then get checked against the original. In any case, the manuscript will always have to be consulted for scribal detail. It thus becomes increasingly important to engage with methods and principles designed for earlier, also pre-digital, historical dialectal projects, draw on them and supplement them with new material.

An important extension of available dialectal data for the ME period came in the 2000s with the Middle English Grammar Project, run at the University of Stavanger (Stenroos et al. 2011).[3] Building on the LALME tradition, the project provides diplomatic transcriptions of representative samples of texts localised in LALME, tagged for lemmas and annotated with extensive information about the manuscript witness (e.g. layout, corrections and palaeographic detail). It thus follows a similar route as LAEME by constructing a corpus of full texts (or extended samples), but – admittedly – does not engage with detailed semanto-grammatical tagging, which forms the core of the LAEME (and LAOS) methodology (Stenroos 2007; Stenroos et al. 2011). The latest version of the MEG-C corpus (2011.1) comprises 410 texts, rendering more than 800,000 words of running text. The MEG-C initiative was the initial stage for what has since grown into the Middle English Scribal Texts programme (MEST). The latest product of the MEST team and an exciting addition to the diplomatically transcribed digital repositories of localised medieval material is the *Corpus of Middle English Local Documents* (MELD). MELD builds on the LALME coverage by gathering transcriptions of over 2,000 documents from the fifteenth century, which can be treated as individual scribal texts. The compilers' intention is 'to ask "who wrote what where – and for whom"' (Stenroos et al. 2017), which takes the focus off 'unmixed' geographical dialects and introduces a more pronounced sociolinguistic – and explicitly variationist – angle.

There are also ongoing projects aiming to create regional dialectal diachronic corpora, such as the *Seville Corpus of Northern English* (SCONE) (for details, see Fernández Cuesta and Amores Carredano 2012), which has a limited geographical scope – the North – but extended time-depth (700–1600). Apart from widening the existing digital temporal coverage, this project aims to complement the LALME data for the region, especially to enable syntactic analysis. Another repository of texts in dialect, the *Salamanca Corpus: Digital Archive of English Dialect Texts* (García-Bermejo Giner 2012), covers the period from 1500–1950, focusing on literary texts alone.

---

[3] For an aggregated searchable repository of currently available corpora and their metadata, see Corpus Resource Database (CoRD, http://www.helsinki.fi/varieng/CoRD/index.html). Here, we only review data collection initiatives which have an explicit link to pre-1700 dialectal diversity in the British Isles.

3.2 Data presentation and remodelling

Current developments in digital technology have made it possible to transform existing printed resources for the study of historical dialectology. The most influential collection of historical dialectal information, LALME, has recently been remodelled and republished in an electronic format. The electronic version of the atlas, eLALME, had no space constraints, which meant that more data could be put online. As mentioned earlier, Moore, Meech and Whitehall started off in the 1930s with just eleven features for linguistic comparison, the printed LALME offers 280, while eLALME contains over 420, due to the inclusion of the originally separate Appendix of Southern forms.

On the basis of the new, electronically tagged, dialectal atlases, it has become possible to obtain a much broader spread of forms for any attested lexeme or morpheme, thus allowing researchers to enquire about their individual linguistic histories and distributions. In order to answer such questions, authors of the *Corpus of Narrative Etymologies from Proto-Old English to Early Middle English* (CoNE) traced the etymological roots of individual spelling variants in LAEME, via phonological, morphological and orthographic changes, to their pre-Old English origins (Lass et al. 2013). The resultant database of individual form histories provides a unique background to the evolution of dialectal variation in medieval Britain.

Another recent endeavour in repurposing dialectal historical data which already exists in a richly annotated electronic format is the *From Inglis to Scots* (FITS) project at the Angus McIntosh Centre for Historical Linguistics at Edinburgh. With its aim to reconstruct the sound-to-spelling mappings of early Scots, this project takes the Germanic root morphemes from LAOS and subjects them to grapho-phonological parsing (Kopaczyk et al. 2018). Thanks to FITS, scholars interested in dialectal variation within medieval Scots will be able to trace spelling preferences geographically, and draw fruitful comparisons with English dialectal material, informing questions about the extent and character of the earliest stages of the dialectal continuum between England and Scotland.

In the past, various initiatives to do with digital technologies proceeded in a disconnected fashion, with little standardisation of coding procedures, especially in the humanities. For example, LAEME and LAOS, robust and comprehensive as they are, rely largely on an idiosyncratic model of semanto-grammatical tagging, designed for the purposes of these specific resources. In the meantime, part-of-speech taggers and syntactic parsers were being developed for and more widely applied to historical linguistic corpus data. These trends in computational approaches to textual data have been recognised by the PLAEME (*a Parsed Linguistic Atlas of Early Middle English*) team, who have recently produced a syntactically parsed version of LAEME (see Chapter 2 in this book) using syntactic annotation and filling an important historical gap among the existing suite of parsed corpora of historical English.

A different approach to data presentation is characteristic of the MEST corpora, MEG-C and MELD, which concentrate on providing the best diplomatic digital representation of the manuscript text without an additional layer of linguistic interpretation, but with comprehensive textual metadata. This approach enables users to perform their own annotations and analyses. The files are fully downloadable and come in several different formats: for MEG-C – the base text (.txt), the readable html and pdf versions, as well as a concordance-friendly version of the base text intended for further work with concordancing software (AntConc 3.2.1., Anthony 2007). To these formats, MELD adds a diplomatic version which retains manuscript letter shapes and other signs without heavy coding. Thus, various research questions can be addressed on the basis of this material, ranging from word geography to sociolinguistic and pragmatic enquiries into medieval dialects, while the base text can also be subjected to automatic spelling normalisation, lemmatisation or parsing.

3.3 Data visualisation and analysis

Maps are a key visualisation tool in historical dialectology and their digital format is constantly evolving. There is a growing suite of readily available maps for LAEME, where the most interesting features of morphology and spelling have been picked by the compilers. These maps can be combined to trace several variants in one visualisation and one can also produce maps for features extracted from user-defined searches. The new electronic format of eLALME includes a tool which produces user-defined maps for selected questionnaire items and their variants, relating them to the rest of the information from a given LP. The user needs to remember, however, that eLALME maps are generated on the basis of pre-digital procedures of data collection, which determine what the maps represent. Therefore, in order to interpret the maps, one should always engage with the underlying methodology.[4]

Similarly, the 'fit' technique, discussed in section 2, was typically performed in the past by overlaying dialectal feature maps on top of each other. An electronic procedure mimicking the fit-technique was developed (Williamson 2004; Laing and Williamson 2004) but its complexity could not be replicated for external users with the web technology available at the time of publication of eLALME. The web-based application provided at present in eLALME works by building up patterns of occurrence rather than eliminating areas of non-occurrence and as such could be said perhaps to be less powerful than the elimination method, but is at least more user-friendly.

The discipline of historical dialectology is thus constantly evolving and drawing on new technologies of data collection, annotation and presentation, while continuing the work that was commenced several decades ago. There is always room for improvement and further development of tools, resources and ideas, which the contributions to the present volume aptly illustrate.

4. Doing historical dialectology in the digital age: Chapter overviews

The volume's remaining ten chapters are split up into three parts. Part 1: *Creating and Mining Digital Resources* contains three papers that all report on the creation of

---

[4] A useful set of guides to LAEME and eLALME, including visualisation features, has been prepared by Alcorn (2017a, 2017b).

new digital resources for historical dialectology, and how to use them. In Chapter 2, 'A Parsed Linguistic Atlas of Early Middle English', Robert Truswell, Rhona Alcorn, James Donaldson and Joel Wallenberg report on the construction of a new resource, the *Parsed Linguistic Atlas of Early Middle English* (PLAEME). As word orders and constructions in verse texts are likely to reflect the demands of metre and rhyme, prose texts are usually regarded as more reliable for the purposes of syntactic investigations. Prose is underrepresented in the period 1250–1350, however, which is why this period is also underrepresented in the *Penn Parsed Corpora of Historical English* (PPCHE, Kroch and Taylor 2000; Kroch, Santorini and Delfs 2004; Kroch, Santorini and Diertani 2016). This is unfortunate, as there is evidence that this particular period is transitional for many syntactic phenomena. PLAEME aims to address this data gap by transforming material from the *Linguistic Atlas of Early Middle English* (LAEME, Laing 2013–) into the same format as the PPCHE. The authors present a detailed account of its construction, as well as three case studies replicating three recent studies of ME syntax: the establishment of *not* as the expression of sentential negation (Ecay and Tamminga 2017); the fixing of the syntax of the dative alternation in ditransitive constructions (Bacovcin 2017); and the introduction of argumental headed *wh*-relatives (Gisborne and Truswell 2017). These case studies show that PLAEME allows these changes to be charted in greater detail. They also show that verse texts can be a useful resource in syntactic investigations, as the syntax of the verse samples in PLAEME is in line with that of the prose texts, at least with respect to the topics of these case studies.

The following chapter, Klaus Hofmann's 'Approaching Transition Scots from a Micro-perspective: The Dunfermline Corpus, 1573–1723', also describes the compilation of a new digital resource for historical dialectology. The Dunfermline Corpus belongs to the Late Middle Scots period (c.1550–1700), recently relabelled as 'Transition Scots' (Kopaczyk 2013). Transition Scots is of particular interest as it shows the outcome of a contact situation of two written varieties – Scots and Southern English – that are both on the verge of standardisation. As a result of the political, economic and cultural unification with England, Southern English won out, so that Transition Scots typically shows the replacement of markedly Scots features by Southern English equivalents. Hofmann subjects the corpus to a diachronic analysis of five linguistic variables that are known to be distinctive features of Older Scots as opposed to Southern English usage. His findings confirm that Anglicisation proceeded at a faster page at supralocal levels than at local levels; local records were particularly slow to adopt the English forms. Hofmann's sociolinguistic, palaeographic micro-approach reconstructs the 'community of practice' that was responsible for the lag in this convergence process, i.e. the town clerks, and investigates their recruitment and training. Recruitment seems to have been almost that of a family-run business, with many clerks and scribes being trained by their own fathers. It is only when the transmission of the orthographic idiolect of this community was disrupted by a new clerk from outside the immediate scribal network that we see bursts of change towards the English forms.

Chapter 4, 'Early Spelling Evidence for Scots L-vocalisation: A Corpus-based Approach', by Benjamin Molineaux, Joanna Kopaczyk, Warren Maguire, Rhona

Alcorn, Vasilis Karaiskos and Bettelou Los, showcases the *From Inglis to Scots* (FITS) project database, which comprises texts from the *Linguistic Atlas of Older Scots* (LAOS), of the period 1380–1500. This new resource makes it possible to test earlier assumptions about the history of Scots, in particular claims about changes that are characteristic of Scots and not shared with Southern English. One such change is L-vocalisation, which entails the loss of coda-/l/ following short back vowels, with concomitant vocalic lengthening or diphthongisation (as in Old English *full* > OSc *fow*). L-vocalisation has been claimed to date from the early fifteenth century and to have completed by the beginning of the sixteenth. Based on attestations of <l>-less forms and reverse spellings, including /l/~ø alternations in borrowed items from (Norman) French (as in *realme~reaume* 'realm'), the authors map the spread of <l> loss in different phonological contexts over time and space. They find evidence of <l> loss in less than 1 per cent of relevant environments, with the final position as an important locus, but with no evidence of a spread.

Part 2: *Segmental Histories* contains four chapters that take on the challenge of matching spellings to sounds in ME data, where the existence of many local substitution sets and messy scribal transmission requires scholars 'to calculate with noise' (Stenroos, Chapter 7). Given the dialectal fragmentation of the data, it is remarkable that some processes, like the one investigated by Minkova in Chapter 8, present a geographically-uniform picture, so that the investigation can concentrate on the timing of the process instead.

Chapter 5, 'Old and Middle English Spellings for OE *hw*-, with special reference to the 'qu-' Type: In Celebration of LAEME, (e)LALME, LAOS and CoNE', by Margaret Laing and Roger Lass, celebrates Angus McIntosh's scholarly legacy, particularly the creation of a *Linguistic Atlas of Late Mediaeval English* (LALME). They demonstrate how the four main electronic resources created in the same tradition as LALME, i.e. LAEME, LALME itself (and its electronic version eLALME), a *Linguistic Atlas of Older Scots* (LAOS) and a *Corpus of Narrative Etymologies from Proto-Old English to Early Middle English and accompanying Corpus of Changes* (CoNE) can be used in tandem to support an investigation into the initial cluster in words such as *when, where, what, who, which*. LAEME, eLALME and LAOS (supplemented by the *Dictionary of Old English* (DOE) Web Corpus and *Middle English Dictionary*) provide an exhaustive list of no fewer than fifty-seven different spellings for this cluster, from the earliest attested Old English (OE) to c.1500. The authors show how LAEME, eLALME and LAOS provide the data that allow for these spellings to be analysed as reflecting various scribal choices, whether determined by orthographic variation (including traditional contextual rules for the use of <v> or <u>), phonological variation, geographical variation and/or diachronic variation. The final section showcases CoNE, with a diachronic account, reconstructed on the basis of this classification of the spellings, revealing a coherent, if extremely complex, picture of lenitions, fortitions and reversals.

Gjertrud F. Stenbrenden in Chapter 6, 'The Development of OE $\bar{æ}$: Middle English Spelling Evidence', presents the range of spellings for the reflexes of $\bar{æ}^1$ and $\bar{æ}^2$ in ME dialects, as found in SED, LAEME and LALME. OE $\bar{æ}$ appears to have raised early in ME, as the dominant spelling is <e(e)>; this is further supported by the fact that <a/æ/ea> spellings are more frequent in the early LAEME texts than in the later ones. The data from LAEME support the East Saxon retraction of $\bar{æ}^2$ to [aː], as proposed in the literature, but only for Essex. As $\bar{æ}^1$ and $\bar{æ}^2$ would have been merged as [æː] already in OE, it is no surprise to find <a> to be almost as frequent for $\bar{æ}^1$ as for $\bar{æ}^2$ in Essex. There was geographic variation in OE, with $\bar{æ}^1$ and $\bar{æ}^2$ appearing to have merged in some dialects but kept apart in others. Their reflexes are not kept apart orthographically in any systematic fashion in any ME dialects, but a detailed analysis of the spellings suggest that there are pockets where spellings are not random. The greater proportion of <a/æ/ea> spellings for the reflex of $\bar{æ}^1$ might indicate an opener quality of this vowel than that of $\bar{æ}^2$, which has a greater proportion of <e(e)> spellings. The reverse situation is suggested by spellings in the *Ormulum*, where the different use of <a> vs. <æ> vs. <e> for the two $\bar{æ}$'s points to a closer quality for $\bar{æ}^1$ instead. As the sound changes affecting the two $\bar{æ}$'s took some time to reach completion, so that they overlapped in time with the early stages of the Great Vowel Shift, the author argues that they must be seen as part of the Great Vowel Shift rather than as similar but unrelated changes.

Merja Stenroos in Chapter 7, 'The Development of Old English *eo/ēo* and the Systematicity of Middle English Spelling', uses a new resource, the Middle English Grammar Corpus (MEG-C), a corpus of fourteenth- and fifteenth-century English texts, to answer an old question: is it possible to find traces of a systematic distinction between the reflexes of OE *e/ē* and *eo/ēo* in ME? The investigation first charts the spellings of twenty-seven lexical items that contain a vowel representing OE *eo/ēo* as well as the equivalent Old Norse element, *jó*. This search throws up a wide range of spellings, the vast majority of which show <e>/<ee>. Spellings which might suggest a rounded pronunciation are also fairly robustly present, however, particularly <eo>, with the South-West Midlands as its core area. The second part of the investigation takes the opposite approach and retrieves all words that were spelled with the digraph <eo>. The vast majority of these turn out to be reflexes of OE *eo/ēo*, and almost all of them are localised to the South-West Midlands. An investigation of unhistorical spellings reveals that they occur either as reflexes of OE *y/ȳ*, or in unstressed syllables, or in words where <eo> follows <w> – three groups for which a rounded pronunciation would be plausible. Stenroos speculates that in a community where texts are read intensively and continuously, traditional spellings may persist and acquire a regional identity-marking function, even if the scribes' own spoken systems did not include rounded front vowels (cf. also Hofmann's findings in Chapter 3). However, the remarkable accuracy with which the spellings continue to be used across the entire timespan of the study, even in less frequent words, suggests that the phonemic distinction remained in some spoken systems well into the fifteenth century.

In Chapter 8, 'Examining the Evidence for Phonemic Affricates: ME /t͡ʃ/, /d͡ʒ/ or [t-ʃ], [d-ʒ]?', Donka Minkova addresses the question of how we can decide whether two adjacent phonetic units form a single segment or a sequence of two separate ones. According to Ladefoged and Maddieson (1996: 90), affricates represent a category intermediate between simple stops and a sequence of a stop and a fricative, and Minkova notes that intermediate categories are analytical challenges, suggesting diachronic instability. In the case of the history of English, the special status of affricates is confirmed by affricates being rare or absent in related languages; where affricates *are* attested, they are usually innovations, or are only found in loanwords. The chapter traces the historical evidence for the development of OE [c], a single segment, to palatal [cʲ], assibilated [tʃ], the sequence [tʃ], and back to a single segment contour /t͡ʃ/, building on diagnostics like the blocking property of medial clusters versus singletons in resolution in OE verse, alliteration, metrical treatment in terms of syllable weight, data from language acquisition, phonetics in terms of durational properties, the interaction with sound changes like those described in CoNE (Open-Syllable Lengthening and Pre-cluster Shortening), as well as the early neutralisation of the singleton-geminate contrast. Further support comes from spelling, including a possible Celtic origin for OE <cg>, and <ch> spellings in LAEME as evidence supporting orthographic remapping of palatal [c]. Finally, Minkova considers the impact of Old French loanwords, and the interaction between ME and Anglo-Norman, where the simplification of affricates in the latter is argued to be delayed (compared to Central French) due to the existence of the sequences [tʃ] and [dʒ] in ME. The findings of this chapter make a number of valuable additions to CoNE, not only in terms of fleshing out its description of velar palatalisation, but also offering corroboration that the change which CoNE identifies as palatal hardening can be argued to be a genuine phonetic process.

Part 3: *Placing Features in Context* groups together three chapters that look at the minutiae of the use of certain features in geographically-defined subsets of texts. Daisy Smith looks at the use of a particular abbreviation (<ꝭ>) in order to feed into an answer to the larger question of the status of <is/ys> spellings in the system of plural marking in Older Scots (Chapter 9). Ad Putter's chapter redefines the place and date of one particular manuscript, by means of an investigation into mostly phonological features (Chapter 10), and also demonstrates how historical corpora can be employed for a variety of different scholarly purposes, bringing the reader back to work carried out by Michael Samuels and Jeremy Smith in the 1980s. Finally, Trinidad Guzmán-González's chapter addresses a particularly knotty problem: the historical depth of a particular gender feature of Modern South-West English.

In Chapter 9, 'The Predictability of {S} Abbreviation in Older Scots Manuscripts According to Stem-final *Littera*', Daisy Smith presents an analysis of the orthographic realisation of the Older Scots plural noun {S} morpheme. The realisation of this morpheme as <is> or <ys>, as in *acctionis* 'actions', has been claimed to be a diagnostic of the 'Scottishness' of a text (e.g. Kniezsa 1997: 41). In a *Linguistic Atlas of Older Scots* (LAOS), the most common realisation of {S} (61 per cent) is in fact the abbreviation <ꝭ>; of non-abbreviated realisations, <is/ys> is indeed the most frequent realisation, although it only accounts for 25 per cent of all tokens. The abbrevation <ꝭ> is often assumed to be functionally identical to <is/ys>, rather than to <(e)s>, in the literature. To test this assumption, Smith uses generalised additive modelling (GAM), with text date, text location, text type and stem-final letter included as independent variables. The independent variable which turned out to be the best predictor for the use of <ꝭ>, as opposed to a full form such as <is>, is the identity of the stem-final letter. A closer inspection reveals why: the salient feature triggering <ꝭ> is whether the stem-final letters terminate in a horizontal stroke or not.

The realisation of the plural morpheme {S} in Older Scots legal texts, then, appears to be primarily motivated by palaeographical convenience.

Ad Putter in Chapter 10, 'An East Anglian Poem in a London Manuscript? The Date and Dialect of *The Court of Love* in Cambridge, Trinity College, MS R.3.19' investigates *The Court of Love*, which has come down to us in a single manuscript (Cambridge, Trinity College, MS R.3.19, folios 217r–234r). It passed for a long time as a poem by Chaucer, a notion which was debunked by Skeat as a neo-medieval fabrication dating from the fourth decade of the sixteenth century at the earliest (a judgement which was so influential that the poem was excluded from the corpus of sources for the MED). This chapter presents a new appraisal of the date, which Putter tentatively pinpoints as the middle of the fifteenth century, and provenance of the poem, which he localises in East Anglia based on broad phonological evidence as indicated by rhymes and some spellings. What we know about the Trinity scribe who copied the poem makes it likely that he was from London, while the poet was from further north and writing earlier. Frequent failures of rhyme point to the linguistic differences between the poet and the scribe, as reconstructed from rhyme, metre and possible 'relicts'. In this case, the eLALME dot maps proved to be more useful than the 'fitting' facility because the transmission history makes it difficult to reconstruct the poet's original spellings. The hypothesis that the poet was from East Anglia and the scribe from London also throws new light on Skeat's claim of 'false grammar' in the poem. The instances of 'false grammar' are in fact examples of syntax that is true to the poet's own dialect.

Chapter 11 – '"He was a good hammer, was he": Gender as Marker for South-Western Dialects of English. A Corpus-based Study from a Diachronic Perspective' – by Trinidad Guzmán-González investigates assumptions that the gender system peculiar to present-day South-West English might have its origins in similar patterns in that area in ME. The present-day dialect uses masculine pronouns as the general reference for most nouns denoting inanimate and countable referents, so that it is not the default gender as in the standard. The earliest reports of this system date from the end of the eighteenth century. On the basis of all the textual files specifically localised as SW in the relevant subsections of LAEME, the *Helsinki Corpus of English Texts* (HC) (Rissanen et al. 1991) and the *Middle English Grammar Corpus* (MEG-C) (Stenroos et al. 2011), the author investigates whether the seeds of these systems might already have been present in the ME ancestors of those dialects, but concludes that this is not the case – in the ME SW texts, it can already be considered as the default gender for all nouns denoting non-living things (barring a small number of exceptions discussed in detail). What this investigation ultimately demonstrates is that traditional dialects are not living fossils and have had their own share of extralinguistic circumstances to affect them in their long histories.

References

Alcorn, Rhona (2017a). a *Linguistic Atlas of Early Middle English (LAEME): A Guide for Beginners*, version 2 (available at http://www.research.ed.ac.uk/portal/en/publications/a-linguistic-atlas-of-early-middle-english-laeme-a-guide-for-beginners(d435f862-a290-4db7-a458-85194c83bd8f).html).

Alcorn, Rhona (2017b). An electronic version of a *Linguistic Atlas of Late Mediaeval English* (eLALME): A Guide for Beginners, version 2 (available at http://www.research.ed.ac.uk/portal/en/publications/an-electronic-version-of-a-linguistic-atlas-of-late-mediaeval-english-elalme-a-guide-for-beginners(e0ab645c-31d9-4313-8930-e82d4761e3a4).html).

Anthony, Laurence (2007). AntConc (3.2.1) [Computer Software], Tokyo: Waseda University (available at http://www.laurenceanthony.net/).

Bacovcin, Hezekiah Akiva (2017). 'Modelling interactions between morphosyntactic changes', in Mathieu and Truswell, pp. 94–103.

Benskin, Michael (1981). 'The Middle English dialect atlas', in Michael Benskin and Michael Samuels (eds), *So Meny People Longages and Tonges: Philological Essays in Scots and Mediaeval English Presented to Angus McIntosh*, Edinburgh: The Editors, pp. xxvii–xli.

Benskin, Michael (1991). 'The "fit"-technique explained', in Felicity Riddy (ed.), *Regionalism in Late Medieval Manuscripts and Texts*, Cambridge: D. S. Brewer, pp. 9–26.

Boberg, Charles, John Nerbonne and Dominic Watt (eds) (2018). *The Handbook of Dialectology*, Oxford: Wiley Blackwell.

Dantas Bezerra, Byron Leite, Cleber Zanchettin, Alejandro H. Toselli and Giuseppe Pirlo (eds) (2017). *Handwriting: Recognition, Development and Analysis*, New York: Nova Science Publishers.

Dees, Anthonij with Pieter T. van Reenen and Johan A. de Vries (1980). *Atlas des Formes et Constructions des Chartes Françaises du 13e Siècle*, Tübingen: Niemeyer.

Dees, Anthonij, with Marcel Dekker, Onno Huber and Karin van Reenen-Stein (1987). *Atlas des Formes Linguistiques des Textes Littéraires de l'Ancien Français*, Tübingen: Niemeyer.

Dossena, Marina and Roger Lass (eds) (2004). *Methods and Data in English Historical Dialectology* [Linguistic Insights 16], Bern: Peter Lang.

Ecay, Aaron and Meredith Tamminga (2017). 'Persistence as a diagnostic of grammatical status: The case of Middle English negation', in Mathieu and Truswell, pp. 202–215.

Fernández Cuesta, Julia and José Gabriel Amores Carredano (2012). 'The SCONE Corpus of Northern English', in Nila Vázquez (ed.), *Creation and Use of Historical English Corpora in Spain*, Cambridge: Cambridge Scholars Publishing, pp. 75–99.

Fischer, Andreas, Horst Bunke, Nada Naji, Jacques Savoy, Micheal Baechler and Rolf Ingold (2012). The HistDoc Project. Automatic analysis, recognition, and retrieval of handwritten historical documents for digital libraries, Proceedings of the International and Interdisciplinary Aspects of Scholarly Editing Symposium 2012, Bern, Switzerland. ResearchGate, pp. 81–96. (Available at https://www.researchgate.net/profile/Andreas_Fischer9/publication/267026475_The_HisDoc_Project_Automatic_Analysis_Recognition_and_Retrieval_of_Handwritten_Historical_Documents_for_Digital_Libraries/links/5441361a0cf2e6f0c0f604a7.pdf)

García-Bermejo Giner, María (2012). 'The Online Salamanca Corpus of English Dialect Texts', in Nila Vázquez (ed.), *Creation and Use of Historical English Corpora in Spain*, Cambridge: Cambridge Scholars Publishing, pp. 67–74.

Gisborne, Nikolas and Robert Truswell (2017). 'Where do relative specifiers come from?', in Mathieu and Truswell, pp. 25–42.

Kniezsa, Veronika (1997). 'The origins of Scots orthography', in Charles Jones (ed.), *The Edinburgh History of the Scots Language*, Edinburgh: Edinburgh University Press, pp. 24–46.

Kopaczyk, Joanna (2013). 'Rethinking the traditional periodisation of Scots', in Robert McColl Millar and Janet Cruickshank (eds), *After the Storm: Papers from the Forum for Research on the Languages of Scotland and Ulster Triennial Meeting*, Aberdeen 2012, Aberdeen: Forum for Research on the Languages of Scotland and Ulster, pp. 233–260.

Kopaczyk, J., B. Molineaux, V. Karaiskos, R. Alcorn, B. Los and W. Maguire (2018). 'Towards a grapho-phonologically parsed corpus of medieval Scots: Database design and technical solutions', *Corpora* 13(2): 255–269.

Kroch, Anthony and Ann Taylor (2000). *Penn–Helsinki Parsed Corpus of Middle English*, 2nd edition, release 4. University of Pennsylvania (available at https://www.ling.upenn.edu/hist-corpora/PPCME2-RELEASE-4/index.html).

Kroch, Anthony, Beatrice Santorini and Lauren Delfs (2004). *Penn–Helsinki Parsed Corpus of Early Modern English*, release 3, University of Pennsylvania (available at https://www.ling.upenn.edu/hist-corpora/PPCEME-RELEASE-3/index.html).

Kroch, Anthony, Beatrice Santorini and Ariel Diertani (2016). *Penn Parsed Corpus of Modern British English*, 2nd edition, release 1. University of Pennsylvania (available at https://www.ling.upenn.edu/hist-corpora/PPCMBE2-RELEASE-1/index.html).

Ladefoged, Peter and Ian Maddieson (1996). *The Sounds of the World's Languages*, Oxford: Blackwell.

LAEME: see Laing, Margaret. 2013–.

Laing, Margaret (2004). 'Multidimensionality: Time, space and stratigraphy in historical dialectology', in Dossena and Lass (eds), pp. 49–96.

Laing, Margaret (2013–). *A Linguistic Atlas of Early Middle English*, 1150–1325, version 3.2, University of Edinburgh (available at http://www.lel.ed.ac.uk/ihd/laeme2/laeme2.html).

Laing, Margaret and Keith Williamson (eds) (1994). *Speaking in our Tongues: Proceedings of a Colloquium on Medieval Dialectology and Related Disciplines*. Cambridge: D. S. Brewer.

Laing, Margaret and Keith Williamson (2004). 'The archaeology of Middle English texts', in Christian J. Kay and Jeremy J. Smith (eds), *Categorization in the History of English* [Current Issues in Linguistic Theory 261], Amsterdam: Benjamins, pp. 85–145.

LALME: McIntosh, Angus, Michael L. Samuels and Michael Benskin with Margaret Laing and Keith Williamson (1986). *A Linguistic Atlas of Late Mediaeval English*. Aberdeen: Aberdeen University Press.

LAOS: Williamson, Keith. 2013–. *A Linguistic Atlas of Older Scots*, Phase 1: 1380–1500, version 1.2, Edinburgh: University of Edinburgh (available at http://www.lel.ed.ac.uk/ihd/laos1/laos1.html).

Lass, Roger, Margaret Laing, Rhona Alcorn and Keith Williamson (2013–). *A Corpus of Narrative Etymologies from Proto-Old English to Early Middle English and accompanying Corpus of Changes*, version 1.1, Edinburgh: University of Edinburgh (available at http://www.lel.ed.ac.uk/ihd/CoNE/CoNE.html).

McIntosh, Angus (1973). 'Word geography in the lexicography of Middle English', *Annals of the New York Academy of Sciences* 211: 55–66.

Mathieu, Éric and Robert Truswell, eds (2017). *Macro-change and Micro-change in Diachronic Syntax*, Oxford: Oxford University Press.

Milroy, James (1992). 'Middle English dialectology', in Norman F. Blake (ed.), *The Cambridge History of the English Language*, vol. 2, *1066–1476*, Cambridge: Cambridge University Press, pp. 156–206.

Moore, Samuel, S. B. Meech and Harold Whitehall (1935). 'Middle English dialect characteristics and dialect boundaries', in *Essays and Studies in English and Comparative Literature*, Ann Arbor: University of Michigan [Publications in Language and Literature XIII], pp. 1–60.

Oakden, James P. (1930). *Alliterative Poetry in Middle English: the Dialectal and Metrical Survey*, Manchester: Manchester University Press.

READ Project (Recognition and Enrichment of Archival Documents) (available at https://read.transkribus.eu/ (accessed 3 March 2018)).

van Reenen, Pieter T. and Marijke Mulder (1993). 'Een gegevensbank van 14de eeuwse Middelnederlandse dialecten op computer'. *Lexikos* 3: 259–281.

Rissanen, Matti, Merja Kytö, Leena Kahlas-Tarkka, Matti Kilpiö, Irma Taavitsainen, Terttu Nevalainen and Helena Raumolin-Brunberg (1991). *The Helsinki Corpus of English Texts*, Helsinki: University of Helsinki (available at http://www.helsinki.fi/varieng/CoRD/corpora/HelsinkiCorpus/index.html).

SED: *Survey of English Dialects:* Harold Orton and William James Halliday (eds) (1962–1969), 4 vols, Leeds: E. J. Arnold.

Stenroos, Merja (2007). 'Sampling and annotation in the Middle English Grammar Project', in A. Meurman-Solin and A. Nurmi (eds), *Annotating Variation and Change* [Studies in Variation, Contacts and Change in English 1], Helsinki: University of Helsinki (available at http://www.helsinki.fi/varieng/series/volumes/01/stenroos/).

Stenroos, Merja, Kjetil V. Thengs and Geir Bergstrøm (2017). 'Manual'. *A Corpus of Middle English Local Documents*, version 2017.1, University of Stavanger (available at www.uis.no/meld (accessed 1 July 2017)).

Stenroos, Merja, Martti Mäkinen, Simon Horobin and Jeremy Smith (2011). *The Middle English Grammar Corpus*, version 2011.1, University of Stavanger (available at http://www.uis.no/research/culture/the_middle_english_grammar_project/ (accessed 1 April 2011)).

Toselli, Alejandro H., Luis A. Leiva, Isabel Bordes-Cabrera, Celio Hernández-Tornero, Vicent Bosch and Enrique Vidal (2017). 'Transcribing a 17th-century botanical manuscript: Longitudinal evaluation of document layout detection and interactive transcription', *Digital Scholarship in the Humanities* fqw064. DOI: https://doi.org/10.1093/llc/fqw064.

Williamson, Keith (2004). 'On chronicity and space(s) in historical dialectology', in Dossena and Lass (eds), pp. 97–136.

Williamson, Keith (2012). 'Middle English dialects', in Alexander Bergs and Laurel J. Brinton (eds), *English Historical Linguistics: An International Handbook*, vol. 1, Berlin: de Gruyter Mouton, pp. 480–505.

Part I Creating and Mining Digital Resources

2

A Parsed Linguistic Atlas of Early Middle English[1]

Robert Truswell, Rhona Alcorn, James Donaldson and Joel Wallenberg

1. Introduction

We describe a new parsed corpus which enriches material from the *Linguistic Atlas of Early Middle English* (LAEME, Laing 2013–) with explicit annotation of syntactic structure in the format of the *Penn Parsed Corpora of Historical English* (PPCHE, Kroch and Taylor 2000; Kroch, Santorini and Delfs 2004; Kroch, Santorini and Diertani 2016). This corpus is known as the *Parsed Linguistic Atlas of Early Middle English* (PLAEME).

In this chapter, we will introduce the PPCHE format and identify a data gap in the Middle English portion of the corpora (section 2), and then demonstrate how LAEME can fill the data gap (section 3). Section 4 describes the process of constructing PLAEME from LAEME materials, and section 5 extends recent studies of Middle English syntax based on the PPCHE to PLAEME data.

2. The Penn Parsed Corpora of Historical English

The PPCHE represent written English from the period c.1150–1914 by means of some 5.8 million words of running prose (with a small amount of verse) in more than 600 texts. They include the *Penn–Helsinki Parsed Corpus of Middle English*, 2nd edition (Kroch and Taylor 2000), the *Penn–Helsinki Parsed Corpus of Early Modern English*

---

[1] Thanks to Meg Laing and two anonymous reviewers for comments on an earlier draft. The construction of PLAEME was supported by a British Academy/Leverhulme Small Research Grant, while the collaboration between Alcorn, Truswell and Wallenberg emerged from a networking event in Campinas, Brazil, funded by the British Council and organised by Susan Pintzuk and Charlotte Galves. Thanks to Susan Pintzuk and Aaron Ecay for helping Truswell get started with the automatic parsing procedure, to Akiva Bacovcin, Aaron Ecay and Meredith Tamminga for making their scripts publicly available, and to Meg Laing for constant encouragement and support.

(Kroch et al. 2004) and the *Penn Parsed Corpus of Modern British English*, 2nd edition (Kroch et al. 2016). The *York–Toronto–Helsinki Corpus of Old English Prose* (YCOE) (Taylor et al. 2003), though not technically one of the PPCHE, follows almost identical annotation guidelines and provides the same type of data for the entirety of extant Old English prose, with manuscript dates from the 9th through early 12th centuries.

Each word in the PPCHE is annotated with a part-of-speech tag, sometimes indicating basic morphological information as well (e.g. BEP for a present-tense form of *be*). Phrases at various levels of syntactic constituency are grouped with brackets, which are labelled for their syntactic category (e.g. NP). These labels are often extended to indicate grammatical function as well (e.g. NP-SBJ for a subject noun phrase), and movement (i.e. displacement phenomena) and other nonlocal dependencies are indicated with various 'trace' and empty category tags. Each sentence tree in these corpora is also associated with a unique ID node, so that it is clear where each piece of data comes from in the output of a given search.[2] As an example, the full sentence token (i.e. matrix clause) in (1a) is shown in its PPCHE format in (1b). This illustrates the labelled bracketing format that is used in the corpus itself. Figure 2.1 gives the same information in a tree representation.

(1) a. *All things were made by it* 'all things were made by it'
     b. ```
((IP-MAT (NP-SBJ (Q All) (NS thinges))
          (BED were)
          (VAN made)
          (PP (P by)
              (NP (PRO it)))
          (. ,))
  (ID TYNDNEW-E1-H,I,1J.10))
```

The PPCHE format is designed for practicality rather than theoretical accuracy. Thus, the syntactic parses in these corpora, for example, do not identify VP nodes: instead, verbs and their associated arguments and adjuncts are grouped under a single IP node with no indication of internal sub-structure (as shown in (1b) and Figure 2.1). This decision allows the corpora to remain agnostic on the difficult question of the boundaries of VP in sentences from various stages of historical English. It also makes querying the corpora more straightforward, with no loss in search accuracy. This is characteristic of the kinds of decisions made in the PPCHE: the great advantage of this format is that it can be consistently implemented and easily queried.

Moreover, the stability of the PPCHE format is such that it can be generalised across different languages and genres, making possible controlled studies of syntactic variation across time, genre and language. For example, the *Icelandic Parsed Historical Corpus* (Wallenberg et al. 2011) uses essentially the same notation with, as far as is possible given the constraints of a different language, identical parsing decisions. There exist similar parsed diachronic corpora for historical French (Martineau et al. 2010)

---

[2] Tree IDs can also be useful in controlling for text-specific idiosyncrasies in mixed-effects statistical models.
```

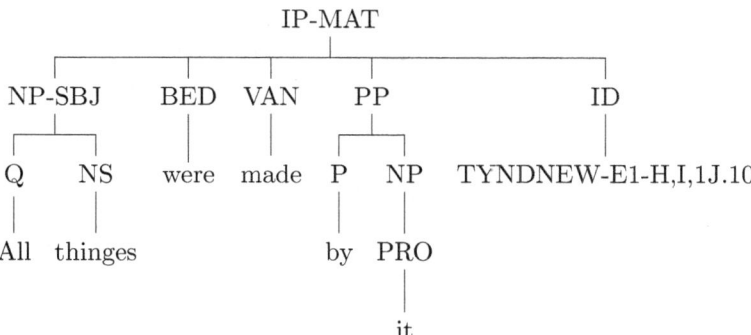

Figure 2.1 An example of a full sentence token in PPCHE format, represented as a tree diagram

and historical Portuguese (Galves and Faria 2010); these – along with the YCOE mentioned above, the *Parsed Corpus of Early English Correspondence* (Taylor et al. 2006), the *HeliPaD for Old Saxon* (Walkden 2016), the *Parsed Corpus of Early New High German* (Light 2011) and the *Parsed Corpus of Middle English Poetry* (Zimmermann 2014–) – form sister corpora to the PPCHE. The approach to parsing is similar enough in all of these corpora that queries (especially using the CorpusSearch query language; Randall 2000/2013) can be run on all of them with only minor modifications, yielding quantitatively comparable output. Because of its great flexibility and portability, the PPCHE format has become the pre-eminent format for diachronic syntax research.

The PPCHE do, however, have a number of limitations. They are built from published editions rather than manuscript texts, which means there is always at least one extra layer between analyst and primary data. Further, many of the source manuscripts are of unknown provenance, so information about time and place of composition is often limited in scope and precision – in particular, most texts are localised only to coarse-grained dialect areas. A third limiting factor is the absence of lemmatisation. A significant portion of PPCHE materials – especially those which pre-date the emergence of a national written standard – exhibit a great deal of non-semantic textual variation, due partly to differences in pronunciation, e.g. ME *mon, hond, lond* (with Southern rounding of Old English /ɑː/) vs. *man, hand, land* (without), and partly to different spelling practices, e.g. *ðu, þou, þu, you, yow, yu, thu* 'thou'. Controlling for such extensive spelling variation is a laborious process and one which is especially prone to error.

A major shortcoming of these corpora is the paucity of data for the period c.1250–1350. Only one text (the 3,534-word *Kentish Sermons*) is included from the late thirteenth century, while the earliest fourteenth-century text is the *Ayenbite of Inwyt*, from 1340. This data gap is no accident: with very few exceptions, the PPCHE are composed of prose texts, whereas the surviving English material from 1250–1340 is overwhelmingly verse. The gap is, however, extremely limiting for research on this period of English, and especially its syntax: recent corpus studies have emphasised that 1250–1340 is a transitional period for many syntactic phenomena, including the establishment of *not* as the expression of sentential negation (Ecay and Tamminga 2017), the fixing of the syntax of the dative alternation in ditransitive constructions

(Bacovcin 2017), and the introduction of argumental headed *wh*-relatives (Gisborne and Truswell 2017).[3] Any further parsed material from the late thirteenth and early fourteenth centuries would naturally help piece together the details of this period of wild change in English grammar.

3. LAEME: a solution to the PPCHE data gap

Since long before the advent of modern corpus linguistics, many different types of corpora have been compiled to feed and support all kinds of historical linguistic enquiry. Many of these corpora are tailored to the requirements of specific research communities. As a result, an efficient alternative to creating a corpus from scratch is often to adapt an existing corpus for other purposes. This approach has been pursued successfully in many cases: the PPCHE initially adapted the unparsed *Helsinki Corpus of English Texts* (Rissanen et al. 1991) by adding syntactic annotation, while the *Penn Discourse Treebank* (Prasad et al. 2008) consists of stand-off annotation of discourse relations designed to supplement the *Penn Treebank* (Marcus et al. 1999).

In a similar vein, the PLAEME project consists of adapting an existing corpus, namely a *Linguistic Atlas of Early Middle English* (LAEME), to remedy the PPCHE's data gap. First published online in 2008, LAEME was compiled from 167 samples of Early Middle English amounting to some 650,000 words in all. As a corpus, it contains all the necessary ingredients for adaptation to the PPCHE format.

First, all of the LAEME materials were written between c.1150 and c.1325, with a sizeable portion falling within the period for which PPCHE materials are lacking. The samples – a mixture of official records, prose, poetry and lyrics – are admittedly more diverse than are usually found in syntactic corpora. Moreover, they are weighted significantly towards verse texts, a genre dispreferred by syntacticians since authors may manipulate word order for reasons related to metre and rhyme.[4] Nonetheless, verse texts can help address many types of question relating to syntactic variation and change. It is possible to assess the magnitude of the effect of verse on the syntactic phenomenon of interest, and we sketch one method for addressing this issue in the conclusion. Moreover, in the case of English c.1300, there is little choice, as there are not enough surviving prose texts.[5]

Second, most of LAEME's samples are rich in metadata: 120 (72 per cent) are localised to a particular county – many to a particular town[6] – and most are dated to within

---

[3] In addition to these recent studies, overviews of these phenomena are included in standard reference works on Middle English syntax, including Mustanoja (1960), Visser (1963–73) and Fischer (1992). For background on Early Middle English syntax, see Moessner (1989).

[4] The PPCHE contain very few verse texts, but do include the *Ormulum*.

[5] Perhaps for this reason, no attempt is made in PPCHE to eliminate certain other potential sources of noise. For example, the *Kentish Sermons* (Laud Misc. 471), the only late thirteenth-century text in the PPCHE, is a collection of five sermons translated from French. According to Hall (1963: 669), the English translations are markedly literal and show French interference in their word order and idiom.

[6] The unlocalised samples exhibit regionally colourless types of language or are not consistent with a single variety.

25 years of their likely production date. Third, all of the samples were diplomatically transcribed from original manuscripts rather than printed editions, thus minimising the number of layers between analyst and primary evidence.

One further, enormous advantage of LAEME lies in its system of tagging. Although LAEME was constructed primarily for the benefit of historical dialectologists, its compiler had an eye on the possibility of future parsing from the outset and annotated the samples accordingly. As a result, LAEME tags have a number of features that make this corpus eminently suitable for automatic parsing.

Each tagged object in LAEME has the structure $lexel/grammel_FORM, with the lexel element identifying the word lexically (in much the same way as a lemma but often with additional information about word sense),[7] and the grammel identifying it grammatically. Grammels minimally specify word category but typically add morphological information such as number, person, tense and mood. The tag is attached to a form which represents the unit of analysis, i.e. the word or morpheme (inflectional and derivational morphemes are tagged separately in LAEME to facilitate the study of their histories). Words and morphemes are transcribed using upper case for plain text manuscript letters; capitalisation is indicated by a leading asterisk, e.g. manuscript *man* and *Man* ('man') are transcribed MAN and *MAN respectively. Lower-case letters are reserved for special characters: y for thorn ('þ'); d for edh ('ð'); z for yogh ('ʒ'); g for insular 'g' ('ᵹ'); m and n for abbreviated forms of these letters, etc. Word-internal morpheme boundaries are generally indicated by +.

Our ability to parse LAEME efficiently and accurately depended primarily on LAEME's grammels. A basic requirement for a syntactically parsed corpus is, of course, part-of-speech tagging. However, although many corpora incorporate this feature, LAEME's grammels are an order of magnitude more informative than usual. This can be seen by comparing the number of distinctions made: the PPCHE POS tag set contains ninety-two distinct tags, while LAEME (even disregarding distinct tags for affixes) uses over 2,000 distinct grammels. This is largely because the grammels indicate a word's grammatical function as well as basic part-of-speech information.

This makes it possible to automatically reconstruct a great deal of information about constituency and other syntactic relations implied by LAEME's grammels, and to automatically annotate the texts with that information in the PPCHE format. For example, the LAEME representation of (2a), given in (2b), can be identified as a noun phrase (NP) on the basis of constituent adjacency and information contained in the constituents' grammels: TN identifies yE as a determiner; aj identifies IUELE as an adjective; and n identifies MAN as a singular noun.

(2) a. *þe iuele man* 'the evil man'
    b. $/TN_yE
       $evil/aj_IUELE
       $man/n_MAN

---

[7] LAEME only provides lexels for content words, not function words like yE in (2b).

LAEME's grammels also identify grammatical function. In (3b), for example, the `Od` element identifies `yE RIzTE LAWE` as a direct object NP. (Indirect objects are identified by `Oi`, and the absence of any functional element in the grammels in (2b) identifies it as a subject NP.)

(3) a. *þe riȝte lawe* 'the right law'
   b. `$/TOd_yE`
      `$right/ajOd_RIzTE`
      `$law/nOd_LAWE`

In (4b), `NER yE SE` can be recognised as a prepositional phrase on the basis of `pr` in its constituents' grammels: `pr` alone identifies `NER` as the preposition, `<pr` identifies `yE` and `SE` as its dependents, and `<` indicates the relative position of the preposition to its dependents.

(4) a. *ner þe se* 'near the sea'
   b. `$near/pr_NER`
      `$/T<pr_yE`
      `$sea/n<pr_SE`

LAEME's grammels additionally project certain nonlocal dependencies. In (5b), for example, `HEOM` is tagged as a 3pl personal pronoun (`P23`) governed by a following preposition (`>pr`), and `TO` is tagged as a preposition (`pr`) that governs an object in a marked position, i.e. to its left (`<`).

(5) a. *& heom co(m) to þe halȝa gast* 'and the holy ghost came to them'
   b. `$&/cj_&`
      `$/P23>pr_HEOM`
      `$come/vSpt13_COm`
      `$to/pr<_TO`
      `$/TN_yE`
      `$holy/aj_HAL+gA $-ig/xs-aj_+gA`
      `$ghost/n_GAST`

The discontinuous PP in (5) can be reconstructed by matching the elements tagged `pr<` (the preposition) and `>pr` (its object).

In example (6) `RTIOd` identifies `dAT` as a relative pronoun (`RT`) with inanimate reference (indicated by `I`) in direct object function (`Od`), but there is nothing to indicate that it is an argument of `BRING+EN`. We have discovered, however, in the course of constructing PLAEME (see next section) that almost every relativised object is an argument of the next main verb encountered in the narrative. On that basis we have automatically annotated these dependencies with a high degree of accuracy.

(6) a. *ðat ghe ne migte hi(m) bringen on* '... that she may not prove against him'
   b. `$/RTIOd_dAT`

```
$/P13NF_GHE
$/neg-v_NE
$may/vpt13_MIGTE
$/P13>prM_HIm
$bring/vi_BRING+EN $/vi_+EN
$on{p}/pr<{rh}_ON
```

Despite the large amount of syntactic information contained in LAEME's grammels, some useful syntactic distinctions are not represented. The `cj` grammel, for example, is used for both subordinating and coordinating conjunctions, in contrast to the standard syntactic treatment of the former as complementisers. On the whole, however, the grammels' rich morphosyntactic information makes this particular corpus of tagged texts a near-perfect quarry for constructing a new syntactically parsed corpus of Early Middle English.

4. The construction of PLAEME

4.1 Text selection

We intend PLAEME as a bridge between the bodies of research carried out by historical dialectologists (using LAEME) and diachronic syntacticians (using the PPCHE). Historical dialectologists can use PLAEME to investigate syntactic variation and change, in addition to the lexical, phonological, morphological and orthographic variation that has typically occupied users of LAEME (e.g. Laing and Lass 2009; Gardner 2011; Studer-Joho 2014; Alcorn 2015; Lass and Laing 2016; Stenbrenden 2016). Diachronic syntacticians can use PLAEME to fill the data gap in existing parsed corpora, and can begin to investigate geographical variation, in addition to variation over time.

Parsing all of LAEME would allow us to include a wide range of Early Middle English texts, including multiple parallel versions of a number of individual texts for focused analysis of dialectal and idiolectal variation. Unfortunately, we are presently unable to parse the whole of LAEME for lack of resources. We have therefore initially chosen to maximise the diversity of the texts included in PLAEME, and we hope in future to be able to expand PLAEME to include parallel versions of texts.

PLAEME currently consists of sixty-eight texts (172,624 words). This is an exhaustive sample of LAEME texts which meet the following criteria:

1. The text is from 1250–1325;
2. no parsed version of the text currently exists;
3. the text is longer than 100 words.

Where multiple versions of the same text meet those criteria, we have chosen a single version with a view to balancing material across dialects as far as possible; all else being equal we parsed the longest version.

LAEME files do not correspond to conventional texts, but to samples of individual text languages, in the sense of Laing (2010: 237, fn. 1). Accordingly, there is a many-to-many relationship between LAEME files and conventional texts. Because of this, we have split LAEME files into their component texts and only included those texts in PLAEME which meet the above criteria. For instance, the LAEME file digby86mapt contains nineteen verse texts from the manuscript Digby 86 that are in unmixed South-West Midlands language. Several of these verse texts (for instance, *The Fox and the Wolf*) have already been parsed in at least one version (in this case, in the *Parsed Corpus of Middle English Poetry*). We have not reparsed those texts, but have split digby86mapt into nineteen files corresponding to those nineteen texts, and included those (e.g. digby86bede, the *Sayings of Bede*) of 100 words or more which have not previously been parsed. Again, this makes PLAEME more accessible to researchers familiar with the PPCHE, where files correspond to texts rather than text languages. The documentation for PLAEME details the correspondences between PLAEME files and LAEME files.

Figure 2.2 shows how material from PLAEME fills the PPCHE data gap. The combination of material from the PPCHE, the YCOE (Taylor et al. 2003) and PLAEME now offers unbroken coverage of the history of English, from the start of the written record to 1914.

The most common reason why texts included in PLAEME were omitted from the PPCHE is because PLAEME is composed of verse texts, with the exception of a few small legal documents. We have included three sample analyses in section 5 to show

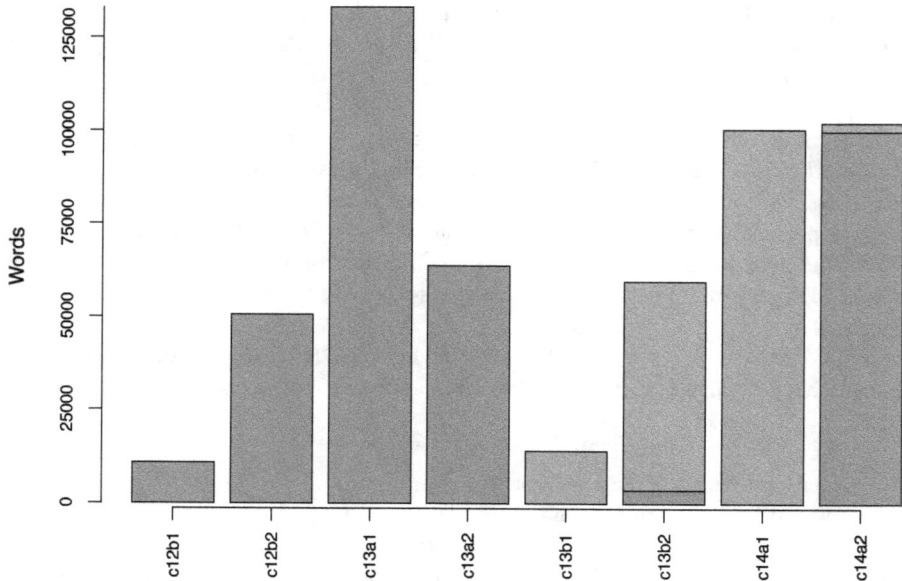

Figure 2.2 Material from the PPCHE (in blue) is complemented by material from PLAEME (in red)

the prospects for use of PLAEME in syntactic analysis and to indicate that use of verse texts does not produce outlandish results.

4.2 Annotation

We used an automatic annotation process to project a first-pass representation of syntactic structure based as far as possible on the information contained in LAEME's grammels (see section 3), supplemented by inferences based on basic English grammar (for example, sentences do not have two subjects; or if a sentence has a direct object but no subject, the subject is probably either null or displaced).

The automatic annotation process, which uses the corpus revision function of CorpusSearch (Randall 2000/2013), inserts labelled brackets around likely constituents, as well as many empty categories. For example, the information in (4) tells us that *ner þe se* is a prepositional phrase, but also indirectly implies that *þe se* is an NP, because *þe* and *se* are tagged as determiner and noun respectively, both dependent on the immediately preceding preposition. Accordingly, we automatically project the following labelled bracket representation of (4).[8]

(7) (PP (P ner-near)
        (NP (D +te-the)
            (N se-sea)))

Similarly, we automatically project (8a) on the basis of (6): the *T* ('trace') indicates that the relative clause appears to contain a direct object gap, while *ICH* ('insert constituent here') indicates that the NP *him* is a nonlocal complement of *on*. During manual correction of this automatically generated parse, indices are added to indicate that (WNP 0) is associated with the direct object trace, (NP-OB1 *T*), and the pronoun *him* with the complement of *on*, (NP *ICH*). Moreover, the context surrounding this example, in the Middle English *Genesis and Exodus*, makes it clear that this is actually a free relative: *And seið ioseph hire þulde don ðat ghe ne migte hi(m) bringen on* 'And (she) says that Joseph would do to her what she could not prove against him'. The LAEME annotation does not systematically distinguish between headed and free relatives, so the distinction has to be made manually in this, and most other, cases. This manual editing leads to the final representation in (8b).[9]

(8) a. (CP-REL (WNP 0)
              (C +dat-that)
              (IP-SUB (NP-OB1 *T*)

---

[8] In addition to projecting the syntactic structure implicit in (4), (7) shows the LAEME transcription converted to PPCHE norms (where +t, rather than y, represents thorn, for example), the preservation of LAEME lexels as lemmata, and the postulation of lemmata for function words like *the*, which were not annotated with lexels in LAEME.

[9] (8) also shows the -RH dash tag, an addition to the PPCHE format. This tag marks rhymes, as indicated by {rh} in LAEME's grammels.

```
                (NP-SBJ (PRO ghe-she))
                (NEG ne-ne)
                (MD migte-may)
                (NP him-him)
                (VB bring+en-bring)
                (PP (P-RH on-on)
                    (NP *ICH*))))
    b.  (CP-FRL (WNP-1 0)
                (C +dat-that)
                (IP-SUB (NP-OB1 *T*-1)
                        (NP-SBJ (PRO ghe-she))
                        (NEG ne-ne)
                        (MD migte-may)
                        (NP-2 him-him)
                        (VB bring+en-bring)
                        (PP (P-RH on-on)
                            (NP *ICH*-2))))
```

Almost all of the information in (7) and (8a) is implicit in the LAEME tags, but the automatic conversion process makes that information visible in a format that can be queried by standard software like CorpusSearch, and more readily assimilated by syntacticians used to thinking in terms of constituent structure.

This initial annotation process is error-prone. Some errors can be corrected automatically with adjustment rules (for example, LAEME tags both *that* and *and* as conjunctions, as mentioned in section 3, so we automatically retag *that* as a complementiser, while leaving *and* as a conjunction), but a substantial residue of errors remains, in part because of the lack of explicit indication of sentence boundaries in Early Middle English manuscript material. We have therefore hand-corrected all automatically annotated texts using Annotald (Beck, Ecay and Ingason 2011), bespoke software for rapid and accurate correction of PPCHE-format corpora. The virtues of this two-stage process are a combination of speed and accuracy: correction of automatically annotated text is both faster and more accurate than manual annotation typically is.

5. Case studies

As mentioned earlier, the Early Middle English period saw rapid syntactic change, and in many cases the quantitative investigation of those changes has been severely hampered by the paucity of parsed material from 1250–1350, which we will refer to below as the 'PLAEME window'. In many respects, despite dramatic changes in inflectional morphology and basic word order, the morphosyntax of the *Ormulum* or *Ancrene Wisse* hadn't moved far beyond Old English. By the mid-to-late fourteenth century, the time of the *Ayenbite of Inwyt* or Chaucer, a recognisably modern syntax had emerged. How this happened in the space of a few generations is quite unclear. We hope that PLAEME can help to cast light on this period of change.

We illustrate the use of PLAEME in relation to an opportunistic selection of three studies of Middle English syntax recently published in Mathieu and Truswell (2017). In none of these cases do we intend to delve too deeply into our findings, or engage with the broader theoretical points made by the authors; rather, we aim to show that, in these PPCHE-based studies, much of the action happened while our back was turned, so to speak. In many cases, investigation of the early stages of a grammatical change has revealed unseen details (see, for instance, Ecay 2015 on properties of affirmative *do* in the early stages of the rise of *do*-support). We hope that investigating the early stages of these rapid changes using PLAEME will be similarly revealing.

5.1 The expression of negation

In Old English, sentential negation was typically expressed by the preverbal particle *ne* (9). Since c.1450, postverbal *not* has been universally used instead (10). Middle English is the transitional period between these two systems.

(9) ... ac   hie   ne   dorston þær   on   cuman
          But they not dared   there in   come
    '... But they did not dare enter there' (Traugott 2008: 267)

(10) It is not neccessari to declare what it was (Capgrave, Chronicle, a1464)

The details of the transition have been debated in a recent string of papers (Frisch 1997; Wallage 2008; Ecay and Tamminga 2017). Much of the debate concerns the status of a hybrid system, in which both preverbal *ne* and postverbal *not* appear, as in (11).

(11) he ne shall nouȝt deceive him
     (*Earliest Prose Psalter*, c.1350; Frisch 1997, cited in Ecay and Tamminga 2017: 206)

Ecay and Tamminga give a graphical representation of the diachrony of these three competing variants; Figure 2.3 is based on their Figure 13.2, p. 207.[10]

Figure 2.3 shows that PPCHE data indicates a stable Early Middle English system that held until c.1250, with *ne* as the majority variant, c.25 per cent of tokens using *ne . . . not*, and near-complete absence of *not*. By 1350, *ne* had largely vanished, with most texts using simple *ne* less than 10 per cent of the time. In the late fourteenth

---

[10] Figure 2.3 is not identical to Ecay and Tamminga's figure in one salient respect: they have a very large point representing a large amount of text from the year 1300. Inspection of their corpus queries (freely available at https://github.com/aecay/digs15-negative-priming) indicates that this is a result of an error in their query, which results in several fourteenth-century texts being dated at precisely 1300, and several fifteenth-century texts at precisely 1400. Correcting this error also leads to markedly different regression curves for the diachronic trajectories of the different variants, compared to Ecay and Tamminga's figure. We hasten to add that this parochial error does not affect any of Ecay and Tamminga's theoretical arguments.

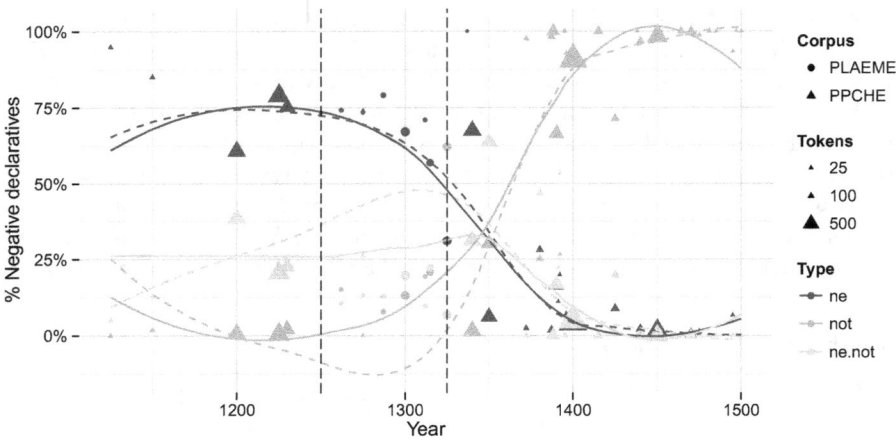

Figure 2.3 Competing expressions of sentential negation in Middle English. Vertical lines indicate the PLAEME window. The dashed lines represent lowess regression lines taking only PPCHE data into account. The solid lines are based on both PPCHE and PLAEME data

century, both *ne . . . not* and *not* are found in significant proportions, with *not* approaching 100 per cent usage by 1400.

What happened between 1250 and 1350 is not clear from the PPCHE data. The only substantial text in this period is the *Ayenbite of Inwyt* (1340), which looks largely similar to texts from 100 years earlier in terms of negation, with majority *ne* use, some use of *ne . . . not*, and no simple *not*.[11] However, the *Earliest Prose Psalter*, just ten years later, favours *ne . . . not* and *not*, and almost never uses simple *ne*. Lowess regression curves based on PPCHE data alone (represented with dashed lines in Figure 2.3) suggest that the frequency of *ne* declines from c.1275, following an S-shaped trajectory as it loses ground initially to *ne . . . not*, which follows a 'failed change' trajectory peaking around 1300, and then to *not*, which increases steeply in frequency after 1325.

Because there is almost no PPCHE data in the PLAEME window, the dashed regression lines in Figure 2.3 during that period are based on interpolation between pre-1250 and post-1340 data, plus the minimal amount of data gathered from the 3,534-word *Kentish Sermons*, c.1275. The PLAEME data suggests several refinements to this picture, as represented by the solid lines in Figure 2.3.[12] The trajectory for

---

[11] As Laing (2013–) observes, the *Ayenbite* was written by a seventy-year-old scribe and so its language may be taken as representative of the late thirteenth rather than the mid-fourteenth century.

[12] See also Laing (2002) for an examination of the distribution of different forms of negation on the basis of an early version of LAEME. Laing's research is partly a response to research by Jack (1978a, 1978b) describing constraints on the syntactic contexts in which *ne . . . not* occurs. Jack's work, on the basis of Middle English prose texts, informed Wallage's response to Frisch and was extended by Iyeiri (1992), who examined verse texts including several that appear in LAEME. Thanks to Meg Laing for pointing us to this body of literature.

simplex *ne* is almost unchanged by the addition of the PLAEME data, but the 'failed change' trajectory for *ne . . . not* becomes much less apparent, as the PLAEME data suggests a more or less stable rate of c. 25 per cent *ne . . . not* use throughout the thirteenth and early fourteenth centuries, followed by a decline in tandem with simplex *ne* in the late fourteenth century. Meanwhile, the emergence of simplex *not* is taken to be more gradual (the solid regression line for *not* moves above 0 about a generation earlier once PLAEME data is added to the analysis). Although *not* remains a marginal variant throughout the PLAEME window, there are some examples as early as the late thirteenth century; (12) is one of the first.

(12) *Suyc richesse p(re)yse ic nout* 'I do not praise such riches'
(tr323bt, Homily for the anniversary of St Nicholas, c13b1)

All of these adjustments to the diachronic picture that emerges can be seen as consequences of a reduced emphasis on the *Ayenbite* and *Earliest Prose Psalter*. Both of these are outliers in certain ways: the *Ayenbite* is the last major text with a majority of *ne* and almost no *not*, while the *Earliest Prose Psalter* is the only major text to use >50 per cent *ne . . . not*. Adding the PLAEME data reduces the influence of these two texts over the regression lines.

5.2 Case and word order in ditransitives

Bacovcin (2017) describes a complex series of changes in the syntax of recipient–theme ditransitives like *give*, leading ultimately to the emergence of the Present-Day English grammar, which allows an alternation between *give* $NP_{recipient}$ NP_{theme}, and *give* NP_{theme} *to* $NP_{recipient}$. Bacovcin is particularly interested in the diachrony of a 'failed change', in which a third variant, *give to* $NP_{recipient}$ NP_{theme}, as in (13), initially gains ground before gradually disappearing over the course of Middle and Early Modern English.

(13) *he ne shal nouʒt ʒeven to God his quemeyng* 'he shall not give God his appeasement'
(Earliest Prose Psalter, c.1350)

Two approaches to the modelling of failed changes, and their relationship to successful changes, have recently been proposed. Postma (2010, 2017) models the U-shaped diachronic trajectory of a failed change as the first derivative of the S-shaped trajectory of a successful change, implying that each failed change is directly linked to a successful change. Bacovcin proposes instead, based on the diachrony of the order in (13), that failed changes result from interactions among multiple successful changes, in this case a first change introducing *to* as a marker of dative case on recipients in both word orders, and a second change introducing the modern split system, in which *to* only surfaces in theme–recipient orders. The first change feeds the rise of examples like (13); the second change bleeds it.[13]

---

[13] The hybrid *ne . . . not* negator described in section 5.1 is also a failed change, as an Early Middle English innovation which disappeared in the fifteenth century. To our knowledge it

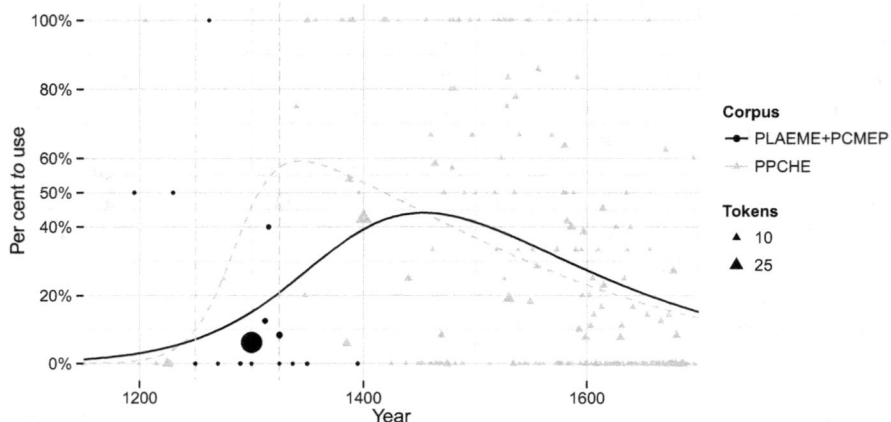

Figure 2.4 Competition between recipient–theme ditransitives with and without *to* in Middle and Early Modern English. The vertical lines indicate the PLAEME window. The dashed curve represents the fit from the Probability Multiplication Model adopted by Bacovcin (2017). The solid line represents the fit from the same model to PPCHE, PCMEP and PLAEME data combined

Bacovcin's Probability Multiplication Model predicts a trajectory for examples like (13) as shown in Figure 2.4 (based on Bacovin's Figure 7.2, p. 98), where the proportion of V NP$_{recipient}$ NP$_{theme}$ orders that contain *to* before the recipient rises throughout Middle English to a peak at approximately 1350.[14]

Unfortunately, data concerning the relevant variants in Early Middle English is very scarce: Bacovcin's analysis of the failed change applies specifically to ditransitives with transfer-of-possession meanings (canonically *give*), where the recipient precedes the theme, both arguments are realised as full NPs, and neither argument is topicalised. Although this strict specification is empirically justified, it means that a very large amount of data is discarded, and only a handful of examples retained. Bacovcin has only four such examples that he dates to within the PLAEME window (one with *to*) and fifty-one from the century prior to the PLAEME window (nine with *to*). Eight of these examples with *to* occur in the same text, namely the *Brut Chronicle*, normally dated to the end of the fourteenth century but dated in Bacovcin's data at 1215. Disregarding this possibly misleading data point, the PPCHE data amounts to forty

---

has not yet been studied from the modelling perspective of Postma or Bacovcin. In principle, PLAEME data could also be used to ground a model of the interactions between the failed change introducing *ne* . . . *not*, and the successful replacement of *ne* by *not*.

[14] Bacovcin's original scripts and datasets for the analysis of Middle English ditransitives are available as online supplementary materials accompanying Mathieu and Truswell (2017), at http://www.oup.co.uk/companion/DiGS15. Although Bacovcin's data covers both recipient–theme and theme–recipient orders, here we only show data concerning recipient–theme orders, as the spread of *to* in theme–recipient orders was clearly well on its way to completion by the start of the PLAEME window.

tokens pre-1250 (one with *to*) and four tokens during the PLAEME window (one with *to*). After the PLAEME window, data is plentiful, supporting the gradual decline of the failed change, but the abruptness of the rise of V *to* $NP_{recipient}$ NP_{theme} is very much open to question.

Because of the scarcity of data, Figure 2.4 shows the addition of data from both PLAEME and the Parsed Corpus of Middle English Poetry (PCMEP, Zimmermann 2014–), which contains thirty-eight poems (107,299 words) from c.1150–1420. This adds 128 further data points (sixteen from PCMEP, of which nine are within the PLAEME window, and 112 from PLAEME, although sixty-four of these are from a single file, namely buryFft, the English texts from the Sacrist's Register of Bury St Edmunds, dated to c.1300). In Figure 2.4, we have also adjusted the date of the *Brut Chronicle* to 1400.

The effect of adding these extra data points can be seen by comparing the dashed regression line (PPCHE data only) with the solid line (data from PPCHE, PCMEP and PLAEME). The revised estimates for the diachrony of V *to* $NP_{recipient}$ NP_{theme} show a more gradual increase in frequency, and a lower and later peak frequency. We have not investigated the implications of these findings for Bacovcin's theoretical claims about the modelling of failed changes. In particular, the asymmetry of Bacovcin's curve (based on only PPCHE data) is crucial to his argument for the Probability Multiplication Model. The revised curve including PLAEME and PCMEP data appears visually to be more symmetrical, and so to offer less strong support for Bacovcin's model, but we have not attempted any quantitative model comparison.

A reviewer comments that the choice of ditransitive construction in PLAEME texts could be affected by factors such as weight, animacy, information structure, metre and rhyme. Bacovcin investigated the first three of these for his data, but we have made no effort to do so in this brief report. In principle, though, the method described in section 6 below could be used to investigate whether there is any systematic effect of metre and rhyme on choice of ditransitive construction.[15]

5.3 Argumental and adverbial *wh*-relatives

Gisborne and Truswell (2017) describe the introduction of headed *wh*-relatives in Middle English, and the division of labour between interrogative and demonstrative forms as relativisers. One of their key claims is that there is no straightforward replacement of demonstrative with interrogative forms. In other words, it is not the case that interrogative forms are co-opted into the system of relative pronouns as direct replacements for the demonstrative forms that were radically levelled at the start of the Middle English period. Rather, interrogative *where* and demonstrative *there* coexisted as relativisers throughout Middle English, while there was a 100-year gap between the disappearance of the *se*-series of argumental demonstrative relatives and the first uses of argumental *which* (and later *whom* and *who*) as relativisers. That 100-year gap is the period labelled as M2 in the PPCHE, spanning 1250–1350, almost perfectly coextensive with the PLAEME

---

[15] Note that most relevant examples in PLAEME come from wills and other legal documents, rather than verse texts, particularly buryFft.

window. Of course, given the scarcity of data from that period, any claims of absolute absence are crying out for re-evaluation in the light of further data.

Further analysis of PPCHE data concerning *where* and *there* as relativisers, beyond that carried out by Gisborne and Truswell, suggests that little of interest happened during the PLAEME window. Although the two forms did indeed coexist for centuries, they were functionally specialised: *where* was an R-pronoun in the sense of van Riemsdijk (1978): it could precede a preposition in relativisers such as *whereby* or *wherethrough* (14), but there are no instances of *where* as a strictly locative relativiser in the PPCHE until the *Ayenbite* in 1340. *There* remains the locative relativiser throughout Early Middle English, including the PLAEME window, in examples such as (15), and is rapidly replaced by *where* in the late fourteenth century. Moreover, although *there* clearly is used as an R-pronoun in Old and Early Middle English, it is apparently not an R-pronoun when used as a relativiser. That is, there are no examples like (14) with *there* replacing *where*.

(14) For þe eareste Pilunge, hwer of al þis uuel is, nis buten of pride 'For the first peeling, where all this evil comes from, is just of pride' (*Ancrene Riwle*, c13b)

(15) bi hald inwart þer ich am & ne seh þu me naut wið uten þin heorte 'Look inward, where I am, and you don't see me without your heart' (*Ancrene Riwle*, c13b)

This refines the empirical picture presented by Gisborne and Truswell but supports the basic claim of largely stable coexistence of *where* and *there* as relativisers throughout Middle English, including the PLAEME window. PLAEME data indeed supports this claim: *where* is used in relative clauses only as an R-pronoun, and *there* as a locative relative.

Of more interest is the diachrony of argument gap *wh*-relatives in PLAEME. Figure 2.5 graphs the percentage of argument gap relatives with a *wh*-relativiser in Middle English.

The PPCHE indicate that complementiser *that* is by far the most common relativiser prior to 1250, despite sporadic use of *wh*-forms. After the PLAEME window, the *Ayenbite* (1340) shows almost no argument gap *wh*-relatives (less than 1 per cent of the 1,117 argument gap relatives use *which*, and other *wh*-relativisers are not used at all for argument gap relatives). Around ten years later, the *Earliest Prose Psalter* uses *which* in 12.3 per cent of the 413 headed relatives with an NP argument gap, and argument gap *wh*-relatives are clearly beginning to be established by the late fourteenth century, for instance in Chaucer and the Wycliffite Bible.

As for the PLAEME window, most texts behave in line with Gisborne and Truswell's claims, and categorically use *that* (or zero) for argument gap relatives. However, there are some occasional examples of *which* or *who*, such as (16), in line with the sporadic earlier argument gap *wh*-relatives noted above.

(16) al erue and prim and pilde der. // Qpel man mai sen on perlde her. 'all cattle and serpents and wild animals which one may see in the world here'

(genexodt, *Genesis and Exodus*, c14a1)

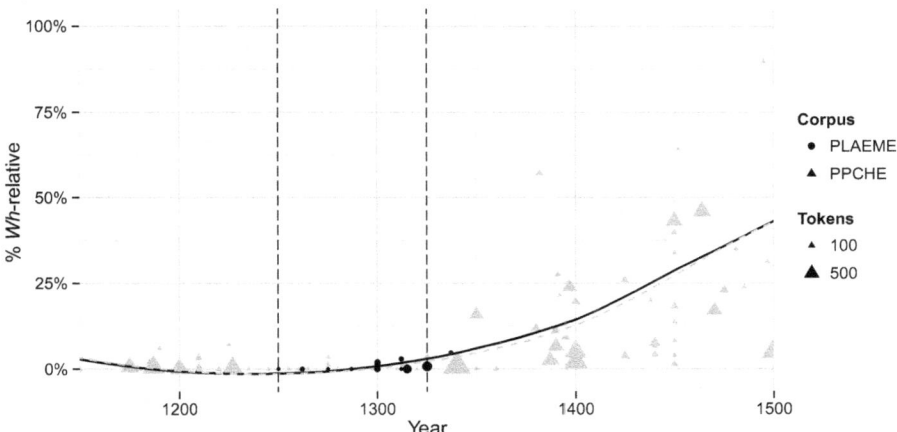

Figure 2.5 Use of *wh*-forms in argument gap headed relative clauses in Middle and Early Modern English. Vertical lines indicate the PLAEME window. The dashed and solid lowess regression lines (PPCHE data only and PPCHE + PLAEME data combined) are virtually identical

This may suggest that argument gap *wh*-relatives were available at a very low frequency for some time prior to their late fourteenth-century diffusion. Alternatively, the emergence of argument gap *wh*-relatives may reflect repeated sporadic innovations throughout Middle English that only began to diffuse in the second half of the fourteenth century.

6. Conclusion

The Parsed Linguistic Atlas of Early Middle English is a fairly small parsed corpus, but it can be of significant use as a supplement to the Penn Parsed Corpora of Historical English in tracking the multiple overlapping rapid changes that take place in the sparsely documented period 1250–1325. The case studies in section 5 show how PLAEME can inform our understanding of changes in the morphosyntax of negation, ditransitives and headed relative clauses. We expect that PLAEME will be of similar use in investigating other grammatical changes in Middle English.

In many respects discussed in the case studies in section 5, PLAEME data is conservative, in the sense that syntactic variables observed in texts from 1250–1325 have more in common with texts from before 1250 than with texts from after 1325. This suggests that the grammatical changes in question were often more abrupt than previously thought. Alternatively, it is possible that the results we have presented reflect some systematic difference between PLAEME and PPCHE texts, such as a difference between verse and prose.

A possible method for investigating the influence of verse on the syntax of a text may be to use the PCMEP. PCMEP overlaps temporally with PLAEME to an extent, but also overlaps significantly with the prose texts of the PPCHE. By comparing results from PCMEP and the PPCHE, it is possible to assess whether verse texts behave differently from prose texts with respect to the variable of interest. If they do not, then properties of verse texts in PLAEME are probably also not attributable to an effect of verse.

PLAEME currently covers approximately one-third of the material included in the unparsed Linguistic Atlas of Early Middle English. We hope in future to expand PLAEME to cover the period 1150–1250, and parallel versions of a single text, to open up these Penn-format resources to canonical historical dialectology methods. Also for the future is the possibility of parsing the Linguistic Atlas of Older Scots (Williamson 2008–), which is in a similar format to LAEME, to facilitate the quantitative investigation of the much-neglected diachrony of Scots syntax.

References

Alcorn, Rhona (2015). 'Pronoun innovation in Middle English', *Folia Linguistica Historica* 36: 1–17.
Bacovcin, Hezekiah Akiva (2017). 'Modelling interactions between morphosyntactic changes', in Mathieu and Truswell (2017), pp. 94–103.
Beck, Jana, Aaron Ecay and Anton Karl Ingason (2011). Annotald, version 1.3.8 (available from https://annotald.github.io/).
Ecay, Aaron (2015). 'A multi-step analysis of the evolution of English *do*-support', PhD thesis, University of Pennsylvania.
Ecay, Aaron and Meredith Tamminga (2017). 'Persistence as a diagnostic of grammatical status: The case of Middle English negation', in Mathieu and Truswell (2017), pp. 202–215.
Fischer, Olga (1992). 'Syntax', in Norman Blake (ed.), *The Cambridge History of the English Language*, vol. 2, 1066–1476, Cambridge: Cambridge University Press, pp. 207–408.
Frisch, Stefan (1997). 'The change in negation in Middle English: A NEGP licensing account', *Lingua* 101: 21–64.
Galves, Charlotte and Pablo Faria (2010). The Tycho Brahe Corpus of Historical Portuguese, Department of Linguistics, University of Campinas (UNICAMP) (available at http://www.tycho.iel.unicamp.br/~tycho/).
Gardner, Anne-Christine (2011). 'Word formation in Early Middle English: Abstract nouns in the *Linguistic Atlas of Early Middle English*', in Paul Rayson, Sebastian Hoffmann and Geoffrey Leech (eds), *Studies in Variation, Contacts and Change in English 6: Methodological and Historical Dimensions of Corpus Linguistics* (available at www.helsinki.fi/varieng/journal/volumes/06/gardner).
Gisborne, Nikolas and Robert Truswell (2017). 'Where do relative specifiers come from?', in Mathieu and Truswell (2017), pp. 25–42.
Hall, Joseph (1963). *Selections from Early Middle English 1130–1250. Part I*, 2nd edition, Oxford: Clarendon Press.
Iyeiri, Yoko (1992). 'Negative constructions in selected Middle English verse texts', PhD thesis, University of St Andrews.
Jack, George (1978a). 'Negative adverbs in Early Middle English', *English Studies* 59: 295–309.
Jack, George (1978b). 'Negation in later Middle English prose', *Archivum Linguisticum* n.s. 9: 58–72.

Kroch, Anthony and Ann Taylor (2000). Penn–Helsinki Parsed Corpus of Middle English, 2nd edition, release 4, University of Pennsylvania (available at https://www.ling.upenn.edu/hist-corpora/PPCME2-RELEASE-4/index.html).

Kroch, Anthony, Beatrice Santorini and Lauren Delfs (2004). Penn–Helsinki Parsed Corpus of Early Modern English, release 3, University of Pennsylvania (available at https://www.ling.upenn.edu/hist-corpora/PPCEME-RELEASE-3/index.html).

Kroch, Anthony, Beatrice Santorini and Ariel Diertani (2016). Penn Parsed Corpus of Modern British English, 2nd edition, release 1, University of Pennsylvania (available at https://www.ling.upenn.edu/hist-corpora/PPCMBE2-RELEASE-1/index.html).

Laing, Margaret (2002). 'Corpus-provoked questions about negation in Early Middle English', *Language Sciences* 24: 297–321.

Laing, Margaret (2010). 'The reflexes of OE *beon* as a marker of futurity in Early Middle English', in Ursula Lenker, Judith Huber and Robert Mailhammer (eds), *English Historical Linguistics 2008, Vol. 1: The History of English Verbal and Nominal Constructions*, Amsterdam: John Benjamins, pp. 237–254.

Laing, Margaret (2013–). A Linguistic Atlas of Early Middle English, 1150–1325, version 3.2, University of Edinburgh (available at http://www.lel.ed.ac.uk/ihd/laeme2/laeme2.html).

Laing, Margaret and Roger Lass (2009). 'Shape-shifting, sound-change and the genesis of prodigal writing systems', *English Language and Linguistics* 13: 1–31.

Lass, Roger and Margaret Laing (2016). 'Q is for what, when, where? The 'q' spellings for OE hw-', *Folia Linguistica Historica* 37: 61–110.

Light, Caitlin (2011). Parsed Corpus of Early New High German, University of Pennsylvania (available at http://enhgcorpus.wikispaces.com/).

Marcus, Mitchell, Beatrice Santorini, Mary Ann Marcinkiewicz and Ann Taylor (1999). Treebank-3 LDC99T42, Philadelphia, PA: Linguistic Data Consortium (available at https://catalog.ldc.upenn.edu/LDC99T42).

Martineau, France, Paul Hirschbühler, Anthony Kroch and Yves Charles Morin (2010). Modéliser le changement: les voies du français. Université d'Ottawa (available at http://www.arts.uottawa.ca/voies/voies_fr.html).

Mathieu, Éric and Robert Truswell, eds (2017). *Macro-change and Micro-change in Diachronic Syntax*, Oxford: Oxford University Press.

Moessner, Lilo (1989). *Early Middle English Syntax*, Tübingen: Niemeyer.

Mustanoja, Tauno (1960). *A Middle English Syntax, Part I*, Helsinki: Société néophilologique.

Postma, Gertjan (2010). 'The impact of failed changes', in Anne Breitbarth, Christopher Lucas, Sheila Watts and David Willis (eds), *Continuity and Change in Grammar*, Amsterdam: John Benjamins, pp. 269–302.

Postma, Gertjan (2017). 'Modelling transient states in language change', in Mathieu and Truswell (2017), pp. 75–93.

Prasad, Rashmi, Nikhil Dinesh, Alan Lee, Eleni Mitsakaki, Livio Robaldo, Aravind Joshi and Bonnie Webber (2008). 'The Penn Discourse Treebank 2.0', in *Proceedings of the 6th International Conference on Language Resources and Evaluation* (LREC), Marrakech.

Randall, Beth (2000/2013). CorpusSearch 2: A tool for linguistics research (available at http://corpussearch.sourceforge.net/CS.html).

Riemsdijk, Henk van (1978). *A Case Study in Syntactic Markedness: The Binding Nature of Prepositional Phrases*, Dordrecht: Foris.

Rissanen, Matti, Merja Kytö, Leena Kahlas-Tarkka, Matti Kilpiö, Saara Nevanlinna, Irma Taavitsainen, Terttu Nevalainen and Helena Raumolin-Brunberg (1991). The Helsinki Corpus of English Texts, University of Helsinki (available at http://www.helsinki.fi/varieng/CoRD/corpora/HelsinkiCorpus/).

Stenbrenden, Gjertrud Flermoen (2016). *Long-Vowel Shifts in English, c.1050–1700: Evidence from Spelling*, Cambridge: Cambridge University Press.

Studer-Joho, Nicole (2014). *Diffusion and Change in Early Middle English: Methodological and Theoretical Implications from the LAEME Corpus of Tagged Texts*, Tübingen: Francke Verlag.

Taylor, Ann, Anthony Warner, Susan Pintzuk and Frank Beths (2003). The York–Toronto–Helsinki Parsed Corpus of Old English Prose (available at http://www-users.york.ac.uk/~lang22/YcoeHome1.htm).

Taylor, Ann, Arja Nurmi, Anthony Warner, Susan Pintzuk and Terttu Nevalainen (2006). York–Helsinki Parsed Corpus of Early English Correspondence, University of York and University of Helsinki. Distributed through the Oxford Text Archive (available at http://ota.ox.ac.uk/desc/2510).

Traugott, Elizabeth Closs (2008). 'Syntax', in Richard Hogg (ed.), *The Cambridge History of the English Language, Volume 1: Beginnings to 1066*, Cambridge: Cambridge University Press, pp. 168–289.

Visser, Fredericus Th. (1963–73). *An Historical Syntax of the English Language*, Leiden: Brill.

Walkden, George (2016). 'The HeliPaD: A parsed corpus of Old Saxon', *International Journal of Corpus Linguistics* 21: 559–571.

Wallage, Phillip (2008). 'Jespersen's Cycle in Middle English: Parametric variation and grammatical competition', *Lingua* 118: 643–674.

Wallenberg, Joel C., Anton K. Ingason, Einar F. Sigurðsson and Eiríkur Rögnvaldsson (2011). Icelandic Parsed Historical Corpus (IcePaHC), version 0.9 (available at http://www.linguist.is/icelandic_treebank).

Williamson, Keith (2008–). A Linguistic Atlas of Older Scots, Phase 1: 1380–1500, version 1.2 (available at http://www.lel.ed.ac.uk/ihd/laos1/laos1.html).

Zimmermann, Richard (2014–). Parsed Corpus of Middle English Poetry (available at http://pcmep.net/).

3

Approaching Transition Scots from a Micro-perspective: The *Dunfermline Corpus*, 1573–1723

Klaus Hofmann

1. Introduction

This chapter explores the potential of early modern Scottish manuscript evidence for linguistic enquiry. In doing so, the chapter pursues two major objectives. Its first goal is to assess the merits of recasting the one-and-a-half centuries between the Scottish Reformation (1560) and the Union of the Parliaments (1707) as a linguistically insightful period in its own right regarding the study of written Scots. This view represents a shift in perspective since previous literature has either treated this period as one of language (re-)standardisation through Anglicisation (Devitt 1989; Agutter 1990; Bugaj 2004), or as a showcase for linguistic diffusion of selected orthographic, grammatical and lexical features in various socio-pragmatically defined text genres and geographical space (Devitt 1989; Meurman-Solin 1993, 1997, 2000). It will be argued that existing studies have barely scratched the surface of a linguistically unique contact situation involving two related but markedly different written varieties on the verge of standardisation.

The second goal places this chapter firmly in the realm of digital approaches to historical linguistics as it aims to introduce and publicise a new electronic corpus of early modern Scottish legal-administrative texts, compiled from archive material. This corpus – named the Dunfermline Corpus after the burgh where the material originated – can be regarded as an initial effort to expand the Edinburgh-based *Linguistic Atlas of Older Scots* (LAOS) into the early modern period. In contrast to most corpus projects, the *Dunfermline Corpus* is narrowly focused on scribal idiolects of individual town clerks and scribes, conceptualised here as a community of practice (Lave and Wenger 1991). It is argued that this sociolinguistic micro-approach is uniquely suited for capturing linguistic diversity in local records while making the best use of the historical evidence. It manages to unite linguistic features with crucial extralinguistic information contained in the manuscript sources to arrive at a comprehensive analysis of patterns of language variation and change.

The chapter is structured as follows: section 2 reviews the literature on Early Modern Scots and discusses new avenues for approaching this period. Section 3 introduces the Dunfermline material within both its academic and socio-historical contexts. Two short pilot studies in section 4 illustrate the functionality of the corpus. Section 5 concludes the chapter with a brief summary and outlook.

2. Anglicisation and Transition Scots

The term 'Scots' generally refers to the Germanic language of Lowland Scotland, which has historically diverged from Southern English and developed its own phonological, grammatical and lexical characteristics, also as a result of different pathways of language contact. Modern Scots is mostly a spoken variety that can be described in terms of a continuum of registers oscillating between broad rural and urban dialects and Scottish Standard English (Aitken 1984; Macafee 1997: 514–520). As a written variety, Scots looks back at a rich historical tradition spanning more than 300 years of the late medieval and early modern period. At its end stood the replacement of Scots by metropolitan Southern English for major functions in professional and administrative text production and other written genres. This chapter concerns the final one-and-a-half centuries of writing in Older Scots.

Following Aitken (1985: xiii), Older Scots is traditionally divided into early Scots (c.1375–1450), Early Middle Scots (c.1450–1550) and Late Middle Scots (c.1550–1700). Much of the scholarly attention has been concentrated on the language of the second sub-period. This was the time of the most celebrated Scots poets (the 'makars') and the period when the Scots vernacular functioned as the language of choice over Latin for most written discourse, including parliamentary acts, religious pamphlets, histories and private documents (cf. Meurman-Solin 1993: 74–124). The subsequent 150 years have received less scholarly attention. So far, this period has mostly been treated from the perspective of Anglicisation, that is the replacement of markedly Scots features by Southern English equivalents as a consequence of political, economic and cultural unification with England (MacQueen 1957; Devitt 1989; Meurman-Solin 1993: 125–185). Typically, Scots features – such as the emblematic <quh>-trigraph, the present participle ending <-and>, the plural suffix <-is> or the past suffix <-it> – were substituted by their English counterparts, <wh>, <-ing>, <-es> and <-ed>.[1] Below, these features are illustrated by two excerpts from parliamentary acts. Example (1) pre-dates Anglicisation, whereas in example (2) no notable Scots features remain.

(1) The **quh**ilk day our soverane lord in this present parliament, the thre estat**is** of this realme be**and** gader**it**, exponit ... (RPS, 1532/5, emphasis added)

(2) **Wh**ich petition, be**ing** heard, read and consider**ed**, the meeting of the estat**es** doe declair ... (RPS, 1689/3/90, emphasis added)

---

[1] For an overview of linguistic and scribal variants diagnostic of the English-Scots contrast, see Meurman-Solin (1993: 126–131). For variants in Scots more generally, see Aitken (1971).

Encapsulated in the term 'Anglicisation' is a wistful conceptualisation of this period as one of decline for the Scots language, particularly regarding its function as a vehicle for literature. From a purely linguistic standpoint, however, the period is arguably a time characterised by striking dynamism due to increased contact between Scots and English standardising usage.

This change in perspective is compatible with a recent proposal to revise the traditional periodisation put forward by Kopaczyk (2013a). Based on various intra- and extralinguistic criteria, she argues that the label 'Middle Scots' should be reserved for the earliest surviving texts in the vernacular. The period of Anglicisation (or else 'Late Middle Scots') is recast as 'Transition Scots' in the revised timeline. Thereby, Kopaczyk effectively parts with any evaluative connotations of language decline, highlighting the period's dynamic character instead. The author insists that 'the history of forms and functions of Scots between the Unions (1603–1707) is yet to be written' (Kopaczyk 2013a: 253), emphasising the untapped potential of this period for linguistic enquiry.

The few empirical studies that deal with the transitional period adopted a classical variationist methodology, tracing the diffusion of novel (i.e. Southern English) forms in the population of Scottish texts. Devitt (1989) and Meurman-Solin (1993: 125–185, 1997, 2000) studied distinctive orthographic, phonological and grammatical features, observing marked differences in the adoption of Southern English variants in different text types. Two main results were that printed texts Anglicised faster compared to handwritten ones (Devitt 1989: 63; Meurman-Solin 1993: 144–148, 1997: 15–16; cf. Bald 1926) and that official records were the slowest to Anglicise, especially in regional and local institutions such as burgh courts (Devitt 1989: 58–59; Meurman-Solin 1993: 152–153, 2000: 158–159; cf. MacQueen 1957: 76–77).

It should be noted that both Devitt (1989) and Meurman-Solin (1993) based their empirical investigations on early prints and modern editions, which is perfectly adequate for published texts, but poses important methodological problems for originally handwritten material such as burgh records (see sections 3.1 and 3.2). These limitations are quite obviously due to the nascent state of corpus research at the time, as well as the sheer scale of the projects and their general focus on macro-level sociopragmatic predictor variables such as genre and register.

As a further consequence of their size and scope, these studies have remained unspecific regarding the actual channels of linguistic contact responsible for the spread of novel forms.[2] Similarly, they have offered little insight into the social and institutional structures promoting the conservation of Scots forms, apart from rather vague references to genre-specific styles, the lack of a wider audience, or unconscious nationalism (Devitt 1989: 65–66; Meurman-Solin 1997: 16).

---

[2] Admittedly, scholars do pay attention to the influence of printers, who favoured Anglicised publications due to the larger English market (Meurman-Solin 1993: 137–147; cf. Görlach 2002: 9–10, based on Bald 1926). However, Meurman-Solin makes the point that it is usually far from obvious whether it was the printers who Anglicised texts or whether authors themselves Anglicised their works proactively in order to reach a wider audience. In any case, the fact that printing vastly increased the dissemination of texts functioned as a catalyst for Anglicisation in published genres.

In pursuit of the mechanisms behind language change and language maintenance (cf. Milroy and Milroy 1991: 57–59), advances in sociolinguistic methodology have made some of the relevant micro-level links between language users amenable to systematic enquiry. Insightful concepts have been borrowed from the social sciences, including social networks (Milroy 1980; Bergs 2005; Nevalainen and Raumolin-Brunberg 2017: 215–231) and communities of practice (Holmes and Meyerhoff 1999; Kopaczyk and Jucker 2013). These conceptual frameworks are still making their way into scholarship on Scots, opening new research pathways. Meurman-Solin (2001) has argued for the importance of social networks for the comparison of linguistic practices in women writers' correspondence. More recently, Kopaczyk (2013b) has provided an analysis of legal formulae in burgh records, embedded in an elaborate socio-pragmatic frame where legal professionals are conceptualised as a community of practice (cf. Kopaczyk 2013c). The latter studies have been central in inspiring the systematic inclusion of extralinguistic information in the *Dunfermline Corpus* (see section 3.3).

A second aspect on which the literature has remained unspecific is idiolect-internal mixing and, particularly, the use of non-canonical forms. One conspicuous example of the latter are forms such as <-et> and <-id> for the past suffix instead of Scots <-it> or English <-ed>. Evidence for such forms emerges in the data at the time when formal variation across and within texts is at its highest (Devitt 1989: 44–45). Since Devitt (1989) and others have treated diachronic variation mostly within the 'Anglicisation-as-diffusion' paradigm, these forms have remained underexplored, their status as erratic variants not being readily compatible with the notion of a linguistic innovation spreading through the language community. Referred to as 'transitional forms' (Devitt 1989: 44) or 'hybrids' (MacQueen 1957: 75), these variants have essentially been treated as confusions by scribes unable to adhere to either Scots or English conventions. While such forms may be more prevalent in the idiolects of less experienced writers (Meurman-Solin 2001: 36–37), their treatment as scribal confusions does not do justice to the extent and consistency of their use by individual writers. As the case study in section 4.2 will suggest, transitional forms may be interpreted as writers' structured responses to the competition between two orthographic models.

Having dealt at some length with the academic motivations for engaging with Transition Scots, the remainder of this chapter aims to start a discussion on how the described desiderata may be tackled methodologically. One prerequisite is the availability of adequate empirical data. The following section sketches out the format that such a dataset may take.

3. The Dunfermline Corpus: A new digital resource for historical dialectology

3.1 Placing the *Dunfermline Corpus* within the study of historical Scots

Over the past few decades, a number of electronic resources have been compiled from Older Scots material. The first to mention is the *Helsinki Corpus of Older Scots* (HCOS; Meurman-Solin 1993, 1995). A supplement to the *Helsinki Corpus of English Texts*, the HCOS follows the same principles concerning text selection, temporal subdivision and textual annotation and is entirely based on modern editions and early prints. It covers the 250 years between 1450 and 1700, that is the period traditionally referred to as 'Middle Sots'. Among the main extralinguistic variables are time period (in seventy-year intervals), geographical space and text type/genre, accompanied by a number of secondary indicators based on the Helsinki model. With more than 830,000 words, the HCOS is the largest and most comprehensive structured resource for the diachronic study of Older Scots. It is also the primary resource for the study of Transition Scots (cf. Meurman-Solin 1993, 1997, 2000).

For the *Dunfermline Corpus* presented here, two recent projects have served as more direct models, particularly regarding the use of manuscript sources and the scope and focus of the resultant electronic resource in the Scottish context. These are the *Helsinki Corpus of Scottish Correspondence* (ScotsCorr), also compiled by Meurman-Solin, and LAOS. ScotsCorr consists of letters written by Scottish authors predominantly from the sixteenth and seventeenth centuries. It covers c.417,000 words and is entirely based on manuscripts. Since personal correspondence counts as one of the more involved and dialogical among the written genres (Koch and Oesterreicher 1985), epistolary prose serves as a valuable substitute for spoken discourse in historical linguistics. Letters are also an exceptionally revealing source for sociolinguistics, as the authors are usually known by name and interpersonal relations can be reconstructed for network-based approaches (cf. Bergs 2005).

The most immediate predecessor of the Dunfermline Corpus is the Edinburgh-based LAOS project, which, like ScotsCorr, relies on manuscript transcripts. Its text corpus mostly consists of Older Scots legal-administrative documents, covering the period from the late fourteenth century to 1500. The choice to focus on this particular genre was motivated by the fact that it includes some of the earliest surviving sources written in the Scots vernacular, and that local documents provide unambiguous information on geographical provenance (Williamson 2001: 5–7). Like its sibling, the *Linguistic Atlas of Early Middle English* (LAEME), LAOS rests upon a large collection of extensively lexico-grammatically tagged corpus texts (c.390,000 words). Continuing in the tradition of historical dialectology as pioneered by McIntosh (1963) and the *Linguistic Atlas of Late Mediaeval English* (LALME, McIntosh, Samuels and Benskin 1986), the primary focus of LAOS is on diatopic (i.e. spatial) variation, which also determines the mode of exposition. However, the linguistic data can also be accessed in dictionary style format and the tagged corpus texts themselves can be retrieved by geographic provenance or date of composition. These features make LAOS the most versatile repository of Older Scots material currently available.

The Dunfermline Corpus complements both LAOS and ScotsCorr, but in different ways. Its contents are roughly contemporaneous with the material contained in ScotsCorr. Thus, it essentially covers the transitional period, starting roughly a half-century after where LAOS leaves off. With LAOS it shares the same focus on local legal-administrative texts, although it zooms in on only one institutional locale, namely the Dunfermline burgh court and council. In contrast to letters, legal and administrative sources are situated at the formal end of the register continuum. Legal language is detached, monological and characterised by a high degree of text planning and elaboration (Koch and Oesterreicher 1985). What the Dunfermline Corpus has in common with both LAOS and ScotsCorr is an analytic focus on the idiolectal behaviour of individual writers, as well as the conviction that empirical analyses should be based on original manuscript material in order to avoid the creation of 'pseudo-data' (Lass 1997: 102). Most notoriously, these include linguistic artefacts deriving from editorial practices rather than the textual evidence (Lass 1997: 99–103).

The *Dunfermline Corpus* is intended as a modest first step towards continuing LAOS into the early modern period. At the same time, it incorporates principles of compilation inspired by ScotsCorr, making use of extralinguistic information for reconstructing social and institutional ties among the producers of the written material. Following Kopaczyk (2013b, 2013c), these ties are conceptualised in terms of a community-of-practice approach. In the following sections, the principles of composition for the *Dunfermline Corpus* are laid out in more detail.

3.2 Compilation and contents

The data included in the *Dunfermline Corpus* consist of samples from the records of the town court and council of the royal burgh of Dunfermline. The registers considered for the present version cover the time between 1573 and 1723. While the start date has been dictated by the accidentals of textual transmission, the end date is arbitrarily set after 150 years, deemed appropriate for studying Transition Scots.[3] In total, the manuscript material consists of ten register books of 250 to 600 pages, filled with record entries of varying lengths.[4]

Dunfermline was chosen for both conceptual and practical reasons. Some twenty miles north of Edinburgh across the Firth of Forth, Dunfermline is in an interesting geographic location, halfway between Scotland's socio-political centre and the rural periphery (cf. Meurman-Solin 2000). Its size suggested that enough legal-administrative material must have been produced during the period under investigation, while the amount still seemed manageable for this small-scale corpus project. As one express aim was to approach the texts from a sociolinguistic micro-perspective, it was crucial that the town's administrative structure be compact and relatively easy to understand. Finally, both quantity and accessibility of the relevant records were guaranteed by the fact that the documents have survived as an almost continuous series of register books, stored at the National Records of Scotland in Edinburgh.[5]

The registers document the proceedings of two major institutional bodies of burgh government, namely the court and the council. Reading the texts, it becomes

---

[3] There is one earlier court book containing records from 1488 to 1584 (NAS B20/2/1). For this book, a carefully crafted edition is available (Beveridge 1917), which, however, does not indicate linguistically vital information. The manuscript itself was not available due to conservation concerns. Smaller samples of this book are included in LAOS.

[4] There exists an edition of the Dunfermline court and council records up to 1680 (Shearer 1951). Linguistically, the edition is relatively faithful, as even some contractions are indicated. However, it only includes a small selection from the records.

[5] National Records of Scotland, Dunfermline Court and Council Records, B20/10/1-B20/10/6, B20/13/1-B20/13/5.

clear that the former was responsible for administering justice according to national and municipal law, while the latter represented the legislative and administrative branches. Due to the wide range of responsibilities assumed by court and council, the contents of the records are highly diverse. The various entries include trial verdicts, local statutes, legal suits, contracts, arbitrations, debt obligations and sureties, inheritance proceedings, appointments of legal guardians, as well as a host of administrative matters. Example 3 illustrates what the beginning of a typical record entry looks like:[6]

(3) Curia burgj de dunfermling tenta in pretorio eiusdem per wi*llel*mum waluod et wi*llel*mum cowper balliuos dictj burgj con*iun*ctim et diuisim xxvj^{to} Julij 1575 sectis vocatis et curia legiti*m*e affir*m*ata
The quhilk day in ye actioun persewit be Bessie Levingstoun aganis m*a*rgaret Levingstoun hir sistir *and* dauid clerk hir spous for his int*e*res In the te*r*me assignit to ye said m*a*rgrate to depoun vpoun ye p*ar*t of ye clame referrit to hir aith conforme to ye last act Comperit ye said m*a*rgrat and deponit as confessit as eftir followis . . .
(B20/10/2: 26 July 1575)[7]

The Latin header contains information about the type of the meeting (*curia* 'court'), the chairpersons (*balliuos*, i.e. the two bailies), place (*in pretorio* 'in the tolbooth, town hall') and date (26 July 1575). The entry itself is composed in Scots. It starts with a formulaic reference to the date given in the header (*the quhilk day* 'the which/same day'), followed by the details of the individual case (in this example a deposition regarding outstanding debt). Only the Scots texts have been transcribed for the corpus, while the Latin headers were mined for extralinguistic information (place, date, type of session, chairpersons). Scribal abbreviations for recurrent words, morphemes or individual letters have been systematically marked following the transcription practices used by LAOS.[8]

Apart from providing manuscript-based data, the second goal of the project was to enable linguistic analysis on the level of idiolects rather than text types. As mentioned earlier, a similar depth of analysis has been pursued by ScotsCorr for letters, where a good amount of extralinguistic information about individual writers is often available. In contrast, legal and administrative texts are notorious for their impersonal and formalised style, which is assumed to suppress linguistic variation (Milroy 1994: 25–26).

Crucially, the immediate producers of legal-administrative texts cannot be regarded as their authors. These professional writers merely carried out the recording

---

[6] Here and henceforth, contractions are indicated in italics.
[7] References to entries from the Dunfermline records are given in the following format: [archive signature of manuscript book]: [date of session]. Thus, this citation refers to the record book with the signature NAS B20/10/2, and specifically to an entry dated 26 July 1575.
[8] Following LAOS, run-on text is in upper case, expansions are in lower case. Superscript letters are marked by circumflex (^).

of court decisions and administrative proceedings. A specialist vocabulary and a (more or less) static set of legal phrases and formulae served as their linguistic toolkits (cf. Kopaczyk 2013c: 24–30).[9] The writers thus fade into the background behind the texts themselves, which receive their authority and their whole communicative purpose from the institutions whose proceedings they document. In the Dunfermline burgh records, this is reflected by the fact that the individual entries do not usually specify who entered them into the books (with some notable exceptions; cf. section 3.3).

In the absence of metatextual identifiers of authorship, it is necessary to rely on other criteria for attributing texts to individual writers, one obvious candidate being palaeographic evidence. In the Dunfermline material, a considerable number of hands can be safely distinguished. Nine of them supplied enough material to include them in the first version of the corpus.[10] The earliest book of the selection (covering 1573–1575) was accepted as a single text witness due to the insufficient amount of text provided by each hand, which violates the principle that corpus texts should represent idiolects. However, linguistic variation within this book was minimal (cf. section 4.1) and, therefore, treating it as a single witness seemed justified for the pilot version.

The ten resulting text witnesses are represented in the *Dunfermline Corpus* by a sample of approximately 5,000 words each, consisting of entries of varying lengths. The samples cover as best as possible the range of subject matters recorded by any given writer. With about 50,000 words in total, the present version of the corpus is rather modest in size. Yet, for demonstrating how the study of diachronic change in burgh records can be combined with a sociolinguistic micro-perspective focusing on the immediate text producers, the size of the present version of the corpus is sufficient. At present, the *Dunfermline Corpus* is still undergoing lexico-grammatical tagging, partly based on the LAOS form dictionary (LAOS, Form Dictionary).

3.3 Town clerks and scribes in Dunfermline: Reconstructing a community of practice

After extracting text samples attributable to individual writers from the manuscript sources, a number of questions pertaining to the texts' historical setting remain to be addressed. What was the institutional frame within which these writers performed their duties? How did writers acquire the required skills? And to what extent can any social and institutional relationships among those writers be reconstructed, in particular the ones that may be relevant for the transmission of scribal and linguistic practices?

The records essentially represent the town's efforts to regulate and manage itself as a community. Since these activities also included the appointment of the town officials

---

[9] For a book-length study on the development of formulaic language in Scottish burgh records, see Kopaczyk (2013c).
[10] The fact that some hands could not be included in the corpus because they simply did not meet the predetermined threshold of enough surviving text is an important caveat for the validity of the conclusions drawn in the analysis (see section 4.1).

responsible for various legislative, executive and, crucially, documentation tasks, snippets of text constantly afford small windows into the historical reality of the burgh's legal-administrative apparatus. Thus, we learn that the official in charge of records and documents produced and issued on behalf of the burgh was the town clerk. Chosen by the council, he seems to have held his office for life, even though he was formally re-elected every year. A considerable number of town clerks can be identified in the record books. Their names are mentioned in entries concerning their own appointments to office. For example, one entry from 1633 starts:

(4) The quhilk day the counsale foirsaid electit nominat and creat Patrik Kingorne, notar publict, yair comoun toun clerk fra ye dait heirof to ye feist of michaelmiss nixttocum.

(B20/10/5: 14 Jan 1633)

The above excerpt is about a Patrick Kingorne, chosen by the town council to serve as their 'comoun toun clerk' until Michaelmas, when town officials were annually (re-)inaugurated. Importantly, Kingorne is described as a 'notar publict', a notary, licensed by royal authority to issue legal documents (Carswell 1967: 48).

All town clerks of Dunfermline seem to have been active as notaries in addition to their employment by the burgh. This is additionally confirmed by notarial docquets and signs, scattered in the record books. These means of authentication were used by the town clerks in their function as notaries (not as clerks) to authorise sasines[11] and other legal documents (Donaldson 1952: vi, cited in Kopaczyk 2013c: 134). Notarial documents form only a marginal subset of the entries in the burgh records, since they were usually recorded in the notary's own protocol book (Carswell 1967: 48). Their survival in the record books is fortunate as the docquets and signs make it possible to match the town clerks' names to individual hands.

Knowing that one had to be a notary to become town clerk provides important clues concerning the writers' training, including language usage. Much of what is known about notaries in early modern Scotland comes from a series of parliamentary acts, which repeatedly set provisions concerning qualifications and competence to rein in forgery and corruption (Carswell 1967: 51–52). Among other measures, central registration and examinations of notaries were introduced in 1563 (Finlay 2009: 397–399; RPS A1563/6/16). With respect to training, an act from 1587 is particularly noteworthy. It stipulates that applicants were required to serve a seven-year apprenticeship, for example under a sheriff or town clerk, before they would be admitted as notaries (Finlay 2009: 400–401; RPS 1587/7/39). This suggests that while there was some form of centralised supervision of the notaries of the realm (or at least attempts to establish such supervision), the transmission of the necessary knowledge and skills for drafting legal documents and dealing with the idiosyncrasies of their language was more devolved, taking the form of apprenticeships at local courts.

---

[11] The Instrument of Sasine was a form of deed that documented and put into effect the transfer of land (Carswell 1967: 48).

Town clerk/scribe	Sample period	ID	
Book A (John Cunninghame)	1573–1575/6	A	James Kingorne
David Broun	1607–1611	B	(regality clerk 1588)
Assistant Scribe B'	*1606–1607*	B'	
William Broun	1607–1613	C	
Patrick Kingorne	1633–1635	D	
John Auchinwallis	1642–1643	E	
Assistant Scribe E'	*1643–1648*	E'	
David Anderson (*mentioned*)	no sample	F	Clerk-assistant relationship
Henry Elder (*mentioned*)	no sample	G	
Andrew Simpson (Sr)	1662–1681	H	Family relationship
Assistant Scribe H'	*1669–1674*	H'	
Thomas Simpson	no sample	I	Identity of last names
Andrew Simpson (Jr)	1698–1723	J	

Figure 3.1 Town clerks and assistant scribes in the Dunfermline court and council records

The palaeographic evidence from the Dunfermline record books certainly seems to support this conclusion. During any given clerk's term of office, more than one hand can usually be distinguished in the manuscripts. Significantly, additional hands stop whenever a clerk departed (usually by death), while a new set of hands commences whenever a new clerk took office. This suggests that the town clerks of Dunfermline personally employed assistant scribes, who, it may be assumed, were in many cases also their trainees as indicated by the statutes cited above.

The clerks' personalised notarial signs make it possible to separate the masters' hands from those of assistant scribes. Following this procedure, the hands of nine informants (leaving aside the earliest book) break down into six town clerks and three assistants. As indicated earlier, these do not exhaust the total number of different hands found in the books. The number of samples in the corpus is restricted by the requirement that every informant should meet a threshold of holograph text. Unfortunately, this criterion prevents a considerable number of hands, even some town clerks, from inclusion in the present version of the corpus.[12]

Figure 3.1 provides an overview of the included clerks and assistant scribes, the latter remaining anonymous for lack of surviving signatures.[13] Apart from the names

[12] The rationale underlying the word count threshold was that the corpus should be balanced, which is certainly preferable for research questions such as those pursued in section 4. However, there is a case to be made that any major gaps in the sequence of scribal idiolects may jeopardise the goal of providing a dependable resource for the study of transmission links between writers. Future versions will also need to incorporate informants who fail to meet the word count requirement, even at the expense of balance.

[13] Writers are assigned identifiers in the form of capital letters. Assistant scribes are identified by their master's ID with a prime added (hence Scribe B' is assistant to David Broun). Assistants are chronologically placed after clerks even when appearing first in the manuscript. Known clerks without samples in the corpus are included in the graph, anonymous additional writers are excluded.

of town clerks, a number of other noteworthy pieces of information can be recovered. Intriguingly, relationships between two writers sometimes extended beyond the professional. Thus, William Broun (C) is named as a "substitut" (NAS B20/10/3: 8 Oct 1611) to David Broun (B), probably his father, and eventually succeeds him as town clerk (NAS B20/10/4: 11 Oct 1619). More explicitly, another entry introduces Thomas (I) and Andrew Simpson (J) as sons to Andrew Simpson (H), the three men occupying the office in direct succession. Moreover, one of the assistants to Andrew Sympsone Sr (H) is referred to as Henry Elder (NAS B20/10/6: 3 Nov 1971), possibly related to Sympsone's predecessor of the same name (NAS B20/13/2: 9 May 1662).[14] Finally, a James Kingorne is mentioned elsewhere as clerk of the regality[15] in 1588 (Torrie 1986: 144), suggesting a relation with Patrick Kingorne, town clerk since 1633. While some of these family links must remain speculative, the frequent recurrence of the same surnames gives the impression that local clerkship was at times not too far removed from being a family-run business. Adding to what has been said earlier about the training of notaries, it can be assumed that the earliest writing teachers of many clerks and scribes must have been their own fathers.

What is still missing at this point is a cogent theoretical frame for conceptualising this interconnected group of writers in a way that usefully informs sociolinguistic analysis. Considering the personal ties among the Dunfermline informants, a networks approach suggests itself. Ever since Milroy's (1980) Belfast study, it has been part of received wisdom in linguistics that close-knit social networks are conducive to the maintenance and stability of linguistic features, while looser networks are more susceptible to innovations (Milroy and Milroy 1991: 57–59). Thus, the more local and self-contained a network of language users, the less their shared language is given to change. An interpretation along those lines has also been offered for Transition Scots (Meurman-Solin 2000: 163), based on the finding that local records constitute the type of texts that resisted the adoption of English forms the longest (cf. MacQueen 1957).

While a classical networks approach would represent various interactional ties, it falls short of fully capturing the described group of writers and their production of written discourse within a local institutional context. Network theory's preoccupation with the strength and density of social ties comes at the cost of neglecting qualitative distinctions between different kinds of ties (Holmes and Meyerhoff 1999: 179–180). For instance, the crucial fact that the relationship between a town clerk and his assistant is the very specific one between a master/instructor and an employee/trainee would not be represented.

Another closely related sociological concept with an explicit emphasis on the transmission of knowledge and professional skill is that of communities of practice. Developed within the field of ethnology, this framework is part of a social theory of learning focused on personal interaction. The three defining features of a community

---

[14] This assistant may be identical with Scribe H', but the palaeographic evidence is not conclusive.

[15] The regality court had jurisdiction over the wider region outside the burgh. Regalities were comparable but superior to baronies (Goodare 2001).

of practice are (1) mutual engagement among its participants, (2) a joint enterprise, and (3) a shared repertoire (Wenger 1998: 72–85). This triad merges a (micro-)social (mutual engagement), a functional (joint enterprise) and a formal (shared repertoire) dimension of analysis, which makes it particularly valuable for sociolinguistic analysis.

In the case of Scottish burgh records, the community-of-practice approach serves as a coherent model covering the specific interactional ties among town clerks and their assistants, their joint involvement in the production of texts for municipal self-government, as well as their common repertoire of written language usage appropriate to the discourse type of legal-administrative texts. The last point includes, crucially, the transmission of language usage from one generation of notary clerks to the next through apprenticeship. In fact, the community-of-practice framework fits the historical context of clerks and assistant scribes so well that it is not surprising it was originally developed to describe the very process of learning through apprenticeship (Lave and Wenger 1991; cf. Kopaczyk and Jucker 2013). Importantly, conceptualising the Dunfermline town clerks and scribes as a community of practice does not preclude their subsequent inclusion in a broader perspective, such as that of discourse communities (Swales 1990; Kopaczyk 2013c: 45–46), which sees the linguistic structure of genres (or 'discourse types') as a function of the communicative goals of language users (Meurman-Solin 2001). Rather, communities of practice provide a micro-perspective to complement the analysis of discourse communities on a higher level. Similarly, the entanglement of personal ties with professional ones found in Dunfermline makes it clear that the communities-of-practice perspective adopted here should be understood as an extension to the network paradigm, not a replacement.

4. Aspects of formal variation and change: Two case studies

4.1 Anglicisation as discontinuation: change and maintenance in a community of practice

This section presents the results of a diachronic analysis of five linguistic variables, which are among the most distinctive features of Older Scots when contrasted with contemporaneous Southern English usage. This set of variables represents a slightly modified version of the selection in Devitt (1989: 16–17).[16] Devitt's study also functions as the main point of comparison for the present analysis and discussion. All forms are a priori regarded as graphemic variants, regardless of their probable realisations in the spoken mode. The selected features are:

---

[16] Devitt's (1989: 27–28) variable 'negative particle' was excluded from the analysis because Devitt's definition of the variable was found unconvincing. The forms *na* 'no' and *nocht* 'not' cannot be regarded as instantiations of the same variable as there is no reason why their shared negative meaning should have caused the two features to have a common trajectory of change. Devitt's own data (Devitt 1989: 88, 90) show that the two forms display very dissimilar diffusion patterns. In addition, Devitt's variable 'relative clause marker', which blends orthographic, phonological and morphological aspects, is replaced here by the variables WH and ICH.

Table 3.1 Occurrence of English variants in the *Dunfermline Corpus* (raw frequencies)

Text witness	Sample period	wh-	n	-ed	n	a(n)	n	-ing	n	-ich/each	n
Book A	1573–1575/6	0	59	0	191	1	48	11	44	0	42
David Brown B	1607–1611	0	50	12	136	0	21	17	74	0	33
Scribe B'	1606–1607	0	43	2	137	0	30	19	64	0	34
William Brown C	1607–1613	0	37	18	149	0	30	30	82	0	35
Patrick Kingorne D	1633–1635	0	54	2	158	1	40	61	89	0	33
John Auchinwallis E	1642–1643	6	63	3	172	0	42	68	85	2	41
Scribe E'	1643–1648	2	86	14	195	1	49	66	95	0	58
Andrew Simpson (Sr) H	1662–1681	32	59	93	150	16	45	63	71	28	31
Scribe H'	1669–1674	44	46	99	140	0	40	72	104	43	45
Andrew Simpson (Jr) J	1698–1723	46	57	153	156	53	53	76	76	31	31

1. WH: the trigraph <quh-> vs. English <wh->, e.g. *quhat* vs. *what*
2. ED: the past and past participle inflection <-it> vs. English <-ed>, e.g. *producit* vs. *produced*
3. A(N): the indefinite article <ane> vs. English <a>/<an>, e.g. *ane aith* vs. *an oath*; *ane bed* vs. *a bed*
4. ING: the present participle inflection <-and> vs. English <-ing>, e.g. *payand* vs. *paying*
5. ICH: the related word forms *(quh)ilk* vs. *(wh)ich* (disregarding onset spelling) and *ilk* vs. *each*, e.g. *the quhilk day* vs. *the which day*

The results are displayed in Table 3.1[17] and Figure 3.2.[18]

It is obvious that the trajectories of change for the individual linguistic variables do not necessarily coincide, which corresponds to findings in Devitt (1989: 17–18). Concerning the advance of English spelling types in general, there is a marked time

---

[17] In Table 3.1, frequencies of English variants are represented as raw numbers. Columns headed by *n* represent the total number of occurrences for all variants (English, Scots or other forms, cf. section 4.2). Every writer is represented by a sample of 5,000 words (cf. section 3.2).

[18] In Figure 3.2, the y-axis represents the proportion of English variants in the samples; the x-axis represents the succession of informants over time (but not real time!). Assistants are placed after clerks even when appearing first in the manuscript. Known clerks without samples in the corpus are included in the graph, anonymous additional writers are excluded. The bars represent the five variables. The red line represents the normalised mean across all variables. For reference to previous results, dashed lines represent Anglicisation in prose genres and national public records up to 1659 based on Devitt (1989: 17, 58), but adjusted to exclude Devitt's variable 'negative particle' (cf. n. 16).

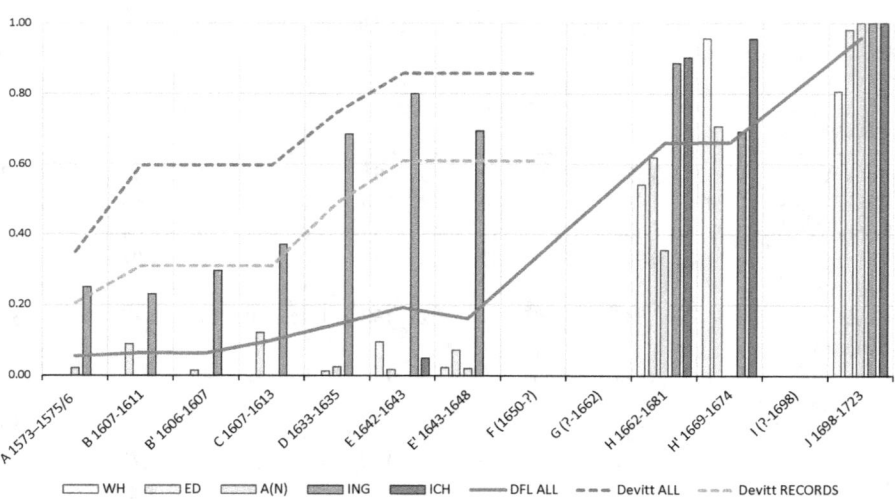

Figure 3.2 Anglicisation in the *Dunfermline Corpus* (relative frequencies)

lag between Anglicisation in the *Dunfermline Corpus* – represented here as an average measure across the five features – compared to prose genres in general (Devitt 1989: 17) and national public records in particular (Devitt 1989: 58). This corroborates results by Meurman-Solin (1997, 2000) and MacQueen (1957: 76–77), who found that local records were particularly slow to adopt the English forms.

In addition to these broad trends, however, the Dunfermline material allows a much more fine-grained view of the change as it zooms in to the level of idiolects. In this light, Anglicisation in the *Dunfermline Corpus* appears as a progression of pulses and pauses. Sequences of writers marked by relative stability in the distribution of forms are disrupted by innovative bursts towards English variants. The first four informants (A, B, B' and C) exhibit very similar usage patterns, mostly adhering to the Scots model. Southern English forms only slowly become more common in the subsequent scribal idiolects. The first variable that is affected in this way is the present participle ending, which sees a decided move towards the English variant with incoming town clerk Patrick Kingorne (D) (C vs. D, [ING]: p<0.001, *Fisher's exact test*). The first significant leap towards an English-looking orthography in all variables comes as late as the second half of the seventeenth century with Andrew Simpson Sr (H) (E vs. H, [WH; ED; A(N); ICH]: p<0.001, *Fisher's exact test*). The last significant step towards Anglicisation occurs with Andrew Simpson Jr (I) (H vs. J, [WH; ING]: p< 0.01, [ED; A(N)]: p<0.001, *Fisher's exact test*), whose idiolect represents a state where the Anglicisation of the five features is practically completed.

When viewing the pattern of pulses and pauses in connection with the extralinguistic information about the texts' producers, one observation that stands out is that assistant scribes' profiles display Anglicisation rates that are similar to the town clerks they served. This is most conspicuous in Andrew Simpson Sr (H) and his assistant's (H') written idiolects, halting at the same overall Anglicisation rate of 66 per cent. Similarly, William Broun's (C) profile is almost indistinguishable from that provided by his master and assumed father David Broun (B), although Anglicisation rates are generally much lower at that point. In contrast, the idiolects of the second pair of writers linked by family ties, i.e. Andrew Simpson Sr (H) and his son Andrew Jr (I), do differ significantly from each other. While the former is the most internally variable in the whole set, the latter's orthography is almost entirely Anglicised.

As indicated earlier, any generalisations based on these observations must be taken as provisional because not all idiolects in the sources have been sampled for the present version of the corpus. Also, this pilot study is only based on five (rather obvious) diagnostic variables, while many more would have been eligible. Nevertheless, what the analysis so far suggests is that, prior to about 1700, the advance of Anglicisation was generally slowed down by professional and personal ties among writers in the books. Such an interpretation is consistent with the idea that the clerks and scribes of Dunfermline formed a community of practice, sharing a common repertoire of legal language usage transmitted through apprenticeship as a form of mutual engagement. It is conceivable that existing entries in the record books functioned as templates for familiarising assistants with recurrent subject matters and legalistic diction. This would inevitably have shaped their use of orthography as well, even if that was not an explicit part of their training. Thereby, transmission links between successive writers would have had the effect of keeping Southern English innovations to a minimum while preserving existing conventions.

Conversely, discontinuities in transmission would have created opportunities for English innovations to come in. In the *Dunfermline Corpus* significant strides towards an English-looking orthography only seem to have taken place when a closely interlinked set of writers was succeeded by a new clerk from outside the immediate scribal network. This applies to Patrick Kingorne (D) and the concomitant early change in the present participle form, as well as to Andrew Simpson Sr (H), whose profile introduced significantly increased levels of English variants across the board. The latter clerk's appointment in 1662 (B20/13/2: 9 May 1662) is particularly noteworthy because it ends a period of twelve years for which no burgh records exist, the gap largely coinciding with the Civil War and Cromwell's Commonwealth. The fact that the records recommence after the hiatus with a decisively Anglicised orthography mirrors similar developments elsewhere, which have been attributed to the 'Civil War effect' (Raumolin-Brunberg 1998). The upheavals of the war may have accelerated the diffusion of Southern English forms throughout the British Isles. To date, a comprehensive study of the linguistic consequences of the British Civil War is still outstanding.

By 1700, orthographic transmission between clerks and assistants finally seems to have broken down, as is evidenced in the markedly different linguistic profiles of Andrew Simpson Sr (H) and his son Andrew Jr (J). It is not surprising that by then other channels of transmission of orthographic conventions – notably through schools and printed texts, including early dictionaries – should have superseded the conservational effect of a local network of clerical writers and their shared linguistic practices.

4.2 Anglicisation as transition: internal variation and the use of non-canonical forms

Although tracing the advance of Southern English forms is useful for appreciating the general rate and manner of Anglicisation, such an analysis conceals the actual amount of variation found in the texts. This concerns particularly non-canonical, or 'transitional forms' (Devitt 1989: 44–46) which are neither typically Scots nor English, but which appear to combine features of both. A case in point is the past and past participle inflection. In addition to Scots <-it> and English <-ed>, a search in the *Dunfermline Corpus* also finds the variants <-t>, <-d>, <-et> and <-id>, accounting for more than 25 per cent of all instances in some idiolects. The details regarding their distribution are presented in Table 3.2 and Figure 3.3.

It will be noticed that the idiolects displaying the largest numbers of alternative forms are the ones in the middle of the investigation period (Patrick Kingorne (D) to Scribe H'), whose spelling systems may thus be regarded as 'transitional'. Their idiosyncratic character suggests that the Scots spelling conventions, still apparent in the consistent use of <-it> in Book A, gave way to a phase of relative orthographic openness, during which there was room for individual scribal interpretations of the past suffix. The evidence points to a period of approximately fifty years in the mid-seventeenth century, during which such forms as <-et>, <-t>, <-id> and <-d> could materialise as part of individual spelling repertoires. It is worth noting that the two idiolects with the highest incidence of transitional forms are those of assistant scribes (E' and H'). Moreover, Scribe H' seems to have stopped using any form other than <-ed> halfway through his sample. These observations are consistent with the interpretation that auxiliary hands are those of trainees, with more idiosyncratic but also still malleable usage patterns.

Table 3.2 Distribution of past suffix variants in the *Dunfermline Corpus*

Text witness	Sample period	-it	%	-ed	%	-et	%	-id	%	-t	%	-d	%	Total
Book A	1573–1575/6	191	100	0	0	0	0	0	0	0	0	0	0	191
David Brown B	1607–1611	116	85	12	9	0	0	1	1	6	4	1	1	136
Scribe B'	1606–1607	130	95	2	1	4	3	0	0	0	0	1	1	137
William Brown C	1607–1613	129	87	18	12	0	0	0	0	2	1	0	0	149
Patrick Kingorne D	1633–1635	123	78	2	1	24	15	0	0	7	4	2	1	158
John Auchinwallis E	1642–1643	140	81	3	2	14	8	8	5	4	2	3	2	172
Scribe E'	1643–1648	127	65	14	7	41	21	1	1	10	5	2	1	195
Andrew Simpson (Sr) H	1662–1681	43	29	93	62	0	0	0	0	14	9	0	0	150
Scribe H'	1669–1674	4	3	99	71	0	0	13	9	5	4	19	14	140
Andrew Simpson (Jr) J	1698–1723	0	0	153	98	0	0	0	0	2	1	1	1	156

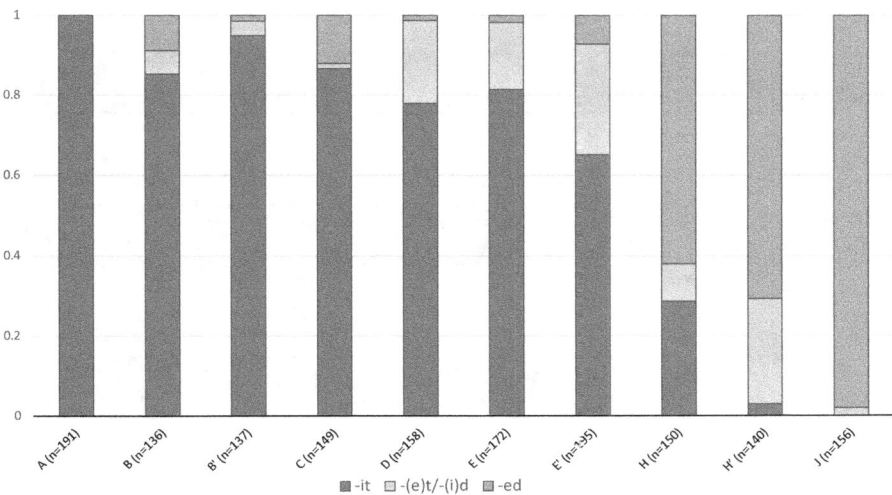

Figure 3.3 Distribution of past suffix variants in the *Dunfermline Corpus*

A closer examination of all past inflection variants within their linguistic contexts reveals that transitional forms were not only a regular part in the writers' repertoires, but that their distribution may be shaped by intralinguistic conditioning factors, in particular phonology. In Figures 3.4 and 3.5, the seventeenth-century group of 'transitional' writers is divided into a pre-war and a post-war subset, while past inflection variants are categorised according to the type of the stem-final sound preceding the inflection. In both groups, transitional forms overwhelmingly occur after sonorants and sibilants, while stops almost categorically select the canonical Scots or English variants. More specifically, <-t> occurs exclusively after the letter <s> when it stands for a voiceless fricative, as in *confest* 'confessed' or *purchest* 'purchased'. In addition to phonological conditioning, graphemic preferences might also play a role in this case, since the letter <s> is realised as a 'long s', yielding the common ligature <ſt> (cf. Smith, this volume).

The forms <-id> and <-d> probably reflect voicing assimilation. They occur almost always in sonorant contexts, notably liquids and nasals, as in *compeirid* 'appeared (before a court)' or *summond* 'summoned'. The somewhat higher likelihood of English <-ed> variants to occur after sonorants compared to other environments might also be attributed to voicing assimilation.[19] The use of <-et> in both sonorant and sibilant environments is more intricate but may also partly be explained by graphemic factors. In Patrick Kingorne's (D) idiolect, the variant is found in forms such as *producet* 'produced', *namet* 'named' or *verifiet* 'verified', which already take a final <-e> in their base forms. In John Auchinwallis' (E) and his assistant's samples, the <e> before the dental is more difficult to interpret but may still be part of their stem spellings

[19] But see Devitt (1989: 22–23), who did not detect any conditioning effect by voiced stem-final segments.

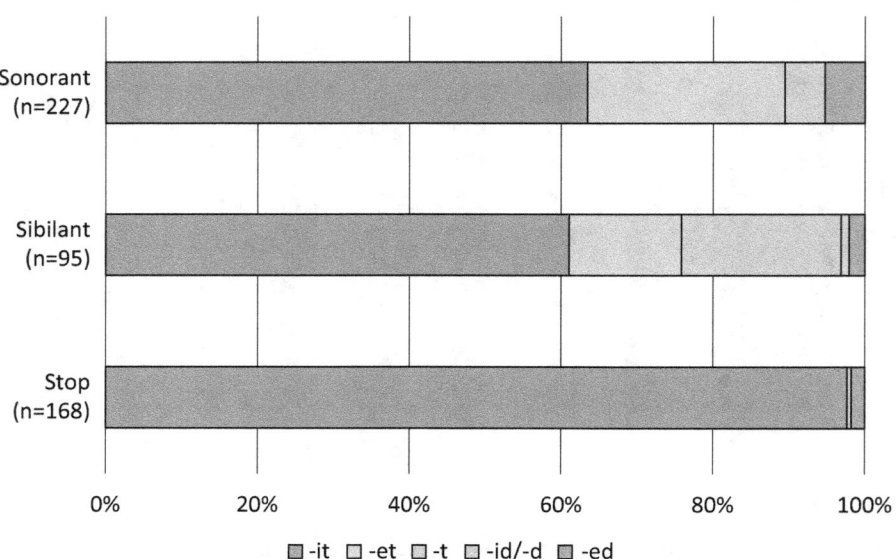

Figure 3.4 Distribution of past suffix variants according to stem-final segment, pre-war group (D, E, E')

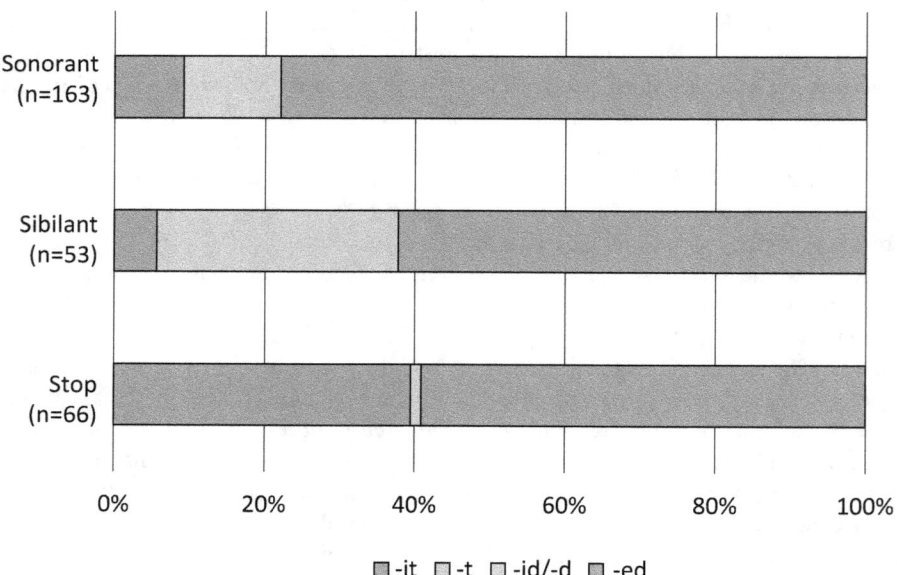

Figure 3.5 Distribution of past suffix variants according to stem-final segment, post-war group (H, H')

(cf. *payet* 'payed', *conteinet* 'contained'). In the post-war writers, <-et> is completely absent. In sum, these observations suggest that the <e> in the form <-et> might only be apparent, which effectively leaves <-t> alone as a variant of canonical Scots <-it>. It should be noted that different variants can be found for the same verb stems even within idiolects (*restorit* vs. *restoret* 'restored', *considerit* vs. *considered*), the level of lexical consistency varying across writers.

Needless to say, the present analysis is based on a small set of writers and the number of occurrences in each idiolect is relatively low (hence the grouping into sets of pre- and post-war writers). Nevertheless, the patterns are striking and warrant further study in idiolect-level corpora, especially in combination with other features that might reflect phonological spellings. If the depiction of the transitional period as a time when writers increasingly took recourse to alternative heuristics for selecting variants is essentially correct, then this would mark Transition Scots as a valuable source of evidence for the study of phonological change.

5. Conclusion

This chapter had two goals. The first was to emphasise that the transition period in the history of Scots is a worthwhile area of linguistic enquiry. The inherent dynamism of this period promises stimulating insights with respect to language variation and change in a contact scenario involving two highly developed written varieties. The second goal was to present a new electronic resource, which allows initial forays into some of the questions that Transition Scots has in store. By way of illustration, the first of two pilot studies in this chapter has suggested that Anglicisation in local records was impeded by close professional and personal ties among town clerks and their assistants, sustaining the transmission of shared linguistic practices. The second pilot study has drawn attention to the range of variant forms for one linguistic variable, the past suffix, suggesting that variation might have been constrained by intralinguistic factors such as phonology.

Limited as it is to a single type of sources from a single historical locale, both size and coverage of the *Dunfermline Corpus* are relatively modest. However, the strength of the corpus lies in providing the opportunity to approach manuscript-based data from a sociolinguistic micro-perspective. It represents the idiolects of individual language users and makes visible some of the historical relationships among them. For the present version, the reservoir of linguistic and extralinguistic data from Dunfermline has by no means been exhausted. Apart from the inclusion of more sparsely represented writers, much further biographical detail may be obtained by consulting other contemporary sources, such as protocol books, regality records or even records from national institutions. For future versions, it is hoped that these additional materials can also be integrated.[20] Finally, to make the insights gained from building this

---

[20] For example, Finlay (2009: 399) mentions that the central register of admissions for notaries, created after the 1563 legislation (see section 3.3), has survived (National Records of Scotland, NP2 series). Apparently, these books include details about the applicant's age and qualifications.

resource relevant for the study of Scots more generally, the same principles of text selection and philological-historical analysis may be extended to manuscript material from other burghs and institutional contexts, or even other text genres, so that the writing of 'the history of the forms and functions of Scots between the Unions' (Kopaczyk 2013a: 253) can begin in earnest.

References

Agutter, Alex (1990). 'Restandardisation in Middle Scots', in Sylvia Adamson, Vivien Law and Susan Wright (eds), *Papers from the 5th International Conference on English Historical Linguistics*, Amsterdam: John Benjamins, pp. 1–11.

Aitken, Adam J. (1971). 'Variation and variety in written Middle Scots', in Adam J. Aitken, Angus McIntosh and H. Pálsson (eds), *Edinburgh Studies in English and Scots*, London: Longman, pp. 177–209.

Aitken, Adam J. (1984). 'Scots and English in Scotland', in Peter Trudgill (ed.), *Language in the British Isles*, Cambridge: Cambridge University Press, pp. 517–532.

Aitken, Adam J. (1985). 'A history of Scots', in Mairi Robinson (ed.), *The Concise Scots Dictionary*, Aberdeen: Aberdeen University Press, pp. ix–xvi.

Bald, Marjory A. (1926). 'The Anglicisation of Scottish printing', *Scottish Historical Review* 23: 107–115.

Bergs, Alexander (2005). *Social Networks and Historical Sociolinguistics: Studies in Morphosyntactic Variation in the Paston Letters, 1421–1503*, Berlin: Mouton de Gruyter.

Beveridge, Erskine (ed.) (1917). *The Burgh Records of Dunfermline, 1488–1584*, Edinburgh: William Brown.

Bugaj, Joanna (2004). 'Middle Scots as an emerging standard and why it did not make it', *Scottish Language* 23: 19–34.

Carswell, R. D. (1967). 'The origins of the legal profession in Scotland', *American Journal of Legal History* 11(1): 41–56.

Devitt, Amy (1989). *Standardising Written English: Diffusion in the Case of Scotland, 1520–1659*, Cambridge: Cambridge University Press.

Donaldson, Gordon (ed.) (1952). *Protocol Book of James Young, 1485–1515*, Edinburgh: Scottish Record Society.

Finlay, John (2009). 'The history of the notary in Scotland', in Mathias Schmoeckel and Werner Schubert (eds), *Handbuch zur Geschichte des Notariats der Europäischen Traditionen*, Baden-Baden: Nomos, pp. 393–428.

Goodare, Julian (2001). 'Local government to 1707', in Michael Lynch (ed.), *The Oxford Companion to Scottish History*, Oxford: Oxford University Press, pp. 397–398.

Görlach, Manfred (2002). *A Textual History of Scots*, Heidelberg: Winter.

HCOS = Anneli Meurman-Solin (1995). *The Helsinki Corpus of Older Scots, 1450–1700*, Helsinki: University of Helsinki (manual available online at http://www.helsinki.fi/varieng/CoRD/corpora/HCOS/ (last accessed 31 August 2017)).

Holmes, Janet and Miriam Meyerhoff (1999). 'The Community of Practice: Theories and methodologies in language and gender research', *Language in Society* 28: 173–183.

Koch, Peter and Wulf Oesterreicher (1985). 'Sprache der Nähe – Sprache der

Distanz: Mündlichkeit und Schriftlichkeit im Spannungsfeld von Sprachtheorie und Sprachgeschichte', *Romanistisches Jahrbuch* 36: 15–43.
Kopaczyk, Joanna (2013a). 'Rethinking the traditional periodisation of Scots', in Robert McColl Millar and Janet Cruickshank (eds), *After the Storm: Papers from the Forum for Research on the Languages of Scotland and Ulster Triennial Meeting, Aberdeen 2012*, Aberdeen: Forum for Research on the Languages of Scotland and Ulster, pp. 233–260.
Kopaczyk, Joanna (2013b). 'How a community of practice creates a text community: Middle Scots legal and administrative discourse', in Joanna Kopaczyk and Andreas H. Jucker (eds), *Communities of Practice in the History of English*, Amsterdam: John Benjamins, pp. 225–251.
Kopaczyk, Joanna (2013c). *The Legal Language of Scottish Burghs: Standardisation and Lexical Bundles, 1380–1560*, Oxford: Oxford University Press.
Kopaczyk, Joanna and Andreas H. Jucker (eds) (2013). *Communities of Practice in the History of English*, Amsterdam: John Benjamins.
LAEME = Margaret Laing (2013–). *A Linguistic Atlas of Early Middle English, 1150–1325*, version 3.2 (available at http://www.lel.ed.ac.uk/ihd/laeme2/laeme2.html (last accessed 31 August 2017)).
LAOS = Keith Williamson (2008–). *A Linguistic Atlas of Older Scots, Phase 1: 1380–1500*, version 1.1 (available at http://www.lel.ed.ac.uk/ihd/laos1/laos1.html (last accessed 31 August 2017)).
Lass, Roger (1997). *Historical Linguistics and Language Change*, Cambridge: Cambridge University Press.
Lave, Jean and Etienne Wenger (1991). *Situated Learning: Legitimate Peripheral Participation*, Cambridge: Cambridge University Press.
Macafee, Caroline (1997). 'Ongoing change in Modern Scots', in Charles Jones (ed.), *The Edinburgh History of the Scots Language*, Edinburgh: Edinburgh University Press, pp. 514–548.
McIntosh, Angus (1963). 'A new approach to Middle English dialectology', *English Studies* 44(1): 1–11.
McIntosh, Angus, Michael L. Samuels and Michael Benskin (1986). *A Linguistic Atlas of Late Medieval English*, Aberdeen: Aberdeen University Press.
MacQueen, Lilian E. C. (1957). 'The last stages of the older literary language of Scotland: A study of the surviving Scottish elements in Scottish prose, 1700–1750, especially of the records, national and local', PhD thesis, University of Edinburgh.
Meurman-Solin, Anneli (1993). *Variation and Change in Early Scottish Prose: Studies Based on the Helsinki Corpus of Older Scots*, Helsinki: Suomalainen Tiedeakatemia.
Meurman-Solin, Anneli (1995). 'A new tool: The Helsinki Corpus of Older Scots, 1450–1700', *ICAME Journal* 19: 49–62.
Meurman-Solin, Anneli (1997). 'Differentiation and standardisation in early Scots', in Charles Jones (ed.), *The Edinburgh History of the Scots Language*, Edinburgh: Edinburgh University Press, pp. 3–23.
Meurman-Solin, Anneli (2000). 'Change from above or below? Mapping the loci of

linguistic change in the history of Scottish English', in Laura Wright (ed.), *The Development of Standard English, 1300–1800*, Cambridge: Cambridge University Press, pp. 155–170.

Meurman-Solin, Anneli (2001). 'Women as informants in the reconstruction of geographically and socioculturally conditioned language variation and change in sixteenth- and seventeenth-century Scots', *Scottish Language* 20: 20–46.

Milroy, James (1994). 'The notion of Standard English and its applicability to the study of Early Modern English pronunciation', in Dieter Stein and Ingrid Tieken-Boon van Ostade (eds), *Towards a Standard English, 1600–1800*, Berlin: Mouton de Gruyter, pp. 19–29.

Milroy, James and Lesley Milroy (1991). *Authority in Language: Investigating Language Prescription and Standardisation*, Abingdon: Routledge.

Milroy, Lesley (1980). *Language and Social Networks*, Oxford: Blackwell.

Nevalainen, Terttu and Helena Raumolin-Brunberg (2017), *Historical Sociolinguistics: Language Change in Tudor and Stuart English*, 2nd edition, Abingdon: Routledge.

Raumolin-Brunberg, Helena (1998). 'Social factors and pronominal change in the seventeenth century: The Civil-War effect?', in Jacek Fisiak and Marcin Krygier (eds), *Advances in English Historical Linguistics*, Berlin: Mouton de Gruyter, pp. 361–388.

RPS = Keith M. Broun et al. (eds) (2007–). *The Records of the Parliaments of Scotland to 1707* (available at http://www.rps.ac.uk (last accessed 31 August 2017)).

ScotsCorr = Anneli Meurman-Solin (2017). *The Helsinki Corpus of Scottish Correspondence*, 1540–1750. Helsinki: University of Helsinki (manual available online at https://www.kielipankki.fi/wp-content/uploads/ScotsCorr_Manual_2016.pdf (last accessed 31 August 2017)).

Shearer, Andrew (ed.) (1951). *Extracts from the Burgh Records of Dunfermline, in the 16th and 17th Centuries*, Dunfermline: Carnegie Dunfermline Trust.

Swales, John (1990). *Genre Analysis: English in Academic and Research Settings*, Cambridge: Cambridge University Press.

Torrie, Elizabeth (ed.) (1986). *The Gild Court Book of Dunfermline, 1433–1597*, Edinburgh: Scottish Record Society.

Wenger, Etienne (1998). *Communities of Practice: Learning, Meaning, and Identity*, Cambridge: Cambridge University Press.

Williamson, Keith (2001). 'Spatio-temporal aspects of Older Scots texts', *Scottish Language* 20: 1–19.

4

Early Spelling Evidence for Scots L-vocalisation: A Corpus-based Approach

Benjamin Molineaux, Joanna Kopaczyk, Warren Maguire, Rhona Alcorn, Vasilis Karaiskos and Bettelou Los

1. Introduction

L-vocalisation (henceforth LV) is a common feature among regional and social varieties of the Insular West Germanic languages, both historical and contemporary.[1] It is also one of the phonological changes that are deemed 'characteristic' of Scots (McClure 1994: 48), representing 'a persistent and vigorous feature of working-class speech' (Stuart-Smith, Timmins and Tweedie 2006: 77) in present-day Scotland. Why is it then important to revisit LV in the context of the earliest extant Scots documents, dating back to the fourteenth and fifteenth centuries? First, this study highlights the need for in-depth corpus-based engagement with historical material to cast light on a phonological process that is perceived as a regional diagnostic. Second, the inception and operation of the change has usually been illustrated in reference literature with a series of stock examples, which are recycled and repeated by consecutive authors, giving the impression of a systematic, uncontroversial, across-the-board process. A close reading of the literature, however, may cast some doubt on this purported systematicity and (degree of) completion of the change in the pre-modern period. Finally, the process has not been studied in a quantitative, corpus-based fashion, in order to contrast spellings indicative of LV with those indicative of its absence. This type of data can now be provided through the FITS Project database,[2]

---

[1] An earlier version of this chapter was published in *Papers in Historical Phonology I* (2016). The authors would like to thank Patrick Honeybone and Pavel Iosad, as well as the audience at the First AMC Symposium on Historical Dialectology for their feedback on previous versions of this chapter. Special acknowledgements also go to Pavel Iosad for developing the R code allowing us to generate maps of the type presented here, and to Caroline Macafee for her careful, critical and constructive comments on the text.

[2] *From Inglis to Scots: Mapping Sounds to Spelling* (FITS) is a four-year research project on Older Scots grapho-phonology at the Angus McIntosh Centre for Historical Linguistics at the University of Edinburgh. More information can be found on the project's website at http://www.amc.lel.ed.ac.uk/fits/.

which maps spellings to sounds in a corpus of early Scots documents (see section 2.1.1).

1.1 What is L-vocalisation?

In simple terms, LV can be defined as a process by which a consonantal realisation of syllable-final /l/ – characteristically a 'dark' [ɫ] – becomes more vocalic and is perceptually recognised as a back vowel (for a discussion of the articulatory, acoustic and perceptual properties of vocalised and non-vocalised /l/, see Hall-Lew and Fix (2012)). According to Jones (1997: 319), this vocalic interpretation of coda [ɫ] is '[o]ne of the most common and historically recurrent features of English and Scots phonology'. Examples of LV can be found in most standard varieties, where spellings still reflect the /l/-ful form, such as pre-labial LV in *calf*, or pre-dorsal LV in *folk*. Such processes are more advanced in particular social and regional accents, like Cockney and Glaswegian, where LV can be found in final position (as in *coal, mole*), and even following front vowels (as in *milk*).[3]

In Scotland today, traditional /l/-less pronunciations compete with Standard English /l/-ful ones, in what seems a lexically-dependant pattern. In Caroline Macafee's Glasgow study of the mid-1980s, *aw* 'all' and *caw* 'call' make up 89 per cent of /l/-less forms (Stuart-Smith, Timmins and Tweedie 2006: 74; cf. Macafee 1988, 1994).[4] The complex history of the phenomenon is also manifest in reverse spellings for several Scottish place-names, such as *Kirkcaldy, Culross, Tillicoultry*, where <l> does not respond to an etymological /l/. The use of an apostrophe to mark a deleted /l/ is also a frequent (if contentious) spelling convention in Present-Day Scots: *a'* 'all', *fa'* 'fall', *ca'd* 'called'. Bann and Corbett (2015: 75) include the employment of an apostrophe for a 'vocalised consonant' /v/ or /l/ in their inventory of Innovative Scots spellings of the eighteenth century. Similarly, inserting <l> as 'back-spelling' or dropping it in post-1700 texts is said to 'give a visual sense of Scots' (Bann and Corbett 2015: 65).

In this chapter, we take a Scots-oriented view by focusing on words containing a short back vowel, i.e. /a, ɔ, ʊ/, followed by /l/, i.e. contexts in which LV may cause the vowel to form a diphthong (/au, ɔu/) or lengthen (/uː/).[5] As a result, we do not

---

[3] Note that this does not preclude such types of LV appearing in traditional 'prestige' varieties. As a matter of fact, Przedlacka (2001) provides evidence for their presence in upper- and middle-class RP speakers.

[4] The dataset collected in 1997 was very similar in this respect to the mid-1980s data (Stuart-Smith, Timmins and Tweedie 2006: 77).

[5] In our own analyses, we use the FITS Project convention in referring to these vowels. A. J. Aitken's number-based nomenclature is used when referring to his and others' work in the same tradition, see section 1.2.2. For reference /a, ɔ, ʊ/ are Aitken's V17, V18 and V19, respectively, while /au, ɔu, uː/ are Aitken's V12, V13 and V6 (cf. Aitken and Macafee 2002). Although, for our purposes, the lowest vowel in the short series, /a/, patterns with the back vowels, /ɔ, ʊ/, the exact articulatory quality of the low vowel along the front-back axis is not clear, patterning at times with the front series, and at time with the back (cf. Aitken and Macafee 2002: 4).

discuss early Scots cognates of the Old English (OE) *swilc* type[6] or potential cases of LV after front vowels, as in *milk*, which is a recent development in modern Urban Scots (see Stuart-Smith, Timmins and Tweedie 2006) but is absent from traditional Scots varieties.

1.2 Literature on Scots LV

1.2.1 Spelling evidence

The earliest linguistic studies of Older Scots mention the interchangeability of <a, au, aw> on the one hand and <al> on the other in certain words, for example <behalf>, with etymological /l/, is seen to alternate with <behafe> (1388), while <chalmer> and <walk> surface as back-spellings for *chamber* and *wake*, respectively (cf. Murray 1873: 122–123; Smith 1902: xxii; Girvan 1939: xlvi–xlvii). Murray calls <l> in these environments 'a mere orthoepic sign' (1873: 123). Later accounts also interpret <l> as an orthographic device to indicate vowel length and/or quality, suggesting the completion of LV and, consequently, the lack of any consonantal sound value in the grapheme. Examples in (1) show the earliest attested <l>-less spellings of words with an etymological /l/ in a roughly chronological order (Slater 1952; Aitken 1977; Aitken and Macafee 2002; Macafee 2003; *Dictionary of the Scots Language* (*DSL*) 2004):

(1) Earliest attestations of <l>-less spellings in Scots
a. *as*	'also'	pre-1410	
b. *auter*	'altar'	pre-1410	
c. *kaw*	'call'	1438	Ayr
d. *Hawch*	'halch = corner, nook'	1457	Peebles
e. *Auche*	'halch'	1457	Peebles
f. *how*	'hole'	1459	north-east
g. *Sydwawdyk*	'side'+'wall'+'dyke'	1462	Peebles
h. *bauk*	'balk = beam'	late fifteenth century	
i. *cawk*	'chalk'	late fifteenth century	
j. *pow*	'pull'	late fifteenth century	

Further instances of interchangeable <l>-ful and <l>-less spellings, such as <bahuif> ~ <balhuif>, <chamer> ~ <chalmer>, <wapin> ~ <wawpin>, <hauk> ~ <hawlk> ~ <hawk>, <faut> ~ <fawt> ~ <falt>, lead Aitken to describe a potential 'interchange under certain conditions (before *k*, *p*, *t*) of *au*, *aw*, *al* and (before or after *b*, *f*, *m*, *v* or *w*) of *a*, *au*, *aw*, *al*' (Aitken 1971: 182).[7] The set of environments looks far from systematic

---

[6] Etymological /l/ was often lost in the post-Conquest English dialects before 'highly salient [tʃ]', as in OE *hwylc* > ME *hwich*, in 'high-frequency words with low prosodic prominence', for example OE *ealswa* > ME *as(e)*, and in modals *should* and *would* (Minkova 2014: 130). These types of words, however, do not show concomitant vowel lengthening or diphthongisation.

[7] In their summary of LV and its impact on Scots spelling, Bann and Corbett list a different

and the individual attestations are too sporadic to propose a fully operational phonological rule. Considering other instances of variant spellings in competition, Aitken proposes that there was 'free variation' at play, but also 'spelling tradition and scribal preferences' (1971: 186). It is therefore difficult to interpret the phonological value of the <l> grapheme in sequences conducive to LV during that period. Aitken further says that: 'What were "phonemic" variants for one writer may conceivably sometimes have been merely "orthographic" for another' (1971: 191). Thus, his assessment of the data is guarded but he does acknowledge the fact that 'this series of changes did produce visible effects on OSc spelling practice' (Aitken and Macafee 2002: 101). He also seems to suggest, however, that the retention of <l> in the spelling may have concealed a phonological change: the 'unreduced' doublets (for example <all> alongside <aw>) 'persisted *at least* as orthographic variants' (1971: 195, emphasis added) while the outcome of the phonological change can be gleaned from present-day dialects of Scots.

1.2.2 Phonological environments: Affected vowels and their consonantal contexts

A summary of the operation of LV in Older Scots phonology is offered by Stuart-Smith, Timmins and Tweedie (2006: 74, vowel symbols original, see n. 5): 'Scots l-vocalization affected /l/ in Older Scots after the short vowels /a, o, u/ so that the outcomes of the sequences /al, ol, ul/ in West-Central Scots were respectively /ɔ, u, ʌu/ (cf. Macafee 1983: 38, 1994: 231) ... This process was blocked before /d/, hence *aul(d)* ('old').' In short, LV would be conditioned by the contexts preceding [ɫ] – the short back vowels – and those following it, as in (2).[8]

(2) Contexts for Older Scots LV
    a. word-finally: *fow* 'full'
    b. before labials: *cauf* 'calf'
    c. before coronals: *haud* 'hold', *bouster* 'bolster'
    d. before dorsals: *faucon* 'falcon'

In order to understand proposed LV-related changes to the vocalic system, it is helpful to refer to Aitken's pioneering work on the diachrony of Older Scots vowels. With an outlook to creating a stable frame of reference for the diachronically evolving phonology of Scots, Aitken proposed a system of historical vowels which foreshadowed the now-familiar English lexical sets (Wells 1983).[9] Each vocalic phoneme of Scots of c.1375 was given a number and its development was traced diachronically (Aitken

---

    set of consonantal contexts: '<l> can often be omitted after <a, o> and before <d, m, f, k>' (2015: 27).

[8] Note that, in phonological terms, we treat [a] as a back vowel here (see n. 5, above). Note also that in (2c), <haud> for 'hold' is taken as a lexical exception since /ld/ clusters usually block LV following [a], cf. Old Northumbrian <ald> becoming Scots <ald>, <auld> 'old'.

[9] Johnston (1997) proposes a lexical-set approach for Modern Scots vowels and traces their diachronic development. For the LV contexts, the sets are: CAUGHT (Aitken's V12), OUT (V6) and LOUP (V13) (Johnston 1997: 64, 82–83, 89–90, 97–98).

1977; Aitken and Macafee 2002). If we conceive of the words listed in (2) as members of a historical vowel set, then the natural consequence of LV would be for each of these words to move into a different set as a result of the lengthening or diphthongisation concomitant to [ɫ]-loss. Thus, words with a short back vowel – specifically /ʊ/ (V19), /a/ (V17) and /ɔ/ (V18) – followed by /l/, would enrich the sets of historical long back vowels – /uː/ (V6), /au/ (V12) and /ɔu/ V13 – through the operation of LV (see Figures 4.1–4.3).

For the short /ʊ/, V19, the change is essentially one of quantity (Figure 4.1). The other two vowels enter a slightly more complex path as a result of LV (Figures 4.2 and 4.3). In Aitken's interpretation, /a/ underwent breaking because of a velarised environment, resulting 'in something like [ɑᵘ] or [aᵘ]'. Here, the outcome was a fronter diphthong which merged with V12, /au/. Similarly, in the /ɔl/ context, the 'backer diaphone of the diphthong ... merged with the existing diphthong /ǫu/ vowel 13' (Aitken and Macafee 2002: 61, vowel symbol original corresponding to /ɔu/). He argues this on the basis of the twentieth-century data from the *Linguistic Atlas of Scotland*, for the 'OSc orthographic evidence is meagre' (Aitken and Macafee 2002: 62). Even though Aitken is rather cautious in his account of LV in Older Scots, his charts schematising the change (such as those on Figures 4.1–4.3) have been less carefully reproduced by later scholars, giving the impression that LV advanced more quickly and exceptionlessly than Aitken himself impies. It is thus necessary to revisit the timelines and scope of the change presented in reference literature and set them against systematically-collected corpus data (see sections 2–3 below).

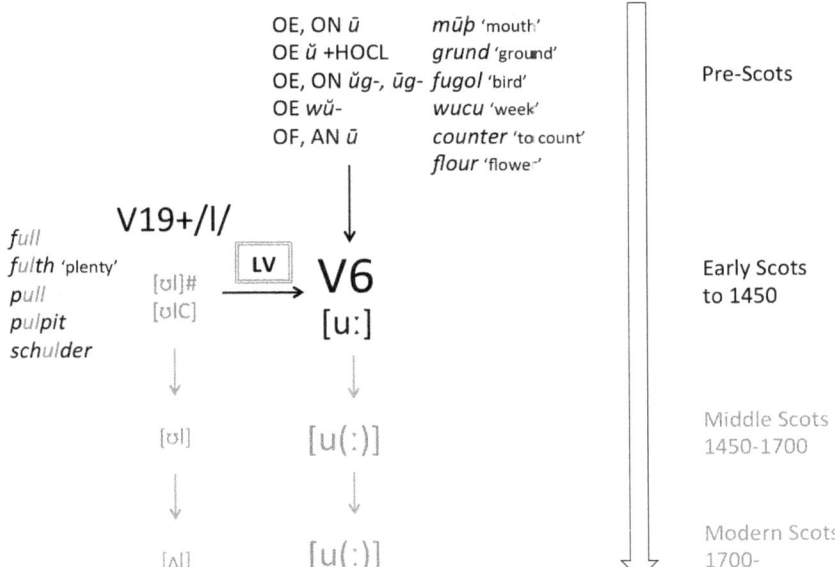

Figure 4.1 The diachronic development of V6 (Aitken 1977; Aitken and Macafee 2002; Macafee 2003) and its enrichment by members of V19 set due to LV

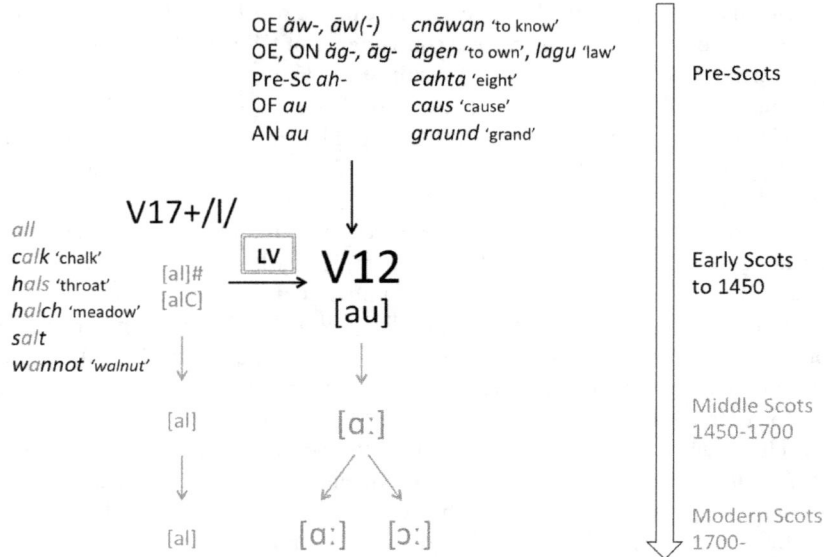

Figure 4.2 The diachronic development of V12 (Aitken 1977; Aitken and Macafee 2002; Macafee 2003) and its enrichment by members of V17 set due to LV

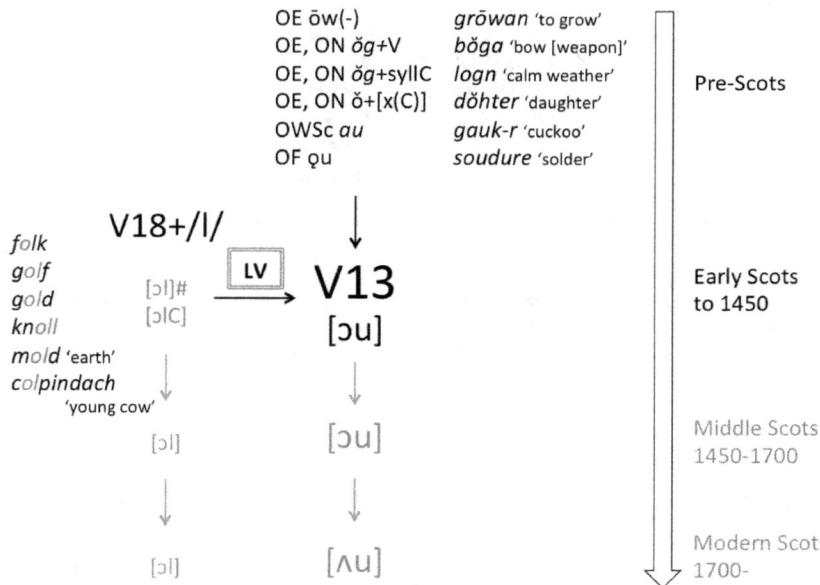

Figure 4.3 The diachronic development of V13 (Aitken 1977; Aitken and Macafee 2002; Macafee 2003) and its enrichment by members of V18 set due to LV

1.2.3 Etymological sources of LV and related back-spellings

In terms of the sources of items with LV environments, we may conclude that word-final LV was restricted to Germanic vocabulary, as this environment is rare in Latin borrowings, excepting words suffixed with *-al(l)* (for example *celestial, special*, and so on), which never vocalise in Scots (Aitken and Macafee 2002: 104).[10] However, borrowing from French with etymological [l]+C clusters did contribute substantially to the emergence of the V12 /au/, V13 /ɔu/ and V6 /u:/ lexical sets. These words may also have been a product of a '[v]ocalisation of [lC] clusters [which] started in OFr in the ninth century' (Minkova 2014: 131; see also Pope 1934: 154–156). Indeed, Johnston (1997: 107) suggests that the Midlanders moving up to south-eastern Scotland after the Norman Conquest could have brought with them a general OE breaking/Old Norman LV rule which in the North and in Scots became more restricted. While individual borrowings could have entered Scots vocabulary after the /l/ had been lost in the donor language, the layering of French and Latin may have produced new alternations. To take an example, the borrowing <faut> 'fault', appearing in its earliest attestation in Barbour's *Bruce* (1375) without the <l>, is a product of French innovation, and its subsequent respelling as <fault> could have happened under the influence of Latin on Scots (either directly or via Midland dialects of Middle English (ME)). The historical <l> was 'put back' by some writers between the fifteenth and seventeenth centuries. The *DSL* gives examples from the second-half of the fifteenth century: <fault> from Gilbert of the Haye's MS (1456) and <fawlt> from Peebles Burgh Records (1478). Note that <l>-less forms are earlier, which suggests <l>-ful forms – at least for this word, in Scots – originated either through Latin influence or via a more general process of back-spelling. No active process of LV is necessary for such items in Scots.

As for back-spellings, while they occur in both native and borrowed items, they are necessarily subsequent to the relevant phonological change that modifies the relationship between a grapheme and its original sound substance. In the case of LV, the sound substance of <l> became reduced or lost altogether, while the preceding vowel changed – it lengthened or diphthongised. Thus, the new members of the groups pronounced with V6, V12 and V13 could continue to employ <l> as an empty length or diphthongisation diacritic. This new spelling option could then spread to the original members of a given group which had never had a <l> or /l/. Back-spellings are thus expected to be later than the inception of the change. Some examples of such back-spellings in the literature are given in (3) and (4), from Murray (1873), van Buuren (1982: 62) and Aitken and Macafee (2002: 103).

(3) Back-spellings in Germanic vocabulary
    a. *Fallkirk* vs *Fawkirk*   1381
    b. *half*   'have'   ?1425

---

[10] Of course, whether such endings were realised as stressed is contentious for the fifteenth century, outside verse. Regarding the native vocabulary, Aitken and Macafee consider the modal verb *sall* 'shall' to be an exception to word-final vocalisation (2002: 104; Macafee 2003: 148, but see section 3).

c. *walle*	'waw, measure of weight'	?a1434
d. *nolt*	'nowt, cattle' (Ayr)	1437
e. *haltyn ~ hautane*	'proud'	1488
f. *walter*	'water'	1491
g. *wall*	'wave'	late fifteenth century
h. *rolpand, rolpit* <OE *hrōpan*/ON *raupa*	'to shout, to boast'	c.1515
i. *bollis*	'ox-bows'	1516

(4) Back-spellings in Romance vocabulary

a. *calse*	'causeway' (Glasgow)	1434
b. *chalmer ~ chawmer*	'chamber'	1473
c. *saulfgarde*	'safeguard'	1473
d. *pulder ~ pouder*	'powder'	1479
e. *beaulte*	'beauty'	fifteenth century
f. *salf*	'safe'	c.1515

English back-spellings in the same context are earlier than those found in Scots. Minkova (2014: 131) lists several of these from the *Middle English Dictionary* before labials and coronals: <palcker> 'packer' (1282), <walke> 'wake' (c.1384), <salme> 'same' (a.1399), <salke> 'sake' (c.1400). For Scots, we do not have substantial written data from before the late fourteenth century. Examples in (3) and (4), however, do not start immediately after continuous written record emerges, which suggests that LV could not have been in full swing before 1400. Interestingly, a quick look at the timing of the first reported back-spellings in the scholarly literature shows the Romance forms in (4) to lag slightly behind the Germanic forms in (3). The use of <l> in unetymological contexts in these words seems to follow on from the native LV process rather than the much earlier operation of the same change in OF.

1.2.4 Claims regarding the inception and operation of LV in Scots

Previous analyses are not unanimous regarding the placement of Scots LV on a timeline, and the characterisation of the change in terms of scope and systematicity remains unclear. Several scholars, for instance, make a case for its inception being traceable to the fourteenth century. Girvan (1939: lxiv) finds the first occurrences in the late fourteenth century. On the basis of the dictionary record, mainly from Robinson (1985), Johnston claims that for V6 [uː], '[c]ombinations of <uv> and <ulC> are realised as OUT words from early on, as the various consonant vocalisation rules are of fourteenth-century date (compare *scowk* for *skulk*; Robinson 1985: 589), or earlier' (1997: 83, see Figure 4.1).[11] He continues with mergers enriching V12 [au]: 'The CAUGHT class was

---

[11] We have changed the brackets from /uv/ and /ulC/ to <uv> and <ulC>, as it seems clear the author is referring to graphemes, rather than phonemes. The input vowel would have been V19, [ʊ].

added to in the fourteenth century, if not before, by a process inserting an epenthetic vowel between the CAT vowel [i.e. V17] and /l/ as in *old* [...]; <au> forms date back as far as the late 1300s' (1997: 89, see Figure 4.2). In turn, Macafee offers a succinct outline of LV: 'A group of conditioned changes known as L-vocalisation took place in the late fourteenth or early fifteenth century' (2003: 148).

Proponents of the fifteenth-century operation of LV start with Murray who lists 'mute *l*' among 'obvious peculiarities' of 'the Middle Period', that is fifteenth century onwards (1873: 53). Aitken and Macafee propose that LV emerges in the fifteenth century, while the earliest attestations, such as <hawhes> 'haugh, nook of land' (OE *healh*) in a c.1240 charter from Kelso or a 1383 spelling of <hafthrepland> (a place-name with *half* as the initial element) were 'perhaps casual or idiosyncratic' (2002: 103). McClure places the occurrence of LV in 'the first quarter of the fifteenth century', resulting in 'a *widespread* use of the digraphs <al, ol> and <au/aw, ou/ow> as free variations, in words both with and without the historical /l/' (1994: 48, emphasis added). In their discussion of present-day new types of LV in Glaswegian, Stuart-Smith, Timmins and Tweedie concede that these new pronunciations add to 'an existing form of l-vocalization continued from Scots, which was *completed* by the mid-fifteenth century' (2006: 73, emphasis added). Most authors would thus see the change well advanced, if not completed, by 1500. Analysing the spelling and grammar in the Asloan MS (c.1515), van Buuren observes that when /l/ followed short vowels (V17, V18, V19), 'it was *evidently* pronounced with a velar or /u/-modification' (1982: 52, emphasis added).

Aitken (1977) captured the proposed history of all Scots vowels in a series of helpful figures and tables, with a subtitle: 'a rough historical outline'. To the main inventory, he added three segments: V6a /ʊl/, V12a /al/ and V13a /ɔl/, which would merge with their respective main counterparts after the operation of LV (Table 4.1).

Table 4.1 Aitken's (1977) outline of V6, V12 and V13

	Early Scots c.1400	Middle Scots (sixteenth century)		Older Scots spellings
V6	uː	uː	uː	ou, ow : ow#
V6a	ʊl			ul, (w)ol : ull#
V12	au	au	aː	au, aw : aw#; a#
V12a	al			al : all#
V13	ou	ou	ou	ou, ow : ow#
V13a	ɔl			ol : oll#

Aitken probably did not consider LV to be complete in the sixteenth century, since he left the vowel + /l/ sequences, potentially affected by LV, out of the tabular presentation of the early Scots inputs to the Scottish Vowel Length Rule (SVLR, Aitken 1981: 132–133), see Table 4.2. He did include items affected by LV in the examples of the SVLR, though, which allowed him not to commit to LV being completed during a specific period. All in all, while some authors have taken schemata such as those in

Table 4.1 as claims for the completion of change,[12] Aitken himself approached LV with more caution: 'In certain orthographic environmental conditions and in particular words, some interchange of graphemes took place' (1977: 5). This statement, although somewhat vague, is a springboard for the quantitative investigation offered below.

Table 4.2 Aitken's (1981) outline of V6, V12 and V13[13]

	Early Scots, c.1400	Middle Scots (sixteenth century)	Modern Scots	SVLR?	Examples
V6	uː	uː	u	yes	*about, mouth, loud, bouk* 'bulk', *shouder* 'shoulder', *hour, cow, fou* 'full', *pou* 'pull'
V12	au	aː	aː ɔː	invariably long in most dialects (cf. Aitken and Macafee 2002: 126)	*faut* 'fault', *saut* 'salt', *fraud, auld* 'old', *mawn* 'mown', *cause, law, snaw* 'snow', *aw* 'all', *faw* 'fall'
V13	ou	ou	ʌu	yes	*nout* 'cattle', *louse* 'loose', *four, owre, chow* 'chew', *grow* (and words such as *about, loud, house* in ScStE)

2. LV in fifteenth-century Scots: A corpus-based assessment

2.1 Why a corpus approach?

As we have noted, the original claims in the literature about the nature and extent of early Scots LV are ultimately unable to assess the degree to which the presence or absence of historical <l> is an artefact of the spelling or an actual feature of the phonology. Although the complex interaction of spelling representation and sound in potential LV contexts will never allow an unambiguous interpretation, the quantification of the spelling alternants (in both etymological /l/ and back-spelling contexts) should give us important insights into the process, establishment, regional and lexical spread, phonological and lexical conditioning, and degree of completion.

---

[12] Bann and Corbett (2015:53–56) transform Aitken's phonological tables taking orthographic units as their starting point. For LV contexts, they list orthographic 'vowel+<l>' combinations as 'vowels', on a par with their respective phonological merger targets. The presentation of data suggests that LV is an across-the-board change, with no phonological or lexical restrictions, so that, for instance, the sequence <aw> could be pronounced as either /au/ or /al/ in pre-GVS Scots, or that the OSc word /huːs/ (OE *hūs* 'house') could be spelled *<hul(l)s>.

[12] Note that, for practical purposes, we use Standard English labels for our examples, where these are available.

Previous accounts, as we have seen, rely on the selected attestations in the dictionary record and more or less *ad hoc* searches of the literature, where <l>-less spellings for etymological /l/ and unetymological <l>-insertion appear as noteworthy. In opposition, <l>-ful and <l>-less spellings in the etymologically-expected contexts are uninteresting, so they are not compiled and tend to receive no direct comment. The discrepancies in frequency can be huge, however. Aitken (1971: 199), for instance, logs the spelling <staw> for the preterit of 'steal', as a single attestation in the c.300 folios of the Scots *Boece*, but does not provide a count for the prevalent <stall>-type spellings in the text.

One of the advantages of diachronic corpus studies is that they afford us a look not only into incoming variants, but also to their relative frequency in relation to the traditional ones. Further to this key advantage, the FITS Corpus allows us to consider the linguistic contexts in which different variants surface (phonotactic, graphotactic, morphological, and so on), and to assess their spatio-temporal distribution, thus providing a more nuanced picture of variation and change quite generally.

Looking beyond the confines of the phenomenon of LV in Scots, a close examination of this feature is informative as regards the advantages and challenges of doing historical corpus phonology more generally. The period we are concerned with (1380–1500) is interesting because we have a fairly clear idea of the sound-system of the preceding (OE) and following (Present-Day Scots) stages of the language, but we can only bridge the gap by establishing plausible sound-spelling mappings based on the highly variable, non-standardised spelling system of early Scots. The result of such a study – the basis for the FITS Project database described in Section 2.2 – should allow a window into the progress of sound change, and the changing orthographic conventions by which changing sounds were represented.

2.2 The corpus

The data presented below is taken from the *From Inglis to Scots* (FITS) project database,[14] comprising material from some of the earliest extant non-literary texts in Scots, mostly administrative and legal documents composed in multiple locations throughout Lowland Scotland. These texts were diplomatically transcribed and semantico-grammatically tagged for the *Linguistic Atlas of Older Scots 1.1* (LAOS, Williamson comp. 2008). In all, LAOS contains around 1,250 text files (c.400,000 words) from manuscripts of the period 1380–1500.

Resolving the relationships between sound and spelling units in the FITS database – or, grapho-phonological parsing (cf. Kopaczyk et al. 2018) – allows for quick targeted searches of the graphotactic and phonotactic contexts where we expect LV (and back-spellings) to occur. Also, given various proposed timelines for the rise of LV in Scots (see section 1.2.3), the timespan of the database is extremely well suited to test them out. The fact that locations and dates are provided for most texts affords us an even more fine-grained look at the regional and diachronic development of this phenomenon.

[14] The language variety of the corpus was originally referred to as *Inglis*, though it eventually came to be labelled as *Scottis* 'Scots' during the period represented in the corpus.

2.3 Research questions

The issues arising from the literature on LV in Scots lead us to propose a quantitative, corpus-based analysis of five key questions on the topic of LV in fifteenth-century Scots:

1. *How prevalent are <l>-less spellings in LV contexts?*
   The most fundamental question is whether, in the native word-stock, <l>-less spellings constitute an important part of the data for the period we are concerned with, particularly if we take into account all the <l>-ful spellings in the same contexts.
2. *When and where are <l>-less spellings attested?*
   Drawing on the fact that most of our texts are dated and localised, we contrast the timing and location of <l>-less and <l>-ful spellings in the purported LV contexts for native words.
3. *In what phonic/graphemic environments do <l>-less spellings surface?*
   Given that we find evidence of /l/-vocalisation after all three etymologically short back vowels, we explore the contexts following the etymological /l/ and relate them to the rate of absence/presence of <l> in the spelling.
4. *Is the evidence for LV different for Germanic and Romance vocabulary?*
   As words of Romance stock may have undergone LV type processes before their borrowing (see section 1.2.2), we contrast the Romance vocabulary with Germanic in terms of their proportions of <l>-less and back-spellings.
5. *Does <l> act as a diacritic for length/diphthongisation?*
   We examine back-spellings as important indirect evidence for LV, that is the presence of an <l> in words where it is not etymological but which share the proposed outcome vowel of LV.

3. Corpus-based findings

3.1 How prevalent are <l>-less spellings in proposed LV contexts?

3.1.1 Search parameters

In order to examine the direct spelling evidence for LV in our corpus, our searches focused on lexical items with an etymological /l/ following stressed, short back vowels [a, ɔ, ʊ][15] in codas, that is morpheme-finally and before a consonant.[16] Importantly, as

---

[15] In a previous version of this work, published in *Papers in Historical Phonology 1* (2016), we claimed, based on preliminary searches of *A Dictionary of the Older Scottish Tongue* (www.dsl.ac.uk), that LV after long back vowels was 'conceivable and indeed attested for later periods'. Unfortunately, our examples proved to be misinterpretations, as rightly pointed out by Caroline Macafee. We are grateful for this critique.

[16] FITS transcription procedure captures some palaeographic detail: double inverted commas stand for a trailing stroke, ± signifies non-continuous spelling of a root, abbreviations are expanded in parentheses, a tilde represents a horizontal line over one or more characters. Potential compounding of the root with a preceding or following morpheme in the source text is indicated by a set of empty parentheses either preceding or following the root.

regards verbs, our searches included only forms in a paradigm such that the expected vowel is /a, ɔ, ʊ/. Hence for *sell* we included only past tense and past participle forms. Furthermore, in the few cases where the expected back vowel is spelled with a grapheme which potentially represents frontness, such as <sell> for *shall*, we have excluded the token altogether. Finally, as the FITS database deals only with root morphemes of Germanic origin, we report – in sections 3.1–3.4 – on these elements alone. In section 3.5, this data is contrasted with that from Romance vocabulary, gathered outside the core FITS material, in order to assess the potential impact of the latter on Scots LV.

3.1.2 Search results

The FITS database search, in line with the parameters outlined above, returned thirty-nine root morphemes which match the target environment, twenty-one of which display <l>-less spellings, as summarised in Table 4.3.[17]

While a glance at the type-data – the individual distinct target morphemes – shows well over half of the target words displaying signs of LV (21/34), a closer look at the data for tokens shows <l>-less spellings to be far rarer than the types would suggest, being attested only seventy-four times across the entire corpus. If we consider all potential contexts for LV, <l>-less spellings make up no more than 0.94 per cent of the total (7,909), while if we only take into account the words where <l>-less spellings are attested (7,272), the proportion is only 1.02 per cent.

Turning to the distribution of <l>-less and <l>-ful spellings by morpheme, Figure 4.4 shows that the <l>-less forms are not the prerogative of any particularly frequent morpheme(s). The proportion of <l>-less spellings is ultimately very low in most morphemes, and it is more prevalent only in infrequently attested morphemes.

3.2 When and where are <l>-less spellings attested?

One of the major advantages of the FITS database is that the vast majority of the texts are dated and localised, due to their legal nature. That said, the problem with this record is that it is unbalanced both in the temporal and the spatial dimensions. In terms of the diachrony, we have a greater density of texts towards the end of the period, as records become more numerous. In terms of the regional imbalance, we find a greater density of texts in more populous or administratively important locations. Still, the geographical spread of texts is reasonable for the areas where Scots was spoken, allowing us some perspective on dialectal distributions.

---

[17] An apparent candidate for this environment is the adverbial *as*, which is found in the FITS data predominantly without <l>, representing etymological /l/ (< Anglian *al(l)swa*). We have excluded it from our dataset, however, as it most likely surfaced in phrasally unstressed positions (cf. n. 5).

Table 4.3 Potential LV contexts in the FITS database

FITS morpheme	LV+ or LV-	<l>-ful token count	<l>-less token count	<l>-less forms
afald 'one-fold'	+	17	2	ane"±favde, ane"±fawde
all	+	2255	5	haw, au, aw
almost	-	1	0	-
alms	-	18	0	-
also	+	349	7	assua, asua, ausua, awssa
behalf	+	76	6	be±haff, be±hauff, behaw, behawf, behofe
boll	+	33	2	bow, ()bov
bolster	+	0	1	boust(er)
bulk	-	1	0	-
calf	+	2	3	cauf, kauf, caff(is)
call	+	479	8	caw, kaw, cawit, kawʒyt
cold	-	3	0	-
fall	+	51	1	tofawis
fold	-	11	0	-
folk	-	18	0	-
full	+	549	7	fow, fowely, fwfyl, fuwullyt
gold	+	36	1	gowd
golf	-	1	0	-
half	+	290	3	haf, haff, hawff
hall	+	7	5	haw
haugh	+	4	1	hewgh~, hewygh~, hawthis
hold	+	626	7	haud, haudyn, haudy(n), hawdyn~, hawdy(n), hawtdy(n)
holm	-	1	0	-
malt	+	12	1	mawyte
old	-	283	0	-
palm	+	1	1	pamesonday
pull	-	1	0	-
salt	-	17	0	-
shall	+	1982	1	sa
should	+	268	4	sad, sowd, sud, suid
small	-	11	0	-
sell vpp/vpt/aj	-	154	0	-
stall	-	1	0	-
stouth	-	1	0	-
tell vpp/vpt/aj	-	5	0	-
toll	-	107	5	toyboith~, towbuth, towbut
wall	-	21	0	-

EARLY SPELLING EVIDENCE FOR SCOTS L-VOCALISATION 75

Table 4.3 Continued

FITS morpheme	LV+ or LV-	<l>-ful token count	<l>-less token count	<l>-less forms
waulk	-	14	0	-
would	+	128	3	wad, wayd
TOTAL		7835	74	*All tokens: 7,909*

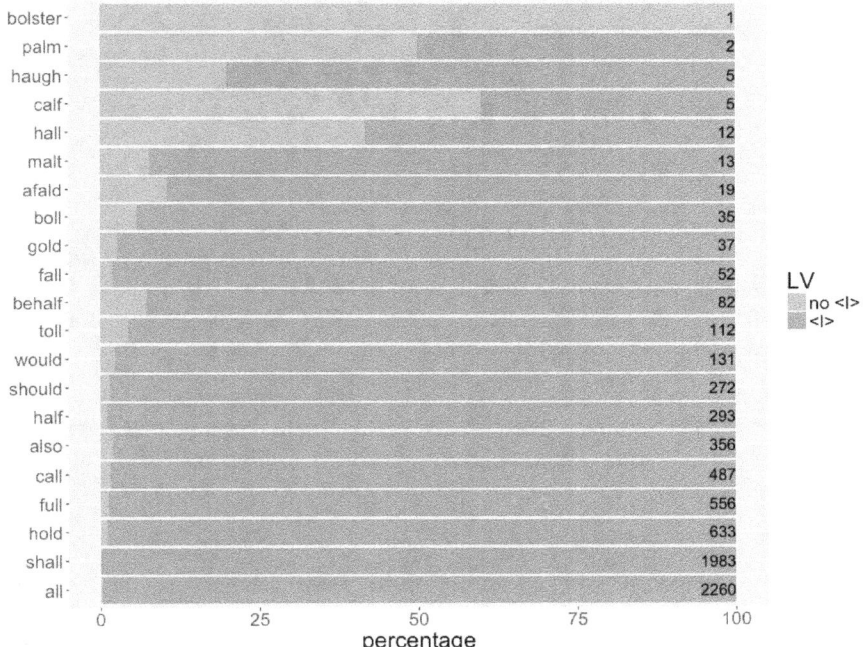

Figure 4.4 Relative proportions of <l>-less and <l>-ful spellings by morphemes presenting <l>-less spellings, with a total number of attestations for each morpheme

3.2.1 Temporal distribution

The literature on LV seems to suggest that the period of our corpus is, roughly, the correct timeframe for /l/-loss to have taken hold or even, potentially, come to completion (see section 1.2.3). With this in mind, we take a closer look at the proportions of <l>-less and <l>-ful spellings by decade in our corpus (Figure 4.5). The difference between overall frequencies in the early decades, as opposed to the later ones, is an artefact of the imbalance in the data we mentioned above. In order to make this plain, we have overlaid a temporal density line for the entire word count of the corpus, which closely follows the overall trend for the LV contexts.

Although <l>-less attestations are rare in the corpus, they seem to follow the overall frequency trend for the corpus over time. No pattern of growth seems apparent.

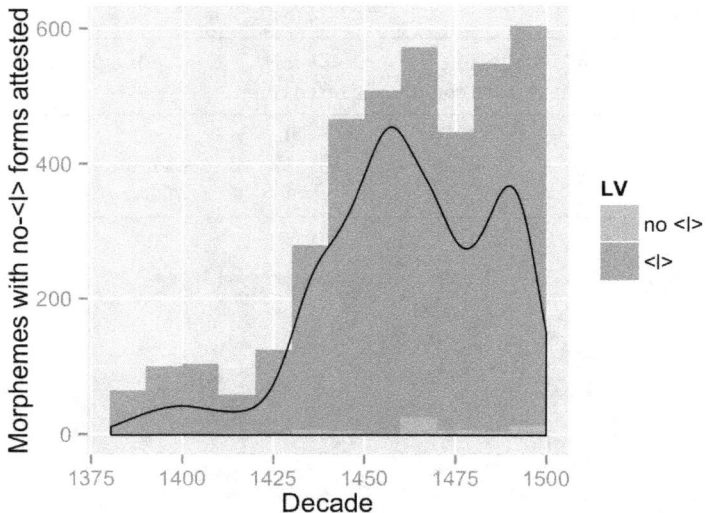

Figure 4.5 Distribution of <l>-ful and <l>-less spellings in words with <l>-less forms attested in the FITS Corpus, by decade. The black line represents a density plot for the temporal distribution of the overall number of words in the entire corpus

Rather, the evidence seems to point to LV as a constant very low-level phenomenon throughout the fifteenth century, at least in the direct spelling evidence.

3.2.2 Regional distribution

Since we are concerned with a feature that has been claimed to be 'characteristic' of early Scots, we try to pinpoint whether its earliest attestations in the spelling are restricted to a core area of Lowland Scotland, or whether they are more diffuse. However, the regional pattern of <l>-less spellings, as seen in Figure 4.6, is not robust. This is mostly due to the fact that the <l>-less attestations are confounded with density of texts overall.

Even though numbers are too low to make any strong claims, what we do see is that the largest number of <l>-less spellings are concentrated around the firths of Forth and Tay, which would have been relatively populous areas at the time. Other important foci, such as Ayr, Peebles and Aberdeen, may be showing hierarchical diffusion from one larger centre of population to another, though this remains speculative.

More interesting, perhaps, is the fact that a large proportion of the attested <l>-less spellings can be traced to twenty-nine tokens associated to Newburgh, and dated to an eighteen-year period between 1461 and 1479. As is evidenced from the map, this particular area has a large concentration of texts overall, which might explain the propensity of these forms to a certain extent. However, temporal proximity of the texts suggests that these attestations may be the work of a single person or a local commu-

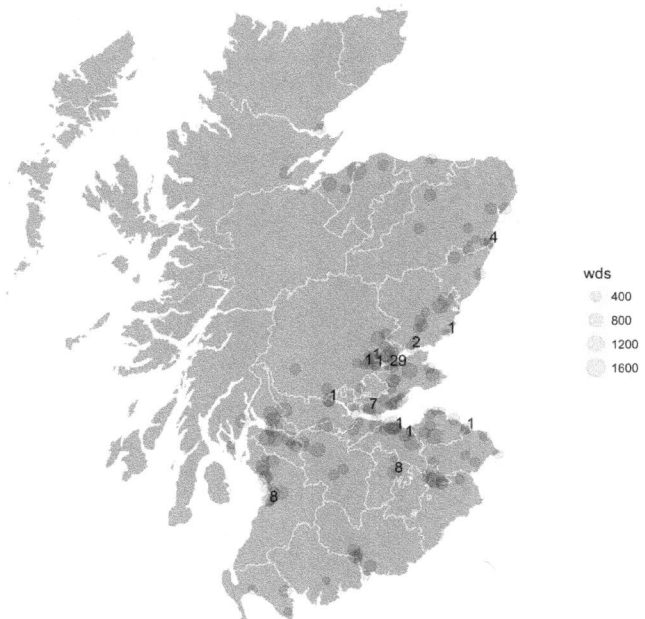

Figure 4.6 Regional distribution of <l>-less spellings in view of regional coverage in the corpus: <l>-less spellings in LV contexts are given in red, with exact counts in black. The overall density of words by location is given in blue

nity of practice (Kopaczyk 2013: 46, 133, 242; see also Hofmann this volume).[18] Still, it remains difficult to assess whether this represents an idiolect, an idiosyncratic spelling system or a broader regional pattern.

3.3 In what phonic or graphemic environments do <l>-less spellings surface?

As discussed in section 1.2.2, the literature on early Scots identifies the environments for LV as those which follow a short back vowel and precede: a) a word boundary; b) a labial consonant; c) a velar consonant; or, variably, d) a coronal consonant. Taking these claims as our starting point, we have organised the relevant lexical items from our corpus (cf. Table 4.3) into these four categories, as presented in Table 4.4, in which morphemes with attested <l>-less spellings are underlined.

Looking at the word-type data alone, <l>-less spellings seem to occur in all the relevant categories, with pre-velar being far rarer, and pre-coronal being more common, than existing descriptions would seem to imply. Examining individual tokens from a quantitative perspective, as in Figure 4.7, these attestations show a different pattern

---

[18] Unfortunately for our historical dialectology pursuits, the vast majority of scribes in the LAOS Corpus are anonymous.

Table 4.4 FITS morphemes by grapho-phonological context fitting the LV environments

Final	/l/+labial	/l/+velar	/l/+coronal
<u>all</u>, <u>boll</u>, <u>call</u>, <u>fall</u>, <u>full</u>, <u>hall</u>, pull, <u>shall</u>, small, stall, <u>toll</u>, wall	almost, alms, <u>behalf</u>, <u>calf</u>, golf, <u>half</u>, holm, <u>palm</u>	bulk, folk, <u>haugh</u>, waulk	<u>afald</u>, <u>also</u>, <u>bolster</u>, cold, fold, gold, <u>hold</u>, <u>malt</u>, old, salt, <u>should</u>, sold, stouth, told, <u>would</u>

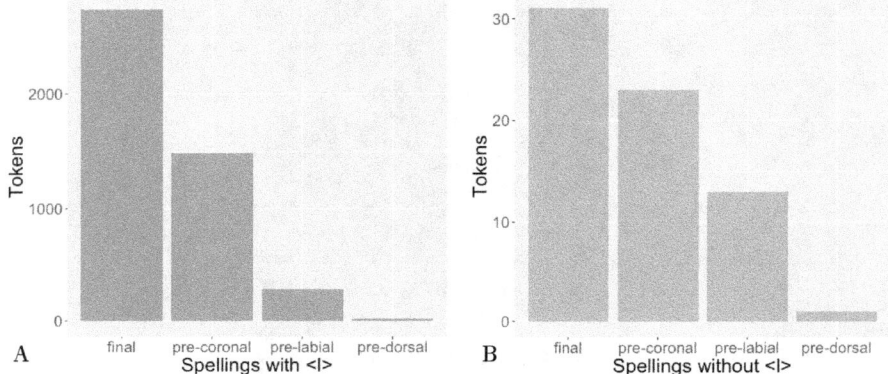

Figure 4.7 Attested spellings with and without <l>, by phonological environment

which, as elsewhere, seems to follow the general frequency of words, albeit at a very low level. No particular context is shown to be especially conducive to LV.

Although rare, <l>-less forms in final and labial contexts are consistent with the literature. Velar contexts are extremely rare in our corpus overall (thirty-eight tokens), so having a single attested <l>-less spelling (<hauthis> for Scots *haugh* 'flat, alluvial land' < OE *healh* 'nook, corner') is unsurprising.

In pre-coronal contexts, the relatively high rate of <l>-less spellings is somewhat unexpected, given that the literature claims that LV did not happen after original /a/ (> /au/) and before /d/, as evidenced by *cold/cauld* and *old/auld* in Scots dialects today (Johnston 1997: 90). Still, the data in Figure 4.8 show that the Older Scots instances of LV closely match those attested in Modern Scots. LV is attested in *also*, *gold*, *malt*, *should* and *would* where it is expected. It also occurs at low levels in *hold* and *afald*. Although the first of these is clearly an exception to the rule that LV does not occur between /a(u)/ and /d/, it is also an exception in all Modern Scots dialects, as the typical modern spelling <haud> shows. LV in *afald* may also be an exception, but as a morphologically complex word with stress potentially falling on the first syllable (as in English *one-fold*), it may be that the very small number of cases of LV in this word reflect other factors. Indeed, the two <l>-less forms that are attested have a coda nasal in the first element, as well as a gap in the spelling (cf. <ane" favde>, <ane" fawde> vs. <afalde>), suggesting that main stress was not on the syllable with etymo-

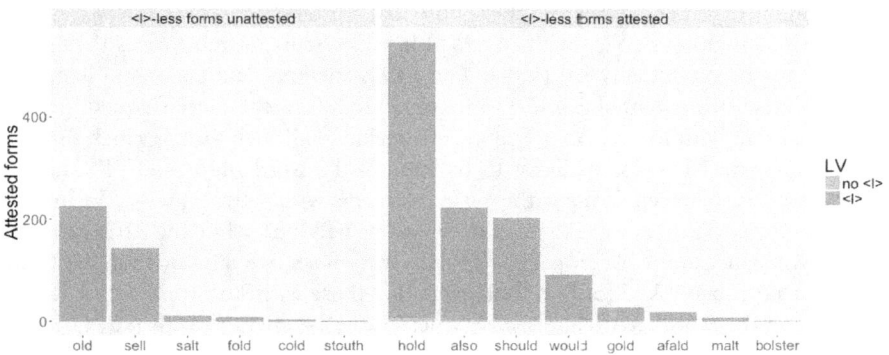

Figure 4.8 Comparison of tokens for morphemes with <l>-less forms attested and not attested in pre-coronal contexts

logical /l/. In contrast to *afald* and *hold*, very frequent items such as *old* and *sold* do not show <l>-less attestations, which matches the distribution of LV in Modern Scots.

3.4 Back-spellings and the use of <l> as a diacritic

While the only reasonably direct evidence for LV in the early Scots record is the non-realisation of etymological /l/ in spellings, it is possible that the spelling system remained conservative, and kept <l> spellings despite its lack of phonic contents in the LV environments. The result of such a process would be the repurposing of <l> as a diacritic for length or diphthongisation of the vowel, as discussed in section 1.2.2. We must assume, therefore, that following the operation of LV, writers would have no longer had access to any way of distinguishing the words with etymological /l/ from those without. Supposing that LV was widespread, we expect to find the use of <l> as a diacritic in all contexts where a long or diphthongal back vowel preceded a consonant or a word boundary. If this was indeed the case, it would lend support to Murray (1873), Bann and Corbett (2015) and other researchers in interpreting <l> in LV contexts as a marker for vowel length or diphthongisation, rather than a true lateral. As a result, spellings like <half> could be taken to represent [hauf] at the level of the phonology.

3.4.1 Search parameters

The key environments for our back-spelling searches are those where a word's etymological stressed vowel matches one of the output vowels of LV, that is [uː], [au] or [ɔu] (Aitken's V6, V12 and V13, respectively) before a consonant or word-finally. The target root morphemes – here only for the Germanic vocabulary – were identified on the basis of the items and categories proposed by Aitken and Macafee (2002) for the target vowels. These results were divided into two groups: those that are attested with an unetymological <l>, and those that do not attest this feature.

Although Aitken and Macafee (2002) note that words such as *bound, found, ground* and *pound* sometimes surface with [uː] (V6) in early Scots, in most cases they argue that the vowel was actually [ʊ] (V19). The FITS spelling data make no distinction between these two potential sounds, so we opted to follow the more frequent pattern (also consistent with Present-Day Scots), and excluded all such forms, which furthermore display no <l>-less spellings. In the case of the word *truth* the FITS data do show a contrast between forms with <ou> and forms with <ew, ev, eu>. We include only the former types, as we take them to represent V13 [ɔu], while the latter types are probably instances of V14a [iu]. For *daughter* and *trough*, we only include the forms with <ou> (probably V13 [ɔu]) as well, excluding those with <o> (probably V18 [ɔ]). We include the words *weak* and *water*, where [aː] (V4) merged with [au] (V12, cf. Aitken and Macafee 2002: 122). To this set we also add the noun *wax*, which has the lengthened form spelled <waux> elsewhere. Finally, we include forms of the word *week* spelled with <ou> and <o>, representing [uː] from OE *wucu* with lengthening after [w] (Aitken and Macafee, 2002:80).[19]

Our search parameters yielded forty-three morphemes with contexts for LV back-spelling. Ten of these types showed at least one instance of unetymological <l>, as presented in Table 4.5, in which morphemes with attested unetymological <l> are underlined.[20]

Table 4.5 Back-spelling environments by phonological context

V6, 12, 13 +__#	V6, 12, 13 +labial	V6, 12, 13 +velar	V6, 12, 13 +coronal
bow, cow, draw, ewe, know, law, mauch, now, own, row, show, sow, trow, <u>waw</u>	dovecot	bouk, brouk, daughter, <u>hawk</u>, owe, stook, trough, <u>wax</u>, <u>weak</u>, <u>week</u>	aloud, brown, <u>could</u>, down, foud, house, loose, mouth, <u>neither</u>, <u>nowt</u>, sloth, south, sound, town, truth, trout, <u>water</u>, wood

In the analysis of the 3,059 tokens with the target environment, a total of twenty-three tokens showed unetymological <l> spellings. Back-spellings, then, make up no more than 0.75 per cent of contexts in which <l> may function as a diacritic. Amongst the twenty-three forms that display such spellings, the most frequent morphemes are *wax* and *week*, as can be seen in Figure 4.9.

A closer look at the back-spellings shows their strong tendency to appear with a

[19] It is not clear whether the single attestation of *smolt* (young salmon), spelled as <smot+is> represents a case of back-spelling or LV, since the word's etymology is not fully known. On these grounds, the token was excluded from our analyses.

[20] FITS forms of *owe* are overwhelmingly spelled with <ch> and variants thereof, as in <aucht>, most likely representing [x]. We have therefore included the morpheme among pre-velar contexts. For the morpheme *own* we also get some verbal forms in [x] (such as <acht>) but these are rare in contrast with the forms derived from a root attaching a past participial ending *-en*, for example <awin> or <aw>. Thus *own* is included among root-final contexts.

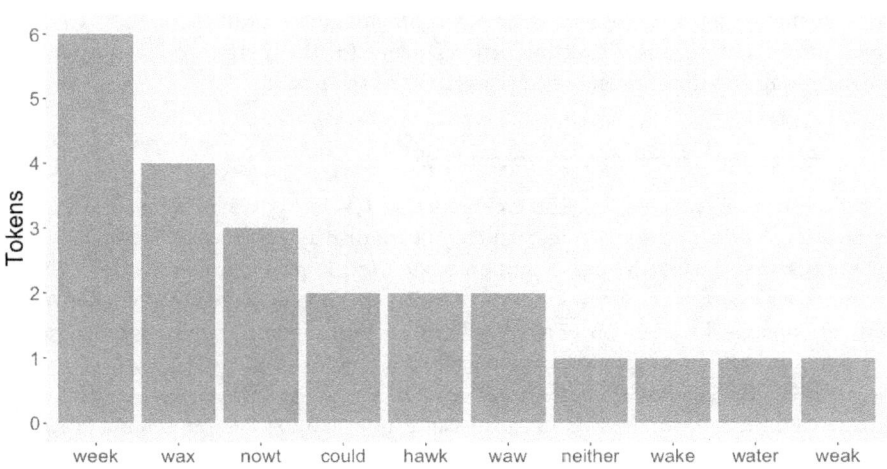

Figure 4.9 Back-spellings: Germanic vocabulary with an unetymological <l>

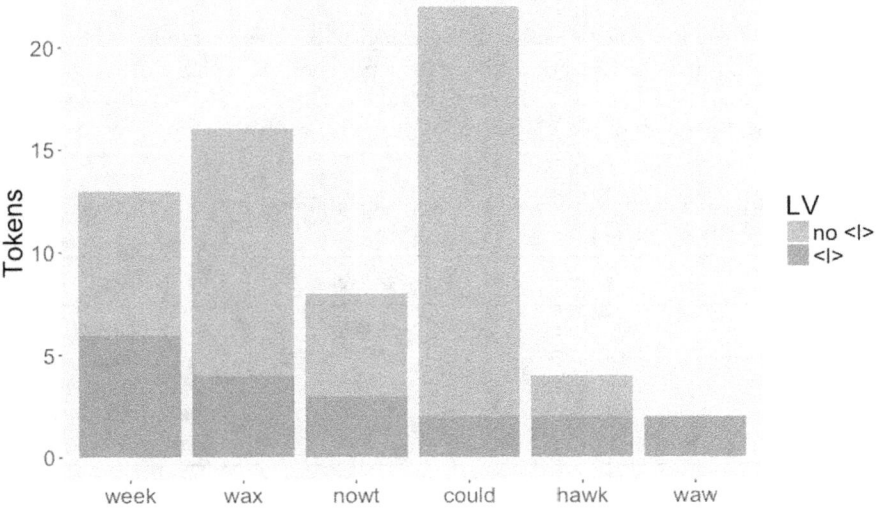

Figure 4.10 Proportions of unetymological <l> in Germanic roots

velar element either preceding or following the target vowel. As a matter of fact, forms with velars both preceding and following the target vowel seem to be most likely to have an <l> in the spelling (see Figure 4.10).

Overall, then, although velar contexts are rare in the actual LV environments of our corpus, these seem to be the most well-established contexts for LV based on the back-spelling data. For the non-velar environments, diacritical use of <l> is vanishingly rare in our corpus, providing little evidence for the merger of LV outputs and existing long and diphthongal vowel categories of the period.

3.5 Evidence for LV in Romance vocabulary

As discussed in section 1.2.2, the emergence of LV in Scots could be linked to the large intake of French borrowings, which, in turn display evidence of pre-consonantal [ɫ] vocalisation during the pre-Conquest period (cf. Pope 1934: 154–156). With this in mind, we examine the attestations of <l>-less spellings in words of Romance origin with etymological <l>. In order to complete our counterpoint examination, we survey the data for back-spellings in the Romance word-stock as well.

As the FITS database excludes non-Germanic lexis, the data for Romance has been extracted directly from the LAOS Corpus and subjected to the same general processes laid out above for the native vocabulary. In this case, for <l>-less spelling contexts, we have considered words plausibly stressed on a syllable with etymological /l/ in Latin, where the LAOS spellings suggest a short back vowel.

3.5.1 <l>-less spellings in Romance vocabulary

Our survey of the Romance items with etymological back vowels followed by /l/ in pre-consonantal and final position yielded thirty types, of which fourteen display <l>-less spellings (see Table 4.6). In terms of tokens, there are 262 <l>-less spellings, making up 31.4 per cent of the 834 potential contexts for LV.

Table 4.6 Romance items in the LAOS Corpus by grapho-phonological context fitting the LV environments

Final	/l/+labial	/l/+velar	/l/+coronal
anull, bull, defoul, null, roll, suppoule	*almond, aumry, dissolve, malvesie, realm, salmon, safe*	*calculate, defalk, malgre*	*altar, cauldron, causey, chalder, default, false, fault, loyalty, herald, multiple, multitude, multure, penult, vault*

Note that a number of words would likely have had vocalised pre-consonantal /l/ well before entering Scots. To this we add the fact that the alternation between <l>-less spellings and <l>-ful ones may be the result of a tradition of learned spellings based on Latin, which would have been continued by Scots scribes. In any case, some of the words where <l>-less spellings are attested show a fair proportion of tokens with the feature, as evidenced by Figure 4.11.

This data makes plain that Romance and Germanic vocabulary do not follow the same pattern, in particular with regard to <l>-less spellings in final position. Although such forms are the most frequent in the native vocabulary, they are only

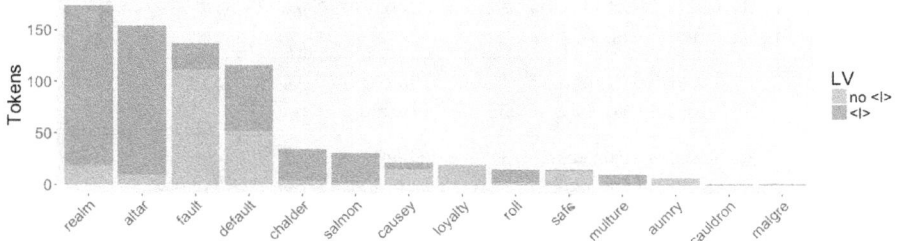

Figure 4.11 Romance morphemes with <l>-less and <l>-ful spellings

attested three times for Romance, in participial forms of the verb *roll* (spelled <rowit> /<rowyt>). The main environment for <l>-less spellings in Romance forms, in contrast, is pre-coronal, with *fault*, *default* and *loyalty* making up the bulk of all attestations.

5.3.2 Back-spellings in Romance vocabulary in LAOS

Using the same procedure as for the Germanic vocabulary, we searched for instances of <l> where it is not justified by etymological [l] in contexts following short back vowels. Surprisingly, as we see in Table 4.7, only three types display back-spellings in the Romance data, amounting to no more than eighteen tokens.

Table 4.7 Back-spellings: Romance vocabulary with an unetymological <l>

LAOS word	<l>-ful token count	<l>-less token count	<l>-ful form
cattle	1	25	caltal
chamber	3	6	chalmyr, chalm(er)
chamberlain	14	40	chalm(er)lane~, chalm(er)lan+eʒ, chalm(er)lan~
Totals	18	71	

The rarity of these eighteen tokens becomes apparent when we survey all words potentially satisfying the environments for back-spelling, as seen in Table 4.8. Since stress position in longer Romance borrowings can be contentious for this period (see Minkova 2014: 306–310 for the ME situation), we have separated out monosyllables and words likely to have initial stress on the target vowel, from words which may have had stress on the same vowels in final syllables. In any case, the numbers are overwhelming in comparison to those with unetymological <l> in Table 4.7.

The data for back-spellings does not support the idea that Scots used <l> as a diacritic for vowel length or diphthongisation in Romance words. Rather, it seems that the use of <l> in words which likely underwent LV in the pre-Conquest period (such as *fault*, *realm*, *causey* or *safe*) are learned spellings, constructed on the basis of Latin (either directly in Scots or via Midlands dialects of ME) and are unlikely to have any phonic content.

Table 4.8 Potential contexts for back-spellings (sample words with stressed V6, V12 and V13) in Romance vocabulary

	Monosyllables and initially stressed words	Final (possibly) stressed syllable	Totals
	cause, croun, counsail, coup, doute, grand, saucer, trouble, etc.	*allow, commoun, famous, merchaunt, prisoun, ordinaunce, person, treason*, etc.	
LAOS types	55	176	231
LAOS tokens	1995	5016	7011

4. Conclusions

Contrary to the generalised assumptions in the literature on Scots, our corpus study provides no evidence for the growth of LV during the fifteenth century. The change, though attested at a low level throughout the period, is by no means nearing completion in the spelling, nor, we contend, in the phonology. The key facts here are that <l>-less spellings make up less than 1 per cent of the potential contexts for LV, while back-spellings are only attested in 0.75 per cent of the relevant environments.

In our corpus, <l>-less spellings are also somewhat regional, with the bulk of attestations found where population and documentary evidence is densest. Although this may represent a case of hierarchical diffusion, direct spelling evidence for LV is still too sporadic to make a firm claim to this effect.

Lack of etymological coda <l> following short back vowels seems to be a low-level variant in all target phonological environments for the Germanic morphemes. However, back-spellings suggest that dorsal environments are further ahead in the establishment of the process. The <l>-less spellings also suggest the final position as an important locus for LV, as compared to pre-consonantal environments, though, again, this is a rather rare phenomenon overall.

With the potential exception of pre-velar contexts, there is not enough alternation in the use of <l> in the spelling to claim it is freely used as a diacritic. Although the argument could be made that <al> and <ol> are spellings of a long vowel [ɑː], as in *half*, and a diphthong [əʊ], as in *folk* in Present-Day English, and that <l> has some kind of diacritic function (a 'marker' in Venezky's 1967 terms), this is probably not the case for Scots in the period of our database. The use of <l> is not frequent enough in non-etymological /l/ contexts, and there aren't enough <l>-less spellings of purportedly vocalised forms. Basically, the availability of <al> as a potential spelling for [au] would produce far more than 0.75 per cent <l>-ful spellings in words with no etymological /l/, due to them being undistinguishable on the surface. The lack of more forms of this type is particularly striking when we consider the amount of spelling variation we find in a non-standardised medieval language like fifteenth-century Scots.

One of the generalisations that we can make is that Romance vocabulary is further advanced in the process of LV than Germanic vocabulary. This, however, can be attributed to LV in the Old French period, rather than to the incipient fourteenth-/ fifteenth-century Scots process. The lack of interaction between the two changes finds evidence in the almost total absence of <l>-less spellings in final position for Romance forms, which contrasts with the native vocabulary of Scots, where it is the most frequent environment for LV. The greater paucity of back-spellings in the Romance word-stock compared to the slightly better established process in native words is another key clue to the independence of the process in the two etymological categories.

Finally, we may begin to assess whether LV can be considered a 'characteristic' feature of early Scots. From a strictly quantitative standpoint, the 'characteristic' variant in our corpus is that which preserves <l>, rather than that which loses it, at least in the spelling. Given the scanty evidence for back-spellings, it is also unlikely that LV had made important inroads in the phonology of the language by 1500. If we are to take 'characteristic' to mean simply that the attested, though rare, early Scots <l>-less and back-spelled forms are unique in some way, then we must compare this data with other historically-related, local varieties. This could be a future research topic, applying the methods proposed here to digital resources available for ME dialects, especially northern, and contrasting both sets of results.

From a methodological standpoint, our corpus approach has proved critical in allowing a view of actual counts, rather than individual – albeit salient – spelling attestations in the dictionary record. In this sense, the quantification of variants allows us to assess the purported pre-eminence of LV in the period, as well as the claims regarding overlap of spelling variants in etymological and non-etymological [l] contexts.

We must acknowledge, of course, that our results are dependent on the legal/ administrative corpus materials that underlie them, and may therefore be register or genre bound. Indeed, Macafee and Aitken (2002: §9.3.7) point out that 'low-life' comical poetry such as *flytings* and *lampoons*, for instance, display a noticeably higher proportion of vocalised forms, evidenced not only in spellings, but also in rhyme-patterns alone. Insofar as this stylistic variation can be extrapolated to social variation, LV may have been more typical of particular sociolects or registers. Further corpus-based studies of this and other genres would be necessary, however, to substantiate these suggestions.

While traditional accounts may ascertain the earliest potential instances of a process of change, or describe the end-state of a development, a corpus approach is not swayed by expectations based on first attestations and later developments, allowing us a view into the progress of changes. As we have seen here, sound change need not move quickly through the grammar once begun, but may persist at a very low level rather than becoming a categorical part of the system.

References

Aitken, Adam J. (1971). 'Variation and variety in written Middle Scots', in Adam J. Aitken, Angus McIntosh and Hermann Pálsson (eds), *Edinburgh Studies in English and Scots*, London: Longman, pp. 177–209 (available online, with a new introduction by Caroline Macafee, at http://www.scotslanguage.com/aitken-papers).

Aitken, Adam J. (1977). 'How to pronounce Older Scots', in Adam J. Aitken, M. P. McDiarmid and D. S. Thomson (eds), *Bards and Makars: Scots Language and Literature Mediaeval and Renaissance*, Glasgow: Glasgow University Press, pp. 1–21 (available online, with a new introduction by Caroline Macafee, at http://www.scotslanguage.com/aitken-papers).

Aitken, A. J. (1981). 'The Scottish Vowel-length Rule', in Michael Benskin and M. L. Samuels (eds), *So Meny People Longages and Tonges: Philological Essays in Scots and Medieval English Presented to Angus Mcintosh*, Edinburgh: Edinburgh University Press, pp. 131–157 (available online, with a new introduction by Caroline Macafee, at http://www.scotslanguage.com/aitken-papers).

Aitken, A. J. and Caroline Macafee (2002). *The Older Scots Vowels: A History of the Stressed Vowels of Older Scots from the Beginnings to the Eighteenth Century*, Edinburgh: The Scottish Text Society.

Bann, Jennifer and John Corbett (2015). *Spelling Scots: The Orthography of Literary Scots, 1700–2000*, Edinburgh: Edinburgh University Press.

van Buuren, Catherine (ed.) (1982). *The Buke of the Sevyne Sagis*, Leiden: Leiden University Press.

Dictionary of the Scots Language (DSL) (2004). Scottish Language Dictionaries Ltd (available at http://www.dsl.ac.uk/ (accessed 25 August 2016)).

Girvan, Ritchie (1939). *Ratis Raving and Other Early Scots Poems on Morals*, The Scottish Text Society, Edinburgh and London: William Blackwood & Sons.

Hall-Lew, Lauren and Sonya Fix (2012). 'Perceptual coding reliability of (L)-vocalization in casual speech data', *Lingua* 122(7): 794–809.

Johnston, Paul (1997). 'Older Scots phonology and its regional variation', in Charles Jones (ed.), *The Edinburgh History of the Scots Language*, Edinburgh: Edinburgh University Press, pp. 47–111.

Jones, Charles. 1997. 'Phonology', in Charles Jones (ed.), *The Edinburgh History of the Scots Language*, Edinburgh: Edinburgh University Press, pp. 267–334.

Kopaczyk, Joanna (2013), *The Legal Language of Scottish Burghs: Standardization and Lexical Bundles (1380–1560)*, Oxford: Oxford University Press.

Kopaczyk, Joanna, Benjamin Molineaux, Vasilis Karaiskos, Rhona Alcorn, Bettelou Los and Warren Maguire (2018). 'Towards a grapho-phonologically parsed corpus of medieval Scots: Database design and technical solutions', *Corpora* 13(2): 255–269.

Macafee, Caroline (1983). *Glasgow*, (Varieties of English Around the World 3), Amsterdam/Philadelphia: John Benjamins.

Macafee, Caroline (1988). 'Some studies in the Glasgow vernacular', unpublished PhD dissertation, University of Glasgow.

Macafee, Caroline (1994). *Traditional Dialect in the Modern World: A Glasgow Case Study*, Frankfurt: Peter Lang.

Macafee, Caroline (2003). 'The phonology of Older Scots (incorporating material by the late A. J. Aitken)', in John Corbett, J. D. McClure and Jane Stuart-Smith (eds), *The Edinburgh Companion to Scots*, Edinburgh: Edinburgh University Press, pp. 138–169.

Macafee, Caroline and Adam J. Aitken (2002). 'A history of Scots to 1700', in *A Dictionary of the Older Scottish Tongue*, vol. XII, Aberdeen: Aberdeen University

Press, pp. xxix–clvii (available at http://www.dsl.ac.uk/about-scots/history-of-scots/).

McClure, J. Derrick (1994). 'English in Scotland', in Robert W. Burchfield (ed.), *The Cambridge History of the English Language*, vol 5, Cambridge: Cambridge University Press, pp. 23–93.

Minkova, Donka (2014). *A Historical Phonology of English*, Edinburgh: Edinburgh University Press.

Murray, James A. H. (1873). *The Dialect of the Southern Counties of Scotland: Its Pronunciation, Grammar, and Historical Relations*, London: The Philological Society.

Pope, Mildred K. (1934). *From Latin to Modern French with Especial Consideration for Anglo-Norman*, Manchester: Manchester University Press.

Przedlacka, Joanna (2001). 'Estuary English and RP: Some recent findings', *Studia Anglica Posnaniensia* 36: 35–50.

Robinson, Mairi (ed.) (1985). *The Concise Scots Dictionary*, Aberdeen: Aberdeen University Press.

Slater, Jane (1952). 'An edition of early Scots texts from the beginnings to 1410', 2 vols, unpublished dissertation, University of Edinburgh.

Smith, G. Gregory (1902 [1975]). *Specimens of Middle Scots*, Edinburgh and London: William Blackwood & Sons.

Stuart-Smith, Jennifer, Claire Timmins and Fiona Tweedie (2006). 'Conservation and innovation in a traditional dialect. L-vocalization in Glaswegian', *English World-Wide* 27(1): 71–87.

Venezky, Richard L. (1967). 'English orthography: Its graphical structure and its relation to sound', *Reading Research Quarterly* 2(3): 75–105.

Wells, John (1983). *Accents of English*, Cambridge: Cambridge University Press.

Williamson, I. Keith (2008). LAOS: A Linguistic Atlas of Older Scots, Phase 1: 1380–1500, The University of Edinburgh (available at http://www.lel.ed.ac.uk/ihd/laos1/ laos1.html).

Part II Segmental Histories

5

Old and Middle English Spellings for OE hw-, with Special Reference to the 'qu-' Type: In Celebration of LAEME, (e)LALME, LAOS and CoNE: In Memoriam Angus McIntosh

Margaret Laing and Roger Lass

> For the second type of spelling variation one might take the alternative conventions for rendering OE /hw/. These are listed ... as being <wh>, <w>, and more rarely <qu>, <qw>; a fifth alternative ... is <qwh>. Unlike <sh> and <sch>, these spellings, and especially those with <q->, very properly invite the hazarding of at least wide phonic solutions; I believe however that it may well be a mistake to work on the assumption that <q-> had the same 'phonic value' in all areas. (McIntosh 1969: 213, review of Kristensson 1967)

1. Introduction

This chapter celebrates Angus McIntosh's scholarly legacy, in particular as a medieval dialectologist. We illustrate how the four main electronic resources, hosted by the Angus McIntosh Centre for Historical Linguistics and in the tradition of LALME (a *Linguistic Atlas of Late Mediaeval English*), can be used in harness to underpin an integrated scholarly investigation.[1]

LAEME (a *Linguistic Atlas of Early Middle English*) covers varieties of English c.1150–1325. (e)LALME (the electronic version of LALME) covers varieties c.1350–1450. LAOS (a *Linguistic Atlas of Older Scots*, Phase 1) covers varieties in documentary texts produced in Scotland 1380–1500. CoNE (a *Corpus of Narrative Etymologies from Proto-Old English to Early Middle English and accompanying Corpus of Changes*) traces the form histories and reconstructs the phonetic realisations of words appearing in the LAEME Corpus of Tagged Texts (CTT).

---

[1] A version of this chapter was presented at the first Angus McIntosh Centre for Historical Linguistics Symposium, University of Edinburgh, 9–10 June 2016. We thank The Arts and Humanities Research Council (LAEME, eLALME, LAOS and CoNE) and the Andrew W. Mellon Foundation (eLALME) for funding the resources used. We thank Rhona Alcorn for comments on earlier drafts and we are grateful to Donka Minkova and an anonymous reviewer for further helpful observations.

After some preliminaries in section 1 below, in section 2 we give a taxonomy of the attested spellings for (reflexes of) Old English *hw*- from Old English (OE) to late Middle English (ME). Section 3 is a diachronic account of the complex and interchanging patterns of lenition and fortition, including reversals, involved in the history of this cluster in OE and ME. Section 4 is an excursus on the 'q-' forms for OE *hw*-, with reference to their geographical distributions and to their possible phonetic realisations. In section 5, we present a CoNE-style etymology of OE *hw*- showing the changes as listed in CoNE's Corpus of Changes.

This chapter deals with the OE and ME parts of the dataset that is the subject also of Lass and Laing (2016). That paper's primary concern is the interpretation of the 'q' spellings for OE *hw*- and the case for assuming that they represent fortition of earlier [xw] to [kw]. In this chapter, we present a taxonomic and diachronic overview of all the attested reflexes at these periods and illustrate how the interface between sounds and spellings may have come about.

1.1 Variation

Variationist historians know that it is not enough to consider the question of *when* a sound change occurred. One must always ask *when* and *where*?

Even then the answer will never be Neogrammarian – not at least until long after the event. So the question must be further qualified: *when, where* and *to what extent*? Or to put it another way: *when, where* and *varying with what else*?

1.1.1 The dataset

There is a wide array of spellings attested from OE through ME and into Older Scots for the initial cluster in words such as WHEN, WHERE, WHAT, WHO, WHICH. We will refer to this cluster as 'OE *hw*-'.

This category derives from one of the sound changes that defines the Germanic family itself: the late Indo-European (IE) spirantisation of voiceless stops in Grimm's Law. The initial change that leads to all the forms we display below is IE **k** > PGmc ***x**, so the origin of these forms is PGmc ***xw-**.[2]

For the initial letters of OE *hw*- words we have isolated the following fifty-seven spellings from the earliest attested OE to c.1500.[3] They have been gleaned from searches of the Dictionary of Old English (DOE) Web Corpus, LAEME, eLALME (supplemented by the *Middle English Dictionary – MED*) and LAOS:

---

[2] We follow the CoNE convention of indicating reconstructed items in asterisked bold type. For the argument that IE ***kw** could have been a cluster rather than a labiovelar (a single consonant with labial coarticulation), and the assumption that PGmc ***xw** was a cluster, see Lass and Laing (2016: fn. 17).

[3] We follow the convention employed in LAEME and (e)LALME that in the context of Roman type, italic indicates the expansion of some kind of abbreviation sign. When citations are in italic the opposite convention applies – expansion of the abbreviation is in Roman. Dates are given as they appear in LAEME, viz: C = century, a = first half, b = second half, a1 = first quarter, a2 = second quarter, b1 = third quarter, b2 = last quarter.

ch-, chu-, chp-, cu-, fw-, h-, hh-, hu-, huwh-, hVw-, hv̄-, hw-, hp-, ku-, q-, qh-, qhw-, qu-, q*u*-, q*u*u-, qv-, qvv- qvh-, qw-, qp-, quh-, qwh-, qw^h-, u-, uu-, v-, vh-, vu-, vVh-, vv-, w-, wch-, wh-, w^h-, whh-, whw-, wVh-, ww-, w3-, 3-, 3h-, 3hw-, 3u-, 3w-, 3p-, þ-, þw-, þp-, p-, ph-, pu-, pv-

As will become apparent, some of these spellings are period defined and many of them are region defined. Not surprisingly, no one period or place attests them all.

1.1.2 'Purely orthographic' vs. phonetic variation

Given fifty-seven spellings for the same etymological category, it is likely that some variation will be due to scribal choices between *litterae*[4] that represent the same sound. But at least some of the orthographic variation is likely to represent some phonic non-identity. We know that there is lenition of [xw] > [hw] and eventually to [w] – as most varieties of PDE testify. Judging by the spellings, this began as early as OE. Both spellings and evidence from alliterative verse show that it continued, variably and partially lexically conditioned, throughout ME and it continues today, still eroding areas of surviving [hw].

2. Taxonomy of the fifty-seven spellings

As a necessary preliminary to the CoNE-style etymology of this cluster shown in section 5, we provisionally divide the spellings according to the phonetic types we think they represent.[5]

2.1 The 'hw-' type: *hu-, hv-, hw-, hp-* [4]

OE runic 'p' indicates [w], as does the ligatured double 'v' (i.e. 'w') that gradually (by c.1300) supersedes it. The *figurae* <u> and <v> are historically the same *littera* and (whether or not doubled or ligatured to form 'w') were used largely interchangeably in the periods in question. Singly they normally stood for [u] or [v], but they could each also represent [w]. It might be considered anachronistic to insist on the designation of e.g. *hu-* and *hv-* as different spellings. There were, however, traditional contextual rules for the use of the *figurae* <v> or <u> depending on their position in the word, and including their use in clusters. In general, <v> (whose shape goes back to the majuscule version of the *littera* 'u' in classical Latin) is found more often word-initial (whether it is being employed for [v] or [u]) and <u> is found word-medial or -final. As the second element in clusters, both would normally represent [w] (rather than [v])

---

[4] *Littera* is the superordinate 'letter', *figura* is the graphic shape and *potestas* the sound value. We follow our usual notational practice of placing *litterae* in single quotes, *figurae* in angle brackets and *potestates* in square brackets. For more details, with acknowledgement to Michael Benskin who first developed the notation, see LAEME, Introduction, §2.3.1.

[5] These figures in square brackets after each heading represent the number of attested spellings within each superordinate type.

but <u> is much more commonly employed than <v>: *du-, hu-, qu-, su-, tu-*. So there are good variationist, orthographic and taxonomic reasons for keeping <u> and <v> separate because they represent scribal choices. In what follows we treat them as separate *litterae* and enclose them not in angle brackets but in single quotes: 'u', 'v'. We can say therefore that the 'hw-' type spellings (*hu-, hv-, hw-, hp-*) would have represented 'the same thing', i.e. [xw] where [x] includes its reflex [h].

2.2 The 'w-' + V type: *u-, uu-, v-, vu-, vv-, w-, ww-, p-, pu-, pv-* [10]

As explained in section 2.1 above, these may all be taken as orthographic variants representing [w].

2.3 What about *vh-, wh-, w^h-, whh-, ph-*? [5]

These use a subset of the same combinations of *litterae* as the '*hw-*' type above, but reversed. They seem likely to have represented the same thing as each other (with probable dittography in the case of *whh-*), but did they also represent the same thing as the '*hw-*' type or some different development?

One common and influential interpretation is that the '*wh-*' type implies a 'voiceless w', which is usually given as [ʍ] or sometimes [w̥]. The standard textbook story is that this [ʍ] in the south later revoiced to [w] and thus merged in ME with existing [w]. The [ʍ] in these accounts implies either a labiovelar or a labial-velar (i.e. a double, simultaneous articulation). Our simpler account is that the category remained a cluster, the [x, h] element gradually leniting to zero and thereby merging with original [w] without needing to be revoiced: [xw] > [hw] > [ʰw] > [w]. See further Lass and Laing (2016: §2.4 (c)) and references.

The '*wh-*' type spellings first appear in late OE (Dietz 2006: 277–278) and start to become common at the same time as other C+ '*h-*' digraphs in Early Middle English (eME): *s(c)h-, ch-, th-*. The use of 'h' as a diacritic for fricativeness had long been known from the Latin representations for Greek aspirates ('th' for 'θ', 'ph' for 'φ', 'ch' for 'χ'). These were pronounced as aspirated stops in classical Latin but spirantised around the turn of the eras, hence their uses for fricatives and affricates in European vernaculars. French usage of 'ch' for [tʃ] seems to have spread quite quickly in post-Conquest English (Scragg 1974: 44–46), and *s(c)h-* for [ʃ] is generally thought to have been modelled on it, gradually winning out over rivals *sc, ss-* etc. The use of 'th' for [θ, ð] (already present in OE following Latin) in variation with 'þ' (and also 'ð' until 1300) progresses more gradually though ME.[6] We suggest that the reordering of the 'h' and 'w' *litterae* for OE *hw-* represents not a phonetic change, but simply an orthographic response to similar use of 'h' as a diacritic for fricativeness in the other initial digraphs, causing it to become visually one of the set.

---

[6] First in lexical words rather than function words, especially in the North and North-East Midlands coinciding with the area where <þ>/<y> were a single *figura*. See Stenroos (2004).

2.4 Forms with 'placement uncertainty': huwh-, hVp-, vVh-, whw-, wVh- [5]

There may be some orthographic support for our argument that '*hw-*' and '*wh-*' represent the same thing. Two of the spellings above, *huwh-* and *whw-*, apparently recognise the innovative reversal, but also seem to be determined to have a [h] element before the [w] somehow or other. There might seem at first to be some sort of placement uncertainty – the writer in each case is unclear as to whether he is hearing the [h] or the [w] first. But the sequence [w] (voiced) and [h] (voiceless) followed by a vowel, seems most unlikely to be a monosyllable. A phonetic sequence like [what] for *what* could only be heard as disyllabic, a syllabic approximant followed by a voiceless fricative followed by a vowel. If voicing is turned off and turned on again the product is another syllable nucleus. It is this impossibility that presumably led to the claim that '*wh-*' stood for voiceless [ʍ] which we have already dismissed as unparsimonious (section 2.3), because it involves devoicing and then revoicing again in order to account for later (including Present-Day English (PDE)) [w] for this segment. So whatever the reversal of former 'hw' to 'wh' represents, it is probably not phonetic but rather an orthographical tidying-up, simply removing the one odd 'h' + C pattern, and matching the pattern already developed in *th*, *ch*, *sh*. (Note that by the time these reversed forms become prevalent – gradually increasing in number from post-Conquest OE, through eME to late ME – the old *hn-*, *hl-*, *hr-* clusters have disappeared.)

There are, however, two types of attested (if very rare) spellings in LAEME CTT that do suggest genuine placement uncertainty. The first is a single occurrence of *hepðer* WHETHER in Lambeth Homilies, language 1 (LAEME text # 1200 lamhomA1t.tag, ca 1200) placed in Worcestershire. The other, with *wVh-* (and *vVh-*) for OE *hwV-*, appears in the work of two different scribes: Laʒamon A, hand B (LAEME text # 278 layamonAbt.tag, C13b1) in Worcestershire and *Estorie del Euangelie* in Dulwich College MS XXII (LAEME text # 182 dulwicht.tag, ca 1300) in Lincolnshire. Laʒamon has *weht* WHAT, *wahr* WHERE and *wuhlc* WHICH (once each) beside much more common *whV-* and *wV-*. The scribe of Dulwich XXII has *waht* WHAT *wehn*, *vehn* WHEN, *weher*, *wehr* WHETHER, *wihlc* WHICH, *wih¦* WHILE, *wahm* WHOM. The vast majority of his spellings for OE *hw-* have 'w' + V with no sign of 'h', and indeed he has no *wh-* spellings. All these oddities suggest perception of friction noise but uncertainty where in the syllable it was. The *hepðer* spelling suggests friction is heard in the onset and the periodic noise of [w] in the coda. The *wVh-* type indicate the opposite, the periodic noise being heard in the onset and friction in the coda. One form *weher* suggests possible epenthesis in the onset and a disyllabic pronunciation. A reasonable explanation for both *hVp-* and *wVh-* would be simply that [h] is noisy, so the friction and the periodic noise of [w] could interfere perceptually with each other. Certainly the one of us (RL), who has not lost the friction in *hw-* words, often has some difficulty on close attention in locating the frication with certainty; it seems rather to be just a 'syllable prosody' as Firth would have called it.[7]

---

[7] See Firth (1948), and cf. Lass (1984: chapter 10).

2.5 The 'h-' type spellings: h-, hh- [2]

We take *h-* to imply [h] with deletion of [w]. Such forms were mainly confined to (and subsequently generalised in) only WHO, WHOM, WHOSE, with non-northern ME [ɔː] from the raising and rounding of earlier [aː] (cf. the deletion of [w] before rounded vowels in NGmc, e.g. OE *wulf* vs. OIc *ulfr*). *hh-* seems to be an error. It occurs once in *Havelok* (LAEME text # 285 havelokt.tag) in the word *hhan* WHEN, beside (in all *hw-* words) *hw-* 116x, *w-* 33x, *qu-* 17x and *hu-* 1x. This shows again how important it is always to ask what is varying with what and in what numbers.

2.6 Remaining spelling sets

Having identified forms implying [hw], [w] and [h], this leaves three other main sets of spellings (which may themselves have subdivisions):

(a) forms implying [kw];
(b) forms implying [xw];
(c) a few further forms that we can put in an 'oddities' bag.

We will deal with (a)–(c) in reverse order.

2.6.1 Oddities: *fw-*, *þ-*, *þw-*, *þp-* (cf. Lass and Laing 2016: fn. 21)

fw- is found only three times in LAEME CTT (in *fwi* WHY 2x and *fwider* WHITHER 1x) and is confined to the work of a single scribe in Maidstone Museum MS A. 13 (LAEME text # 67 maidsdwct.tag and # 68 maidststt.tag). We take the *f-* to represent labial friction similar to that found in NE Scots [f]-initials in [fan] WHEN, [far] WHERE, [fɪt] WHAT.

þw- is found only twice (*þwit* and *þwyte* WHITE) in a very short text in London, British Library, Additional 11579 (LAEME text # 19 candet7t.tag). Similarly, the form *þp-* appears only twice (both times in *þpen* WHEN) in Oxford, Bodleian Library, Tanner *169 (LAEME text # 124 tannert.tag). Neither of these writing systems has any other OE *hw-* words for comparison. Both these scribes elsewhere use 'þ' to represent [θ, ð] as normal and 'w' (and also 'p' in the case of the Tanner scribe) to represent [w]. Neither system shows any 'þ/p/y/ʒ' substitution (Laing and Lass 2009), so we assume that these spellings could also represent labial friction for the initial cluster.

þ- appears once only (in *þich* WHICH) in the work of Trinity Homilies, Hand B (LAEME text # 1300 trhomBt.tag), beside very numerous (*h*)*p-* spellings in OE *hw-* words. Its isolation in this system suggests that *þich* is most likely an error for *pich*.

2.6.2 Forms implying continuing [xw] as opposed to lenited [hw]:[8] *ch-*, *chu-*, *chp-*, *qh-*, *qhw-*, *qvh-*, *quh-*, *qwh-*, *qw^h-*, *wch-*, *wȝ-*, *ȝ-*, *ȝh-*, *ȝhw-*, *ȝu-*, *ȝw-*, *ȝp-* [17]

Each of these sequences contains at least one *littera* that is typically used to represent an oral obstruent: 'c', 'q', 'ȝ'.

The *chu-* (three times), *chp-* (once) spellings are found only in the C10 Lindisfarne Gospels for what is elsewhere in the text spelled *hu-* (thirty+ times). It is generally accepted that these represent [xw]. *Wch-* is attested much later. It occurs in the list s.v. *wh-* in MED, but we have not been able to trace its manuscript source. We assume that it falls into the '*wh-*' type, but that the 'ch' may indicate [x] rather than [h].

In ME, 'ȝ' and (in early texts) its precursor 'ȝ' (insular 'g') were used for [j], [x] and (again in earlier texts) surviving intervocalic [ɣ] (before its change to [w]). Word-initially, 'ȝ' would normally represent [j]. Word-medially before consonants and -finally it would most commonly represent [x]. However, in a reflex of OE *hw-*, what is required is a voiceless fricative, and 'ȝ' seems a natural scribal choice to indicate [x] rather than [h]. The variants in combination with *litterae* implying [w] (including *ȝhw-* with added 'h') are parallel to the '*wh-*' and '*hw-*' types discussed above, but with overt indication of a stronger fricative. For those without indications of [w] see section 2.6.3 below.

We will come shortly to the discussion of 'q' itself. Here we will just say that we assume the addition of 'h' to 'q' in *qh-*, *qhw-*, *qvh-*, *quh-*, *qwh-*, *qw^h-* is a diacritic for fricativeness added later to an established spelling for a velar stop to indicate that it has now become [x] rather than [k].

2.6.3 Subset of above lacking *litterae* for [w]: *ch-*, *ȝ-*, *ȝh-*, *qh-* [4]

The first three of these are found only in eME, the last only in Late ME.

ch- appears only once. It is found in the work of Hand A of the C14a manuscript Edinburgh, Royal College of Physicians, *Cursor Mundi* MS (LAEME text # 296 edincmct.tag, placed in York). It is in the form *achone* A FEW (< OE *hwōn*). The same text also has *quon*er FEWER. It is possible that this is a rare member of the WHO, WHOM, WHOSE set but with a stronger fricative than [h].

The single attestation of *ȝh-* is from Gospatric's Writ (Carlisle, Cumbria RO, D/Lons/L Medieval Deeds C1: LAEME text # 132 gospatrict.tag, placed in Cumbria), a C13 copy, apparently of a mid-C11 original. This text's orthography is very idiosyncratic and interpretation is difficult because of its shortness. The spelling appears in the word *no-ȝhar* NOWHERE. The C13 scribe uses 'ȝ' for what was presumably 'ȝ' in the original. Elsewhere in the text 'ȝ' stands for all the possible functions of 'ȝ' in OE, viz. [g], [j] and [ɣ]. There is only one other OE *hw-* word in this text for comparison: *loc-hyylkun* for OE *lōc-hwylc* WHICHEVER. The first 'y' is presumably for OE 'ƿ' so this *hy-* would be an expected representation of OE *hw-*, but it does not help us with the phonetic value of *ȝh-*. There are no words with historical [x] in the very short text,

---

[8] Of the seventeen forms listed, four seem to indicate loss of [w]. We will treat these in section 2.6.3.

but nevertheless is seems most likely that '3' in combination with 'h' here implies [x]. So this form too could be a member of the WHO, WHOM, WHOSE set with a stronger fricative.

The single example of *3-* alone appears in the word *3at* WHAT (beside *3wat* 65x), in the work of Hand A of Oxford, Bodleian Library, Laud Misc 108 (LAEME text # 1600 laud108at.tag, ca 1300, placed in Oxon). In this category the scribe has *wuch* (2x) WHICH beside *3wuch(e)* (13x). Otherwise in OE *hw-* words he has only *3w-* (over 200x) except in the word *ho-so* (16x and the only spelling) WHOSO. These numbers strongly suggest that *3at* is an error for *3wat*.

The *qh-* forms are found in small numbers in nine LALME Linguistic Profiles (LPs) all in the northern or North-East Midlands counties. Given the strong traditional association of 'q' with [kw], the absence of an overt indication of [w] may not mark its absence. The presence of 'h', however, does suggest a fricative rather than a stop.

2.6.4 Forms implying [kw]: *cu-, ku-, q-, qu-, q*u-, *quu-, qv-, qvv-, qw-, qp-* [10]

We take these spellings at face value and assume that the first element of the cluster represents what it would normally represent in environments other than OE *hw-*, that is [k].

In Lass and Laing (2016), we propose this interpretation of the '*qu-*' type spellings for OE *hw-*. Our arguments there are based on the full range of relevant materials in LAEME and eLALME, including evidence from alliterative texts. We also use onomastic evidence, the earliest of which is an example of *Qu-* for OE *hw-* from *Domesday Book*: *Queldale* (< OE *hwēol* WHEEL) for PDE Wheldale, in the West Riding of Yorkshire (Darby and Versey 1975: 512, column 2). For ME onomastic evidence Kristensson (1967) and (1995) are invaluable sources. In addition, we reference modern dialect surveys (EPED, EDG, EDD and SED) where there is surviving (if exiguous) evidence for the change of [xw] to [kw] in this category. We also offer a modification to previous accounts of the relationship of '*qu-*' type spellings for *hw-* with the lenition of original [kw] (e.g. in [(h)wik] for 'quick') in some of the areas where '*qu-*' for earlier [xw]/[hw] was found. It is a very long and complex paper and we do not attempt to summarise its arguments here. The main claims are quoted in section 4.2.3 below.

3. Diachrony of OE *hw-*

Now that we have the corpus of forms, the next stage is to embed them in history. We will do this by listing sets of variants according to their temporal occurrence. The forms are arranged alphabetically within each time period; not all would necessarily have overlapped with each other in a more fine-grained chronology.

3.1 Variants found in OE (from DOE Web Corpus but normalised (h)w- is given here as (h)p-)[9]

chu-, chp-, h-, hu-, hp-, p-, ph- [7]

The first two spellings are confined to OE and even there are found only in Northumbrian, in the gloss to the Lindisfarne Gospels; these belong in the [xw] type. Those in bold continue into eME and belong in the groups we have referred to as the 'h-', 'hw-', 'w-' and 'wh-' types. The ones with 'ch' are relevant to our account of the 'qu-' type, because they establish the presence in the North of a [xw] variant as opposed to already lenited [hw].

3.2 Variants found in Early Middle English (LAEME)

ch-, fw-, **h-**, hh-, hu-, hVp-, hv-, **hw-**, hp-, **qu-**, q*u*-, quu-, **qv-**, **qw-**, qp-, u-, uu-, v-, vu-, vVh-, vv-, **w-**, **wh-**, wVh-, ww-, **w3-**, 3-, 3h-, 3hw-, **3w-**, ȝp-, þ-, þw-, þp-, p-, ph-, pu-, pv- [38]

The spellings in bold continue into late ME. There is an explosion of new forms after OE, including the 'oddities' with 'f' and 'þ'. 'w' and 'v' appear for the first time for the [w] element in variation with 'p' and 'u'. Very prominent are the six new variants with 'q' (none of these with added 'h') and also six with '3'/'ȝ'.

3.3 Variants found in late Middle English (eLALME)

h-, hw-, <u>**q-**</u>, <u>**qh-**</u>, <u>**qhw-**</u>, qu-, q*u*-, qv-, <u>**qvh-**</u>, qw-, <u>**qwh-**</u>, <u>**qw^h-**</u>, v-, <u>**vh-**</u>, w-, wh-, <u>**w^h-**</u>, <u>**whw-**</u>, w3-, 3w- [20]

'New' variants *not* already recorded in eME are underlined bold. Note that of the nine, six involve 'q'. Also, there has been a considerable weeding out of variants. All spellings with 'p' have disappeared in favour of 'w' or to a lesser extent 'v'. Spellings involving '3' have reduced to two. But there are now ten different variants with 'q', some of which have the addition of 'h' (unlike those in the eME set).

3.3.1 Further late ME variants added from *MED* not recorded in eLALME

cu-, huwh-, ku-, wch-, whh-, 3u- [6]

Of these, *cu-* and *ku-* are of great importance to our account of the 'qu-' type spellings, since they are two further apparently unambiguous representations of [kw]. The first is cited in *MED* as a place-name *Cuelpou* with the first element from OE *hwelp* WHELP. *Ku-* (as we will see later) is in *kuyt* (< OE *hwīt* WHITE). *3u-* clearly belongs with the rest of the '3' set in the [xw] type. *huwh-* has already been mentioned in relation to placement uncertainty. *whh-* probably represents simple dittography of 'h' and

---

[9] We do not normally include here unique forms listed in DOE with the annotations 'xii' and 'xiii' (for C12 and C13) because there is overlap in these cases with texts appearing in LAEME (c.1150–1325). Even late C11 and early C12 texts in English (whether or not copied from earlier OE) may show influence of French orthographic practices.

belongs with the '*wh-*' type. There are four examples of *whh-* in *MED* Corpus, each from a different MS, each of which has very numerous other examples without 'h' doubling. We have not been able to find the source of *wch-*, but if it is not an error the 'ch' may imply a stronger fricative than [h] and belong in the [xw] type.

3.3.2 Variants found in Older Scots, 1380–1500 (LAOS, made up of local documentary texts)

q-, quh-, qwh-, qu-, q*u*- qv-, qvh-, qvv- qw-, v-, w-, wh- [12]

Here the 'q' type spellings are vastly in the majority, with *quh-* the norm (and unique to Scots) followed by *qwh-* and then the 'h'-less 'q' types. *wh-* is not at all commonly found. The word WHITSUNDAY is responsible for almost all *w-* and rare *v-*, spellings; it seems that the etymology of this word (WHITE SUNDAY) had become opaque as early as eME, and in Older Scots where lenition of OE *hw-* was at best rare, it had been reanalysed (by some at least) as a *w-* word. The form WHITSUNTIDE found as early as C14a1 shows that WHITSUN was seen as a separate element divorced from both WHITE and SUNDAY.

3.4 Summary

Original [xw] varying with [hw], and already showing variable signs of lenition to [w] and debuccalisation to [h], was attested only as 'expected' spellings for those respective circumstances. In eME, regional spelling diversification becomes more pronounced, and French (and Latin) orthographic traditions are also more commonly adopted. These factors, combined with the continuing progress of lenition and debuccalisation, lead to an explosion of new combinations for the reflexes of OE *hw*. By late ME this large number of variants had settled into a smaller number showing some regional consensus. Prominent among these are the 'q' type spellings, which suggest that alongside lenition, fortition in this initial cluster could also occur.

4. The 'qu-' type spellings for OE *hw-* in ME

These are the most controversial and intensely discussed of all the *hw-* reflexes, not least because of their coherent distribution.

4.1 Geographical distributions

These forms occur almost exclusively north and east of a line starting in Norfolk, running northwest through Cheshire.[10] They are therefore characteristic of the

---

[10] DOE notes some forms (viz *qwo* (twice) for WHO and *quilke* (once) for WHICH) that might appear to come from Leicester and thus lie somewhat south of this area. All three forms are in the same C13 copy of an OE document, Osulf and Leofrun to St Edmund's Abbey (Leicester) (Sawyer 1968: 1608), and appear in a Bury cartulary, London, British Library, Harley 1005. Kathryn Lowe (pers. comm.) confirms that the copyist is in fact likely to be from Norfolk, possibly the King's Lynn area.

North-East Midlands, parts of the North-West Midlands, the North and Scotland. The area showing this type is quite small in LAEME (pre-1325) – just Norfolk, North Lincolnshire and Yorkshire.[11] It is much more extensive in eLALME (c.1350–1450).[12]

> In LAEME, all the text languages showing this development are from just before or just after 1300, that is late in the period covered by the survey (ca 1150–1325). The restricted distribution may partly be because of the smaller number of surviving texts at this period, especially in the North; but it seems probable that it also (at least partly) reflects the chronology of the development. It is important also to note that in the LAEME CTT none of the '*qu-*' type spellings for OE *hw-* combine with 'h'. In the later period covered by eLALME, spellings with added 'h', *qwh-* and *quh-* (the latter only in Scotland) begin to appear, though never in England in such numbers as those without 'h'. (Lass and Laing 2016: §1.2.1)

4.2 What do the 'qu-' type spellings represent?

Until now the consensus has been that they must imply something stronger than [hw] (starting with the evidence of Lindisfarne *chu-* and *chp-* beside more common *hu-*) and that this could only be [xw] (e.g. Kristensson 1967, 1995; Benskin 1989; Laker 2002; Minkova 2003, 2004; Dietz 2006).

4.2.1 Variability

Angus McIntosh (1969) suggested that <q-> in these spellings might mean different things in different contexts, as our opening quotation makes clear. Very characteristically he put in qualifiers: 'these spellings, and especially those with <*q-*>, very properly *invite* the *hazarding* of *at least wide* phonic solutions' (emphasis added). Angus was of course the subtlest of variationists. In his 'wide phonic solutions' he presumably was still including <*wh*> and <*w*>, and he was certainly including <*qwh*> which he draws particular attention to. The wide phonic solutions among all these spellings presumably therefore included [w], [hw] and [xw]. Whether he also considered [kw] as a possibility is now unknowable. He was also very aware of 'qu-' type spellings for OE *hw-* in the poems of the alliterative revival, and although he does not elaborate in this rather cryptic little remark, he always had in mind scribal copying strategies and the likelihood of internal dialectal and idiolectal variation whether in spontaneous writing or literatim copying or constrained selection.

4.2.2 Idiolectal variation

It is important to note that a surprisingly large number of the variants listed in section 1.1.1 can occur in a single scribe's output. Late ME evidence from eLALME shows this

---

[11] LAEME Feature Map 28285405: WH-: *qu* + V (incl abbr 'u'), rare *qw/qp* + V (no 'q' spellings plus 'h' attested).
[12] eLALME Dot Map Item 44: WH-: *q-*, all spellings.

most strikingly (Lass and Laing 2016, appendix 2). In Lincolnshire, Suffolk and especially Norfolk, most LPs show a wide variety (partially lexically conditioned) within single orthographies, and indicating that spellings representing both fortition and lenition could coexist. LP 4621 in Norfolk, for example, has *h*-, *qu*-, *ꝗu*-, *qw*-, *qwh*-, *qw^h^*-, *w*-, *wh*-.

4.2.3 Lenition of original [kw]

There is another change that needs to be considered in the history of 'qu-' type spellings for OE *hw*-. Modern English evidence shows variable lenition of original [kw] in the North: [kw] > [xw] > [hw] > [w]. SED has five relevant headwords: QUARRY, QUART, QUARTER, QUICK, QUILT. Of these only QUICK shows extensive lenition (e.g. [hwɪk], [wɪk]) with some spread from the North also into the West and East Midlands (LAE maps Ph212 and Ph213). Laker (2009: maps 1–4) provides more evidence for lenition in QUICK and also in QUEY (HEIFER). Twentieth-century Cumberland may have had more extensive lenition; see Benskin (1989: 28) quoting Prevost (1905: 5): 'the older dialect speakers use *w* or *wh* for *qu* in all cases'. This surviving evidence of a variable change is unsurprising in the light of our hypothesis (see section 4.2.5 below) that widespread fortition of original [xw] to [kw] and its subsequent reversal provoked lenition also in a subset of original [kw], with QUICK especially switching allegiance to [xw]/[hw] in part of the original fortition area.

When did this lenition start? Unfortunately, the (e)LALME questionnaire has no original [kw] items. However, *MED* s.v. **qu-** (cons. clust.) gives a wide range of examples, which the editors refer to as 'reverse spellings' predicated on the presence of 'qu-' type forms for OE *hw*-. Given the modern evidence, it seems more likely that at least some of these were genuine phonetic occurrences. Most of the attestations are from the second half of C14 onwards. They are mainly in northern texts but there are a few sporadic instances from further south, including Norfolk.

Before 1350 the evidence is much sparser, which may be a function of text survival but may also reflect that this change began later than our proposed fortition of [xw] to [kw], which would be consistent with our hypothesis.

> There are just a few spellings in LAEME CTT that show [lenition]. The earliest attestation is completely isolated in both time and space: *hpakien* (< OE *cwacian* QUAKE) beside only *qu*- or *ꝗu*- from text # 2001 lamhomA2t.tag (N Worcs). Other examples are forms of a single lexeme (reflexes of the past tense singular of OE *cweþan* SPEAK), in two texts placed in W Norfolk and dated in LAEME C14a1. Text # 285 havelokt.tag has two examples of *hwat* and one of *wat* beside 19 spellings with expected *ꝗu*-; the text also shows *guot* and *couth* once each. Text # 155 genexodt.tag has two examples of *pað* beside 30 forms in expected *qu*- or *ꝗu*-. These Norfolk forms occur in the heartland of 'qu-' type spellings for OE *hw*- at the same date and, in these cases, in the same texts. There is no evidence of the persistence of this change in Norfolk in modern times. (CoNE, The CC, s.v. ((KWL)) – kw-Lenition).

4.2.4 Alliterative evidence

A great deal of data about reflexes of OE *hw-* have been gathered from late OE and ME alliterative verse (e.g. Oakden 1930: 79; McLaughlin 1963: 124–126; Laker 2002: 188–189; Minkova 2003: 348–369, 2004: §5; and see further Lass and Laing 2016: §3.3.3). Here we confine ourselves to a few examples suggesting at least variable alliteration on [kw], first from *The Wars of Alexander* cited from Minkova (2004: 20). We embolden the alliterating elements and give their glosses in small caps to the right of each example:

1679: **Qu**irris furth all in **qu**ite | of **qu**alite as aungels [WHIRR WHITE QUALITY]

4640: For h[i]m was **qu**artirs of **qw**ete vm**qu**ile out of nombre [QUARTERS WHEAT WHILE]

Compare also these lines from *The Destruction of Troy* cited from Laker (2002: 189), himself quoting from Schumacher (1914: 147–148):

633 **Wh**erfore I be**qw**ethe me | to your **qw**eme spouse [WHEREFORE BEQUEATH OE *cwēme* (PLEASING)]

1809 **Qwh**erfore, to **qw**eme | **qw**yt of all other [WHERE OE *cwēman* (PLEASE) QUIT]

1928 **Qw**erfore vs **qw**emes noght | now his **qw**aint speche [WHERE *cwēman* (PLEASE) QUAINT]

11509: **Wh**erfore, to **qwh**eme, | & to **wh**ite vs of skaithe [WHERE *cwēman* (PLEASE) QUIT]

11783: Of **qwh**ete, & of **qwh**ite syluer | **qw**emly to-gedur [WHEAT WHITE *cwēm-* (PLEASINGLY)]

In these poems, and others in the North and North-West Midlands, we can see that OE *hw-* words alliterate with historical [hw] and [kw] (as well as elsewhere with historical [w]). These examples show that the spellings *wh-*, *qw-* and *qwh-* can all be used for both historical [xw] and historical [kw]. One of these reflexes we take to have been [kw] as we argue in detail in Lass and Laing (2016). We cannot of course know whether the alliteration was on [kw] or on [xw] (cf. section 4.2.2 above) or indeed whether [kw] and [xw] were considered 'close enough' to alliterate with each other. There is also the possibility that the alliteration itself was variable.

Of potential interest also is another example from *The Destruction of Troy* (Panton and Donaldson 1869), lines 4968–4974, (in part cited in *MED* s.v. **whīt** (adj.)):[13]

---

[13] *The Destruction of Troy* is from Glasgow, University Library, Hunterian 388 (V.2.8) dated by *MED* as late as c.1540; both hands in it are localised by eLALME in Lancashire. *The Wars of Alexander* is from Oxford, Bodleian Library, Ashmole 44 dated in *MED* c.1450. Its language is not included in the eLALME maps, but it is 'substantially of Durham, or possibly S

The braunches were borly, su*m* of bright gold,
Sum syluer for sothe, semlist of hew ;
W*ith* leuys full luffly, light of þe same ;
W*ith* burions aboue bright to be holde ;
And frut on yt fourmyt fairest of shap,
Of mony **kynd** þat was **kuyt, knagged** aboue, [KIND WHITE ME *knagged* TIED, HUNG]
Þat shem*ert* as shire as any shene stonys.

This describes an artificial, decorative tree in gold and silver. We quote the context of the emboldened forms at greater length than in the other examples because there is some disagreement as to the meaning of *kuyt*. It appears in the form list in *MED* s.v. whīt (adj.) and this very quotation is given as an example of the sense 'white, whitish, pale-coloured'. *Oxford English Dictionary* (*OED*) s.v. white, *adj.* (and *adv.*) and *n.* does not use *kuyt* in any of its quotations for this word, but it does appear in the form list at the head of the entry. This entry in *OED* was updated in 2015. The 1901 *OED* editors, however, did not accept the interpretation of *kuyt* as WHITE. They use this same example in a different entry s.v. knagged, *v.* (which has not yet been updated for *OED*3) and say: 'c1540 (?a1400) *Dest. Troy* 4973 *A tre, þat was tried, all of tru gold,... And frut on yt fourmyt fairest of shap, Of mony kynd þat was knyt [1874 kuyt], knagged aboue*'.[14] The 1901 editors were perhaps not familiar with the numerous 'q' spellings for OE *hw*-. In any case they do not seem to have considered the possibility of an equivalent 'ku' spelling or a [kw] variant for the cluster in spite of Panton and Donaldson's reading of it as *kuyt* (glossed by them WHITE). Instead, *OED* assumes minim confusion of 'u' and 'n', which certainly in many scribal hands is all too possible. We have not seen the manuscript and cannot judge on palaeographic grounds whether the 'n' or 'u' reading is more, less or equally likely. But on semantic and literary grounds we consider the 1869 editorial reading to be better. The *kuyt* (WHITE, SHINING) fruit goes with the glistening silver branches and bright stones. If this reading is accepted, given the *k-* spellings and the fact that the other alliterating elements are original [k] words, not either original [hw] words or original [kw] words, it is hard to see how the alliteration could be on anything other than [k] in this example.

From the same poem, lines 3027–3028, have:

Hir forhed full fresshe & fre to be-holde,
Quitter to **qweme** þen þe **white** snaw [WHITER *cwēman* (PLEASE) WHITE]

Northumberland, but with odd features of apparently NW Midland origin'. eLALME maps scribal dialects rather than authorial ones unless the two happen to coincide. The copying strategies of scribes (whether *literatim* or 'translating' or a mixture) may affect any inferences made about alliteration.

[14] This quotation is in fact from the first volume of the text dated 1869 not 1874, which is the date of EETS 56, part 2 of the text.

Here the alliterating lexeme WHITE occurs with variant spellings in the same line, *qu-* and *wh-*, both alliterating on original [kw] with *qweme* (< OE *cwēman*) PLEASE.

The *OED* reading becomes even less likely if one turns to their entry s.v. knit *v.* under 5. c. (also the 1901 entry, not yet updated for *OED*3). Here the editors give a specialised horticultural usage of KNIT, which they define 'Of fruit: To form, "set". Also of the tree, or of the blossom: To form fruit'. They quote a different line from *The Destruction of Troy* to exemplify: '*c*1540 (?a1400) *Destr. Troy* 2737 In the moneth of May. . . frutes were knyt [1874 *mispr.* kuyt]'. Immediately beneath this they add also the example used s.v. knagged *v.* (line 4973) but without quoting it or commenting on it for this entry. The passage at line 2737 is about the spring and the condition of nature at the time. A fuller quotation (2734–2739) makes it clear that the *OED* reading and definition in this case is probably right:

> In the moneth of May, when medoes bene grene,
> And all florisshet with floures þe fildes aboute;
> Burions of bowes brethit full swete,
> ffflorisshet full faire; frutes were kuyt [read: knyt];
> Greuys were grene, & þe ground hilde;
> Hit was likyng in Laundys ledys to walke;

That the flowers of fruit trees are past the blossom stage and have set their fruit is exactly right for this example; it is May not autumn, and the fruits have not even begun to grow, let alone to ripen. But it would be totally ludicrous to assume this meaning for an artificial tree with full-sized, fully-formed artificial fruits, especially when the description is entirely about appearance and not about the fruiting process. So the example at line 4973 must be wrongly interpreted in *OED*.

4.2.5 The 'q' spellings: Our hypothesis

In Lass and Laing (2016) we propose that, in the areas where 'q' spellings for the reflexes of OE *hw-* were found in ME, at least a subset of these reflexes came (at least variably) to be pronounced [kw]. We argued that the evidence (also presented here in sections 2 and 3) suggests that this pronunciation, and the spellings that indicate it, existed variably alongside surviving [xw], lenited [hw] and [w], as well as [h] after deletion of [w]. Others (notably Laker 2002) have argued that the lack of significant survival of [kw] into modern times, as well as the lenition of [kw] to [hw]/[w] in (some of) the same geographical areas, indicates rather a realisation for the 'q' spellings in [xw]. We maintain that the 'qu-' type spellings without added 'h' are attested for a significant period before the *qwh-* and (in Scotland) the *quh-* spellings are found, and that these spellings with 'h' do probably indicate a fricative pronunciation – [xw] rather than [kw]. But we also maintain that, given the wide variety of spellings for the initials of OE *hw-* words throughout the ME period, none of the changes in progress could have been anything like Neogrammarian in effect. In our previous words (2016: section 1.4):

Historical [xw] words *as a set* never merged with historical [kw] words *as a set*. Moreover, the [kw] pronunciation was not destined to prevail. The initial cluster [xw] was also variably undergoing lenition, at least to [hw] and often to [w], in the same areas, and frequently in the same idiolects, as it underwent fortition to [kw]. In those circumstances, the pronunciation as a stop and the pronunciation as a fricative or approximant were in competition [...] Gradually lenition wins out against fortition, and even in areas where the cluster is preserved today, it is normally [hw].

The lenition of original [kw] (section 4.2.3) fits well with our hypothesis. When the strengthened [kw] variants of earlier [xw] in OE *hw-* words began to undergo lenition back to [xw] (and thence to [hw] or even [w]), a subset of original [kw] words (variably and only in some areas) would have (not unnaturally) fallen in with them and also undergone lenition to [xw] > [hw] (> [w]).

We therefore assume, alongside lenition and debuccalisation, also the change xw-Fortition for the illustrative CoNE type narrative etymology that follows.

5. CoNE type narrative etymology of *hw-*

We use the term narrative etymology to distinguish our praxis from that of standard etymological dictionaries. We narrate the trajectories of items with inputs, changes and outputs specified (including spelling developments). In other words, our etymologies are histories rather than cognate sets with a single primary etymon. In CoNE itself, we etymologise morphemes from the LAEME CTT. We do not normally etymologise segments or clusters divorced from morphemes, which we will be doing in this chapter. Here we also include the later spellings from LALME, *MED* and LAOS as listed earlier. Again, unlike CoNE, we will present our etymology in two stages: section 5.2 shows the phonological development with spelling *types* only as taxonomised in section 2. Section 5.3 also interleaves the orthographic developments responsible for the *rest* of the spelling variation.

5.1 General shape

| | *reconstructed input form ((change)) > *resulting reconstructed form >
[phonetic substance underlying citation form] > *citation form*

Each fork in the etymology is numbered. The change in double parentheses is always an initialism.[15]

---

[15] Initialisms are spelt out (and the changes explained) in section 5.3. In CoNE the initialisms are linked to their interpretations in the Corpus of Changes (the CC), which forms part of CoNE. For the most part, these are extended versions of the commentaries we give in this chapter.

5.2 Narrative etymology of OE hw-: phonological development with all orthographic variants by type

‖ *kw ((GLVS)) >

1 [xw] > *ch-, chu-, chp- qh-, qhw-, qvh-, quh-, qwh-, wch-, w3-, 3-, 3h-, 3hw-, 3u-, 3w-, ʒp-*
   ↓
2 *xw ((CXL)) > [hw] > *hu-, huwh-, hv-, hVw-, hw-, hp-, vh-, vVh-, wh-, wh-, whh-, whw, wVh-, ph-*
   | ↓
   | 3 *hw ((CLHD)) > [w] > *þ-, u-, uu-, v-, vu-, vv-, w-, ww-, p-, pu-, pv-*
   ↓   ↓
         4 *hw ((CWD)) > [h] > *h-, hh-*

5 *xw ((ICA)) > [fw] > *fw-*
   ↓
6 *xw ((?)) > [?] > *þw-, þp-*
   ↓
7 *xw ((XWF)) > [kw] > *cu-, ku-, q-, qu-, ɋu-, quu-, ɋv-, qvv- qw-, qp-*
   ↓
   8 *kw ((KWL)) > [xw] > any subset of [xw] spellings above
     ↓
     *xw ((CXL)) > [hw] > some subset of the [hw] spellings above
     ↓
     *hw ((CLHD)) > [w] > some subset of the [w] spellings above

Key to the changes
((CLHD)) = Cluster h-Deletion
((CWD)) = Cluster w-Deletion
((CXL)) = Cluster x-Lenition
((GLVS)) = Grimm's Law Velar Spirantisation
((ICA)) = Initial Cluster Assimilation
((KWL)) kw-Lenition
((XWF)) xw-Fortition

5.3 The changes in detail – for full versions see CoNE, the CC

5.3.1 Grimm's Law Velar Spirantisation

IE *k > PGmc *x. Grimm's Law is one of the changes that defines Gmc as a family. All the IE obstruents except *s (the only fricative) change manner of articulation. For the velar stops, our concern here, taking Latin as standing for unshifted IE: e.g. L *cord-* = OE *heorte* HEART.

5.3.2 Cluster x-Lenition

[xl] > [hl], [xn] > [hn], [xr] > [hr], [xw] > [hw]. [x] in initial sonorant clusters lenites to a glottal fricative [h]. The timings of these lenitions are difficult to determine because both [x] and [h] initially are likely to have been representable by 'h'. In what follows, cf. also section 5.3.3 Cluster h-Deletion. We asume that loss of the fricative is preceded in each case by the lenition, which may give some indication of possible chronology. In the case of [xw] (our topic here) [x] remained (at least variably) in North-East Midlands, parts of North-West Midlands and the North well into the ME period. Its survival is necessary to account for the numerous 'qu-' type spellings in those areas right into late ME and even later in Older Scots.

5.3.3 Cluster h-Deletion

[hl] > [l], [hn] > [n], [hr] > [r], [hw] > [w]. The glottal [h] in initial sonorant clusters undergoes the final stage of lenition (i.e. deletes). Here we deal only with [hw] > [w]. *p*V- (and later *w*V-) spellings from OE onwards indicate the beginnings of this change. Such spellings became increasingly common throughout eME and into LME (see the feature and dot maps for the item WH- in LAEME and eLALME). As well as *w*V-, *hp*- and *hw*- persist in eME beside *ph*- (from lOE) and later *wh*-, cf. ((OMIC)), section 5.4. For alternative accounts of [hw] involving a stage [ʍ] (voiceless [w]), with subsequent revoicing before merger with already existing [w], see Minkova (2003: 348–369) and Dietz (2006: chapter VI).

5.3.4 Cluster w-Deletion

[hw] > [h]. In this highly restricted change, the sonorant element [w] deletes (debuccalisation), leaving [h] as remainder. The commonest examples are in the WHO(M), WHOSE set (< OE *hwā(m)*, *hwās*). This change allows PDE *wh*- spellings for original *h*- words, e.g. *whole* (< OE *hāl*) and *whore* (< OE *hōre*).

5.3.5 Initial Cluster Assimilation

[xw] > [fw]. Two texts in the same hand (C13a) in LAEME have *fw*- for OE *hw*-. They are too short to place, but a longer text in the same hand (text # 66 maidspat.tag) belongs in South-West Northamptonshire. Text # 67 maidsdwct.tag has *fwi* (twice) WHY and text # 68 maidststt.tag has *fwider* (once) WHITHER. Here the place of articulation of the first element of the cluster has apparently changed from velar to labial.

5.3.6 xw-Fortition

[xw] > [kw]. See evidence already presented, and for full discussion of the change and its context see Lass and Laing (2016).

5.3.7 kw-Lenition

[kw] > [xw] > [hw]. Mainly confined to late ME or later. Survives into Modern English in rural North, e.g. in [hwɪk], [wɪk] for QUICK.

5.4 Narrative etymology – phonological development including under each phonological type the orthographic changes involved

‖ *kw ((GLVS)) >
1 [xw] >
1a ((CHFX)) > *ch-, chu-, chp-*
1b ((ORG)) > *ʒp-*
  1c > ((OR3)) > *ʒu-, ʒw-* ([PSE]) > *ʒ-*
    1d > ((HDF)) > *ʒhw-* ([PSE]) > *ʒh-*
    1e > ((OMIC)) > *wʒ-*
1f ((EOQ)), ((HDF)) > *qh-, qhw-, qvh-, quh-, qwh-*
1g ((CHFX)), ((OMIC)) > *wch-*

2 *xw ((CXL)) > [hw] >
2a *hu-, hv-, hw-, hp-*
2b ((OMIC)) > *vh-, wh-, w^h-, ph-*
  2c > ([DCD]) > *huwh-, whh-, whw-*
  2d > ([PU]) > *hVw-, vVh-, wVh-*

    3 *hw ((CLHD)) > [w] >
    3a *u-, uu-, v-, vu-, vv-, w-, ww-, p-, pu-, pv-* ([PSE]) > *þ-*

    4 *hw ((CWD)) > [h] >
    4a *h-*
    4b ([DCD]) > *hh-*

5 *xw ((ICA)) > [fw] > *fw-*

6 *xw ((?)) > [?] > *þw-, þp-*

7 *xw ((XWF)) > [kw] >
7a *cu-*
7b ((SOK)) > *ku-*
7c ((EOQ)) > *q-, qu-, ǫu-, quu-, qv-, qvv- qw-, qp-*

    8 *kw ((KWL)) > [xw] > any subset of [xw] spellings above
     *xw ((CXL)) > [hw] > any subset of the [hw] spellings above
     *hw ((CLHD)) > [w] > any subset of the [w] spellings above

(For simplicity's sake we have not included the changes that account for the orthographic variation between 'u', 'v', 'p', and 'w', for which see CoNE, CC s.v. ((EOV)) Emergence of v and ((EOW)) Emergence of w.)

The orthographic changes – for their texts see CoNE, CC.
((CHFX)) 'ch' for [x]
((EOQ)) Emergence of 'q'
((HDF)) 'h' as Diacritic for Fricativeness
((OMIC)) Orthographic Metathesis Initial Cluster
((ORG)) Orthographic Remapping of 'g'
((OR3)) Orthographic Remapping of '3'
((SOK)) Spread of 'k'

The special codes
([DCD]) Doubling of Character(s) by Design/Dittography
([PSE]) Possible Scribal Error
([PU]) Placement Uncertainty

References

Benskin, Michael (1989). 'Some aspects of Cumbrian English, mainly mediæval', in Leiv Egil Breivik, Arnoldus Hille and Stig Johansson (eds), *Essays on English Language in Honour of Bertil Sundby*, Oslo: Novus, pp. 13–45.
CoNE = Roger Lass, Margaret Laing, Rhona Alcorn and Keith Williamson (2013–). A Corpus of Narrative Etymologies from Proto-Old English to Early Middle English and Aaccompanying Corpus of Changes, Edinburgh: Version 1.1 © The University of Edinburgh (available at http://www.lel.ed.ac.uk/ihd/CoNE/CoNE.html).
Darby, H. C and G. R. Versey (1975). *Domesday Gazeteer*, Cambridge: Cambridge University Press.
Dietz, Klaus (2006). *Schreibung und Lautung im mittelalterlichen Englisch*, Heidelberg: Universitätsverlag Winter.
DOE Web Corpus = Antonette diPaolo Healey (ed.) (2009). Dictionary of Old English Web Corpus, Ann Arbor: University of Michigan Press (available at http://www.doe.utoronto.ca/pages/pub/web-corpus.html).
EDD = Joseph Wright (1898–1905). *The English Dialect Dictionary*, 7 vols, London: Henry Frowde.
EDG = Joseph Wright (1905). *The English Dialect Grammar*, Oxford: Henry Frowde.
eLALME = Michael Benskin and Margaret Laing (2013–). *An Electronic Version of A Linguistic Atlas of Late Mediaeval English*, with webscripts by Vasilis Karaiskos and Keith Williamson, Edinburgh: © The Authors and The University of Edinburgh (available at http://www.lel.ed.ac.uk/ihd/elalme/elalme.html).
EPED = Alexander J. Ellis (1889). *On Early English Pronunciation. Part V. The Existing Phonology of English Dialects*, London: Trübner & Co.

Firth, John Rupert (1948). 'Sounds and prosodies', *Transactions of the Philological Society* 127–52.
Kristensson, Gillis (1967). *A Survey of Middle English Dialects 1290–1350: The Six Northern Counties and Lincolnshire*, Lund: C. W. K. Gleerup.
Kristensson, Gillis (1995). *A Survey of Middle English Dialects 1290–1350: The East Midland Counties*, Lund: Lund University Press.
LAE = Harold Orton, Stewart Sanderson and John Widowson (eds) (1978). *Linguistic Atlas of England*, London: Croom Helm.
LAEME = Laing, Margaret (2013–). *A Linguistic Atlas of Early Middle English, 1150–1325*, version 3.2 (with R. Lass (Introduction) and webscripts by Keith Willamson, Vasilis Karaiskos and Sherrylyn Branchaw), Edinburgh: © The University of Edinburgh (available at http://www.lel.ed.ac.uk/ihd/laeme2/laeme2.html).
Laing, Margaret and Roger Lass (2009). 'Shape-shifting, sound-change and the genesis of prodigal writing systems', *English Language and Linguistics* 13: 1–31.
Laker, Stephen (2002). 'An explanation for the changes *kw-*, *hw-* > *χw-* in the English dialects', in Markku Filppula, Juhani Klemola and Heli Pitkänen (eds), *The Celtic Roots of English*, Joensuu: Joensuu University Press, pp. 183–198.
Laker, Stephen (2009). 'On the geography and date of the merger /kw/, /hw/ > /χw/', in Esa Penttila and Heli Paulasto (eds), *Language Contacts Meet English Dialects: Studies in Honour of Markku Filppula*, Newcastle: Cambridge Scholars Publishing, pp. 179–198.
LALME = Angus McIntosh, M. L. Samuels and Michael Benskin (1986). *A Linguistic Atlas of Late Mediaeval English* (with the assistance of Margaret Laing and Keith Williamson), 4 vols, Aberdeen: Aberdeen University Press.
LAOS = Keith Williamson (2013–). *A Linguistic Atlas of Older Scots, Phase 1, 1380 to 1500*, version 1.2, Edinburgh: © The University of Edinburgh (available at http://www.lel.ed.ac.uk/ihd/laos1/laos1Z.html).
Lass, Roger (1984). *Phonology. An Introduction to Basic Concepts*, Cambridge: Cambridge University Press.
Lass, Roger and Margaret Laing (2016). 'Q is for WHAT, WHEN, WHERE?: the "q" spellings for OE *hw-*', *Folia Linguistica Historica* 37: 61–110.
McIntosh, Angus (1969). 'Review of Kristensson (1967)', *Medium Ævum* 38: 210–216.
McLaughlin, John C. (1963). *A Graphemic-Phonemic Study of a Middle English Manuscript*, The Hague: Mouton.
MED = Hans Kurath, Sherman M. Kuhn et al. (eds.) (2001). *The Middle English Dictionary*, Ann Arbor: The University of Michigan Press (electronic version available at http://quod.lib.umich.edu/m/med/).
Minkova, Donka (2003). *Alliteration and Sound Change in Early English*, Cambridge: Cambridge University Press.
Minkova, Donka (2004). 'Philology, linguistics, and the history of [hw] ~ [w]', in Anne Curzan and Kimberley Emmons (eds), *Studies in the History of the English Language II. Unfolding Conversations*, Berlin: Mouton de Gruyter, pp. 7–46.
Oakden, J. P. (1930). *Alliterative Poetry in Middle English: The Dialectal and Metrical Survey*, Manchester: Manchester University Press.
OED = Oxford English Dictionary. Online (OED3): http://www.oed.com.

Panton, Geo. A. and David Donaldson (eds) (1869). *The Gest Historiale of the Destruction of Troy*, Part 1 [EETS OS 39], London: Trübner.
Prevost, E. W. (1905). *A Supplement to the Glossary of the Dialect of Cumberland, with a Grammar of the Dialect by S. Dickson Brown*, London: Henry Frowde.
Sawyer, P. H. (1968). *Anglo-saxon Charters: An Annotated List and Bibliography*, London: Royal Historical Society
Schumacher, Karl (1914). *Studien idber den mittelenglischen Alliterationsdichtungen*, Bonner Studienzur englischen Philologie XI, Bonn: Hanstein.
Scragg, Donald George (1974). *A History of English Spelling*, Manchester: Manchester University Press.
SED = Survey of English Dialects
  Harold Orton and William James Halliday (eds.) (1962). *Survey of English Dialects*, vol. 1, *The Basic Material: The Six Northern Counties and the Isle of Man*, Leeds: E. J. Arnold.
  Harold Orton and Martyn Francis Wakelin (eds) (1967). *Survey of English Dialects*, vol. 4, *The Basic Material: The Southern Counties*, Leeds: E. J. Arnold.
  Harold Orton and Michael V. Barry (eds) (1969). *Survey of English Dialects*, vol. 2, *The Basic Material: The West Midland Counties*, Leeds: E. J. Arnold.
  Harold Orton and Philip Michael Tilling (eds.) (1969). *Survey of English Dialects*, vol. 3, *The Basic Material: The East Midland Counties and East Anglia*, Leeds: E. J. Arnold.
Stenroos, Merja (2004). 'Regional dialects and spelling conventions in late Middle English: Searches for (th) in the LALME data', in Marina Dossena and Roger Lass (eds), *Methods and Data in English Historical Dialectology*, Bern: Peter Lang, pp. 257–285.

6

The Development of Old English ǣ: Middle English Spelling Evidence

Gjertrud F. Stenbrenden

1. Introduction

The available evidence for Middle English (ME) long-vowel changes, including the so-called 'great vowel shift' (GVS), is scattered, both temporally and geographically, and notoriously difficult to interpret.[1] The problems are arguably most serious for Old English (OE) ǣ, whose phonetic correspondences and orthographic representations vary considerably even in OE. OE has ǣ from two main sources, as outlined below.

1. ǣ¹ from WGmc *ai+i* is generally retained in all OE dialects except Kentish (Campbell 1959: §197; Sievers 1968: §§57, 62, 90), and it may have been raised before dentals in parts of the country (Luick 1914–40: §§187–188; Jordan 1925: §48, Anm.2).
2. ǣ² from WGmc *ā* is retained in Saxon dialects but is reflected as *ē* in Anglian and Kentish (Wright and Wright 1925: §119; Campbell 1959: §257; Sievers 1968: §57; Hogg 2011: §§3.22–3.25). In the East Saxon dialects, ǣ² is believed to have retracted to [aː] (Kristensson 1997).

When use of <æ>, <ae>, etc. is gradually discontinued after the Norman Conquest, matters only get worse, as the reflexes of both ǣ's come to be spelt <e(e)>, as indeed are reflexes of OE ē. Another complicating factor is the merger of the reflex of OE *ēa* with that of ǣ, at which both were raised to 'long open *e*', possibly in the early eleventh century (Wright and Wright 1928: §63). Thus, the digraph <ea> was also available as an orthographic device to indicate a long front vowel in the open or open-mid area. The orthographic result is a number of cc-variants for what one might call 'eME ǣ', i.e. <ea>, <ae>, <ee>, besides traditional <æ>, which, according to Wright

---

[1] I wish to thank the two anonymous reviewers, the editors and members of the audience at the First AMC Symposium for very useful comments and suggestions, for which this chapter is much the better. All the remaining shortcomings are my own responsibility.

and Wright (1928: §52), was 'preserved in writing until about the end of the twelfth century, and occasionally even later' (cf. Wyld 1914: §161).

The reflex of OE ǣ was raised to /eː/, thence to /iː/, in the GVS, but the raising process to [ɛː] started earlier (Wyld 1914: §§120, 161;[2] Campbell 1959: §292; Lutz 2004; despite Wright and Wright 1928: §52). The terminal value [iː] is in evidence from the sixteenth century, according to Zachrisson (1913: 204) and Dobson (1968: 610). While this is likely true of the ancestor of RP and many other dialects, a distinction between the reflexes of OE ē and OE ǣ is upheld by some dialects into the twentieth and twenty-first centuries (cf. Anderson 2015: sections 3.18–3.31). Nonetheless, forms with <i> and <y> in ME sources probably indicate early vowel shift of both ǣ's, even with the above caveat in mind.

This chapter attempts, first, to present the range of spellings for the reflexes of the two ǣ's in ME dialects, as found in the Corpus of Tagged Texts for a *Linguistic Atlas of Early Middle English* (LAEME; see section 2). As my chapter aims to show the totality of spellings for ǣ^1 and ǣ^2 in all the LAEME texts, it has not been possible to submit all individual scribal systems to detailed analysis (either in terms of co-variants or statistical significance), except in a few cases for illustration. Second, this chapter aims to establish the course of change, phonetically as well as orthographically, for the two ǣ's, and to determine the isoglosses for OE ǣ^2; that is, which ME areas likely had [eː] and which had [æː] for ǣ^2. Establishing the isoglosses for ǣ^2 is important in that it bears on the phonetic interpretation of the spellings thereof. Traditionally, forms with a shortened vowel have been used to determine the quality of the reflexes of ǣ^2 in ME, since the reflexes of both long vowels are spelt <e(e)> in ME. If the shortened reflex is spelled <a>, it presumably goes back to [æː], whereas if the shortened reflex is spelled <e>, it is supposed to go back to [eː]. Shortened forms are, however, infrequent in the main source of ME used here (LAEME), so such forms have not been exploited or analysed systematically for this chapter.[3] A third aim of this chapter is to place the phonetic changes to the two ǣ's in a wider context of long-vowel changes in the ME period.

2. Data and method

The evidence for OE ǣ is culled primarily from LAEME (Laing 2008). As all LAEME sources have been dated and most of them have been localised, it should be possible to determine (a) the orthographic reflexes (across time and space), and (b) the sound correspondences – including any changes – of the two OE ǣ's in the regional varieties of ME. I have examined additional data from a *Linguistic Atlas of Late Mediaeval English*

---

[2] Note that Wyld uses 'ǣ^1' to refer to the reflex of W Gmc ā (PrOE ǣ) and 'ǣ^2' to refer to the reflex of the *i*-mutated product of W Gmc *ai*.

[3] In *LAEME*, there are five tokens for STREET as a suffix, all of which have <e>; they appear in sources localised to Gloucestershire (#10), Herefordshire (#246), Worcestershire (#173), Norfolk (#1400) and York (#296). The simplex is rather more frequent, and all except eight tokens have <e(e)>; four tokens have <a>, in a source from Essex (#4), and four tokens have <æ>, in a source from Worcestershire (#278); the latter also has one form with <e>.

(LALME; McIntosh, Samuels and Benskin 1986) and a *Survey of Middle English Dialects*, c. 1290-1350 (SMED; Kristensson 1967, 1987, 1995, 2001, 2002). For Early Modern English (EModE), I have consulted Zachrisson (1913) and Dobson (1968), who report the statements of the early ortho-epists.

From LAEME, all spellings for a number of words with OE $\bar{æ}$ have been extracted and counted, and the words have been divided into groups according to their origin, $\bar{æ}^1$ or $\bar{æ}^2$, as far as this has been possible to establish. The *Oxford English Dictionary Online* was used to check the etymologies of the relevant words, and only words whose etymology was certain were included. Hence, forms for the following lexical items were counted in localised sources.

1. For OE $\bar{æ}^1$: CLEAN aj., DEAL v., GLEAM n. and v., HÆLEND, HÆLU, HEAL v., HEAT, HEATHEN aj. and n., LEAD v., TEACH, WHEAT (1342 tokens).[4]
2. For OE $\bar{æ}^2$: GREEDY, LET, RÆD n., RÆDAN, READ v., LÆCE, (UN)SÆLIG, SLEEP n. and v., SPEECH, STREET (1502 tokens).

For the verbs, forms for the infinitive, imperative, indicative plural and 1. singular present indicative were counted. The LAEME spellings are found in Table 6.3 and Table 6.4 in the Appendix at the end of the chapter. In the discussion, forms with <a>, <æ/ae> and <ea> have been treated together, as it seems sensible to assume that these spellings all correspond to a front mid-to-open vowel.

3. Discussion and findings

The following discussion is based on the spellings and figures reproduced in Table 6.3 and Table 6.4 (Appendix). But first, an observation on the use of <æ> in ME. As stated in the introduction, Wright and Wright claim that traditional <æ> was 'preserved in writing until about the end of the twelfth century, and occasionally even later' (1928: §52). The LAEME data show, however, that <æ> was in fact retained much longer – at least by certain scribes – in some cases into the late thirteenth or early fourteenth century, cf. Table 6.1.[5] Whether this counts as 'occasional' is for the reader to judge. Wyld (1914: §161) is more accurate in his assessment, stating that <æ> 'is found comparatively rarely after the thirteenth century, and probably not at all after the beginning of the fourteenth'.

[4] Forms for the noun DEAL (with $\bar{æ}^1$) were also extracted, but as OE also had *dāl* besides *dǣl*, these forms were not included in the tables. Additionally, all spellings for THERE, WHERE, HAIR (OE $\bar{æ}^2$) and EVER, NEVER (OE $\bar{æ}^1$) were counted, but their developments are idiosyncratic: they develop into PDE /eə/ and /e/, respectively, rather than to PDE /iː/. Therefore, their spellings have not been reported here; the interested reader is referred to Stenbrenden (2016: chapter 3). Nor has LADY ($\bar{æ}^1$) been counted, as it also has a different development (seen in the fact that it has PDE /eɪ/ rather than /iː/): the vowel of the first syllable underwent early shortening and joined ranks with eME *a*, which lengthened to [aː] in ME open syllable lengthening, and eventually vowel shifted to /eɪ/. The vowel of HEALTH ($\bar{æ}^1$) similarly shortened and has not been counted; the same applies to DEAD and DREAD (with $\bar{æ}^2$).

[5] Table 6.1 contains only lexemes extracted for analysis in the present chapter.

Table 6.1 Incidence of <æ> for OE ǣ in LAEME sources dated after 1200

No.	Loc.	Date	Lexemes with <æ>
304	Ha	1200	HÆLU, LEAD V., TEACH, LET
64	Ex	1200–24	DEAL V., HÆLU, HEAT, LEAN V., LEAD V., TEACH, LET, RÆDAN, RÆD, READ, SÆLIG, SLEEP V.
1900	Wor	c.1200	HÆLU
157	Som	c.1240	LET
6	Wor	c.1250	LEAD V., READ
7	Wor	c.1250	LEAD V.
11	Ex	1258	DEAL N., RÆD
277	Wor	1250–74	DEAL N., LEAN V., LEAD V., RÆDAN, RÆD, SLEEP V., SPEECH
278	Wor	1250–74	DEAL V., HÆLU, LEAN V., LEAD V., RÆDAN, RÆD, READ, STREET
131	Nfk	1272–1302	TEACH

OE $ǣ^1$ (< W Gmc $ai+i$) is believed to have been [æː] in all OE dialects except Kentish, where it was [eː]. Tables 6.3 and 6.4 (Appendix) show that <e> type spellings greatly preponderate in Kent for the reflexes of both OE $ǣ^1$ and $ǣ^2$, as expected. The two <ae> forms for $ǣ^1$ cannot change the conclusion reached by all previous scholars that Kentish had [eː] for both OE ǣ's (despite Hogg 2011: §§3.22–3.25). In the rest of the country also, <e> is the dominant spelling from the earliest period covered by LAEME (1150–1250), but even more so in the later period (1250–1350). Moreover, <e> is more frequent in the East Midlands, the South-East and the North (at 78.8 per cent, 94.74 per cent and 90.15 per cent respectively, for the entire period 1150–1350) than in the West Midlands (at 66.97 per cent for the entire period); this is obviously connected to the high number of <ea> in the West Midlands, to which I will return later. Numbers for the South-West are so low as to preclude any conclusion. The preponderance of <e> is a little surprising: If OE $ǣ^1$ really was [æː] generally in Saxon and Anglian dialects, one would expect a greater proportion of <a/æ/ae/ea> forms, at least in the early period. Still, their infrequency may not be enough to contradict the conventional account. At least this is Kristensson's conclusion based on analysis of the SMED material (2001: 40). It is also perfectly possible that the reflex of OE $ǣ^1$ was [æː] in OE, but started to raise early, and so had reached [ɛː] before 1150, for which <a/æ> may have been deemed inappropriate by the scribes. Of course, it is possible to read too much into the (non-)survival of <æ> in early ME (eME) dialects and scribal systems, and changes in orthography may have no phonetic correlate. However, when changes in orthography are systematic, either in terms of their dating/locus or in respect of how many scribes have adopted the new orthographic pattern, the likelihood that they do indeed reflect pronunciation changes is increased. Such is the case here.

The minor <ai/ay/æi/ei> forms are difficult to interpret (see Table 6.4 and Table 6.6 in the Appendix). If taken at face value, they indicate diphthongs similar or identical to those in words with an etymological diphthong (like OE *cǣg* 'key'), which is not impossible. The <i/y> may also be used as a diacritic device to indicate either a closer vowel, or vowel length (as in Older Scots); such diacritic use of <i/y> in the LAEME Corpus has been reported elsewhere (e.g. Stenbrenden 2016: 108). It is here that considerations of scribal habit and practice may be useful: more detailed analysis of the relevant scribal profiles may reveal whether or not they were capable of using letters diacritically.[6] Use of <ai/ay/æi/ei> is confined to the North and the West Midlands (cf. Table 6.6), with the exception of two texts from East Anglia: #1300 from Suffolk has one <ai> for $æ^2$ (HAIR), and #285 from Norfolk has one <ei> for $æ^1$ (SEA). In northern texts, there are twelve <ai> type spellings for $æ^1$ and two for $æ^2$, whereas for the West Midlands the numbers are three and five, respectively. A few scribes use <ai> type forms for both $æ$'s, but the majority use <ai/ei> etc. for only one of the $æ$'s. Lexically, there are some 'repeat offenders': in the North, <ai> type spellings occur for the (stressed) vowel of HEAT, HEATHEN, HǢLU, SEA ($æ^1$) and HAIR ($æ^2$); in the West Midlands, they are found for the (stressed) vowel of HǢLU, CLEAN, LEAD ($æ^1$) and RǢD, HAIR ($æ^2$). At least for the North, the proportions of different spellings for the two $æ$'s are statistically highly significant, even with the preponderance of <e> for both $æ$'s.

When <a>, <ai> and <e> are measured as separate categories, the chi square is 13.4382 with a p-value of .001208. The result is significant at $p < .01$. Given that the percentages of <e> for both $æ$'s in the North are almost identical (90.15 per cent for $æ^1$ and 90.68 per cent for $æ^2$), it must be the proportions of <a> vs. <ai/ay> which are responsible for this effect. The question is thus how to interpret the <ai/ay> forms – are they indicative of a diphthong or simply of a long, possibly retracted $æ/ā$ [æ: ~ ɑ:] (with <i/y> used as a diacritic device)? If so, the different proportions in northern sources cannot matter (as is confirmed by the chi square test), since there are thirteen <a/ai/ay> for $æ^1$, and eleven <a/ai/ay> for $æ^2$. We are thus back to the interpretation of the <i/y> element in <ai/ay> digraphs; to assess their role, the orthographic system of one LAEME text with one <ei> for $æ^1$, #295 from the West Riding of Yorkshire (dated c.1300–1350), will be examined in some detail in what follows. #295 has <ai> and <ay> very consistently for etymological *ai* (< OE *æg*) and *ei* (< OE *eg*) as well as for *ai, ei* in French loans, e.g. in AGAIN, AGAINST, AWAY, CLAY, DAY, EITHER, FAIR, HAIL, MAIDEN, MAY, NAIL, NAY, RAISE, SAY, WAY, AIR, AVAIL, HEIR, PRAY, TRAITOR. Generally, <ei/ey> are not used for the etymological diphthongs. OE <þ> and <ð> are consistently <y> or <th>. There are a few back-spellings with for the etymological diphthongs *ai* and *ei*; i.e. one <falid> (beside one <failld>) for the third person singular preterit of FAIL, and three <slan> (beside one <slain> and one <slaym>) for the past participle of SLAY, and five <sla> for the infinitive of SLAY. These may suggest that <i/y> merely indicate vowel length, as it is unlikely that SLAY was ever pronounced with [a: ~ ɑ:], unless it is confused with the cognate ON *slá* 'to strike, hit'. Alternatively and less likely, they indicate that the value of <a> had diphthongised already (ME /a:/ > [æi ~ ɛi]). #295 also has 'unetymological' (possibly diacritical) <i/y> in the following lexemes, which had a long monophthong in West Saxon: one <beit> for the past participle of BĒTAN; one <braith> for BRĀÞ;

---

[6] Ideally, all the scribal profiles of LAEME should be submitted to such close analysis, but that is not possible in this chapter, as remarked in the Introduction, for reasons of time and scope: virtually all the scribal texts in LAEME have instances of one or both $æ$'s and would thus have to be analysed along these lines.

seven <broiyer-> for BROTHER; one <deid> for DEATH; one <gait> for the third person singular preterit of GITAN; one <heiten> for the past participle of HĀTAN; one <laith> for LOTH; one <Rais> for the third person singular preterit of RISE; one <seir> for sĒR; one <wayth> for VĀÞI. It should be noted that these spellings in most cases appear alongside completely traditional spellings. The forms adduced appear to support the interpretation that <i/y> are used to indicate vowel length. However, as <ai/ay> are used so consistently for the etymological diphthongs, a diphthongal interpretation cannot be ruled out entirely – the scribe clearly knows what diphthongs are and how to spell them. The interpretation of such <ei/ey> and <ai/ay> for $\bar{æ}$ may thus be as elusive as ever.

Jordan (1925: §48, Anm.2) states that OE $\bar{æ}^1$ raised before 'dentals' in the North and the East Midlands; it is clear from his examples that the 'dentals' in question are the alveolar consonants /t d l n/; perhaps 'coronal' would be a better term, as the precise pronunciation of these sounds in the period covered remains uncertain. Jordan seems to say that this raising started in OE, but he quotes examples from ME texts, e.g. the *Ormulum* and *Havelok*. Kristensson, however, finds no evidence for this change in the SMED data (1987: 47, 1995: 24, 2001: 40). The material examined here shows almost exclusively <e(e)> for OE $\bar{æ}^1$ in the northern sources, regardless of the phonetic context, but the northern material in LAEME is generally very late: all but one of the sources have been dated to the period 1300–1350; only #151 from Lancashire is somewhat earlier and has been dated to the period 1275–1299. Similarly, the SMED sources are from the period 1290–1350. By this date, the reflex of $\bar{æ}^1$ must have raised generally across the country anyway, and the dominant spelling is <e(e)> everywhere. Table 6.5 in the Appendix shows the incidence of <e/ee/éé> for $\bar{æ}^1$ in LAEME sources dated before AD 1200: most of the <e> type spellings do indeed appear before a dental or alveolar consonant, but since in any case most of the words examined in fact have an alveolar post-vocalic consonant, I find it difficult to draw any conclusions regarding this supposed sound change from the material examined here.[7]

OE $\bar{æ}^2$ is supposed to be [æ:] only in Saxon dialects, and [e:] in Anglian and Kentish; Campbell (1959: §257) believes the split goes back to the Continental phase. The exact boundary is of course difficult to establish (cf. Wyld 1914: §162), but Brandl (quoted in Kristensson 1967: 57) finds it started at the Severn, cut right across Worcestershire and the southern part of Warwickshire, then followed the southern border of Northamptonshire. In the East, things are a little less clear, but Brandl appears to state that the dividing line followed the western border of Cambridgeshire and Huntingdonshire. North and east of this line, there was Anglian [e:]; south of this line, there was Saxon [æ:]. Kristensson agrees for the most part (1987: 51–52, map 6 and 1995: 28–32, map 4), except that he thinks the boundary cut across Northamptonshire in a north-easterly direction, then followed the southern border of Peterborough and Ely to the Wash. Thus, Ely, Cambridgeshire, Huntingdonshire, Bedfordshire, Buckinghamshire and Oxfordshire were Saxon territories, in Kristensson's opinion, and the south-eastern part of Northamptonshire and most of Gloucestershire, except

---

[7] A thorough investigation of (late) OE sources might settle the case, but that is beyond the scope of this chapter.

for the northernmost tip, were also [æː] areas. Kitson (1998: 176) finds Kristensson's account much too simplified, and it is certainly not always clear whether Kristensson thinks of these areas as politically Saxon, or linguistically Saxon. For our purposes, it need not matter.

Kristensson (2001: 44) argues that East Anglia had a large Saxon population, and thus must have had [æː] for OE $\bar{æ}^2$ rather than the expected Anglian [eː]. Besides, OE $\bar{æ}^2$ is supposed to have retracted to [aː] in East Saxon dialects. Kristensson's isogloss for this retracted [aː] includes Essex, Hertfordshire, Bedfordshire, Huntingdonshire, Middlesex and most of Cambridgeshire (1995: 31). In the LAEME data, frequent and dominant <a> in the material from Essex (Table 6.4) supports East Saxon retraction there, but not at all in the rest of the supposedly East Saxon territory. The domain of this retraction therefore seems not to extend beyond Essex in the time period covered by LAEME. This is remarkable, given what Kristensson concludes from the SMED material, which is generally dated 1290–1350 and thus overlaps with the later LAEME material. One important difference regarding the material in LAEME and SMED, however, is that the latter is comprised of onomastic data and so contains a rather high number of shortened forms for OE *strǣt* 'street', which traditionally have been used to establish the isogloss between Anglian *ē* and Saxon *ǣ* for $\bar{æ}^2$, cf. the last paragraph of section 1. Tables 6.3 and 6.4 show that <a> is recorded for $\bar{æ}^2$ in the West Midlands also, but one would tend to interpret it as corresponding to Saxon [æː] rather than as evidence of retraction. However, <a/æ/ea> are indeed slightly more common in the East Midlands than in the West, which might indicate retraction, or else simply retention of [æː], in Saxon areas. The story of *ǣ* illustrates perhaps better than that of any other vowel the difficulty linguists face when they attempt to infer the phonetic correspondences of ME spellings.

Above all, analysis of the LAEME material reveals that the reflexes of the two *ǣ*'s are not kept apart as systematically as expected in Anglian (or indeed anywhere). In the South-East, <a/æ> are of course very rare, but do occur. In other places, on the other hand, <a/æ/ea> are very common, not just for $\bar{æ}^1$, but also for $\bar{æ}^2$. Sources localised to the South-West Midlands should in principle have the same number of <a/æ/ea> for both *ǣ*'s – being the heart of the West Saxon territory – but that is not the case: <a/æ/ea> are more frequent for $\bar{æ}^1$. The total number of tokens is very low, and any conclusions must be highly tentative, but if this pattern has any significance at all, it suggests that the value of $\bar{æ}^2$ may always have been a little closer than that of $\bar{æ}^1$, even in Saxon, and even if it goes back to West Gmc *ā*, which a priori would suggest a more *open* value. W Gmc *ā* supposedly goes back to PrGmc *ǣ* (Campbell 1959: §§127–130), so one can only speculate as to the concrete phonetic realisation(s) of $\bar{æ}^2$, in OE as well as in ME. Hogg (2011: §§3.3, 3.22–3.25) argues that PrGmc *ǣ* remained in W Gmc, being /aː/ but phonetically [æː]. His reasoning is that since PrGmc *ǣ* was the only low long monophthong, there was no phonemic front-back opposition, so that /æː/ may have had a number of allophones, front [æː] or [aː], and back [ɑː], as evidenced by later developments.[8] (The same argument applies to the short low vowel /a/.) 'It

---

[8] The latter allophone is likely to have occurred before nasals, since the later development is to /oː/, as in OE and Old Frisian *mōna* 'moon'.

therefore follows that the alleged OE, OFris shift of */aː/ > /æː/ is an artefact of phonemic theory, and that there is no reason to suppose that [...] the Gmc long low vowel retracted significantly at any period in the development of OE' (Hogg 2011: 60), because it had been [æː] all along.⁹ The dating of the Anglian raising of this $\bar{æ}^2$ to $\bar{e}$ is unclear, in Hogg's opinion (2011: 61; but see his fn. 2 on p. 61). If Hogg's hypothesis is correct, it entails that the realisation of $\bar{æ}^2$ may not have been lower than that of $\bar{æ}^1$ (the *i*-mutated product of W Gmc *ai*).

Furthermore, another question raised by the ME spellings is whether $\bar{æ}^2$ really was [eː] in Anglian; there cannot be any doubt that Kentish had [eː]. Wyld claims quite specifically that 'This non-W.Sax. $\bar{e}$ was tense' (1914: §120), i.e. [eː] rather than [ɛː]. If so, the overwhelming majority of forms should have <e>, which they generally do.¹⁰ Still, there is a fair number of forms with <a/æ/ea>: do these correspond to an opener sound, or simply reflect the conservative (WS) nature of spelling? A possibility is that not just non-WS $\bar{æ}^2$, but non-WS $\bar{æ}^1$ also, had raised by this stage, so that the reflexes of both $\bar{æ}$'s had merged, but were somehow phonetically separate from the reflex of OE $\bar{e}$, and were thus distinguished orthographically by whatever means (other than <e>) that the scribes found useful. A statistical analysis of all LAEME spellings for OE $\bar{e}$ and both $\bar{æ}$'s may support or refute such a hypothetical, albeit plausible, course of events, but is beyond the scope of the present chapter (cf. n. 11).

Orm's spellings are worth considering in some detail in this context. From the portion tagged for LAEME #301 (the Dedication and Preface, and parts of the Introduction and Homilies), I have extracted and counted all forms for words with OE $\bar{æ}^1$ and $\bar{æ}^2$, except (a) those forms which show a shortened vowel in Orm's language (i.e. are followed by a double consonant), and (b) those words whose etymology is uncertain (in terms of which $\bar{æ}$ they go back to). Thus, 107 tokens with $\bar{æ}^1$ were counted, of which three have <a> (ANY, NE+ANY, LADY), sixty-eight have <æ> and thirty-six have <e>. One hundred and sixty-four tokens with $\bar{æ}^2$ were analysed, of which nine have , 141 have <æ> (including the highly frequent THERE, which has <æ> in all 110 tokens) and fourteen have <e>. A chi square test reveals that the two vowels have highly significantly different spellings ($p < 0.00001$) in the *Ormulum*, both when <a> and <æ> are amalgamated and measured against <e>, and when all three spellings are measured separately.¹¹ Clearly, <æ> is the dominant spelling for both groups of words, which suggests that $\bar{æ}^2$ may have had an open quality [ɛː] even in Orm's dialect. On the other hand, the higher proportion of <e> for $\bar{æ}^1$ may indicate, somewhat surprisingly, a closer quality for $\bar{æ}^1$ than for $\bar{æ}^2$. Wyld (1914: §161) thinks Orm's <æ> spellings are

---

[9] One could argue that the W Gmc phoneme should be /æː/ rather than /aː/, if it remained essentially unchanged from PrGmc, but Hogg's solution has the advantage of covering the later development in all the W Gmc languages.

[10] In fact, non-WS should have exactly the same spellings for OE $\bar{æ}^2$ as for OE $\bar{e}$. Previous analyses suggest that such is not the case (Stenbrenden 2016), but conducting a thorough comparison of spellings for the two vowels in non-WS is clearly a topic for further research.

[11] When the three spellings are counted separately, the chi square statistic is 27.4009. The *p*-value is < 0.00001. The result is significant at $p < .01$. Similar chi square tests could be calculated for all scribal systems in *LAEME*, but the aim of this chapter is rather to show the totality of the spellings for the two $\bar{æ}$'s in the relevant period.

'remarkable', since his Anglian dialect should have $\bar{e}$. In Wyld's opinion, the <æ>-forms 'must probably be attributed to the domination and persistence of the classical W.Sax. mode of writing among learned persons like Orm' (1914: §161). This is quite possible, although any 'domination and persistence' of the late West Saxon standard 'mode of writing' is not exactly in evidence elsewhere in Orm's system. Given Orm's obviously good ear, I propose that his spellings be taken at face value, as suggesting at the very least that there was a system(at)ic difference in sound, however small, between the reflexes of OE $\bar{e}$ and the two $\bar{æ}$'s even in Anglian. The significant difference in his spellings of $\bar{æ}^1$ and $\bar{æ}^2$ may even suggest a three-way distinction. It could also be that the reflex of $\bar{æ}^2$ was felt to be more similar to that of $\bar{æ}^1$ than that of $\bar{e}$. Whether this difference was phonemic is another question entirely. (A similar case might be seen in Modern French, in which $é$ [e(:)] and $è$ [ɛ(:)] are kept apart in spelling as well as in pronunciation, even if the difference does not reach phonemic status: their distribution is largely predictable from the phonetic context and the syllable structure; cf. Girard Lomheim and Lyche 1991: §3.2.1.3.) Even if alphabetic writing is essentially phonemic (at least at the outset), that does not prevent scribes from observing subphonemic details and differences, especially if they are clearly noticeable.

Wyld also offers some statistics regarding spellings for both $\bar{æ}$'s in southern texts, and he concludes that '*ea* is written with far greater consistency for' $\bar{æ}^1$ than for $\bar{æ}^2$ (1914: §161). This indicates an opener quality of $\bar{æ}^1$, which is the opposite of my conclusions regarding Orm's system. However, Wyld continues, 'but the identity of the sounds is proved by the fact that *e*, *ea*, *æ* are written indifferently for both and further from such rhymes as *þære–were*, *dreden–læden*' (1914: §161). He thus seems to believe that the two $\bar{æ}$'s were identical in southern ME, certainly from the later thirteenth century onwards. This view seems to be supported (for the whole country) by the fact that the same spellings are found for both $\bar{æ}$'s in most counties, as laid out in Table 6.4 (Appendix): that is, <a>, <æ>, <ea>, <e>, <eo>, <ai/ei> are found for both $\bar{æ}$'s. However, the proportions vary, and this is indeed the point: in the absence of clearly distinct letter-sound correspondences, it is the fact that there are dominant vs. minor spelling variants that allows us to postulate a potential pronunciation difference. In fact, a chi square test including all spellings for the two $\bar{æ}$'s as summed up in the final row of Table 6.4 (excluding <eo> and the very infrequent <i>, <y>, <ia> and <o>, because numbers lower than five may affect the validity of the test), indicates that the difference in the spellings of the two vowels is highly significant ($p < 0.00001$).[12] Overall, the spellings point to a closer quality of the reflex of $\bar{æ}^2$, which is as expected.

Regarding the 'new' ME digraph <ea>, or rather its new use for OE $\bar{æ}$, the material from LAEME suggests very strongly that it was a West Midlands 'innovation'. In the early period, <ea> reaches a percentage of 41.16 for $\bar{æ}^1$ here, which is all the more remarkable given its almost complete absence from the East Midlands material (for either $\bar{æ}$ in any period). Forms with <ea> are especially frequent in Shropshire, Cheshire, Worcestershire and Herefordshire, some of which must have been Anglian territory, politically and/or linguistically. For $\bar{æ}^2$, however, forms with <ea> reach

---

[12] The chi square statistic is 66.7755. The *p*-value is < 0.00001. The result is significant at $p < .01$.

only 7–8 per cent in the West Midlands (7.72 per cent for the entire period). The question, therefore, is whether use of <ea> arose as a means to distinguish the two ǣ's orthographically, especially given the change OE ēa > ǣ and the ambiguity of <e(e)>. In this context, <ea> for the short eME æ, ea (whose reflexes had merged) may in fact have acted as a 'bridge' for the long vowel. Lass and Laing (2012: 81) examine all the lexemes for which <ea> is used in LAEME and find that it was used for what they call 'opener front' vowels. They conclude that it was something like a diacritic device indicating a more open e type sound (2012: 92–95), with which I agree. Essentially, the same rationale lies behind both <æ> and <ea>: they are composed of 'e' and 'a' and correspond to a sound intermediate between [e(ː)] and [a(ː)]; it is only the relative chronology of the two parts that differs.

As long as <ea> continues to be used in ME sources, it is possible that the more open quality [ɛː] may have persisted. On the other hand, the earliest evidence of vowel shift of OE ē to [iː] appears around 1200–1250, but the conventional spelling <e(e)> remains, as it does to the present day. Therefore, the reflex of ME ę̄ *may* in fact also have raised, to [eː], around this date – or later – and <ea> simply remained for conventional reasons. All we know for certain is that the two reflexes are generally kept apart (for instance in rhymes) into the Early ModE period, when they merged at /iː/ in some dialects. But whether they were kept apart as [eː] and [ɛː], as conventionally believed, or as [iː] and [eː], is an issue open to argument and to which I will return later.

At this point, it is worth clarifying some principles regarding the chronology and nature of the GVS and the process commonly referred to as ME 'open syllable lengthening' (MEOSL). Briefly, short vowels were lengthened in open syllables at some point during ME, and it seems as if they were simultaneously lowered, e.g. eME *ivel* > ME *ēvel* EVIL (Ritt 1994; Lutz 2004). Conversely, when long vowels are shortened, the resulting short vowel seems to have been simultaneously raised, e.g. eME *sēk* > ME *sick* SICK. However, if the 'Early Vowel Shift Hypothesis' suggested by Stockwell (1985) and Stockwell and Minkova (1988a, 1988b) is correct, and I have concluded previously that it is (Stenbrenden 2016), there is no need to postulate a lowering process for lengthened vowels or a raising process for shortened vowels, as isolative short-vowel raising is historically very rare.[13] In other words, if the vowel shift was already under way when MEOSL started, the new long vowels from MEOSL simply merged with the closest etymological long vowel, which had already been raised in the vowel shift. Thus, the new long vowels from MEOSL merely *seem* to have been lowered, and the new short vowels only *appear* to have been raised, because their spellings have changed, but the spellings correspond to a different phonetic reality (Stockwell 1985: 310–311).

On the topic of vowel shift: the raising of eME [æː] is in evidence from the midthirteenth century. Forms with <i> and <y> are found very early, in sources dated to the period 1250–1330 (LAEME, SMED), as indicated in Table 6.2 (in which the first three spellings are from LAEME and the remaining from SMED). The lexical

---

[13] It has occurred combinatively, especially before nasals or as a result of vowel harmony (Campbell 1959: §111; Hogg 2011: 64–65; Ringe and Taylor 2014: 62).

'leader' in this change may have been SILLY (< OE *sǣlig*). It is unlikely that the vowel of SILLY, or of the other words in Table 6.2, demonstrates raising of a short vowel (which must have arisen from shortening of the long OE vowel) for the following reasons. First, as pointed out in the preceding, unconditioned short-vowel raising is rare in English; second, and with the first argument in mind, regular (early) vowel shift of OE/eME $\bar{æ} > \bar{e} > \bar{\imath}$, then shortening to i, is a more economical development than OE/eME $\bar{æ} > æ > e > i$. It is more economical because it involves the well-known stages of the vowel shift of $\bar{æ} > $ [iː], then well-attested shortening to a vowel of the same height, whereas the alternative involves shortening to a vowel of the same height, then raising of that short vowel in two stages.[14] Yet, variants with [ɛː], [eː] and [iː] probably coexisted for a long time, given the non-merger in ME between the reflexes of eME $\bar{e}$ and $\bar{æ}$ (from whatever source); as noted above, this merger did not take place until the sixteenth century at the earliest (Zachrisson 1913: 204; Dobson 1968: 610). In this respect, it makes sense to distinguish between the standard language and regional/social variants: in the latter, the merger may have taken place earlier.

Table 6.2 Early vowel-shift spellings for OE $\bar{æ}$ (LAEME, SMED)

County	No.	Date	Spelling
Worcestershire	278	1250–74	<spiche> SPEECH ($\bar{æ}^2 >$ non-S $\bar{e}$)
Mixed (NE and SW)	214	1275–99	<silly> SÆLIG ($\bar{æ}^2 >$ non-S $\bar{e}$)
Lincolnshire	159	c.1300	<lydy> LEAD 1.sg.ps. ($\bar{æ}^1$)
West Riding, Yorkshire	–	1327	<Minskip> ($\bar{æ}^1$)
Lincolnshire	–	1327	<Silyman> ($\bar{æ}^2 >$ non-S $\bar{e}$)
Huntingdonshire	–	1327	<Silly> ($\bar{æ}^2 >$ non-S $\bar{e}$)
Suffolk	–	1327	<Rydelingfeld> ($\bar{æ}^2 >$ Saxon $\bar{æ}$)
Dorset	–	1327	<Ridelyngton> ($\bar{æ}^2 >$ Saxon $\bar{æ}$)
Somerset	–	1333	<Brych> ($\bar{æ}^2 >$ Saxon $\bar{æ}$)

Of the spellings reproduced in Table 6.2, the forms from Dorset and Somerset almost certainly indicate early vowel shift of $\bar{æ}^2$ in the South-West, as does the Suffolk form in the South-East Midlands; the forms from the West Riding of Yorkshire and Lincolnshire probably indicate vowel-shift raising of $\bar{æ}^1$. The remaining forms demonstrate vowel shift of non-Saxon $\bar{e}$. In so far as it is possible to conclude anything on the basis of such a low number of forms, the South-West, the South-East Midlands and the North-East stand out as loci of change. Incidentally, the same areas stand out with respect of early vowel-shift spellings for the other ME long monophthongs too (Stenbrenden 2016: chapter 9).

Lutz (2004) sees the early ME raising of OE /æː/ to [ɛː] as a prelude to the GVS, making the latter a push-chain process in traditional terminology (cf. Jones

---

[14] Shortening of long vowels, e.g. $\bar{\imath}$ to i, is commonplace in words of more than one syllable, but is also seen in some frequent monosyllabic words in late ME or early ModE, such as FOOT, GOOD, but only *after* the vowel shift had raised the etymological long vowel, cf. Wells (1982: 198).

1989: 127–141).¹⁵ To determine whether this claim is supported by the spellings, the remainder of this section seeks to establish the chronology of the full set of ME long-vowel changes, in order to place the changes to OE $\bar{æ}$ in the bigger picture.

I concluded in earlier work (Stenbrenden 2010, 2016) that the traditional GVS changes started around 1250, and that they began with the simultaneous raising of eME $\bar{e}$ and $\bar{o}$ and diphthongisation of eME $\bar{\imath}$ and $\bar{u}$. This lends support to the 'Early Vowel Shift Hypothesis' alluded to earlier. The changes affecting the two low vowels, OE $\bar{a}$ and $\bar{æ}$, are not usually considered part of the GVS, even if they are similar in nature. The main reason has been their dating: OE $\bar{a}$ seems to have started raising in the late eleventh century (Stenbrenden 2016: 58), and the raising of OE $\bar{æ}$ appears to have been on its way certainly in the twelfth century, probably quite a bit earlier, as argued in the present chapter. The two processes seem however not to have reached conclusion until much later: <a> and <o> still co-vary for OE $\bar{a}$ in the late ME period (cf. relevant items in LALME), and <a> for OE $\bar{æ}$ persists into the later period covered by LAEME. Thus, given that the incipient stages of the GVS have now been dated to c.1250, one must conclude that there was in fact an overlap in time between the changes affecting $\bar{æ}$ and $\bar{a}$ on the one hand, and the traditional GVS on the other. Hence, the conclusion must be, partly *contra* Lutz, that the changes to OE $\bar{æ}$ should be regarded as *part* of (rather than a *prelude* to) any 'great Middle English long-vowel shift', although this apparent difference of opinion may merely reflect a differece in terminology. The same argument applies to the changes to OE $\bar{a}$, and to OE $\bar{o}$ north of the Humber. Still, this is not to say that there is a causal relationship between any of these changes, but that they are similar processes which overlap chronologically. The eME changes to the reflexes of OE $\bar{e}o$ and $\bar{y}$ seem to be simple processes of unrounding and may be different in kind.

Chronologically, the initial stages of the changes to $\bar{æ}$ and $\bar{a}$ started before the constituent GVS changes, supporting a push-chain interpretation. The terms 'push-chains' and 'drag-chains' are used here merely as descriptive labels, as they have no explanatory power. Similarly, the changes to long vowels in ME and early ModE may be labelled a 'chain shift' *post facto*, in so far as the said changes served to uphold phonemic distinctions, but the term does not in itself explain any of the phonetic processes involved. Besides, the concept of a capitalised unitary vowel shift is hardly tenable. Stockwell and Minkova hypothesise (*passim*) that it was the vocalisation of OE <g> in <ig/īg> and <ug/ūg> that really set the GVS in motion, in that the two high vowel phonemes /iː/ and /uː/ received diphthongal allophones, which destabilised them and triggered their subsequent phonemic diphthongisation.¹⁶ The vocalisation of post-vocalic <g> is tentatively dated to late OE (Jordan 1925: §87; cf. Jones 1989: 19–21), which in turn suggests a drag-chain scenario.

Interestingly, Samuels (2006) claims to find evidence only of vocalic drag-chains, synchronically as well as diachronically, and she thus denies the existence of push-

---

¹⁵ Jones refers to the changes to OE $\bar{a}$ and $\bar{æ}$ as 'The first English vowel shift' (1989: 137), and clearly sees them as instances of (some of) the same tendencies that are observed in the later GVS, i.e. increased palatality ($\bar{æ}$) and labiality ($\bar{a}$) (1989: 127–136).

¹⁶ A different view is proposed by Lass (1988), although he has in fact changed his view of the vowel shift in recent years (personal communication).

chains altogether. At some level, such argumentation may be mere theoretical quibble – after all, changes of this kind are often simultaneous and defy easy categorisation. But if it is true that there is empirical evidence only of drag-chains, it appears to reveal something about vowel *systems*: it is not the danger of merger that triggers chain shifts, but rather the fact that vowel slots are vacated, creating asymmetries, cf. the principle of 'equal phonetic spacing' (Luick 1932; Martinet 1955; Liljencrants and Lindblom 1972).

As for the relationship between the changes reported here and other long-vowel changes in the eME period, the following may be concluded. First, most if not all long-vowel changes taking place between late OE and c.1750 appear to be related, as they overlap temporally. The question of causation in language change is fraught with difficulty, and correlation is not the same as causation. However, when changes affect sounds which are all members of a part-system, such as that of long monophthongs, and it can be established in hindsight that the changes contributed to upholding this part-system, then the case is stronger for seeing them as related. True causation may never be established, even for ongoing changes. Second, the changes to OE ǣ must be part of the great vowel shift, as they overlap with the early stages of the vowel shift as traditionally conceived. Third, we are looking at a very long period of particularly intensive vowel shifting. Fourth, these changes instantiate a small number of recurring processes, that is, raising, fronting and diphthongisation.

In future research, what is needed is more focus on the likely reasons for this tendency in Germanic languages to shift long vowels along these paths. Work on the interplay between qualitative and quantitative vowel changes has much to offer in this regard (Ritt 1994; Britton 2002; Britton and Williamson 2002): they suggest that MEOSL of short/lax vowels produced long vowels of 'intermediate quality' (compared to the etymologically long vowels), and that they therefore upset the system and caused shifting. Similarly, when articulatory and acoustic examinations have been undertaken of present-day vowel shifts, like the Diphthong Shift in Cockney, Estuary English and Australian English (Wells 1982) and the Northern Cities Shift in American English (Labov 1994; Gordon 2001; McCarthy 2010), they give promising clues as to what exactly is going on in vocalic chain shifting. Labov (1994: *passim*) indeed establishes principles of vowel shifting in which acoustic and articulatory factors are seen to interact. There is a distinct possibility that chain shifts may be explained as simple gestural overshoot or undershoot, possibly in combination with prosodic features or coarticulatory phenomena (e.g. assimilation), especially as previous work (Stenbrenden 2016) concluded that that most of the long vowel shifts in ME were in fact combinative, i.e. they started in certain phonetic contexts and then spread through the lexicon.

4. Conclusions

This chapter has concluded that although use of <æ> was gradually discontinued after 1066, it persisted in some cases into the early fourteenth century, although its frequency dropped substantially after 1200. It has been argued that this marked decrease was the result of changes in pronunciation, that is vowel raising, which happened in two or more stages.

Moreover, the reflexes of the two OE $\bar{æ}$'s are not kept apart orthographically in any systematic fashion in any ME dialects: <e(e)> is the dominant spelling everywhere, which indicates that the raising process had begun very early, as indeed all the major textbooks on ME claim.

Additionally, the proportion of <a/æ/ea> is higher in the early part of the period covered by LAEME than in the later part, which suggests that the raising process continued throughout the period for the reflexes of both $\bar{æ}$'s, and the orthography eventually followed suit. It also indicates that as <æ> fell out of use, the scribes resorted to other orthographic means of keeping the reflexes of OE $\bar{e}$, $\bar{æ}^1$ and $\bar{æ}^2$ apart, though not always successfully. In this respect, West Midlands sources stand out with a very high proportion of innovative <ea> for $\bar{æ}^1$, especially in the earliest period. <ea> is also used for $\bar{æ}^2$, but not nearly to the same degree; in the later period, things are more even.

The proposed East Saxon retraction of $\bar{æ}^2$ to [aː] is supported by the spelling evidence from LAEME, but only for Essex. However, as <a> is almost as frequent for $\bar{æ}^1$ as for $\bar{æ}^2$ in Essex, it seems that the reflex of $\bar{æ}^1$ joined in this retraction, which is not at all improbable, given that both would have been OE [æː].

Even if the same types of spellings are used for both $\bar{æ}$'s, their proportions vary, and the differences appear to be statistically significant. The evidence thus indicates that there may have been a phonetic difference between $\bar{æ}^1$ and $\bar{æ}^2$ in West Saxon as well as in the other dialects, which goes counter to what is usually claimed. If so, the reflex of $\bar{æ}^1$ seems to have had an opener quality than that of $\bar{æ}^2$, because there are more <a/æ/ea> for the former and more <e(e)> for the latter. Potential influence from the late West Saxon standard language should not be overlooked, but such influence seems to be ruled out in the case of the *Ormulum*: Orm's different use of <a> vs. <æ> vs. <e> for the two $\bar{æ}$'s is statistically highly significant, and – surprisingly – points to a closer quality for $\bar{æ}^1$.

In the future, close analysis of all or some of the scribal profiles in LAEME should be carried out, both in terms of the proportions of co-variants and orthographic systems, and in terms of statistical significance. In such a study, the spellings of the two $\bar{æ}$'s ought to be compared to those of etymological OE $\bar{e}$, with which non-WS $\bar{e}$ < $\bar{æ}^2$ is supposed to have merged; late OE sources might fruitfully be included.

Finally, it has been shown in this chapter that the sound changes which affected the two $\bar{æ}$'s took some time to reach completion, and that they overlapped in time with the early stages of the GVS. I therefore argue that they must be seen as part of the vowel shift, rather than as similar but unrelated changes.

Appendix

Table 6.3 LAEME spellings for OE $ǣ^1$ and OE $ǣ^2$, by area and date

Area	$ǣ^1$ <W Gmc $ai+i$			$ǣ^2$ <W Gmc $ā$		
	No.	%	<a/æ/ea>	No.	%	<a/æ/ea>
North	1 <a>	0.76	0.76%	9 <a>	7.63	7.63%
	119 <e>	90.15		107 <e>	90.68	
	12 <ai/ei>	9.09		2 <ai/ei>	1.69	
	Total: 132 tokens			Total: 118 tokens		
East Midlands	51 <a>	17.83	<a/æ/ea>	65 <a>	35.91	<a/æ/ea>
1150–1250	25 <æ>	8.74	78	33 <æ>	18.23	98
	2 <ea>	0.7	27.27%	82 <e>	45.3	54.14%
	208 <e>	72.73		1 <ai>	0.55	
	Total: 286 tokens			Total: 181 tokens		
East Midlands	1 <æ>	1.04	1.04%	4 <a>	2.76	2.76%
1250–1350	93 <e>	96.88		140 <e>	96.55	
	1 <ei>	1.04		1 <o>	0.69	
	1 <y>	1.04				
	Total: 96 tokens			Total: 145 tokens		
East Midlands total	51 <a>	13.35	<a/æ/ea>	69 <a>	21.17	<a/æ>
	26 <æ>	6.81	79	33 <æ>	10.12	102 31.29%
	2 <ea>	0.52	20.68%	222 <e>	68.09	
	301 <e>	78.8		1 <ai>	0.31	
	1 <ei>	0.26		1 <o>	0.31	
	1 <y>	0.26				
	Total: 382 tokens			Total: 326 tokens		
South-West	1 <a>	20	<a/æ>	1 <æ>	16.67	16.67%
	2 <æ>	40	3 60%	5 <e>	83.33	
	2 <e>	40				
	Total: 5 tokens			Total: 6 tokens		
South-East	1 <a>	1.75	<a/æ>	2 <a>	2.94	2.94%
	2 <æ>	3.51	3 5.26%	66 <e>	97.06	
	54 <e>	94.74				
	Total: 57 tokens			Total: 68 tokens		
West Midlands	1 <a>	0.26	<a/æ/ea>	1 <a>	0.2	<a/æ/ea>
1150–1250	21 <æ>	5.54	178	17 <æ>	3.42	55
	156 <ea>	41.16	46.96%	37 <ea>	7.45	11.07%
	200 <e>	52.77		424 <e>	85.31	
	1 <ei>	0.26		14 <eo>	2.82	
				3 <ai/ei>	0.6	
				1 <ia>	0.2	
	Total: 379 tokens			Total: 497 tokens		

(*Continued*)

Table 6.3 Continued

Area	$ǣ^1$ <W Gmc *ai+i*			$ǣ^2$ <W Gmc *ā*		
	No.	%	<a/æ/ea>	No.	%	<a/æ/ea>
West Midlands 1250–1350	5 <a>	1.29	<a/æ/ea>	10 <a>	2.05	<a/æ/ea>
	43 <æ>	11.11	69	40 <æ>	8.21	89
	21 <ea>	5.43	17.83%	39 <ea>	8.01	18.27%
	313 <e>	80.88		391 <e>	80.29	
	3 <eo>	0.77		3 <eo>	0.62	
	2 <æi/ei>	0.52		2 <ei>	0.41	
				2 <i>	0.41	
	Total: 387 tokens			Total: 487 tokens		
WEST MIDLANDS TOTAL	6 <a>	0.78	<a/æ/ea>	11 <a>	1.12	<a/æ/ea>
	64 <æ>	8.36	247	57 <æ>	5.79	144
	177 <ea>	23.11	32.25%	76 <ea>	7.72	14.63%
	513 <e>	66.97		815 <e>	82.83	
	3 <eo>	0.39		17 <eo>	1.73	
	3 <æi/ei>	0.39		5 <ai/ei>	0.51	
				2 <i>	0.2	
				1 <ia>	0.1	
	Total: 766 tokens			Total: 984 tokens		
	Total: 1342 tokens			**Total: 1502 tokens**		

Table 6.4 LAEME spellings for OE $ǣ^1$ and OE $ǣ^2$, by county

Area	$ǣ^1$ <W Gmc *ai+i*	$ǣ^2$ <W Gmc *ā*
North		
Durham	3 e	1 a, 2 e
East Riding, Yorkshire	1 a, 28 e, 1 ee, 1 ai	4 a, 27 e, 1 ai
Lancashire		4 e
North Riding, Yorkshire	50 e, 2 ay	4 a, 27 e, 1 ee, 1 ay
West Riding, Yorkshire	9 e, 3 ee, 1 ei	23 e
York	24 e, 1 ee, 6 ai, 2 ei	23 e
East Midlands		
Cambridgeshire	4 e	1 a, 2 e
Ely	3 e	11 e
Essex	51 a, 7 æ, 2 ea, 43 e	65 a, 21 æ, 20 e
Leicestershire		1 e
Lincolnshire	6 æ, 44 e, 1 y	11 æ, 21 e, 1 é
Norfolk	1 æ, 59 e, 1 ee, 1 ei	3 a, 100 e, 5 ee, 1o
Northamptonshire	4 e	8 e
Peterborough	5 æ, 1 e	1 æ, 3 e
Suffolk	7 æ, 142 e	50 e, 1 ai

(*Continued*)

Table 6.4 Continued

Area	$\bar{æ}^1$ <W Gmc $ai+i$	$\bar{æ}^2$ <W Gmc $\bar{a}$
South-East		
Kent	2 ae, 50 e, 2 éé	64 e
London	1 a	
Sussex	1 e	2 e
Surrey	1 e	2 a
South-West		
Hampshire	2 æ, 2 e	1 æ, 5 e
Somerset	1 a	
West Midlands		
Berkshire	1 a, 97 e, 1 eo	46 e
Cheshire	1 a, 22 ea	1 ea, 57 e, 1 eo, 1 ai, 2 ei
Gloucestershire	47 e, 1 eo	1 a, 74 e, 4 ee
Herefordshire	16 ea, 77 e, 1 éé	3 ea, 176 e, 2 é, 1 eo, 1 ei, 1 i
Oxfordshire	58 e	5 a, 52 e
Shropshire	97 ea, 18 e, 1 ei	30 ea, 104 e, 2 é, 13 eo
Staffordshire	1 e	1 e
Wiltshire	1 a, 8 e, 10 éé, 1 ee, 1 eo	24 ea, 29 e
Worcestershire	3 a, 64 æ, 42 ea, 182 e, 8 é(é), 5 ee, 2 æi/ei	5 a, 57 æ, 18 ea, 268 e, 2 eo, 1 æi, 1 i
Total	60 a, 94 æ, 179 ea, 989 e(e), 16 ai/ei, 3 eo, 1 y	91 a, 91 æ, 76 ea, 1215 e(e), 8 ai/ei, 17 eo, 2 i, 1 ia, 1 o

Table 6.5 LAEME <e> spellings for OE $\bar{æ}^1$ in early sources (before AD 1200)

County	No.	Date	Words with <e>
East Midlands			
Peterborough	149	1154	HEATHEN
Essex	4	1150–99	HEAT
Essex	1200	1175–99	CLEAN, HÆLEND, HEAL, HEATHEN, LEAD (DEAL)
Suffolk	1300	1175–99	CLEAN, HÆLEND, HEAL, HEAT, HEATHEN, LEAD, SEA, TEACH (DEAL)
Lincolnshire	301	1175–99	CLEAN, LEAD
West Midlands			
Worcestershire	170	1175–99	HÆLEND
Worcestershire	5	c.1200	HEAT, LEAD, SEA
Worcestershire	2000	c.1200	CLEAN, HÆLEND, HEAL, HEATHEN, LEAD, SEA, TEACH (DEAL)
Worcestershire	2001	c.1200	CLEAN, HÆLEND, HEAL, HEATHEN, LEAD, SEA, TEACH
Oxfordshire	232	1175–1224	LEAD
Worcestershire	1900 (171–173)	1200–49	CLEAN, HÆLEND, LEAD, TEACH, WHEAT

Table 6.6 Incidence of <ai/ay>, <æi>, <ei> for OE $\bar{æ}^1$ and OE $\bar{æ}^2$ in LAEME

Area	No.	Date	$\bar{æ}^1$ <W Gmc $ai+i$	$\bar{æ}^2$ <W Gmc $\bar{a}$	Lexemes
West Riding, Yorkshire	295	1300–50	8 e, 3 ee, 1 ei	19 e	ei HEAT
York	296	1300–50	24 e, 1 ee, 6 ai, 2 ei	23 e	ai HEATHEN; ei SEA
East Riding, Yorkshire	297	1300–50	1 a, 27 e, 1 ee, 1 ai	4 a, 27 e, 1 ai	ai HÆLU; HAIR
North Riding, Yorkshire	298	1300–50	50 e, 2 ay	4 a, 27 e, 1 ee, 1 ay	ay HEATHEN; a/ay HAIR
Suffolk	1300	1175–99	7 æ, 142 e	50 e, 1 ai	ai HAIR
Norfolk	285	1300–24	31 e, 1 ei	3 a, 33 e, 1 o	ei SEA
Shropshire	272	1225–49	26 ea, 1 ei	3 ea, 57 e, 2 é, 2 eo	ei HÆLU
Cheshire	118	1240–50	1 a, 17 ea	1 ea, 51 e, 1 eo, 1 ai, 2 ei	ai/ei HAIR
Worcestershire	278	1250–74	1 a, 24 æ, 2 ea, 3 e, 1 æi	4 a, 24 æ, 2 ea, 1 eæ, 10 e, 1 æi, 1 i	æi LEAD; RÆd
Worcestershire	2	1275–99	7 e, 1 ei	21 e	ei CLEAN
Herefordshire	246	1275–99	10 e	18 e, 1 ei	ei RÆD

References

Anderson, Peter (2015). *A Structural Atlas of the English Dialects*, London and New York: Routledge.
Britton, Derek (2002). 'Northern fronting and the north Lincolnshire merger of the reflexes of ME /uː/ and ME /oː/', *Language Sciences* 24: 221–229.
Britton, Derek and Keith Williamson (2002) (ms.). 'A review of *Northern Fronting* and its developments in England and Scotland', paper read at the 12th ICEHL, Glasgow, Scotland, 23 August 2002.
Campbell, Alistair (1959). *Old English Grammar*, Oxford: Clarendon Press.
Dobson, Eric (1968). *English Pronunciation 1500–1700*, Vol. I, 2nd edition, Oxford: Clarendon Press.
Girard Lomheim, Francine and Chantal Lyche (1991). *Phonétique et phonologie du français*, Oslo: Universitetsforlaget.
Gordon, Matthew J. (2001). *Small-Town Values and Big-City Vowels: A Study of the Northern Cities Shift in Michigan* [Publication of the American Dialect Society 84], Durham, NC: Duke University Press.
Hogg, Richard (2011). *A Grammar of Old English*, Volume 1: *Phonology*, Oxford: Blackwell.
Jones, Charles (1989). *A History of English Phonology*, London: Longman.
Jordan, Richard (1925). *Handbuch der mittelenglischen Grammatik: Lautlehre*, Heidelberg: Carl Winter Universitätsverlag.
Kitson, Peter (1998). 'Review Article of Kristensson 1995', *NOMINA* 21: 169–178.

Kristensson, Gillis (1967). *A Survey of Middle English Dialects 1290–1350. The Six Northern Counties and Lincolnshire*, Lund: CWK Gleerup.
Kristensson, Gillis (1987). *A Survey of Middle English Dialects 1290–1350: The West Midland Counties*, Lund: Lund University Press.
Kristensson, Gillis (1995). *A Survey of Middle English Dialects 1290–1350: The East Midland Counties*, Lund: Lund University Press.
Kristensson, Gillis (1997). 'The Old English Anglian/Saxon boundary revisited', in Jacek Fisiak (ed.), *Studies in Middle English Linguistics*, Berlin: Mouton de Gruyter, pp. 271–281.
Kristensson, Gillis (2001). *A Survey of Middle English Dialects 1290–1350: The Southern Counties. I. Vowels (except Diphthongs)*, Lund: Lund University Press.
Kristensson, Gillis (2002). *A Survey of Middle English Dialects 1290–1350: The Southern Counties. II. Diphthongs and Consonants*, Lund: Lund University Press.
Labov, William (1994). *Principles of Linguistic Change. Internal Factors*, Oxford, UK and Cambridge, MA: Blackwell.
Laing, Margaret (2008). *A Linguistic Atlas of Early Middle English*, University of Edinburgh (available at http://www.lel.ed.ac.uk/ihd/laeme2/laeme2.html).
Lass, Roger (1988). 'Vowel shifts, great and otherwise: Remarks on Stockwell and Minkova', in Dieter Kastovsky and Gero Bauer (eds), *Luick Revisited*, Tübingen: Gunter Narr Verlag, pp. 395–410.
Lass, Roger and Margaret Laing (2012). '"ea" in Early Middle English: From diphthong to digraph', in David Denison, Ricardo Bermúdez-Otero, Chris McCully and Emma Moore (eds), *Analysing Older English: Studies in English Language*, Cambridge: Cambridge University Press, pp. 75–117.
Liljencrants, Johan and Björn Lindblom (1972). 'Numerical simulation of vowel quality systems: The role of perceptual contrast', *Language* 48(4): 839–862.
Luick, Karl (1914–40). *Historische Grammatik der englischen Sprache*, Vol. I, Parts 1 & 2, Oxford: Basil Blackwell.
Luick, Karl (1932). 'Zur neuenglischen Lautgeschichte', *Archiv für das Studium der neueren Sprachen*, 1932: 89–90.
Lutz, Angela (2004). 'The first push: A prelude to the Great Vowel Shift', *Anglia*, 122(2): 209–224.
McCarthy, Corrine (2010). 'The Northern Cities Shift in Chicago', *Journal of English Linguistics* XX(X): 1–22.
McIntosh, Angus, Michael Samuels and Michael Benskin (1986). *A Linguistic Atlas of Late Mediaeval English*, Vols. I–IV, Aberdeen: Aberdeen University Press.
Martinet, André (1955). *Économie des changements phonétiques: traité de phonologie diachronique*, Bern: A. Francke.
Oxford English Dictionary Online (available at http://www.oed.com/).
Ringe, Don and Ann Taylor (2014). *A Linguistic History of English*, Volume 2: *The Development of Old English*, Oxford: Oxford University Press.
Ritt, Nicolaus (1994). *Quantity Adjustment. Vowel Lengthening and Shortening in Early Middle English*, Cambridge: Cambridge University Press.
Samuels, Bridget D. (2006). 'Nothing to lose but their chains: Rethinking vocalic chain shifting', BA thesis, Harvard University.

Sievers, Eduard (1968). *An Old English Grammar* [translated and revised by Albert Cook], Boston: Ginn.
Stenbrenden, Gjertrud F. (2010). 'The chronology and regional spread of long-vowel changes in English, c.1150–1500', PhD dissertation, University of Oslo.
Stenbrenden, Gjertrud F. (2016). *Long-Vowel Shifts in English, c.1050–1700: Evidence from spelling*, Cambridge: Cambridge University Press.
Stockwell, Robert P. (1985). 'Assessment of alternative explanations of the Middle English phenomenon of high vowel lowering when lengthened in the open syllable', in Roger Eaton et al. (eds.), *Papers from the 4th International Conference on English Historical Linguistics*, Amsterdam, Philadelphia: John Benjamins, pp. 303–318.
Stockwell, Robert P. and Donka Minkova (1988a). 'The English Vowel Shift: problems of coherence and explanation', in Dieter Kastovsky and Gero Bauer (eds), *Luick Revisited*, Tübingen: Gunter Narr Verlag, pp. 355–394.
Stockwell, Robert P. and Donka Minkova (1988b). 'A rejoinder to Lass', in Dieter Kastovsky and Gero Bauer (eds), *Luick Revisited*, Tübingen: Gunter Narr Verlag, pp. 411–417.
Wells, John C. (1982). *Accents of English*, Cambridge: Cambridge University Press.
Wright, Joseph and Elizabeth M. Wright (1925). *Old English Grammar*, Oxford: Oxford University Press.
Wright, Joseph and Elizabeth M. Wright (1928). *An Elementary Middle English Grammar*, Oxford: Oxford University Press.
Wyld, Henry C. (1914). *A Short History of English*, London: John Murray.
Zachrisson, R. E. (1913). *Pronunciation of English Vowels 1400–1700*, Göteborg: Wald. Zachrissons Boktryckeri.

7

The Development of Old English eo/ēo and the Systematicity of Middle English Spelling

Merja Stenroos

1. Introduction

This chapter presents a study of the spelling of words containing Old English *eo* and *ēo* in fourteenth- and fifteenth-century English texts. The main question considered is to what extent it is possible to find traces of a systematic distinction between the reflexes of Old English *e/ē* and *eo/ēo* in this period. To the extent that such traces can be found, a further question is whether they might reflect conservative spelling or the survival of distinct phonemes. This question involves central problems in the use of spelling as evidence for earlier English speech, in particular with regard to the interpretation of 'back-spellings' or unhistorical uses of a distinctive spelling unit.

Several fourteenth-century West Midland texts contain intriguing usages with regard to the distinction between Old English *eo/ēo* and *e/ē*, the two categories being distinguished in spelling to a remarkable extent, but always with exceptions, including back-spellings. Such texts include the well-known miscellany in BL Harley 2253, the compilation of (mainly) Romance texts in Lincoln's Inn 150 and the autograph poems by William Herebert in BL Add. 46919. The scribal practices of these texts are of considerable interest in their own right, and have been the subject of individual studies (McSparran 2000: *passim*; Stenroos 2005: *passim*, 2013: 174–175); however, in order to place these usages in context it will make sense to study them as part of a larger corpus. The present study is based on a corpus of fourteenth- and fifteenth-century English texts, *The Middle English Grammar Corpus* (MEG-C), version 2018.1.[1] The corpus covers all areas of England and a wide variety of genres and includes substantial samples of Harley 2253 and Lincoln's Inn 150, as well as the poems of William Herebert in their entirety.

In Old English, the spelling <eo> was used to correspond to (at least) two distinct vowels: a long diphthong and a short vowel that has traditionally also been considered a diphthong. The long diphthong was a development of Germanic *eu and appeared in several high-frequency words, such as *bēon* 'be', *sēon* 'see', *frēo* 'free' and *hēo* 'she'.

---

[1] See http://www.uis.no/meg-c.

The short vowel forms part of a group of 'short diphthongs', also including the vowels usually spelt <ea> and <ie>, which seem to have been the result of various sound changes, most importantly breaking and back mutation (see e.g. Campbell 1959: 54–57, 85–90). Both the realisation and the phonological status of these Old English 'short diphthongs', *ea*, *eo* and *ie*, have been controversial.[2] Minkova (2014: 180) suggests that the realisations of these three vowels, in comparison with the equivalent short monophthongs (*æ*, *e*, *i*) are 'best analysed as "not-yet-integrated semi-contrasts", a status half-way between a phoneme and an allophone (Goldsmith 1995: 12)' rather than fully phonemic entities.

It is assumed in the following discussion that, with the possible exception of <eo> following palatal consonants (*geolu* 'yellow', *geol(o)ca* 'yolk', etc.), both the long and the short vowels spelt <eo> were distinct from those spelt <e> or <o>, whether this distinction was fully contrastive or the kind of semi-contrast suggested by Minkova. This assumption is, however, in no way a prerequisite for the study, but may rather be reviewed in light of the results. Because of the controversial status of the sounds, the Old English spoken categories are here referred to using 'philological notation' rather than phonemic or phonetic symbols.

According to most textbooks, all the Old English diphthongs were monophthongised in late Old English. The *eo* diphthongs are assumed to have become front rounded vowels, sometimes referred to using the IPA symbol [ø]. Eventually they merge either with /e(:)/ or, less commonly, /o(:)/.[3] This development seems to take place at very different rates in different parts of the country. In the northern and East Midland varieties it may have started already in the late Old English period. The *Ormulum*, written around 1200 in Lincolnshire, contains regular <eo> spellings until line 13,000, after which Orm changes to <e> and systematically goes back to delete the <o> from the earlier spellings; this is usually taken to indicate that the merger had taken place either in his own system or in that of speakers around him.

The distinction seems to remain longest in the South-West Midland area. Most earlier scholars have suggested that the rounded vowels survived here until the fourteenth century (cf. Brook 1935: 16, Sundby 1963: 144; Kristensson 1987: 159, 2002), while Jordan (1968: 86 [1925]) suggests that they might have remained in some areas until the fifteenth. Lass (1992: 54) also took the latter view:

> By the early to mid-twelfth century, judging by the testimony of the *Peterborough Chronicle* ... /ø(:)/ had unrounded in the north and east ... This is clear from the confusion of <e> and <eo> ... In the south-west, west midlands and much of the central midlands, on the other hand, both rounded categories remained unchanged into Middle English, and in one form or another persisted into the fifteenth century.

This view, however, was later contested by Lass and Laing (2005: 289) who find no conclusive orthographic evidence for the existence of distinct front rounded vowels in

---

[2] An excellent summary of the various viewpoints is provided by Hogg (1992: 16–24).

[3] Lass and Laing (2005: 289) have suggested that this merger takes place already at the diphthong stage, with no intervening rounded monophthong stage.

Middle English. Instead, they suggest that the Old English *eo* words may simply have gone in two directions from an early stage – some merging with long and short *e*, and some with long *o*:

> The standard story in which /e(:)o/ first monophthongised to a mid front rounded vowel which remained in the West is unnecessarily complex ... All we need to account for subsequent orthographic and phonological developments is a variable split of the diphthongs in which some reflexes merged with those of /e(:)/ and others merged with those of /o(:)/.
> (Lass and Laing 2005: 289)

Lass and Laing find a large amount of spelling variation in Early Middle English, with <eo> as a particularly volatile element; because of this, they do not find grounds for assuming a distinct vowel in Early Middle English that relates to the spelling <eo>.[4] I would like to suggest in the present chapter that the late Middle English evidence presents a different picture, which indicates that the vowel of most Old English *eo* words remained distinct from both *e* and *o* into the later Middle English period in at least some spoken varieties in the West Midland area, and that the written distinction may have become an identity marker for West Midland scribes.

2. Interpreting the evidence: Back-spellings and mergers

For the study of historical sound change, virtually the only evidence available for the Middle English period is derived from spelling: there are no orthoepic writings or detailed comments about accents. The value of Middle English spelling as evidence for the study of phonology is, however, a highly complex issue. Middle English spelling is, of course, highly variable, and local spelling traditions may be assumed to have a closer relationship to the spoken system than most standardised writing systems have today. However, Middle English writing cannot be expected to represent transcriptions of speech: as with any writing, it is based on conventions of its own, and the orthographic variation will reflect other factors besides phonology.

In the last decades, in the tradition of a *Linguistic Atlas of Late Mediaeval English* (LALME, McIntosh, Samuels and Benskin 1986), it has become usual to study spelling variation from a completely orthographic point of view, without any reference to the spoken mode. McIntosh (1956: *passim*, 1963: 24) suggested that, in order to study the details of variation in the written mode, we have to study it as written language: in other words, different spellings, such as *it* and *yt* 'it', should be distinguished in the analysis whether or not they reflect differences in speech. This was an important methodological point in a period when Middle English dialects were identified mainly on the basis of the reconstruction of phonemic systems.

At the same time, the LALME team did not suggest that one should not enquire

---

[4] In the same study, Lass and Laing presented a corresponding argument about Old English *y(:)*, suggesting that it also did not survive as a front rounded vowel into Middle English. This argument has been addressed and to some extent refuted by Stenbrenden (2016: 270–273).

into the phonology behind the written forms: such enquiries simply belong to another level of analysis. Much of the published research connected to the successor project of LALME, a *Linguistic Atlas of Early Middle English* (LAEME, Laing 2008–) focused on spellings as evidence of sound change (see e.g. Laing 1999; Laing and Lass 2003; Lass and Laing 2005, 2016), and this is indeed the focus of the ongoing FITS Project at the University of Edinburgh (see Chapter 4 in this volume). It may be argued that, in order to make sense of spelling variation, as opposed to simply describing it, we have to take into account the spoken system as well; on the other hand, as a research direction in its own right, the study of historical sound change has to take into account the nature of the written evidence. The view taken in the present study is that variation in one mode is not intrinsically more important or interesting than in the other: however, the ways in which we interpret their interaction are central to our understanding of the developments in both modes.

The interpretation of spelling as evidence of pronunciation inevitably works differently in the case of different writing systems. Scholars dealing with periods of language with an identifiable written standard make use of spelling mistakes as evidence of sound change. The classical evidence of phonemic mergers consists of reverse spellings, or 'back-spellings': for example, spellings such as *whater* and *wistle* suggest that the consonants spelt <wh> and <w> respectively have merged in the writer's spoken variety. In a classic article first published in the 1950s, Penzl (1969: 16) formulated this as a rule: 'Orthography indicates phonemic mergers and their results, e.g., by noncontrastive use of two formerly contrasting symbols or by the use of one symbol instead of two initial ones ... Reverse or inverse spellings ... always indicate a phonemic coalescence.'

This kind of evidence, however, is not quite straightforward to evaluate in the Middle English materials, as the absence of a standard model makes the concept of 'spelling mistake' problematic. The earliest Early Middle English texts already seem to show evidence of the distinction between *eo* and *e* being lost, even in the phonologically conservative South-West Midland area. An example of what seems like a very clear back-spelling is found in Cambridge, MS Trinity College 323 (fol. 45v):

Ne mai no mon tellen / hu lodliche is þe qued
Wose lokede him on / of drede **heo** were deed
'No man can tell how loathsome the Devil is
Whoever looked at him, **(s)he** would be dead from fear'

Assuming that the spelling *heo* does not represent a rather unlikely 'generic *she*', the traditional interpretation of the spelling would be that the reflexes of Old English *eo* and *e* are no longer distinguished. However, another possible interpretation of such spellings has been suggested by Margaret Laing (1999: *passim*; see also Laing and Lass 2003), who has developed the concept of 'litteral substitution sets'.

In a variable writing system such as that of Middle English, a single spelling may relate to several different phonemes (or *potestates*, to use the classical terminology employed by Laing and Lass); conversely, the same phoneme (or *potestas*) may be realised by several different spellings. Once two spellings come to be seen as interchangeable in one context they may be interchangeable in other contexts as well:

We thus have the possibility in Middle English that a single *figura* may do service for three *litterae* and therefore may imply also any of the different possible *potestates* of those *litterae*. The logical extension of this phenomenon is the reverse process that many different *figurae* ... may be employed to realise the same *potestas* ... It is apparent that considerable numbers of permutations and combinations of spellings are potentially available to scribes for certain sounds or groups of sounds. (Laing 1999: 256–257)

Assuming that the reflexes of Old English *eo/ēo* remained distinct categories in the West Midland area, scribes would certainly have learnt that <e> was an acceptable spelling corresponding to these sounds. By the late thirteenth century, the distinction had certainly disappeared in most other varieties, and any scribe who came in contact with texts written elsewhere would have encountered mostly <e> spellings in these. In the areas where the two phonemes were still distinct, this might have led to a situation where <eo> and <e> could be used interchangeably for two different sounds. That similar developments took place in the Middle English period is shown by spellings such as *ȝoroȝ* and *thorth* 'through', and the remarkable reference to *our modir kyrke saynt petir of thork* in a Yorkshire text (Cambridge University Library Ee.iv.19, fol. 91r; see Jensen 2012). There are no indications that the initial and final consonants of 'through' would have merged in any spoken variety, nor that /j/ would have merged with the dental fricative; instead, the spellings seem to indicate a complex chain of litteral substitutions, both <th> and <ȝ> being interchangeable with <y> in at least some contexts (cf Benskin 1982: 20–21).

Litteral substitution sets, while a highly useful concept, can be problematic as explanations as they are in principle endless. Laing and Lass (2005: 287–289) themselves illustrate this problem well in their presentation of a seemingly chaotic range of spellings of Old English *eo* in the thirteenth century, something that leads them to conclude that the distinction between *eo* and *e* had not survived Old English. It might, however, be argued that the complex picture that emerges from the Early Middle English materials reflects the relative isolation in which much English writing took place during this period, with a low density of networks in which more uniform conventions could develop. It should, therefore, be useful to consider the evidence in the later Middle English period, when materials are much more plentiful and spelling variation is less extreme.

3. The study: Material and methodology

This study is based on the MEG-C, compiled at the University of Stavanger.[5] MEG-C consists of diplomatic transcriptions of texts mapped in LALME, produced either from the manuscript or from facsimile reproductions, and covers the period 1325–1500. The present version of the corpus, 2018.1, consists of 490 texts. Short texts are

---

[5] MEG-C is available as an open access resource at www.uis.no/meg-c. The current published version is 2011.1, which contains 410 texts; the version used in the present study, 2018.1, will be published during 2018.

provided in their entirety while longer texts are provided in samples of 3,000 words; the corpus contains altogether 778,602 words.

This version of MEG-C contains approximately half the texts mapped in LALME. It is somewhat geographically skewed with regard to the number of texts (235 northern, 162 western, 93 eastern); however, as the northern texts are on average much shorter than the eastern ones, the distribution is much more even in terms of word count (western 311,112; northern 240,823; eastern 226,667). The texts include a wide range of genres, from legal documents and letters to literary works, religious writings and medica.

All texts are referred to with a code consisting of the letter L followed by the LALME Linguistic Profile (LP) code, made up to a four-digit number by prefixing zeros as needed. The abbreviated county label is also given for each texts, e.g. Herefs L7330. Further information about the texts, including their shelfmarks and contents, is available either in the MEG-C catalogue or, using the LALME LP code, in the LALME/eLALME Index of Sources.

The corpus has been searched using the concordancing programme AntConc 3.2.1, which allows both searching for specific strings and scrolling down an alphabetic list of words in order to identify all the spellings of a particular item. Two searches were carried out, approaching the survival of *eo/ēo* from different angles: the spelling of words that had the sound historically, and the actual distribution of <eo> in the material.

For the first search, a questionnaire was compiled, consisting of twenty-seven items that contain a vowel representing either Old English *eo/ēo* or the equivalent Old Norse element, *jó*:

BE (inf. and pres.pl.), BEAR (inf. and pres.pl.), DARK, DEAR, DEEP, DEVIL, EARL, EARTH, FAR, FIEND, FLEE (inf. and pres.pl.), FREE, FRIEND, HEART, HEAVEN, KNEE, LEARN, LEOF, MEEK, PRIEST, SEE, SEVEN, SHE, STAR, TEEN, THIEF, TREE

The list was designed to collect data for both the long and short Old English vowels in different phonotactic environments. In the selection of items, words with forms that could reflect different etymologies were avoided (e.g. LOSE reflecting Old English *lēosan* or *losian* and CHOOSE reflecting Old English *cēosan* or Old French *choisir*). In addition to the Old English words, one word of Old Norse origin, MEEK (ON *mjúkr*) was included; the Old Norse element seems to have become identified with *ēo*, and forms of MEEK appear commonly in Early Middle English with <eo> spellings. The list includes a few items where <eo> spellings in Old English were dialectally restricted, most notably words with potential *eo* from back mutation, such as BEAR, DEVIL, HEAVEN, SEVEN, TEEN.

This search was designed to find out to what extent the *eo/ēo* words in the material show distinctive orthographic patterns. The findings are correlated with geographical location and approximate date. It is important to note here that, for most of the texts in MEG-C, neither location nor date is based on direct historical evidence. The LALME localisations, which are used here, are based on linguistic similarities using the 'fit-technique'; they do not necessarily reflect the place where the text was produced, but rather indicate its position in a reconstructed dialect continuum (Williamson 2000: 119–120; for a description of the technique, see Benskin 1991: *passim*). For the most part, however, it makes sense to assume that the texts localised in a particular place may have been produced in that general area, or produced by scribes from that area.

Many of the dates are based on palaeographical assessment, and are therefore approximate. The dates were collected for MEG-C by the present writer from a wide variety of sources, including catalogues and editions of various dates; as they are not derived from a unified assessment, and are generally approximate, the chronological findings can only be indicative of very general patterns.

The second search was carried out to collect all the <eo> spellings in the corpus, irrespective of which words they appeared in. This search makes it possible to see the whole range of historical *eo/ēo* words in which these spellings appear, as well as to map out the uses of these digraphs in the material, including unhistorical or 'back'-spellings. Together, the searches should provide a reasonably nuanced picture of the development of Old English *eo/ēo* in the late Middle English materials.

The conventions used to refer to spoken and written units are as follows: the etymological sound categories (Old English *eo/ēo*) are given in italics, while Middle English sound categories are given in phonemic brackets (/e:/). Spelling units, whether single letters or di- or trigraphs, are indicated by angled brackets (<eo>).

4. The first search: How were Old English *eo/ēo* words spelt?

4.1 The general distribution of spelling units in the corpus

The first search makes clear that the reflex of Old English *eo/ēo*, in so far as it remained distinct, was certainly not a marginal phoneme: the questionnaire constructed for the study includes several highly frequent words. The search for the twenty-seven words listed above returned as many as 16,877 tokens. Of these, the vast majority (15,724, or 93 per cent) show spellings with <e> or <ee>.

Altogether fifteen different spelling units appear in the material. As Table 7.1 shows, <e> is by far the most common spelling unit for the reflex of Old English *eo/ēo*, both in terms of tokens and distribution: it appears in virtually all texts in the corpus. The second most common spelling unit in terms of texts, <ee>, appears throughout the period and in all geographical areas; it is mainly – but not exclusively – confined to the long vowel, appearing in FLEE, FREE, SEE, TREE (but never BE).

Only 1,062 tokens show a spelling that might suggest a pronunciation with a rounded vowel: <eo>, <o>, <oe>, <oy>, <u> and <ue>. The most frequent of these in terms of texts is <o>. With the exception of one instance of *horte* HEART (Gloucs L6980), all the instances of this spelling represent SHE: *scho* and *sho* appear in fifty-six texts altogether, virtually all of which are localised to the northern or North-West Midland counties, while *ho* appears in six texts, all of which are localised in the North-West Midlands. The rare spelling unit <oy> only appears in *schoy* (YWR L0415b and L0415j).

The spelling <u> is similarly restricted in function. Out of its sixty-seven occurrences, sixty are forms of *buth/buþ* ARE, appearing in fifteen texts all of which are

Table 7.1 Spelling units used for the vowel element in the twenty-seven questionnaire items: Number of texts and tokens and distribution in terms of items

Spelling unit	Number of texts	Number of tokens	Lexical items
<a>	28	62	*far, dark, harte*
<e>	487	15,385	All the questionnaire items
<ee>	120	339	*feer, flee, meek, see, tree,* etc.
<ei>	1	2	*theif*
<eo>	36	543	*beo, beore, deorke, deor, deop, deouelis, eorl, eorthe, feond, fleo, freo, freond, heorte, heouene, kneo, leorne, leof, meoke, preost, seo, heo, teone, theof, treo,* etc.
<ey>	5	6	*theyf*
<i>	2	2	*prist(e)*
<ie>	2	13	*priest(e), thief*
<o>	59	327	*scho, ho, horte*
<oe>	1	81	*boe, boeth, oerþe, doere, froendes, hoeuene, moeke, proest, hoe, stoerre, toene, troe,* etc.
<oy>	2	3	*schoy*
<u>	17	67	*buþ, frunde(s), lurne*
<ue>	1	41	*buen, duere, huerte, luef, hue*
<y>	4	5	*frynd(e)*
<ye>	1	1	*fryend*

localised in the south and west, from Staffordshire and Wales to the north and west to Sussex in the east. It may be noted that all except one of these texts are dated to the fifteenth century, and the spelling is thus not an early one. Apart from *buth/buþ*, <u> appears only in two West Midland texts (Shrops L4239 and Warwicks L4682), in the words *frunde(s)* FRIEND(S) and *lurne* LEARN respectively.

The spellings <eo> and <oe> both appear for a very wide range of the questionnaire items. The <oe> spelling, however, only appears in the poems of William Herebert (Herefs L7410), where it is the majority spelling variant in Old English *eo/ēo* words, besides less frequent <eo> and <e> (cf. also Stenroos 2005: 297–300). Together with <e>, the digraphs <eo> and <oe> are the only spelling units in the material that seem to be used universally in Old English *eo/ēo* words: they appear in thirty-six texts altogether and 538 tokens, representing all the questionnaire items except FAR and SEVEN. Like <oe>, the spelling <ue> is restricted to one text, the Harley 2253 miscellany (Herefs L9260), where it also varies with <eo> and <e> and appears in several items.

Finally, ninety-one tokens show other spellings: <a> is found exclusively before <r> in FAR, DARK, HEART and <ei>, <ey>, <i>, <ie>, <y>, <ye> in occasional forms such as *theif, feynd, heyuen, prist, priest, frynd, fryend*. All these spellings appear in fifteenth-century texts or (in two cases) in texts dated to the end of the fourteenth century, and may be assumed to relate to later developments unrelated to the survival of Old English *eo/ēo*.

Of the spellings that might indicate rounding, the <o> and <u> spellings are clearly lexically limited: both are frequently occurring forms that appear in a large number of texts, but are virtually restricted to the items SHE and ARE respectively. With regard to SHE, Laing and Lass (2014: 224–228) explain the vowels in *s(c)he* and *s(c)ho* (as well as *ho*) as the straightforward result of the merger of Old English *ēo* with either *ē* or *ō*. As they also point out, the geographical spread of the <o> forms is completely different from that of the other spellings of Old English *eo/ēo* that suggest rounding, and they may accordingly be considered a separate development.

The forms *buth/buþ* ARE only seem to become common at a relatively late stage: the earlier texts in the present material that show spellings indicating rounding tend to show either *beoþ/beon* or *boeth*. As they also seem to represent a different development from the other items in terms of their distribution, they have not been included in the overall findings presented in the following.

4.2 The South-West Midland core area: The distribution of <eo> type spellings

Of all the spelling units found in the corpus, only <eo> and <oe> are used generally for Old English *eo/ēo* words, rather than being restricted to specific lexical items. The former may also be the case with the digraph <ue> found in Harley 2253. As both <oe> and <ue> seem to appear as variants of <eo> in individual texts, they are here subsumed in the same category: all three spelling units will be referred to in the following as '<eo> type spellings'. The occasional spellings <u> in *frunde(s)*, *lurne* and <o> in *horte* are also included in the below counts, as they appear to indicate rounded vowels and are found in the same area as the <eo> type. Conversely, all spellings which do not indicate rounding are referred to as <e> type spellings.

Altogether, <eo> type spellings are found in the material for all but two of the questionnaire items (FAR and SEVEN). The proportions of <eo> type spellings vary between lexical items; however, the usages of individual texts are so different that it is difficult to discern general patterns. It may simply be noted that the words which show few or no <eo> type spellings tend to belong to two groups: short vowels followed by [r] except in homorganic clusters (FAR, HEART, BEAR; although EARTH shows a high proportion of <eo> type spellings) and a back-mutation environment (SEVEN, HEAVEN, DEVIL).

The <eo> type spellings of the questionnaire items make up a total of 665 tokens and are found in a total of thirty-five texts. All these texts are localised in a well-defined area consisting of nine counties, making up what might be called a slightly extended version of the 'traditional South-West Midland area': Berkshire, Gloucestershire, Herefordshire, Oxfordshire, Shropshire, Staffordshire, Warwickshire, Wiltshire and Worcestershire (see Figure 7.1).[6]

---

[6] It might be noted here that the *buth/buþ* type forms of ARE appear over a somewhat larger area, which includes the same nine counties but stretches to Wales in the west and Hampshire and Sussex to the south.

Figure 7.1 The counties where texts with <eo> type spellings are localised in LALME (map outline: Abigail Brady)

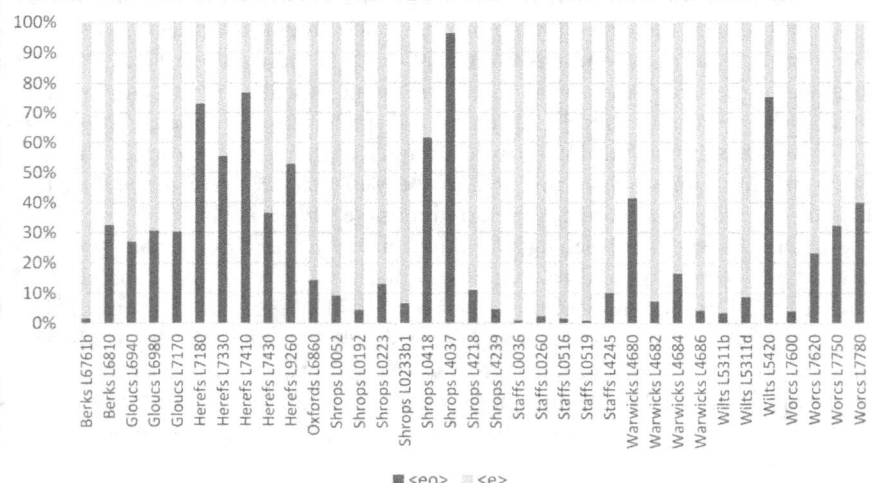

Figure 7.2 Proportions of <eo> and <e> type spellings of Old English *eo/ēo* words in those texts in which <eo> type spellings appear, arranged according to county

Figure 7.2 shows the proportions of <eo>- and <e> type spellings in the thirty-five texts, sorted according to county. It may be noted that the westernmost counties, Gloucestershire, Herefordshire and Shropshire, show relatively high numbers of texts and high proportions of <eo> type spellings, while the presence of <eo> in Staffordshire and Oxfordshire is marginal, and the figures for Berkshire and Warwickshire are relatively low. At least in relation to the LALME localisations, the distribution of <eo> type spellings thus shows a very clear geographical pattern, the highest frequencies within individual texts correlating with locations to the west, adjoining to the Welsh Marches.

In Black (1999), the present writer carried out a study of SHE in texts which LALME localised to Herefordshire. In this material, <eo> spellings for *heo* SHE were retained much longer than they were in any other item. It was suggested that, for functional reasons, the written form *heo* was retained as a distinctive written form, given that the merger of *ēo* and *ē* had made the masculine and feminine pronouns identical in speech; *heo* may therefore have continued to be used for a long period after the merger. Given this initial evidence, it may be worth enquiring into whether the distributions would look very different if the item SHE is excluded altogether. Having done this for the current study, it was found that eight of the thirty-five texts show <eo> type spellings for SHE only, reducing the overall number of texts with <eo> type spellings to twenty-seven. As Figure 7.3 shows, the exclusion of this frequent *ēo* word does make a difference to the proportional frequencies; however, the overall pattern is not dramatically different, especially with regard to those texts which have high proportions of <eo> type spellings.

One might ask, then, how these thirty-five texts compare with the overall data from the nine counties. The patterns here must be treated with caution, as they are not based on statistically sound samples: the MEG-C/LALME samples are necessarily based on the availability of linguistically localisable texts, and the materials for different counties vary considerably both in quantity and date range.

As might be expected, given the generally late date of the material, the <eo> type spellings are less frequent than <e> type spellings even in the nine South-West Midland counties: they appear in 33 per cent of the texts localised in this area

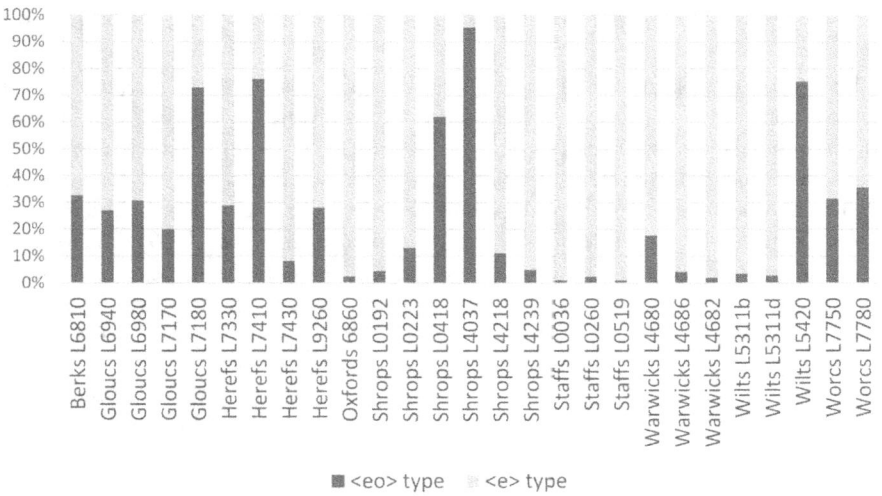

Figure 7.3 Proportions of <eo> and <e> type spellings of Old English *eo*/*ēo* words (not including SHE) in those texts in which <eo> type spellings appear, arranged according to county

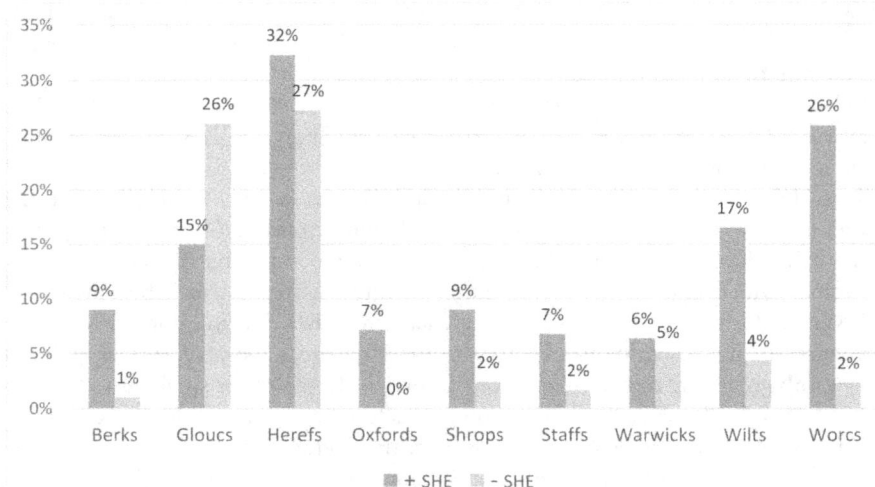

Figure 7.4 The distribution of <eo> type spellings in texts localised in the nine South-West Midland counties (average of proportional figures per text)

and make up 13 per cent of the overall tokens. Figure 7.4 shows the proportional frequency of <eo> spellings in the nine counties. The overall figures confirm the concentration of such spellings in the western part of the area. Gloucestershire and Herefordshire clearly appear as the counties with most <eo> spellings. The comparatively low figures for Shropshire reflect the fact that Shropshire texts in MEG-C (and LALME) are generally of a later date than those localised in Gloucestershire and Herefordshire, and they include a high number of late texts with no <eo> spellings at all.

The chronological spread of the MEG-C Corpus is nearly two centuries, from the early fourteenth to the second-half of the fifteenth century. Figure 7.5 shows the distribution of <eo> type spellings in the nine South-West Midland counties over the four half-centuries of this time period.[7] Again, it is clear that leaving out SHE makes a difference; however, there is no indication of a general survival of *heo* spellings alone, as was suggested by the Herefordshire material studied in Black (1999). The overall trend, unsurprisingly, is that <e> type spellings increase in frequency; however, it may be noted that the figures for the first and second halves of the fifteenth century are remarkably even, showing that the <eo> type spellings linger on for a very long time, even when restricted to a very small proportion of the texts.

Perhaps the most interesting point about this development is that the <eo> type spellings are not restricted to occasional forms in the fifteenth-century material: even in the latter part of the century, they are still found in substantial numbers within individual texts. Figures 7.6 and 7.7 show the thirty-five texts in approximate chrono-

---

[7] Here, eighteen texts had to be omitted from the calculations as they could not be placed within a specific half-century.

THE DEVELOPMENT OF OLD ENGLISH eo/ēo   145

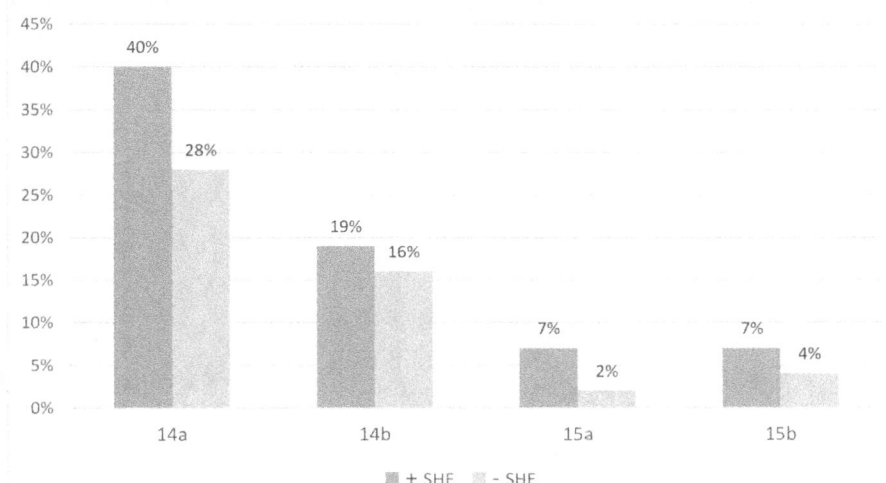

Figure 7.5 The distribution of <eo> type spellings per half-century (average of proportional figures per text)

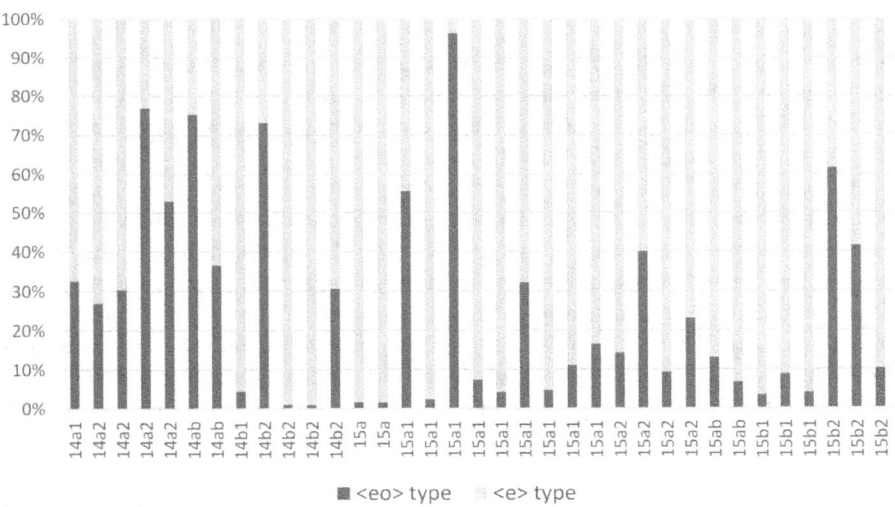

Figure 7.6 Proportions of <eo> and <e> type spellings of Old English *eo/ēo* words in those individual texts in which <eo> type spellings appear, arranged according to (approximate) quarter-century

logical order, including and omitting SHE respectively. It should be remembered here that the dating is very approximate, and the detailed order of the texts is for the most part arbitrary: however, given the wide chronological scope, the broad placing of the texts should be reasonably reliable. It is clear that there is no unidirectional decrease over time in the proportional frequency of <eo> type spellings: some of the latest

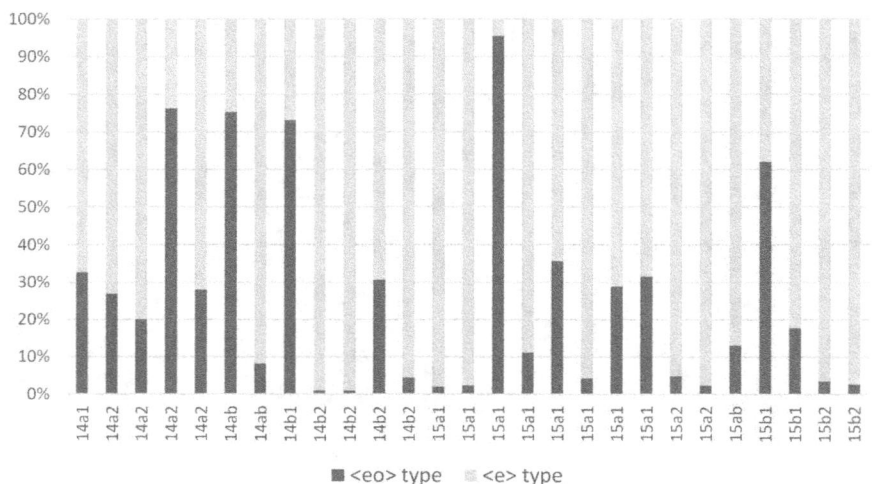

Figure 7.7 Proportions of <eo> and <e> type spellings of Old English *eo/ēo* words (not including SHE) in those texts in which <eo> type spellings appear, arranged according to (approximate) quarter-century

texts in the material still show substantial proportions of them. It is also notable that the retention of the <eo> type is no less solid when SHE is omitted (cf. Figure 7.7): the survival of the spellings throughout the fifteenth century does not simply represent the conventional use of *heo* for functional reasons.

As Figures 7.3, 7.4, 7.6 and 7.7 show, the proportion of <eo> type spellings varies considerably from text to text. A 100 per cent distinction between the historical categories would not be expected in this type of material at any point during the Middle English period: by far most of the texts are the result of scribal copying and may show relict usage from exemplars, especially in the case of rhyming usage (for the term 'relict', see LALME: vol. I, 13). In addition, the lexical distribution of the categories would have varied even in Old English, and lexical diffusion may be expected in the progress of the change. As Figure 7.8 shows, however, several texts show a remarkably high proportion of <eo> type spellings.

Those fourteen texts which show a proportion of more than 30 per cent <eo> type spellings (including SHE) are listed in Table 7.2. It may be noted that the proportions for some texts vary considerably depending on whether data for SHE are included in the count or not: thus, L4680 and L7430 turn out to include very small proportions of <eo> type spellings apart from *heo*. However, for most of the texts, including the five highest scorers, the inclusion of SHE makes little or no difference.

The one text that stands out is Lincoln's Inn 150 (Shrops L4037), which shows a virtually complete retention of <eo> type spellings for the Old English *eo/ēo* words. This is particularly remarkable as this manuscript is dated to the early fifteenth century. The other texts with high rates of <eo> type spellings show a very broad date range, and mainly consist of manuscripts of large works intended for reading for

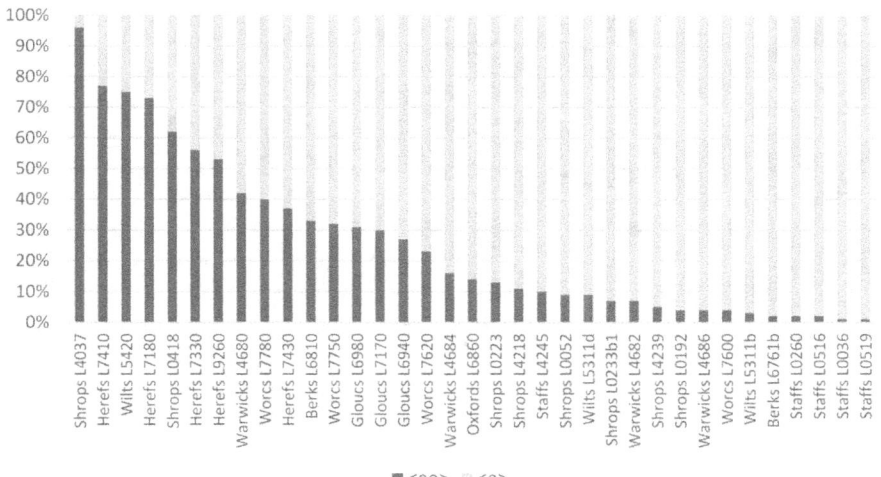

Figure 7.8 Proportions of <eo> and <e> type spellings of OE *eo/ēo* words in those texts in which <eo> type spellings appear: Comparing the individual texts

improvement and entertainment, such as the *Prick of Conscience*, the *South English Legendary* and *Piers Plowman*. Interestingly, however, they also include a Shropshire lease from the late fifteenth century.[8] While several of the texts are copies of the *Prick of Conscience* and the *South English Legendary*, both these texts were extremely popular works and the manuscripts listed here are not particularly closely related. Accordingly, it is very unlikely that there might be a single textual source that would account for the high proportion of <eo> spellings in these particular texts.

It therefore appears that <eo> type spellings survive well into the fifteenth century, not only as occasional relicts but as fairly frequent variants in a varied group of texts. The spellings do not, of course, prove that a phonemic distinction was retained in the speech of this area. In order to make any inferences about the function of the spellings and their possible connection with spoken developments, more context is needed: most importantly, the entire distribution of the spellings should be taken into account. Earlier work has shown that some of the high-scoring <eo> texts, in particular Lincoln's Inn 150 (Shrops L4037), contain several unhistorical <eo> spellings (Stenroos 2005: 302–304, 2013: 174–175); clearly, these have to be considered together with the high number of historical spellings.

5. The second search: Which words were spelt with <eo>?

The aim of the second search was to identify all the actual occurrences of the digraph <eo> in the corpus. No attempt was made to follow up the other, minor units, <o>, <oe>, <u> and <ue>: apart from the two frequent lexical items discussed above (SHE

---

[8] For a brief discussion of this text, see Stenroos (2016: 119–120).

Table 7.2 The texts with the highest proportion of <eo> type spellings

Code	Shelfmark	<eo> +SHE (%)	<eo> – SHE (%)	Content	County	Date
L4037	London, Lincoln's Inn, Hale 150	96	95	Miscellany	Shrops	15a1
L7410	London, BL Add. 46919	77	76	Poems of William Herebert	Herefs	14a
L5420	Canterbury, Cathedral Archives and library, Lit. D.13 (66), fols 1r–144v	75	75	Prick of Conscience	Wilts	14ab
L7180	London, BL Cotton Cleopatra D ix. Hand A, fols 153v–155v	73	73	South English Legendary	Herefs	14b
L0418	London, PRO E 40/7587	62	62	Lease	Shrops	15b1
L7330	Oxford, Bodleian Digby 171	56	29	Piers Plowman C	Herefs	15a1
L9260	London, BL Harley 2253	53	28	Miscellany	Herefs	14a2
L4680	London, BL Harley 875. Hand A, fols 1r–8v	42	18	Piers Plowman A	Warwicks	
L7780	Huntington Lib, San Marino, HM 125	40	36	Prick of Conscience	Worcs	15a1
L7430	London, BL Cotton Cleopatra D ix, hand of fols 156r–167	37	8	South English Legendary	Herefs	14ab
L6810	Cambridge, CCC 145. Hand A, fols 1–210r	33	33	South English Legendary	Berks	14a1
L7750	Oxford, Bodleian Laud Misc 463	32	32	South English Legendary	Worcs	15a1
L6980	Oxford, Bodleian Laud Misc 601. Main hand, fols 1r–115v	31	31	Prick of Conscience	Gloucs	14b2
L7170	Oxford, Bodleian Ashmole 43	30	20	South English Legendary	Gloucs	14a2

and ARE), these spelling units show up rarely as forms of Old English *eo/ēo*, but are instead used frequently in other functions; there is accordingly little point in pursuing them here.

As the MEG-C Corpus is not tagged for morphemes, the search returns all occurrences of adjoining *e* and *o*; the first task was therefore to remove all occurrences of <eo> that cross morpheme boundaries, as in *thereof*. The remaining data consist of 1,147 tokens altogether. These may be divided into five categories:

- Names (*George, Symeon, Theodir, Greogory*): 56
- Spellings of French or Latin loanwords (*dungeon, feoffament, people*): 115
- Reflexes of words with Old English *eo/ēo* or ON *jó*: 834
- Unhistorical spellings: 142

The majority of the names and the loanwords, by far, represent uses where <eo> is conventional and expected in the Middle English context; however, there are very occasional examples of unexpected <eo>: so *laureole* 'laurel', *gregory* 'Gregory' and *galeon* 'Galen'. It is, however, the last two categories that are of most interest here.

The historically 'correct' spellings, that is, those representing the reflexes of Old English *eo/ēo* or ON *jó*, form by far the largest group of <eo> spellings, with 834 tokens. Apart from the twenty-five items covered by the questionnaire survey, they represent a further fifty-six lexical items that may be plausibly identified as Old English *eo/ēo* words:

> *aneowe* 'anew', *beode* 'bede', *bleo* 'blee', *breost* 'breast', *byneoþe* 'beneath', *by-tweone* 'between', *by-ʒeonde* 'beyond', *cheose* 'choose', *cleos* 'claws', *deol* 'dole', *eorldom* 'earldom', *feo* 'fee', *feol* 'fell', *feole* 'fele', *feorþe* 'fourth', *forleose* 'forlose', *gleo* 'glee', *heold* 'held', *heole* 'hide', *heorde* '(shep)herd', *heore* 'their', *heom* 'them', *heowe* 'hue', *kneowe* 'knew', *leode* 'lede', *leofly* 'lovely', *leom* 'leam', *leoned* 'leaned', *leop* 'leapt', *leor* 'leer', *leose* 'lose', *leouede* 'left', *leoynge* 'lying', *meode* 'meed', *neore* 'near', *reod* 'reed', *reowe* 'rue', *seolf* 'self', *seoluer* 'silver', *seothe* 'since', *sheowe* 'show', *sweordes* 'swords', *teon* 'teen', *theodɜ* 'thede', *theose* 'these', *þreo* 'three', *þreow* 'threw', *weole* 'weal', *weop* 'wept', *weopen* 'weep', *weoryour* 'worthier', *ʒeode* 'went', *ʒeold* 'yielded', *ʒeon* 'yon', *ʒeorne* 'yern', *ʒeorsterday* 'yesterday'

While the <eo> spellings in the first two categories are distributed around the entire country, all except two of the remaining spellings, *leoynge* 'lying' (YWR L0406) and *þeo* 'the' (YWR L0592), appear in forty-six texts localised to the same area as the <eo> type spellings of the questionnaire items considered in 4.2: the nine counties of Berkshire, Gloucestershire, Herefordshire, Oxfordshire, Shropshire, Staffordshire, Warwickshire, Wiltshire and Worcestershire (see Figure 7.1).

The second search thus confirms that both historically expected <eo> type spellings for OE *eo/ēo* words and unhistorical spellings are confined to texts localised in a limited area in the South-West Midlands. It is finally time, then, to turn to the unhistorical spellings.

At first sight, 142 unhistorical spellings may seem a large number. However, it turns out that by far most of them, 116 tokens, are found in a single text: the same text that contains the largest number of historical <eo> type spellings, Lincoln's Inn 150 (Shrops L4037). However, the Lincoln's Inn scribe does not use <eo> indiscriminately in all contexts: 107 of the 116 tokens represent two forms: *þeo* 'the' and *weore(n)* 'were'. In addition, the following forms appear in the text: *daweos, eowel, hundreod, neo* 'nor', *seot* 'sat', *wolleoþ* 'will'.

The remaining unhistorical spellings in the material are found in twelve texts and include the following forms:

beo-howeþ 'behoves', *beord* 'burde', *deorne* 'dern', *deorste* 'dared', *eon* 'eyes', *feor, feore* 'fire', *greot* 'great', *sheweode* 'showed', *strengeore* 'stronger', *sonne-beom* 'sunbeam', *þeo* 'the', *weore* 'were'

By far most of these 'unhistoric' spellings seem to fit into three categories:

- Vowel following <w>: *weore(n), weorne*
- Old English *y/ȳ* words: *eowel, beord, feor(e), deorne*
- Unstressed syllables: *beo-howeþ, daweos, hundreod, wolleoþ, sheweode, strengeore* and the normally unstressed words *neo, þeo*

For all these three groups, a spelling indicating a rounded pronunciation would be plausible. A preceding <w> has a general rounding effect on the following vowel, which commonly becomes fully or partly phonemicised (cf. e.g. Minkova 2014: 239–240). The alternation of *wil* and *wol* throughout the Middle English period is an example, and William Herebert's poems (Herefs L7410) show spellings such as *woe, woepinge*.

What seem like crossovers of spelling between Old English *eo/ēo* and *y/ȳ* words in the Early Middle English period have been commented upon by several scholars. Sundby (1963: 146) suggested that the two rounded front vowels, the reflexes of Old English *eo/ēo* and *y/ȳ*, may have merged in some south-western dialects, and Lass (1992: 55) suggests that the reflexes of *eo/ēo* may sometimes have been raised (cf. also Ek 1972: 121). William Herebert's poems (Herefs L7410) show spellings such as *doede* 'did', *moeche* 'much' and *stoede* 'stead', all in words that might show either <e> or <u> in texts localised in the same area. In Stenroos (2005) it was suggested that these spellings might be seen as a way of indicating rounded vowels by a writer whose own spoken system might have had an /e/ in these words (Stenroos 2005: 303). Whatever the precise explanation for the emergence of such spellings may be in each case, once <eo> and <u> became interchangeable in some contexts it would be conceivable for them to enter into a litteral substitution set where they signaled vowel roundness. Such a substitution set would also make sense of the form *deorste* for expected *durste* 'dared' (L5420).

In texts localised to the western area, unstressed syllables – in particular, inflectional suffixes – are very frequently spelt with <u>, a spelling convention that appears in documentary texts at least up to the early sixteenth century (Stenroos forthcoming). It is normally assumed that these spellings indicate a rounded or central quality of the unstressed vowel. Once <eo> and <u> were used interchangeably in some contexts, expanding the use of <eo> to unstressed contexts would be natural. The spelling *þeo* would, in addition, provide a useful written distinction between *þeo* 'the' and *þe* 'thee'.

This argument certainly does not imply that every scribe using <eo> spellings would have rounded front vowels in their own spoken system. Rather, their use might indicate an awareness that spellings indicating rounding were appropriate or expected in certain words. What is notable about the data here discussed is, indeed, the almost complete restriction of <eo> spellings to very well-defined sets: the historical contexts as well as the three groups identified above, for all of which there are good indications of pronunciations with rounded vowels. Only three 'back-spellings' remain: *seot* 'sat', *greot* 'great', *sonne-beom* 'sunbeam'.

In their study of Early Middle English spellings of reflexes of Old English *eo/ēo* and *y/ȳ*, Lass and Laing (2005) constructed diagrams of sound-spelling mappings, showing that the <eo> spellings mapped onto a large number of etymological categories; they suggest that it 'would certainly be difficult to make a case for the graph <eo> being tied to any particular ancestral OE category'. The same would clearly be the case here, if one were to construct such mappings on the basis of all words spelt with <eo>. At the same time, regular sound-spelling correspondences need not be biunique, and the extension of spelling units to other functions does not cancel earlier mappings.

In addition, quantities (which Lass and Laing did not consider in the 2005 paper) clearly play a role. The three 'back-spellings', added to a diagram of sound-spelling mappings, would certainly introduce chaos. Conversely, given the merger of *eo/ēo* and *e/ē* in the great majority of varieties of English at the time and the general fluidity of Middle English spelling practices, the presence of only three such forms might be considered a low figure indeed. Admittedly, we should not forget *greogory*, *galeon* and *laureole*, only one of which, however, appears in the core <eo> area.[9]

The search for <eo> spellings shows that the functions of <eo> in late Middle English were partly geographically restricted, and remarkably consistent. Throughout the country, <eo> appears in names and in French or Latin loanwords. In the South-West Midland area (defined as the nine counties shown in Figure 7.1), it maps onto the following spoken elements:

- Reflexes of OE *eo/ēo* or ON *jó*
- Unstressed vowels
- Other rounded vowels, especially ones that vary with /e(:)/

6. Discussion

The final question, then, is to what extent it is feasible to assume a systemic distinction between the reflexes of Old English *e/ē* and *eo/ēo*. It is certainly true that few texts show anything like a complete distinction; on the other hand, the completely regular written realisation of a regionally restricted contrast is hardly to be

---

[9] *Laureole* appears in Staffs L0357; here, the <eo> might indicate a rounded unstressed vowel. The other two spellings appear in Ches L0246 and Lincs L0492 respectively.

expected, as Middle English spelling and scribal transmission require us to calculate with noise.

A sizeable group of texts show a high proportion of distinctive spellings: in seven texts, more than half the occurrences of the Old English *eo/ēo* words included in the present questionnaire are spelt using a distinctive spelling, almost always the historical <eo>. While unhistoric <eo> spellings do occur, by far most of them are used for a clearly defined group of vowels that would plausibly be pronounced with roundness; only a handful of forms cannot be explained in such a way. The thirty-six texts in total that show <eo> type spellings for the questionnaire items are localised within a limited geographical area, but range across the entire timespan of the study, suggesting a local tradition that is not limited to individual texts or scribes.[10]

Does this tradition reflect a conservative spelling habit or the survival of distinct phonemes? If we take the strict view that back-spellings always indicate phonemic merger, then we have to assume that the <eo> type spellings are a purely orthographic convention – at least in those texts where the back-spellings occur. However, other evidence suggests quite strongly that Middle English spelling simply does not work like this. The example of *saynt petir of thork* suggests that back-spellings could take place simply as a matter of letter substitution; whatever route the scribe took to arrive at this spelling, it certainly does not reflect the merger of /j/ and /θ/.

The retention of <eo> spellings does not necessarily indicate the survival of phonological categories, any more than the present-day use of <wh> spellings does. It could be suggested that, since many of the words included in the first search are very frequent, they might show regular orthographic distinctions that no longer correspond to speech. Such a retention of traditional spellings might work in a community where texts (in the same language) are read intensively and continuously, and could be expected especially if the spellings have some kind of status or identity-marking function. It was suggested in Stenroos (2013) that <eo> spellings might have functioned as regional identity markers in the aristocratic communities of the Welsh Marches, even if they no longer mapped onto a distinct spoken category (see Stenroos 2013: 176–177). The kind of texts which show a high retention of <eo> type spellings in the present material would seem to fit this kind of context very well: most of them are large miscellanies or copies of sizeable texts, manuscripts produced for local patrons rather than working texts.

However, the remarkable accuracy with which the spellings continued to be used throughout the time period, even in less frequent words, would seem unlikely if the distinction had completely disappeared from the spoken mode. The wide range of Old English *eo/ēo* words – altogether eighty-five lexical items – which appear with <eo> type spellings, and the almost total lack of <eo> spellings outside contexts where rounded vowels may be expected, suggest that the speakers who produced these texts

---

[10] It should also be noted that the sample of South-West Midland texts in MEG-C is very far from exhaustive even in terms of the LALME coverage. Another text with a high frequency of both historical <eo> spellings and spellings such as *þeo* 'the' is the Wycliffite lectionary in Longleat, Marquess of Bath's MS 5 (Herefs L7520; see Stenroos 2013: 167–171); so far this text has not been included in MEG-C, largely because it is a nightmare to transcribe.

cannot have been far from a living distinction, even if the usage of some of the texts might reflect the tail end of an S-curve. In other words, while it is not possible to show that any of the scribes themselves retained the spoken distinction, the extent to which the <eo> spellings are historically predictable might suggest that the phonemic distinction remained in some spoken systems well into the fifteenth century.

Accordingly, it is suggested here that the <eo> type spellings in the fourteenth and fifteenth centuries were actively used in the South-West Midland area for several different purposes. Scribes who did not retain the distinction in speech might have used <eo> spellings to disambiguate between what would otherwise have been homographs (*he/heo* and perhaps *þe/þeo*), while scribes both with and without the spoken distinction would have catered for the expectations of an audience, followed learnt writing conventions and, perhaps, signalled a specifically western identity. What the scribes clearly did not do was scatter <eo> spellings around their texts indiscriminately; as with late Middle English spelling in general, their output was variable but certainly not chaotic.

References

Benskin, Michael (1982). 'The letters <þ> and <y> in later Middle English, and some related matters', *Journal of the Society of Archivists* 7: 13–30.
Benskin, Michael (1991). 'The fit-technique explained', in Felicity Riddy (ed.), *Regionalism in Late Medieval Manuscripts and Texts*, Cambridge: D. S. Brewer, pp. 9–26.
Black, Merja (1999). 'Parallel lines through time: Speech, writing and the confusing case of *she*', *Leeds Studies of English* 30: 59–81.
Brook, George L. (1935). *English Sound-changes*, Manchester: [no publisher named].
Campbell, Alistair. (1959). *Old English Grammar*, Oxford: Clarendon.
Ek, Karl-Gustav (1972). *The Development of OE y and eo in South-Eastern Middle English*, Lund: Gleerup.
eLALME = *An Electronic Version of A Linguistic Atlas of Late Mediaeval English* (2013), compiled by Michael Benskin, Margaret Laing, Vasilis Karaiskos and Keith Williamson, University of Edinburgh (available at http://www.lel.ed.ac.uk/ihd/elalme/elalme.html).
Goldsmith, John (1995). 'Phonological theory', in John Goldsmith (ed.), *The Handbook of Phonological Theory*, Oxford: Blackwell, pp. 1–23.
Hogg, Richard M. (1992). *A Grammar of Old English, vol. I: Phonology*, Oxford: Blackwell.
Jensen, Vibeke (2012). 'The consonantal element (th) in some late Middle English Yorkshire texts', in Jukka Tyrkkö et al. (eds), *Outposts of Historical Corpus Linguistics: From the Helsinki Corpus to a Proliferation of Resources*, Helsinki: VARIENG.
Jordan, Richard (1968 [1925]). *Handbuch der mittelenglischen Grammatik: Lautlehre*, 3. Auflage, Heidelberg: Carl Winter Universitätsverlag.
Kristensson, Gillis (1987). *A Survey of Middle English Dialects 1290–1350: The West Midland Counties*, Lund: Lund University Press.

Kristensson, Gillis (2002). *A Survey of Middle English Dialects 1290–1350: The Southern Counties II: Diphthongs and Consonants*, Lund: Lund University Press.
LAEME = *A Linguistic Atlas of Early Middle English, 1150–1325*, version 3.2, 2013 [version 2.1, 2008], compiled by Margaret Laing with accompanying software by Keith Williamson, University of Edinburgh (available at www.lel.ed.ac.uk/ihd/laeme2/laeme2.html).
Laing, Margaret (1999). 'Confusion *wrs* confounded: Litteral substitution sets in Early Middle English writing systems', *Neuphilologische Mitteilungen* 100: 251–270.
Laing, Margaret and Roger Lass (2003). 'Tales of the 1001 nists: The phonological implications of litteral substitution sets in 13th-century South-West-Midland texts', *English Language and Linguistics* 7(2): 1–22.
Laing, Margaret and Roger Lass (2014). 'On Middle English *she, sho:* A refurbished narrative', *Folia Linguistica Historica* 35(1): 201–240.
LALME = *A Linguistic Atlas of Late Mediaeval English*. 1986, compiled by Angus McIntosh, Michael L. Samuels, and Michael Benskin, Aberdeen: Aberdeen University Press. Now available as: eLALME.
Lass, Roger (1992). 'Phonology and morphology', in Norman Blake (ed.), *The Cambridge History of the English Language, vol. 2: 1066–1476*, Cambridge: Cambridge University Press, pp. 23–155.
Lass, Roger and Margaret Laing (2005). 'Are front rounded vowels retained in West Midland Middle English?', in Nikolaus Ritt and Herbert Schendl (eds), *Rethinking Middle English: Linguistic and Literary Approaches*, Frankfurt am Main: Peter Lang, pp. 280–290.
Lass, Roger and Margaret Laing (2016). 'Q is for WHAT, WHEN, WHERE?: The 'q' spellings for OE hw-', *Folia Linguistica Historica* 37(1): 61–110.
McIntosh, Angus (1956). 'The analysis of written Middle English', *Transactions of the Philological Society* 55(1): 26–55.
McIntosh, Angus (1963). 'A new approach to Middle English dialectology', *English Studies* 44: 1–11.
McSparran, Frances (2000). 'The language of the English poems: The Harley scribe and his exemplars', in Susanna Fein (ed.), *Studies in the Harley Manuscript: The Scribes, Contents, and Social Contexts of British Library MS Harley 2253*, Kalamazoo: Medieval Institute, Western Michigan University, pp. 391–426.
MEG-C = *The Middle English Grammar Corpus*, version 2011.1 (2011), compiled by Merja Stenroos, Martti Mäkinen, Simon Horobin and Jeremy J. Smith, University of Stavanger (available at www.uis.no/meg-c).
Minkova, Donka (2014). *A Historical Phonology of English*, Edinburgh: Edinburgh University Press.
Penzl, Herbert (1957). 'The evidence for phonemic changes', in Ernst Pulgram (ed.), *Studies Presented to Joshua Whatmough on his Sixtieth Birthday*, The Hague: Mouton, pp. 193–208. Reprinted in Roger Lass (ed.) (1969). *Approaches to English Historical Linguistics: An Anthology*, New York: Holt, Rinehart and Winston, pp. 10–24.
Stenbrenden, Gjertrud F. (2016). *Long Vowel Shifts in English, c. 1050–1700: Evidence from Spelling*, Cambridge: Cambridge University Press.

Stenroos, Merja (2005). 'Spelling conventions and rounded front vowels in the poems of William Herebert', in Nikolaus Ritt and Herbert Schendl (eds), *Rethinking Middle English*, Frankfurt am Main: Peter Lang, pp. 291–308.

Stenroos, Merja (2013). 'Identity and intelligibility in late Middle English scribal transmission: Local dialect as an active choice in fifteenth-century texts', in Esther-Miriam Wagner, Ben Outhwaite and Bettina Beinhoff, *Scribes as Agents of Language Change*, Berlin: Mouton de Gruyter, pp. 159–182.

Stenroos, Merja (2016). 'Regional language and culture: The geography of Middle English linguistic variation', in Tim Machan (ed.), *Imagining Medieval English*, Cambridge: Cambridge University Press, pp. 100–125.

Stenroos, Merja (forthcoming). 'The "vernacularisation" and "standardisation" of local administrative writing in late and post-medieval England'.

Sundby, Bertil (1963). *Studies in the Middle English Dialect Material of Worcestershire Records*, Bergen: Norwegian Universities Press.

Williamson, Keith (2000). 'Changing spaces: Linguistic relationships and the dialect continuum', in Irma Taavitsainen et al. (eds), *Placing Middle English in Context*, Berlin: Mouton, pp. 141–179.

8

Examining the Evidence for Phonemic Affricates: Middle English /t͡ʃ/, /d͡ʒ/ or [t-ʃ], [d-ʒ]?

Donka Minkova

1. The segment or sequence problem in phonology

This study takes a close look at a case in the history of English which illustrates what Hayes (2009: 55–57) has dubbed 'the segment or sequence problem': when are two adjacent phonetic units to be analysed as a single segment?[1] This long-standing question (e.g. Jones 1918 [1922]: 22–23; Hockett 1958: 109 ff.) can arise both with sequences involving vowels and with consonantal sequences. To frame the issue for diachronic English, and assuming that choices made by poets and their scribes reflect their linguistic competence, their 'internalized grammar', the examples in (1) highlight some sequence-segment options in Middle English (ME):

(1) Ambiguities in ME scansion:
    a. Now makes *moyses* him boun
       Als drightin tald him his lessun
       'Now Moses makes him(self) ready
       As the Lord told him his lesson'
       (*Cursor Mundi* 5843–4)

       "Lauerd," said *moyses*, "wil i tru
       þat pharaon sal me mistru."
       '"Lord," said Moses, "I (will) believe
       that Pharaoh shall distrust me"'
       (*Cursor Mundi* 5807–8)

---

[1] Many thanks to the organisers of the First AMC Symposium (2016), to the editors of this volume, and to two deeply erudite and helpfully thorough anonymous reviewers of my draft submission. Most of their comments are gratefully incorporated; the editors and the reviewers cannot be incriminated in any remaining empirical or analytical faults and misdemeanors.

b. time...he tok : child
    (*William of Palerne* 4674)
    & chased . . . chaunce : child
    (*William of Palerne* 216)[2]

Cursor Mundi illustrates a transitional stage in the adaptation of classical Latin *Mōÿsēs*, Old English and ME *Moyses, Moises* 'Moses'. In (1a) *mɔyses* in line 5843 is trisyllabic, while in line 5807 *moyses* has to be disyllabic, suggesting that the recently borrowed /oi/ diphthong was still peripheral to the system.[3] In the strictly alliterative *William of Palerne* in (1b) the <ch-> of *child* alliterates with [t] in line 4674, while in line 216 (and elsewhere in the poem) it self-alliterates on either a cohesive sequence [tʃ] or a singleton [t͡ʃ].

Discrete units and single segments have distinct phonological properties and effects, so a decision on the segment or sequence problem relates directly to larger questions concerning the evolution of the phonological system, the sources and mechanisms of innovation, and the research methodology in the absence of live speakers' judgements. The study presented here is part of a larger-scale project on tracking the phonological vicissitudes of sequences vs. segments. After some necessary background on the properties of English affricates today, section 2 addresses their behaviour in Old English (OE). Section 3 turns to the evidence for affrication in ME, and section 4 proposes an account of phonemic affrication as an interaction of factors, including Old French and Anglo-Norman influence. The findings are summarised and discussed in section 5.

1.1 Affricates in Germanic and Present-Day English (PDE)

(2) Defining the properties of affricates:
     Affricates are stops in which the release of the constriction is modified in such a way as to produce a more prolonged period of frication after the release . . . the class of affricates has no sharp boundaries. Affricates are an intermediate category between simple stops and a sequence of a stop and a fricative.
     (Ladefoged and Maddieson 1996: 90)

'Intermediate' categories are analytical challenges, suggesting diachronic instability; they also raise the question of how common such categories are. The answer depends on affricate type and on where one is looking: within the older Germanic languages

---

[2] William of Palerne, *An Alliterative Romance*, ed. G. H. V. Bunt, Groningen: Bouma's Boekhuis, 1985, dated c.1340. Line 4674 is cited in Schumacher (1914: 155).

[3] Cited from British Library, Cotton Vespasian A iii (Morris 1874–93). For the record: Orm always treats *Moyses* as trisyllabic (e.g. *þatt Moysœs iss Jesu Crist / þatt ledde þurrh himm sellfenn* 'that Moses is Jesus Christ / who led by himself' (1482-3)), while Chaucer always treats it as disyllabic (e.g. *Of craft of rynges herde they neuere noon / Saue þat he Moyses / and kyng Salomon* (*Squire's Tale* 248–9)) 'They had never heard of ring-craft / except that he Moses and king Solomon'; the full treatment of such loans in ME verse needs to be fully examined.

only Old Frisian and OE are reconstructed as having the palato-alveolar affricates /tʃ/ and /dʒ/. Old and Middle Welsh did not have affricates (Willis 2009), nor did Old Irish, nor does Scots Gaelic. Among all the modern Germanic languages only the newer contact languages Yiddish and Afrikaans have palato-alveolar affricates, and for Modern German the phonemic status of /tʃ/ and especially of /dʒ/ is controversial; the voiced affricate is found only in loanwords.[4] This makes English somewhat of an oddball within its own family.

Strangely, this oddity within Germanic is not paralleled by distributional facts across the world's languages, 45 per cent of which have /tʃ/, though its voiced counterpart is rarer (Ladefoged and Maddieson 1996: 90). In terms of cross-linguistic 'naturalness', therefore, palato-alveolar affricates are unexceptional.

Within English, affricates are among the less frequent consonants. In PDE the overall frequency of occurrence of the affricates is quite low, as shown in Table 8.1.

Table 8.1 Texts frequencies of consonants in General British: percentages of consonants among all phonemes and among consonants only (adapted from Cruttenden 2014: 235). Total all consonants: 60.6 per cent

	% All	% C		% All	% C
/n/	7.62	12.59	...	...	...
/t/	6.95	11.49	/g/	0.99	1.64
/s/	4.79	7.92	/ʃ/	0.89	1.46
/d/	4.63	7.65	/dʒ/	0.62	1.02
/l/	3.79	6.26	/tʃ/	0.47	0.78
/r/	3.57	5.79	/θ/	0.47	0.78
...	...	...	/ʒ/	0.07	0.42

The overall frequency of /dʒ/ is slightly above that of /tʃ/. Only /ʒ/ is rarer than the identically frequent /tʃ/ and /θ/. Similarly, Knowles' phoneme frequencies (1987: 224) show 0.63 for /dʒ/, 0.57 for /θ/ and, even lower, 0.53 for /tʃ/, see also Hammond (1999: 127) and Hayes (2011) for comparable frequency rankings. However, if we look at the word-final frequencies (Muthmann 1999: 404; Hayes 2011), the frequency of affricates in relation to other consonants is significantly different (Table 8.2).

Word-finally /-dʒ/ and /-tʃ/ are slightly below the mid-range, and in onset position they are even more prominent (Table 8.3).
These numbers are not just trivia about the PDE consonants: arguably, the discrepancy between overall occurrence and occurrence at word edges is something that may

---

[4] In some analyses of German only /ts/ and /pf/ are fully phonemically contrastive affricates. Kohler (1990) treats [tʃ] and [dʒ] as allophones, while Prinz and Wiese (1991) argue that all stop-fricative combinations in German are potential phonological affricates. For a commentary on Prinz and Wiese see Rákosi (2014). My understanding of the consonantal system of Modern Frisian based on Hoekstra (2001) is that it does not have phonemic affricates.

Table 8.2 Frequencies of word-final consonants in English (percentages from Muthmann 1999: 404.) Total all word-final consonants: 84.92 per cent

	%		%		%
/-t/	13.71	/p/	2.09	/-g/	0.69
/-n/	11.41	/-v/	1.42	/-θ/	0.64
/-r/	AE 9.81	/-f/	0.98	/-b/	0.53
/-s/	9.49	/-d͡ʒ/	0.98	/-ð/	0.09
/-l/	8.98	/-t͡ʃ/	0.93	/-ʒ/	0.08
/-d/	7.75	/-ʃ/	0.74	/-x/	0.01
...	...	...	...	...	

Table 8.3 Frequencies of word-initial consonants in English (percentages from Hayes 2011)

	%		%		%
/s-/	14.28	...	...	/θ-/	0.76
/k-/	11.07	/d͡ʒ-/	1.73	/z-/	0.27
/p-/	9.55	/ʃ-/	1.34	/ð-/	0.22
/d-/	7.87	/j-/	0.99	/ʒ-/	0.01
/r-/	7.19	/t͡ʃ-/	0.94		

need to be factored into the phonemicisation of the affricates. Another observation based on the frequencies in Tables 8.1–8.3 is that in PDE the voiceless and the voiced members appear to stay together as a subset, yet /d͡ʒ/-/t͡ʃ/ is the only obstruent pair in English in which the voiced member is more frequent; the 'usual' ratio is in favour of the voiceless member, e.g. /t/ > /d/, /ʃ/ > /ʒ/. This reversal of the relative density of voiced-voiceless is another potential indication of the affricates' compositionality. The frequencies are also meaningful in conjunction with the number of minimal pairs: the functional load of the affricates in initial and final position is very strong: *choke:joke*; *cheap:jeep*; *chin:gin*; *age:<h>*; *besiege:beseech*; *liege:leech*; *splodge:splotch*; *bulge:mulch*.

1.2 PDE affricates as contour segments

By way of a reminder, accounts of PDE affricates agree on the functional coherence of the phonetic sequence of stops + fricatives.[5] The autosegmental representation of contour segments is shown in (3):

---

[5] This subsection and section 2 draw on some material included in Minkova (2016).

(3) The structure of contour segments:

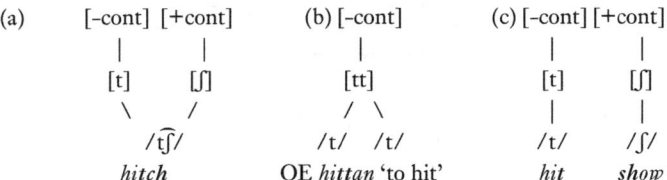

Only (3a) is a singleton; (3b) and (3c) are sequences.[6] The arguments in favour of a unitary treatment are solid: distribution, possibilities of commutation of the elements, native speaker's reaction and speech errors, all identified in Cruttenden (2014: 188 ff.). One additional argument, not included in the list of phoneme vs. sequence criteria for affricates, is acquisition: as reported in Lleó and Prinz (1997) and Gierut and O'Connor (2002), affricates are acquired late, after singletons, but before clusters. Affricates in onset position are acquired before affricates in coda position. Moreover, their acquisition does not depend on 'the prior acquisition of the plosives and fricatives of which they are composed ... in particular the fricative /ʒ/ may be of later occurrence than the affricate /dʒ/, perhaps due to its comparative low frequency of occurrence in the adult language' (Cruttenden 2014: 191).

The early acquisition of singletons against the lateness of affricates and clusters is attributed to the simplicity of non-branching vs. branching structures. Branching occurs on the tier above the segmental level in the contour segment in (3a), while the branching in sequences (3c) is pervasive. Branching, of course, is a representational abstraction needed to account for segment-internal 'edge' effects showing that the components are independently active.

(4) Edge effects of the components of /t͡ʃ/ and /d͡ʒ/ in PDE:

- Feature [-continuant] for [t] independently active in aspiration: [tʰɪp] – [t͡ʃʰɪp]
- Glottal reinforcement and replacement of [t]: [tiː?t͡ʃɪn], [kaʊ?ʃ][7]
- Feature [+strident] for [ʃ] and [ʒ] independently active, matching [s] and [z]
- Omission of [t, d], but not of [ʃ, ʒ] in adjacent affricates[8]
- No initial C + [t͡ʃ, d͡ʒ] or [t͡ʃ, d͡ʒ] + C[9]

---

[6] The most appropriate phonological representation of affricates is still under discussion, see Hall (2012) who discusses alternative representations of affricates, including the Strident Stop Representation, which makes the wrong prediction of affricates patterning only with sibilant fricatives cross-linguistically. The choice between the other two representations, the Contour Segment Representation and the Complex Segment Representation, is in favour of the Contour Representation because of the attested edge effects as in (4).

[7] /p, t, k/ are '... generally subject to reinforcement only when a consonant follows; and to glottal replacement of the [t] element alone' (Cruttenden 2014: 187).

[8] *Much choice* can be realised as [mʌʃ t͡ʃɔɪs] and *large jar* as [lɑːʒ d͡ʒɑː], but omission of the fricative element is unacceptable (Cruttenden 2014: 192).

[9] On /tr, dr/ see also Cruttenden (2014: 192).

All of the edge effects are phonotactically conditioned realisations: aspiration in stressed syllable onset as in *chip*, blocking of adjacency of [+strident], as in *matches*, *bulges*, blocking of adjacency of dental stops as in *mu*ch ch*oice* [mʌʃ t͡ʃɔɪs] and *large* j*ar* as [lɑːʒ d͡ʒɑː], not *[mʌt t͡ʃɔɪs], *[lɑːd d͡ʒɑː], avoidance of cluster complexity.

The precariousness of the boundary between segment and sequence is reflected in the purely durational properties of affricates with [t͡ʃ] and [d͡ʒ] exceeding all singletons in length, but shorter than the sequences [tʃ] and [dʒ] (see Table 8.4 in section 3).

Neither the edge effects nor the greater intrinsic duration of the PDE affricates alter their categorisation as structural singletons; they function like other singletons in the language.

A related observation, not used as a test for the unitary nature of the affricates in the sources that I am familiar with is that the phonotactics of medial intervocalic affricates are practically identical with the liquids /l/ and /r/.[10] They appear before short *and* long vowels freely, except after the 'foreign' /oi/: *lychee, hygiene, debauchery, fraudulent, voucher, gouging, emoji*, even a borrowed *koi-cha* 'tea' (Japanese). Medial clusters, on the other hand, are much more phonotactically restricted. With reference to internalised grammar it is of note that even an astute, basically quantitative poet like Gerald Manley Hopkins, who recognised the syllable weight effect of subphonemic quantity in e.g. *bi*d vs. *bi*t (Kiparsky 1989), did not scan intervocalic affricates as different from any other singleton.

This is how the phonetics and the phonology play out in PDE. For a volume on historical dialectology, the inherited affricates show a rather flat and uniform picture. Areal differences do not challenge the singleton treatment of affricates, in spite of persistent 'edge effects', as in the ongoing variation of [d͡ʒ] ~ [ʒ] in g*enre, adagio, beige* (Cruttenden 2014: 84, 94, 190). There is also both a regional (Caribbean English) and a social dimension, the 'democratisation' of English, in the current expansion of acceptability of affricates for /tr-/, /dr-/ in e.g. *trees, draw*. The variability of [t-j, d-j] ~ [t͡ʃ, d͡ʒ] is a sociolinguistic marker: in General British and American English it is well attested in unaccented syllables, as in *culture, impromptu, soldier, obdurate*, as well as in stressed onsets as in *Tuesday, during*. In 'Conspicuous' General British (Cruttenden 2014: 81), on the other hand, the orthographic <t->, <d-> + [-j], in, for example, *statue, mature, gradual, endure*, continue to be realised as a sequence.

2. Pre-Conquest affricates?

The affricates /t͡ʃ/ and /d͡ʒ/ are regularly included in the OE consonantal inventories, yet dating the reanalysis from stop-fricative sequences to singleton contrastive phonemes remains unaddressed. Another set of questions which bear further scrutiny are the possible discrete stages in the process of velar affrication. Looking at the voiceless velar first: the velar palatalisation ((VP)) entry in CoNE recognises the challenge and admits that it 'glosses over much controversy and complication, including the relationship of the palatalisation with the associated affrication and assibilation'.

---

[10] Pace Hammond (1999: 126–7) who considers -ɔːt͡ʃ-, -ʌɪt͡ʃ-, -aʊd͡ʒ-, -ɔɪt͡ʃ- (author's transcription) as non-occurring.

Crucially, the very extensive and admirably judicious CoNE discussion of the gradualness of velar palatalisation – assibilation – affrication identifies the core 'segment or sequence' problem:

(5) The segment or sequence problem in CoNE:
... we take the palatalisation + assibilation cluster as 'unitary' for the sake of etymologies, but with the background assumption that there was at least one 'intermediate stage' that we need to reconstruct. Thus *k > [tʃ] is a shorthand for (probably) at least *k > *c > [tʃ]. There are probably other stages in between, but we prefer to leave conceptual holes where there is no evidence enabling recovery, and collapse what was almost surely a longer sequence without making up any changes *ex vacuo*. (CoNE, Velar Palatalisation)

Contrary to the consensus in many existing accounts, Minkova (2016) argues that assibilation of the velars continued to be subphonemic in OE at least to the end of the OE alliterative tradition, which goes underground after 1066.[11] The absence of fully assibilated unitary /t͡ʃ/ is based on the continuing identity of the voiceless velars in alliteration and on the behaviour of intervocalic velars with respect to syllable weight:

(6) Palatalised and non-palatalised voiceless velars in alliteration ([k]:[c]:[c^j]):[12]
cynedom 'kingdom' : *ciosan* 'choose'
(*Beowulf* 2376, c. 725)

acennedne 'born' : *cildes had* 'childhood'
(*Guthlac B* 1361)

Hi on Choreb *swylce* : *cealf ongunnan*
'They in Choreb thus : began the calf'
(*Paris Psalter 105*:61)[13]

clene Cudberte 'clean Cudbert' : *cildhade* 'childhood'
(*Durham* 16, c. 1100, em. Holthausen)

From the earliest poetic records to the dated late poems, the palatalised and the non-palatalised initial velar stops were paired in alliteration. The tradition disallows cross-phonemic alliteration, and the cohesive sequences [st-, sp-, sk-] always alliterate with

---

[11] Van Langenhove (1930: 75) sided with earlier sceptics on the dating (Sweet, Wyld, Kaluza, and others) and concluded that 'Even with regard to the eleventh century it seems to me that the indications at our present disposal are momentarily not sufficient to admit as an indisputable fact the beginnings of dentalization + assibilation of OE palatal stops.'

[12] The notation [c^j] (a palatalised palatal) is unorthodox; the modifier is intended as a placeholder for the future fricative. A possible alternative would be a voiceless alveolo-palatal sibilant modifier [ɕ], i.e. [cɕ].

[13] Text from the middle of the eleventh century (Fulk 1992: 414).

each other (Minkova 2003), which makes it probable that if the poets were treating [cj-]/[ce-] as unitary, they would prefer self-alliteration. This does not rule out [cj-]/[ce-] : [k] alliteration completely, nor does it preclude ongoing allophonic palatalisation and assibilation *[k] > [c] >[cʲ]/[cᶜ-] in the right environments. It does, however, suggest strongly that the palatal realisations of the etymological */k-/ in late OE were not internalised as a new contrastive unit.

The [c] ~[cʲ]/[cᶜ-] option for */k-/ is testable in the metrical treatment of the voiceless velar in terms of syllable weight.

(7) Treatment of V̆<c>V in verse:
   Hē æfter recede wlāt (w w w S-w w s)
   'He looked at the hall'
   (*Beo* 1572b)

   for micelnysse (w S-w s w)
   'for greatness'
   (*Judgment Day II* 186b)[14]

   þæt he micel āge (w w S-w s w)
   'that he much should possess'
   (*Exhortation* 38b)

   wudafæstern micel (S-w s w s-w)
   'wood-shelter big'
   (*Durham* 6b)

Resolution, the metrical equivalence of a stressed heavy syllable and a stressed light syllable + another syllable (marked as S-w) in items such as *reced* 'building', *micel* 'much', is required in the verses in (7). Medial clusters block resolution, therefore the metrical evidence for a singleton medial consonant is incontrovertible. Whether the singleton was a palatal stop or a unitary affricate cannot be entirely determined just on the basis of metrical resolution, but cumulatively, as summarised in (8), the evidence is in favour of a palatal stop:

(8) Palatal stop vs. affricate <c> in late OE:

   • Alliterative pairing in late verse, see (6)
   • Inherent duration of affricates
   • Paradigmatic alternations: *micla, miclan, miclum* with [-k-]
   • Scandinavian-influenced North, North-East Midlands variation [c] ~ [k]

Perceptually, the inherent duration of contour affricates, which exceeds the duration

---

[14] *Judgment Day II*, as well as *Exhortation to Christian Living* are 'demonstrably late' (Fulk 1992: 264).

of all other consonants (see Table 8.4), would be a factor in their continuing status as singletons. Paradigmatic and dialectal variation would also inhibit the reanalysis. These considerations plus the ME situation addressed in sections 3 and 4 make it highly improbable that the singleton which licenses resolution in (7) is phonemically a unitary, contour voiceless affricate.

The interpretation of word-final <-c>: *brēc* 'breeches', *rīc-* 'rich', *blēc* 'bleach', *bræc* 'breach', but also *ec* 'eke', *lec* 'leak(y)', *rec* 'reek' in ME allows [c] ~[cʲ]/[cᵉ] and possibly an assibilated sequence (see Lass and Laing 2013). Specifically for *rich*: 'In the early OE runic form *riicnæ* (from the inscription on the Ruthwell Cross (*c*700)) the stem-final consonant is spelt with a *cēn* -rune, indicating palatalization and assibilation of the original velar plosive /k/' (*OED* under *rich*, adj.).

Turning to the voiced affricate: the OE voiced and assibilated velars result either from West Germanic gemination stem-finally, or from post-nasal assibilation as in PrG, as in **sangjan*, OE *sengan* 'singe'.

(9) Sources of OE voiced velar assibilation: [*g(g)] > [ɟ(ʝ)]/[ɟ(j)] > [(?)dʒ][15]
     Goth. *bugjan*   OE *by*cgan '*buy*'
     PrG **brugjō-*   OE *bry*cg 'bridge'
     PrG **sangjan*   OE *sengan* 'singe'[16]

Although [dʒ] is also commonly included in the OE consonantal inventories (Minkova 2013: 75 puts it in parentheses), there is no compelling argument for the reconstruction of a phonemic contour segment. Phonetically, the sequences hypothesised in (9) and the voiceless sequences [cj]~[cɕ] > [tʃ] are what I'd like to call collectively 'pre-affricates'. The assibilation in post-nasal position is most plausibly analysed as subphonemic, in the context of high vowel + nasal, resulting in a voiced palatal stop with subsequent assibilation. Distributionally, the OE pre-affricates were limited to stem-medial and -final position; there were no initial voiced pre-affricates. This is not an argument against phonemic status, but the metrical treatment of inflected forms of items such as *bridge*, *edge*, *secg* 'man', where degemination in word-final position is early, leaves no doubt that the possibly assibilated velar was treated as a sequence:

(10) Stem-final <cg> blocking resolution in OE:
     Forðam secgum wearð (w w S w S)
     'Because to the men happens'
     (*Beo* 149b)

     on þa bricge stōp (w w S w S)
     'on the bridge stepped'
     (*Maldon* 78b)

---

[15] Campbell (1959: 176) posits a possible input stage involving a voiced velar fricative [ɣ]. The 'curly-tail j' [ʝ] is a voiced palatal fricative, an allophone of [j].

[16] Attested only once as *sæncge* (LawRect B14.44), untestable in the verse.

wið þas secgas feaht (w w S w S)
'against those men fought'
Maldon 298b

Comp. *swa he selfa bæd* (w w S w S)
'as he himself bade'
(*Beo* 29b)

wið þæs recedes weal (w w S-w w s)
'against the hall's wall'
(*Beo* 326b)

The metrical treatment of the items in (10) is consistent and unambiguous: a resolved foot for *secgum, bricge* would render the verses unmetrical; whatever <cg> represents phonetically, it is a sequence, or a geminate, not a phonemic singleton.

A short excursus on spelling is in order here. In OE, the palatalised velar geminate is represented either as <gg> or, from quite early on, <cg>.[17] The diagraph spelling with <cg> in, for example, *secg, brycg, ecg*, cannot be relied on as evidence that the realisation went beyond a geminate voiced palatal stop [ɟ] or one of the sequences in (9).

In an obscure footnote, Campbell (1959: 27, fn. 1) refers to the digraph spelling of the velar geminate as 'the only considerable trace in OE spelling of the Celtic use of *p, t, c* for voiced stops'. As far as I know, there have not been any further comments or speculations on the significance of this orthographic transfer, but I would like to suggest, cautiously, that the <cg> spelling in the items that had voiced palatal geminates, or pre-affricate sequences, is a combination of [ɟ] + a palatal approximant [j], for which the OE insular <ȝ> is used regularly.

(11) Interpreting the <cg> spelling in OE:
Celtic use <c> for [g]/[ɟ]
OE Insular <ȝ> for [j]/[j]

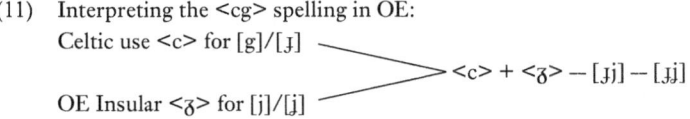

<c> + <ȝ> — [ɟj] — [ɟj]

This is not the place to belabour this point; claiming specific narrow phonetic realisations for the representation of a dead language is never without multiple caveats – for a model discussion see Laing (2008) – but a hetero-segmental sequence as in (11) has the advantage of rendering moot the plausibility of a geminate voiced affricate in the absence of a singleton voiced affricate in OE. Hogg (1992: 37) posits geminate voiced affricates for OE only for the sake of symmetry with the voiceless affricate. What matters for the overall history of the consonantal system is that functionally, a singleton/contour /d͡ʒ/ cannot be reconstructed for OE.

Now that the PDE-OE end-points are more or less clear, I turn to ME in the hope

---

[17] Reminder: <-cg-> in *secgum* behaves like <-lf-> in *selfa* in *Beo* 29b, but not like <c> in *recedes* in *Beo* 326b.

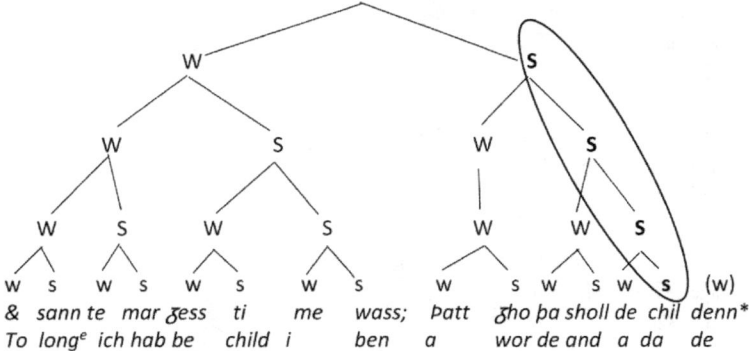

Figure 8.1 The early ME septenary line
Ormulum 3316–17; *Poema Morale* 1.3. On the uniformity of the treatment of the seventh foot in the seven manuscripts of *Poema Morale* see Minkova (2016a).

of identifying additional factors and arguments throwing light on the pathway, or pathways of linking these end-points.

3. Post-vocalic (pre-)affricates in early ME

Sound production and perception depends on the unit's structural position: onsets are typically more salient than codas, coarticulation with adjacent vowels changes the nature of the consonant, and so does stress. The first hypothesis to test, prompted by the behaviour of the velars in OE verse in (7) and (10), is whether intervocalic pre-affricates were treated as bisegmental or as simple obstruents by poets sensitive to syllable weight.

Orm's thoroughly reliable septenary has one property, shared with the similarly metrified earlier *Poema Morale*, namely that the strong position in the seventh foot of each long line of four-and-three is invariably and testably filled by a heavy syllable. This is shown in Figure 8.1.

The strength of the seventh foot in these compositions has been a most useful heuristic for the weight of the syllable that fills that position: both in *Poema Morale* and in the *Ormulum* the line has a feminine ending, but OE words with stressed light syllables such as OE *bacan* 'bake,' *draca* 'snake,' *eten* 'eat,' *bosemm* 'bosom', that is, candidates for open-syllable lengthening, are avoided in this position. Unhelpfully, the number of items eligible for testing is extremely limited by definition: the majority of palatalised intervocalic velars are either historical geminates, or follow a long high vowel: OE *dīc* 'ditch', OE *lǣce* 'physician', OE *cōcel* 'little cake', ME *kechell*. Some frequent words with OE high front short vowel + <c> such as *much*, *cwice* (attested Cleo: *cwich*)[18] are not found in the seventh foot either in Orm or in *Poema Morale*. Recall also that Orm was writing in an in an area of extensive Old Norse influence, so he selects uninflected

---

[18] ?c.1225 *Ancr.* (Cleo C.6): *The English Text of the Ancrene Riwle: BM Cotton MS Cleopatra C.6*, ed. E. J. Dobson, *EETS* 267 (1972). (*MED*). Orm spells the voiceless palatal velar after a long vowel as <ch>, e.g. *læche* 'physician'.

mikell, inflected *miccle*, where <cc> clearly represents a velar stop, as in *flocc*, *bucc* (see also Britton (2005) on *wicke*). What we do find in the seventh foot in the septenary is illustrated in (12):[19]

(12) 'Long' pre-affricates in the *Ormulum* and in *Poema Morale*:
& ec þiss Goddspellwrihte seggþ, Þatt Zakariʒess **macche**[20]
'And also this Gospel says that Zacharia's spouse'
(*Orm* 289–90)

& he badd tatt ʒho shollde himm þa An litell waterr **fecchenn**
'And he bade that she should him fetch some water'
(*Orm* 8633–4)

& ʒiff þu cwemesst tin drihhtin. Wiþþ bedess. & wiþþ **wecchess**[21]
'And if you please your Lord. With prayers and with wakes'
(*Orm* 6740–1)

þach ich elches worldes wele. þer me mahte **feche**
'Though I each worldly wealth. There to me might fetch'
(*Poema Morale* (Lamb. ms) 222)
ho fareð from hete to hete. & hech to frure þe **wreche**
'They go from heat to excessive heat. And each to fire(?) provokes you'
(*Poema Morale* (Lamb. ms) 232)

The bold-faced words: *match*, *fetch*, *watch*, *ditch*, *wretch* straddle the syllable and render it heavy. The matching is completely regular.[22] Such placement does not offer a clue to the phonetic realisation of the medial consonants, but it clearly *precludes* phonemic singletons. The immediate objection to including such negative evidence in the account, however, is that etymologically these are all intervocalic geminates, therefore the usage in (12) may be discarded as irrelevant, yet that would be rash.

One reason why such verse evidence does matter is that elsewhere Orm and the *Poema Morale* the poets use monosyllabic versions of the same words, so in the ambient language such items were subject to phonotactically conditioned degemination as in (13), which shows that a word-final non-geminate was an available realisation in *match*, *wretch*, *stitch* and so on.

---

[19] I have not attempted to represent Orm's 'flat-top' <g> for the velar stop [g]. He uses the Continental <g> for the affricate: *egge, legge, seggen*.
[20] OE *(ge)mæcca*, also WS *gemaca*, Nhb. *maca*; also cp. OI *maki*, eME *mæcche*, ME *mach(e)*. LAEME has a total of four tokens (three cases) of *match*, n., two of which are in the *Ormulum*.
[21] OE *wæcce, wecce* 'wake'.
[22] See further *Ormulum* 368 & ʒho þatt wass hiss *macche* 'And she who was his mate'; 1451 Wiþþ *cnelinng*, & wiþþ *wecche* 'With kneeling and with wake'; 12048 *Acc sinnfull mann* & *wrecche* 'But sinful man and wretched'; 13505 Wiþþ hise ʒæpe *racchess* 'with his gaping hunting dogs', etc.

(13) Etymological geminates in elision environment:
& ʒiff þin macche iss wis & god
'And if your spouse if wise and good'
(*Orm* 6196)

Unnorne & wrecche & usell child
'Simple and lowly and wretched child'
(*Orm* 3668)

All wrecche & wœdle & usell mann
'All miserable and needy and wretched man'
(*Orm* 5638)

We ʒeueð uneðe for his luue a stuche[23] *of ure brede*
'We give uneasily for his love a piece of our bread'
(*Poema Morale* (Lamb. ms) 189)

Reduction of word-final geminates is an OE process which eliminated the phonological distinction between $-C_1\#$ and $-C_1C_1\#$, see the arguments and references in Fulk (1996). The option of word-final degemination for inherited geminates makes an important point: for Orm and for the *Poema Morale* poet(s) the pre-affricates were a special 'intermediate' category: intervocalically they are sufficient to render the stressed syllable heavy, hence the behaviour in (12). The weight of the stressed syllable there, however, does not have to be attributed to the presence of a geminate: an assibilated, or a dental-fricative sequence, will have the same effect.

Orm kept the inherited voiceless pre-affricates spelled <cch> as in (12) and (13) orthographically separate from the pre-affricates after a long vowel, as in *spæche* 'speech', *riche* 'rich'.[24] He also kept them separate from the voiceless velar stops: for the singleton he uses <c>, <k>, <cc>, <x>, <xx> (= /ks/), <q>, and for the historical geminate <ck>, <kk> (Anderson and Britton 1999: 321).[25] The variety of representations is another indication of the difficulties facing the early orthographic

---

[23] OE *stycce*, ON *stykki* < Gmc **stukkjo-m* 'a fragment'.

[24] '... there are no examples of <Vch#> in the text and so <ch> in final position can only be illustrated in the context <C_1C_1ch#> [as in *stinnch* "stench" DM]. Phonologically, /VVtʃ#/ was possible in Orm's dialect, as in an imperative singular /tɛːtʃ/ "teach", and had Orm used the form it would have had a <tæch> spelling' (Anderson and Britton 1999: 316, fn. 31). This is indeed the case, for example line 8662: *þæroffe an litell kechell* 'thereof one little cake' (OE *cēcel* 'cake'). As one of the reviewers suggests, 'the relevant voiceless segments could in principle possibly still (variably?) be /t͡ʃː/ or /iːt͡ʃ/ (with the long vowel providing the heaviness)'. In principle, the logical possibility exists, but the reconstruction would be untestable. The geminate /Vt͡ʃː/ would imply phonetic [Vtt͡ʃ]: that sequence can occur only after short vowels. Since [Vtt͡ʃ] cannot contrast with [Vt͡ʃ], the argument based on the *Ormulum* and *Poema Morale* is valid. We must exclude [VVt͡ʃ] as a possible variant because of the pre-cluster shortening illustrated in (16).

[25] But note Orm's *obacch* 'aback'.

reformer: ongoing assibilation and possibly affrication of the voiceless palatal stop, optional degemination, orthographic remapping of the palatal <c> ((ORPC)) (CoNE); it is not surprising that for the velar he writes <boc~bokes>, <flocc~flokkess>, <bucc~buckess~bukkess> predictably, but the palatal pre-affricates are not straightforward.

Again, the most interesting point about both the voiceless and the voiced singleton and their geminate counterparts even in the earliest ME texts is that 'the two affricate clusters [ttʃ] and [ddʒ] **did not contrast with their singleton correlates**' [emphasis added] . . . the geminates always followed short vowels while the singletons always followed long vowels' (Britton 2012: 237). The existing vs. non-existing strings we can posit on the basis of metrical distribution and spelling are shown in (14):

(14)   Early ME cluster degemination:
        Spelling: <-Vcche>
        Value: -V[tʃ]V-, e.g. *macche* 'match'
        Unattested: *<Vch>

        Spelling: <-VVch>(e)
        Value: -VV[tʃ](e), e.g. *spǣche* 'speech'
        Unattested: *<VVcch>

The absence of <Vch#> spellings in the text renders the lack of medial <ch> after a short vowel in the seventh foot in Orm irrelevant for the tracking of the phonologisation of the affricate: for him <ch> is orthographically equivalent to an orthographic singleton. Admittedly, in this particular text, this is a moot point since all relevant items in Orm's Lincolnshire dialect have the northern voiceless velar: *mikell*, *swillc(e)~swillk(e)*, *cwic(c)~cwike*. This independent argument and the metrical evidence in (12) confirm something that has been argued on different grounds by Fulk (1996, 1998): 'orthographic geminates indicate primarily syllable division rather than length', that is, the syllable division of *macche* is ma[t].[ʃ]ə 'match'.[26]

In Britton's study, the loss of singleton-geminate contrast is seen through the prism of functional load in the ME lexicon – it is the absence of minimal pairs, and not schwa loss or open-syllable lengthening that underpins degemination. He treats degemination as a gradual process, showing that by 1200 only a subset of the consonants could participate in length contrasts: ten in total, with a strong presence of sonorants, voiceless obstruents, /d/, and minimally represented /s/ and /θ/. There was no quantity contrast for the pre-affricates. As an alternative to Britton's proposal, we can treat the lack of functional load as a secondary factor, an artefact rather than a trigger. As Bermúdez-Otero (2012: 193) also notes in reference to Britton's account, there may be a phonetically-driven aspect of the length neutralisation. Neither Britton

---

[26] *Poema Morale*, with its multiple witnesses, is much less helpful: <-VV[tʃ]> strings occur in the seventh foot, see (12). The only <-Vch> word, *michel/muchel* does appear in a position also regularly filled by a heavy syllable, the strong position of the fourth foot: lines 24, 60, 62, 113, 262, 369 (Bodleian 1605, Digby A 4).

nor Bermúdez-Otero elaborate on this, they just recognise the option of treating degemination as a case of 'reduced articulatory energy' which aligns it with lenition. In this phonetically-based alternative, the early and complete neutralisation of the singleton-geminate contrast is then an instantiation of lenition on the basis of constriction duration (Zuraw 2009: 14). Here are the durational properties of the PDE affricates:

Table 8.4 Duration of PDE contour segments vs. bisegmental sequences in ms (from Minkova 2016)[a]

		Sagey	Lavoie		Sagey	Lavoie
Sequence	tʃ	207	n/a	dʒ	192	157
Contour	t͡ʃ	159	133	d͡ʒ	133	92
Singleton	ʃ	139	121	ʒ	125	86
	s	—	113	z	—	75
	t	91	36 ([ɾ])	d	88	71

[a] Measurements are cited from Sagey (1986: 82–83) and Lavoie (2009: 36) whose measurements are averaged across all speakers and all positions. For /t/ Lavoie's study includes only the flap [ɾ] at 36 ms.

In Table 8.4 the intrinsic duration of a geminate bisegmental sequence, or of a contour affricate, where the gemination is assumed to affect the stop portion, would make the constriction duration quite significantly longer, making the long segment a phonetically likely target of degemination. Whatever the rationale, the sequences /tʃ/ and /dʒ/ did not survive as geminates; they merged with the etymological singletons as sequences which are pre-affricates: they are not contour segments yet.

3.1 Pre-affricates and vowel quantity

Britton's innovative account, unlike other approaches to ME degemination, is ostensibly independent of open-syllable lengthening and schwa loss. However, attributing degemination to the salience of the functional load alone cannot be separated from the chronologically concurrent schwa loss, which eliminates the potential singleton-geminate contrast word-finally (bēd(e) 'prayer' – bedd(e) 'bed', dat.sg.), as illustrated in the monosyllabic realisation of the elided items in (13).

If geminate /tʃ/ and /dʒ/ cannot be posited in ME, it is worth exploring the interaction between medial pre-affricates and vowel quantity.

(15)   Pre-affricates and vowel quantity:
       Open-syllable lengthening blocked: No Vtʃ/dʒə(C) > *VVtʃ/dʒə(C)[27]

[27] The CoNE entry on MEOSL is silent on the pre-affricates, but recognises the potential influence of [ʃ]: 'There seems always to have been a phonotactic restriction that at very least disfavours long vowels before [ʃ] in most dialects. (There are a few instances in OE like flǣsc "flesh", but these have shortened; we can probably assume that the phonotactic constraint is of late OE or early ME date.) Except in a very few places in the English dialect range, long

OE *hecel, ME hechil (a1300) > PDE hatchel
ME sachel (a1340) > PDE satchel
OE recils 'incense' > †rechel, v. †rechels, n.
OF lecheor, ME lechur (c.1175) > PDE lecher
OF lachet 'lace, a thong' > PDE latchet
AN, OF rochet 'ecclesiastical vestment' > PDE rochet
OF hachette (a1327) > PDE hatchet
Also match, rache (OE racce) 'a hunting dog', squatch, swatch, wretch, crotchet (c.1394); bratchet 'a kind of hound' (c.1400) etc.

OE hecg > PDE hedge
OE ecg > PDE edge

Compare: OE hwæl > PDE whale, OE blac > PDE Blake

The data for -Vtʃ- in (15) are revealing: I have not been able to identify any potential examples of open-syllable lengthening in which the vowel gets lengthened in front of a 'future' voiceless affricate. For the voiced pre-affricate -Vdʒ- the situation is similar. Ritt (1997: 263) states that for *edge*, *hedge* 'at least phonetically the final affricate can count as a cluster', that is, we should not expect lengthening, not even in schwa-final oblique forms, which is the usual explanation of e.g. OE hwæl > whale, OE blac > Blake.[28] This kind of evidence bears out the assumption that both phonetically and phonemically the pre-affricates remain a sequence for as long as open-syllable lengthening is an active rule.

(16) Pre-cluster shortening: VV[tʃ]- > V[tʃ]-
OE dīc 'ditch', cf. dike
OE līc 'body', cf. like
OE rīc- 'rich', comp. Ryker
OE wīc 'dwelling, salt-pit', cf. wich-house, Wich, now Droitwich (Worcs.)[29]

The shortenings in (16) fit the general pattern of pre-cluster shortening ((PCS)) (CoNE), which serves well as yet another test for the continuous compositionality of the pre-affricates. The relevant examples all have an etymological high front vowel, the proper environment for pre-affricates. The shortening must have been aided by the intrinsic shorter duration of the high vowels. Indeed, if affricates appear after high

vowels and diphthongs don't occur here, except secondary diphthongs from short vowels followed by epenthetic [i], which do not create new phonemes but only special allophones of the vowel preceding /ʃ/.' A link to the intrinsic duration of [ʃ] as shown in Table 8.4 suggests a phonetic basis for the avoidance of long vowels before /ʃ/.

[28] -VVdʒ- non-native forms such as *age*, *page*, *sage*, *wage* are borrowed with a long vowel; its preservation is related to the simplification of the affricate, see section 4.1.

[29] OE brēc 'breech', pl. 'britches', also belongs to this set, showing an interesting case of early raising of OE [eː], compare northern and Scots breek(s).

long vowels in PDE, the vowel is either historically long, as in OE *lǣce* 'physician', or the word is a borrowing, or both, as in *couch* (1340), *vouch*, v. (a1325).

This takes some analytical problems out of the way: the singleton-geminate contrast for pre-affricates was no longer functional in early ME, therefore the syllable weight evidence in the septenary, combined with the cluster behaviour of the pre-affricates with respect to quantitative changes, drives the point home: post-vocalically both the voiced and the voiceless pre-affricates were structural sequences.

The question of when and where the sequence vs. segment reanalysis occurred remains. Next, we look at pre-affricates in onset position.

4. ME onset affricates

The OE alliterative evidence in (6) is a solid indication of the pre-affricate status of the initial palatalised voiceless velar stops. Some suggestive alliterative pairing of /k/:<ch-> appears in one of the 'transitional' ME compositions, Laʒamon's *Brut*, dated between 1189 and the first half of the thirteenth century.

(17) Unexpected alliteration in Laʒamon's *Brut:*
þa þet *child* wes iboren. *wel* wes *Claudiene þer-foren*; (4794)
þo þat *child* was ibore; *wel* was *Claudien þar-vore* (Otho)
'when that child was born; well was to Claudien therefore'

& ladde þes childes moder. for quene nauede he oðer; (4807)
he ladde þ(i)s childes moder; for cwene (n)a(d) + oþer (Otho)
'And he led this child's mother; because he had no other woman'

Cador com to cuðða. bi-uoren Childriche (10729)
Cador com to cuþþe. bi-fore Cheldriche (Otho)
'Cador came to the homeland. Before Childrich'

Minkova (2003: 74–75) is undecided on the phonological value of these examples.[30] A re-examination of the issues does not yield much more certainty. The matching of assibilated [cʲ-/cj] with [k-] is arguably evidence against the contour status of the pre-affricate. The fact that the later Otho manuscript preserves the same patterns makes phonemic identity of [c-]:[k-] more plausible. The <ch> spelling might be a problem, but I believe that the speed and consistency of orthographic remapping ((ORPC)) (CoNE) conceals the true phonetic nature of the palatalised ~ affricated [cj-]. Of the 694 tokens of *child* in LAEME, there isn't a single instance of *<cild> or *<kild>, similarly no *<cide> or *<kide> among the forty-one tokens of *chide*.[31] Since LAEME's cut-off point is c.1325, and since these are the only

---

[30] Alliteration is not the only metrical device in *Laʒamon*, so the matching is less reliable than in OE. Alliteration in the text is structural in only about 75 per cent of the text by Oakden's (1968: 142–143) count.

[31] A fourteenth-century pairing of <church>, with /k/-initial items is most likely to be due to the coexistence of *church* and unpalatalised Scandinavian *kirk*, see Schumacher (1914: 162–168).

lexical items alliterating on [k-], spelled <c-> or <qu->, the uniformity of the <ch> spellings for *child, chide* elsewhere cannot serve as verification of the unitary status of /tʃ-/.

(18) Unexpected alliteration in later ME:
a. *time...he tok : child*
   (*William of Palerne* 4674)
   chese : turnen
   (*Chevelere Assigne* 357)

   chiftanis : twin
   (*The Scottish Prophecy* 122)[32]

b. *Castell : chesez*
   (*Morte Arthure* 1225)[33]

   champayne : schalke 'chalk'
   (*MA* 1226)[34]

   acheued : chaunce, I schal (*ichal?*)
   (*SGGK* 1081)[35]

As adumbrated in the first example in (1b), the usage in (18a) serves as a reminder of the potential compositionality of the affricates, only this time the first element is [t-], allowing a progression from [cj] > [tj] > [tʃ] – one possible phonetic chain linking [cj] and [tʃ]. (18b) shows that like the data from Laʒamon, alliteration suggestive of phonetic compositionality of <ch-> continues to occur in the fourteenth century, with matching based on [cj-] possibly perceptually-overlapping [tʃ].[36]

Admittedly, the practice of matching pre-affricates is exceedingly regular in the corpus and one has to search far and wide for the type of data in (17) and (18). This suggests that inference based on them is defeasible. The normal practice is shown in (19a) for the voiceless and in (19b) for the voiced pre-affricate pairings:

---

[32] Examples from Schumacher (1914: 155). *Chevelere Assigne* is late fourteenth century; *The Scottish Prophecy* is early fifteenth century.

[33] The *Alliterative Morte Arthure: A Critical Edition*. 1976. Ed., with an Introduction, Notes and Glossary, by Valerie Krishna, New York: Burt Franklin. There are no examples of irregular /ch-/ alliteration in *Piers Plowman* (A Text).

[34] *Morte Arthure*, the full line is: *Thurghe a faire champayne, vndyr schalke hyllis* 'Through a fair open country, under chalk hills', *MA* 1226.

[35] *Now acheued is my chaunce, I schal at your wylle* 'Now achieved is my exploit, I shall at your will'. The *ch*-forms in *ichal* are 'chiefly southern' (*MED*).

[36] The perceptual confusability of [cj] and [tʃ] for PDE is documented and discussed in Guion (1998).

(19) Regular alliteration in ME:
   a. *Than was Sir Cherlemayne chosen chefe kynge of Fraunce*
   'Then was Sir Charlemagne chosen chief king of France'
   (*P3A* 520)

   Chymbled ouer hir blake chyn with chalkquyte vayles
   'Wrapped up over her black chin with chalk-white veils'
   (*SGGK* 958)

   In a chosyn chariott as a chefe maister
   'In a chosen chariot as a chief master'
   (*WA* 802)

   Bathe chambirlayn and chaplayne in chalke-quite wedis
   'Both chamberlain and chaplain in chalk-white garb'
   (*WA* 1707)

   b. *Justed ful jolilé þise gentyle kniʒtes*
   'Jousted full jollily these gentle knights'
   (*SGGK* 42)

   Jesus and sayn Gilyan, þat gentyle ar boþe
   'Jesus and Saint Julian who gentle are both'
   (*SGGK* 774)

   In gelosie ioyeles and ianglyng on bedde
   'In jealousy joyless and quarreling in bed'
   (*PP* (AText) 10.190)

   To Iesu the gentil, . that Iewis todrowe
   'To Jesus the gentle that Jews pulled apart'
   (*PP* (AText) 11.27)

There is of course no alliterative evidence comparable to (19b) for native voiced pre-affricates word-initially; the OE palatal counterpart is /j-/.

The available information on the status of word-initial pre-affricates thus allows only a tentative hypothesis: by the end of the fourteenth century assibilated word-initial sequences have fully replaced the initial palatal singletons, opening up an interpretation of perceptual variability between pre-affricates and contour affricates.

4.1 The French connection

The search for regularities and exceptions in the ME alliterative corpus revealed an unexpected density of Old French (OF)/Anglo-Norman (AN) <ch->-initial words. The *Chronological English Dictionary* (1970) records a total of thirty-six items of Germanic origin with affricated initial <ch-> pre-1150, including derivatives (*child, childish, childhood, childly, Childermas*, etc.). The corresponding search yielded forty-two <ch-> items in the *OED*. The number of borrowed items with initial <ch-> first recorded 1150–1450 jumps to 183: *chain, chair, chance, change, chapel*, etc., a substantial increase. The voiced counterpart, of course, is entirely non-native: the PrG voiced initial velar was either a stop or a palatal approximant. The affricates in initial position in ME *gent, giant, gem, judge, joust*, come from OF; this applies to ultimately Latin words recycled through OF: *January, June, July, Jesus, Job*.

The exposure to so many items with potential affricates suggests a possible connection between the history of the pre-affricates in native items and the corresponding developments in OF:

(20) Simplification of [t͡ʃ] and [d͡ʒ] in thirteenth-century OF (based on Pope 1934: 93):[37]
Word-initial
[t͡ʃar] > [ʃar] *char* 'wagon'[38]
[t͡ʃier] > [ʃi̯er] *chier* 'dear'
[d͡ʒanbe̜] > [ʒanbe̜] *jambe* 'leg'

Intervocalic
[tat͡ʃe̜] > [taʃe̜] (*a*)*ttach* 'to fasten'
[sat͡ʃe̜] > [saʃe̜] *sache* 'bag'
[rud͡ʒe̜] > [ruʒe̜] *ruge* 'red'[39]

Pope (1934: 450) makes the point that it is 'probable that these sounds were retained longer in insular speech than on the Continent'. If it was not until later AN that the dental component was lost, the implication is clear: AN affricate simplification was delayed due to the existence of the sequences [tʃ] and [dʒ] in ME. Moreover, the simplification was reversed in the accommodation of the loanwords e.g. *attach, satchel, chain, joust*. The variable realisation of the AN affricates is a good reason to include language contact in the factors leading to reanalysis from a sequence to a segment. The parallel pathways of native and borrowed words with emerging word-initial affricates are sketched in (21) and (22).

(21) Middle English – Anglo-Norman parallels in onset position:

		Early ME		------------- >		Later ME	
a.	OE:	[cʲin]	~	[tʃin]	~	[t͡ʃin]	OE *cinn* 'chin'
	AN:	[t͡ʃar]	~	[tʃar]~[ʃar]	~	[t͡ʃar]	AN *char* 'wagon'
b.	AN:	[d͡ʒuːst]	~	[dʒuːst]~[ʒuːst]	~	[d͡ʒuːst]	OF *jo(u)ster* 'joust'
c.	Onset	C-	~	CC-	~	-C	

---

[37] I am transcribing the OF inputs as contour segments on Pope's authority, although she does not make an explicit argument for a sequence vs. segment analysis. Even if the inputs were sequences licensing the 'edge' effect of deleting the stop portion of the affricate, the arguments on the structural parallelism would be valid.

[38] †*char* (Obs.) *a*1400 (*a*1325, *Cursor Mundi*) (*OED*).

[39] Late ME *rouʒ*, late ME *rowdge*, *a*1425 (*OED*).

The variability of onset CC- ~ C- in the loanwords: [tʃar]~[ʃar], [dʒuːst]~[ʒuːst] suggests a structural parallel for the perception of the same native CC- sequences as singletons. Domain-initially the native pre-affricates and their borrowed counterparts are in a position conducive to the development of a contour segment. Stressed-syllable onset affrication is a plausible pathway of change, especially if we recognise the lack of unity in lenition processes and disassociate the idea of domain-initial position as necessarily inhibiting lenition (see Honeybone 2001, 2012). Honeybone's hypothesis that lenition processes 'can be affected by their prosodic and melodic environment but are not caused by it' (2012: 784) is supported by the divergent directions of change of pre-affricate sequences: towards affrication in English, and towards de-affrication in French. The split is probably related to the difference in the ambient prosodic systems, with affrication occurring preferentially foot-initially in English.

Whether initial affrication should be included in the taxonomy of lenitions, as in the trajectory of lenitions in Lass (1984: 178), or not, depends on the way the term is defined.[40] In the account proposed here, see Table 8.5 below, the simplification of the stop+palatal fricative sequence to a singleton can be qualified as lenition, both in English and in French. Moreover, phonetically affrication in the native lexical set is a 'natural' development:

> alveolar stops are likely to affricate adjacent to close front vowels. The narrow channel created by the stop closure yields a higher volume velocity airflow at the stop release, which may generate frication in the post-alveolar region. Release type error is less frequent in medial and final contexts[.] (from Ohala 2005, cited in Foulkes and Vihman (2015: 308–10).[41]

This is in line with PDE acquisition findings: as noted in 1.2, affricates are acquired prior to clusters, and their acquisition in onsets is earlier than in codas.

The next position where the French connection in the rise of contour affricates could be structurally relevant is in the coda. The parallels are shown in (22):

(22) ME – AN parallels in coda position:

Early ME - > Later ME
a. ME: [wrɛt.ʃ(ə)] ~ [wrɛtʃ] ~ [wrɛ.t͡ʃ(ə)] ~ [wrɛt͡ʃ] OE *wrecche* 'wretch'
   AN: [ta.t͡ʃe̜] ~ [tatʃ] ~ [ta.ʃe̜] ~ [taʃ] (*a*)*ttach* 'to fasten'
b. ME: [ɛd.ʒ(ə)] ~ [ɛdʒ] ~ [ɛ.d͡ʒ(ə)] ~ [ɛd͡ʒ] OE *ecg* 'edge'
   AN: [ru.d͡ʒe̜] ~ [rudʒ] ~ [ru.ʒe̜] ~ [ruʒ] *ruge* 'red'
c. ME   -VC.Cə ~ -VCC ~ -V.Cə ~ **-VC**
   AN   -V.Cə ~ -VCC ~ -V.Cə ~ **-VC**

---

[40] Lavoie 2009 (p. 33): 'Affrication adds complexity to a segment so it seems like strengthening, but historically affrication may lead to deletion, so the evidence is conflicting.'
[41] Foulkes and Vihman's findings indicate that initial release-type error is by far the most frequent type in first language acquisition. More specifically, initial [tʃ] 'error' for /t/ is the most frequent and predictable type in first language acquisition.

22 (a) and (b) show alternating –CC ~ –C realisations of the inherited voiced and voiceless inputs. Once again, AN simplification provides a template for the variation. The structural parallels appear clearly in (22c), especially after the loss of schwa, when the sequence becomes entirely tautosyllabic. Tautosyllabicity is a crucial bridge linking –VCC and –VC realisations, the latter involving a phonemic singleton.

In terms of sonority a coda sequence [stop + fricative] is marginal – the typologically 'optimal' coda cluster would be [fricative + stop]. In OF, AN, and allophonically in Modern English, see the fourth bullet in (4), the simplification of an affricate targets the stop, preserving the more sonorous fricative. Coda position is a typical lenition site, but once again the processes are diverse: loss of the dental in OF, and development from a sequence to a contour segment in English. In addition, as shown in Lass and Laing (2013: 110–111), there may have been sporadic voicing in ME of [tʃ] to [dʒ] in items such as *wretch*, *fetch*.

The structural variation between singletons and stop-palatal fricative sequences in ME points to a possible connection between the sets in (21), (22) and a change which CoNE identifies as palatal hardening:

(23) Palatal hardening ((PH)) in CoNE: [ʃ] > [tʃ]: *charpe* 'sharp'; *chaw* 'show';[42] *fl*ech 'flesh'
This change is sporadic but regionally widespread, occurring in LAEME texts both from the SWML and from the North. We assume that this is a genuine phonetic change rather than a graphic extension of ((ORPSC)). (CoNE, Palatal hardening)

The identification of ((PH)) as a phonetic change, which I propose to analyse as variation between singleton [ʃ] and a sequence [tʃ], is original with CoNE. Stanley (1972: 126) noticed <ch> spellings for <sch> in the Cotton Caligula A ix version of *The Owl and the Nightingale*, but dismissed them as an 'error, which should perhaps be emended'.[43] Positing a template of palatal CC~C variation as outlined in (21–22) offers a structural corroboration to CoNE's assumption that this was a genuine phonetic process. Placed in the context of variability of similar items elsewhere, this initially 'weird'-looking change appears more structurally and phonetically orthodox.

Returning to section 1.1, Tables 8.2–8.4 show that the type frequency of affricates in English is significantly higher in word-initial and word-final position than elsewhere. It is imprudent to equate word frequencies in current English with older

---

[42] (x2) Edinburgh, Royal College of Physicians, MS of *Cursor Mundi*, entry 2, C14a, Yorkshire, North Riding: *Forþi wil I chaw oþer thinges* 'I will therefore show other things'; *Þus-gat spac þis eremyt hi(m) tille \ To ger hi(m) chaw his thohtes ille* 'Like this spoke this hermit to him, to cause him to show his ill thoughts'.

[43] The full quote is: '. . . *ch* for *sch* occurs here [*ofchamed* "ashamed", line 933] and in *ic chadde* 1616, *cliures charpe* 1676, *his chelde* ["shield", DM]; in each case the preceding letter or letters may have led to this error, which should perhaps be emended: *ch* after *ch*, *s* omitted after *s*, or here [line 933] omitted after *f* which is like long *s*.' The *Cursor Mundi* examples in fn. 44 would not fit Stanley's supposition.

English blindly, but the numbers are at least suggestive. Affrication is easily encoded phonetically, therefore we would expect the most frequent frames to be affected first in the corresponding sound change (Phillips 2006: 181). From that point of view, the reanalysis from a sequence to a segment was most advanced at the word edges, and the type frequency increase from the loanwords with initial affricates enhances that pattern.

This ordering of phonetic and phonological events remains hypothetical, of course. Laker (2003) disagrees with Minkova's (2003) assumption that affrication was more advanced in the coda, suggesting that the opposite pattern holds in Old Frisian and Low German. In revisiting affrication, I have not found much evidence for or against either assumption, except for the stronger probability that coda position would be the most likely leader in the reanalysis simplification/lenition of the sequence to a segment. The other new elements here – the reference to tautosyllabicity as a prerequisite and the lexical frequency data (for PDE) – increase the probability of intervocalic/word-medial affrication lagging behind, but they do not tell us anything about the relative chronology of the change in onsets versus codas.

5. Summary and final thoughts

This study attempts to reconstruct the ways in which the stop+palatal fricative sequences based on the OE palatalised velar stops were phonologically reanalysed as contour affricates in ME. The search for answers followed and combined evidence from orthography, use in verse, relation to quantitative changes, phonetic properties and structural argumentation, especially in relation to parallels in the Romance loan vocabulary. Ultimately, these different perspectives converge on several points: bisegmental perception and production of the pre-affricates [tʃ] and [dʒ] is an option until at least the end of the fourteenth century. Full affrication is the end-point of a multiple-stage process initiated by the development of a complex sequence out of a singleton, variation between a CC sequence and a new type of singleton, a pattern reinforced by concurrent CC~C alternations in the loan vocabulary. The same structural template accounts for another phonetic change in ME, palatal hardening (CoNE), hitherto dismissed or considered in isolation, unrelated to other phonological changes.

The evidence from spelling can be helpful, but it is by no means determinative. For the voiced assibilated sequence in OE, section 2 highlights a previously unnoticed Celtic connection between the spelling <cg> and its bisegmental nature, see the schema in (11). In ME the orthographic representation changed and in effect obscured the issue:

> The post-Conquest adoption of Caroline minuscule for the writing ... of English introduced a new *figura* for 'g' (<g>). Some early Middle English scribes ... simply transferred the composite functions of insular 'g' to Caroline 'g'. But there gradually emerged a new consensus. This was to use Caroline 'g' for [g] and [dʒ]. (Laing and Lass 2009: 9)

While the OE scribal techniques do not indicate awareness of a disruptive difference between the non-palatalised and the palatalised voiceless velar stop, using <c> indiscriminately, the twelfth-century modified Caroline minuscule, the Protogothic script as practised by the scribe of the *Second Continuation of the Peterborough Chronicle* (1132–1154), shows a gradual switch to <k> for the velar, and <ch> for the palatal (Roberts 2006: 104–105). The middle of the twelfth century is therefore the beginning of the orthographic remapping of palatal c ((ORPC)) (CoNE). Sampling one frequent item, *much*, in LAEME shows only a small number of <c> spellings: ignoring <k> spellings, out of 1937 tokens for *much*, only twenty-four have <c>.[44] The switch is dramatic and probably indicates an advanced, though not necessarily complete, stage of the reanalysis of the velar stop to a bisegmental sequence, a pre-affricate. Spelling is not helpful with respect to the loss of the singleton-geminate contrast: for *watch*, all nineteen tokens in LAEME have <cch> while for *fetch* the ratio is thirty of <cch> to twelve <ch>, see also sections 3, 4.

Table 8.5 summarises the proposed stages and characterisation of the type of change affecting the pre-affricates for the input voiceless singleton */k/, palatalised to [c] and spelled <c> in OE:[45]

Table 8.5 Pre-affricates to affricates in Middle English (from Old English [c])

	OE [c]	#CV-[b]	-C#	-VCV-	Type of change
OE ——> ME	Palatal [cʲ]	✓	✓	✓	Lenition
	Assibilated [tʃ]	✓	✓	✓	Fortition
	Sequence [tʃ]	✓	✓	✓	Fortition
	Contour /t͡ʃ/	✓?	✓?	✓?	Lenition
		Early ----------> Late ME			

[b] Hall, Hamann and Zygis (2006: 61) characterise assibilation as a process in which 'The trigger is typically to the right of the target.' In English the trigger can be on either side, as in the -C# column in Table 8.5.

Affricates are unique in terms of manner of articulation; they are an 'intermediate' category. The step-wise vertical chronological progression from singleton stops with secondary [+ continuant] articulation to a bisegmental sequence and back to a singleton cannot be dated precisely, but at least negatively it seems that the reanalysis to an underlying phonemic /t͡ʃ/ was not completed before the end of the fourteenth century, possibly even later, hence the question marks in the last row for the contour segment /t͡ʃ/. Absence of affricates in the repertoire of speakers of ON also argues for a late rather than early establishment of phonemic contour affricates in ME. The progression from left to right, early to late ME, is meant to suggest that the change was more advanced at word edges, and was still incomplete at the end of ME.

[44] *Final Continuation of the Peterborough Chronicle* (x21), Cotton Claudius D iii: *Benedictine Rule* (x1), *Laʒamon A*, Hand B (x1), London, British Library, Cotton Nero A xiv, fols. 1r–120v, hand A: *Ancrene Riwle* (x1) There are only two instances of *much* spelled with <cch>.

[45] A similar schema can be constructed for the voiced affricate: the bottom rows would be identical.

To cite CoNE again, the Velar Palatalisation ((VP)) outline "glosses over much controversy and complication, including the relationship of the palatalization with the associated affrication and assibilation". I have tried to address some of those controversies and complications.

In the spirit of 'what remains to be done': I believe that there is more to be learned from separating the instances of initial/onset affrication and final/coda affrication in the voiced series, where the native basis disallowed the former but would have been receptive to the latter. It would also be of interest to study more closely the token rather than type frequencies of the affected items to see whether there are any discernible patterns along these lines. Not least, one point about the ME pre-affricates, which has not been addressed here, is the dialect question. The virtual absence of documentation for Older Scots until the end of the fourteenth century makes a more fine-grained regional reconstruction of the spread of the affricate unfeasible. The northern and Scots contact-induced resistance to palatalisation in e.g. *kirk*, *birk* 'birch', *thack* 'thatch', *rig*, *brig* for *ridge*, *bridge* makes it probable that the contour affricates are borrowed in their fully developed, modern form; an issue which deserves a separate treatment.

References

Anderson, John and Derek Britton (1999). 'The orthography and phonology of the Ormulum', *English Language and Linguistics* 3(2): 299–334.

Bermúdez-Otero, Ricardo (2012). 'Introduction to Part IV: When a knowledge of history is a dangerous thing', in Denison et al., pp. 187–193.

Britton, Derek (2005). 'Orm's *wikenn* and compounds with *-wican* in Annal 1137 of the *Peterborough Chronicle*', *Notes & Queries* 52: 10–11.

Britton, Derek (2012). 'Degemination in English, with special reference to the Middle English period', in Denison et al., pp. 232–244.

Campbell, A. C. (1959). *Old English Grammar*, Oxford: Clarendon Press.

Chronological English Dictionary: Thomas Finkenstaedt, Ernst Leisi and Dieter Wolff (eds) (1970). *A Chronological English Dictionary: Listing 80,000 Words in Order of Their Earliest Known Occurrence*, Heidelberg: Carl Winter.

CoNE: A *Corpus of Narrative Etymologies from Proto-Old English to Early Middle English and Accompanying Corpus of Changes*, compiled by Roger Lass, Margaret Laing, Rhona Alcorn and Keith Williamson, version 1.1, 2013–, © The University of Edinburgh (available at http://www.lel.ed.ac.uk/ihd/CoNE/CoNE.html).

Cruttenden, Alan (2014). *Gimson's Pronunciation of English*, 8th edition, London: Routledge.

Denison, David, Ricardo Bermúdez-Otero, Christopher B. McCully and Emma Moore, with the assistance of Ayumi Miura (eds) (2012). *Analysing Older English*, Cambridge: Cambridge University Press.

Foulkes, Paul and Marilyn Vihman (2015). 'First language acquisition and phonological change', in Patrick Honeybone and Joseph Salmons (eds), *The Oxford Handbook of Historical Phonology*, Oxford: Oxford University Press, pp. 289–313.

Fulk, Robert D. (1992). *A History of Old English Meter*, Philadelphia: University of Pennsylvania Press.

Fulk, Robert D. (1996). 'Consonant doubling and open syllable lengthening in the *Ormulum*', *Anglia* 114: 481–513.
Fulk, Robert D. (1998). 'The role of syllable structure in Old English quantitative sound changes', *NOWELE* 33(1): 3–35.
Gierut, Judith A. and Kathleen M. O'Connor (2002). 'Precursors to onset clusters in acquisition', *Journal of Child Language* 29(3): 495–517.
Guion, Susan Guignard (1998). 'The role of perception in the sound change of velar palatalization', *Phonetica* 55: 18–52.
Hall, Tracy Alan (2012). 'The representation of affricates in Cimbrian German', *Journal of Germanic Linguistics* 24(1): 1–22.
Hall, Tracy Alan, Silke Hamann and Marzena Zygis (2006). 'The phonetic motivation for phonological stop assibilation', *Journal of the International Phonetic Association* 36(1): 59–81.
Hammond, Michael (1999). *The Phonology of English. A Prosodic Optimality-theoretic Approach*, Oxford: Oxford University Press.
Hayes, Bruce (2009). *Introductory Phonology*, Oxford: Wiley-Blackwell.
Hayes, Bruce (2011). English Phonology Search, a program (available at http://www.linguistics.ucla.edu/people/hayes/EnglishPhonologySearch/Index.htm).
Hockett, Charles (1958). *A Course in Modern Linguistics*, New York: Macmillan.
Hoekstra, Jarich F. (2001). 'Standard West Frisian', in Horst Haider Munske (ed.), *Handbuch des Friesischen*, Tübingen: Max Niemeyer Verlag, pp. 83–97.
Hogg, Richard (1992). *A Grammar of Old English, vol. I: Phonology*, Oxford: Blackwell.
Honeybone, Patrick (2001). 'Lenition inhibition in Liverpool English', *English Language and Linguistics* 5: 213–249.
Honeybone, Patrick (2012). 'Lenition in English', in Terttu Nevalainen and Elizabeth Closs Traugott (eds), *The Oxford Handbook of the History of English*, Oxford: Oxford University Press, pp. 773–787.
Jones, Daniel (1918 [repr. 1922]). *An Outline of English Phonetics*, New York: G. E. Stechert & Co.
Kiparsky, Paul (1989). 'Sprung rhythm', in Paul Kiparsky and Gilbert Youmans (eds), *Rhythm and Meter*, San Diego: Academic Press, pp. 305–340.
Knowles, G. (1987). *Patterns of Spoken English: An Introduction to English Phonetics*, 6th edition, London: Routledge.
Kohler, Klaus J. (1990). 'German', *Journal of the International Phonetic Association* 20(1): 48–50.
Ladefoged, Peter and Ian Maddieson (1996). *The Sounds of the World's Languages*, Oxford: Blackwell.
LAEME: A *Linguistic Atlas of Early Middle English*, 1150–1325, compiled by Margaret Laing, version 3.2, 2013, © The University of Edinburgh (available at http://www.lel.ed.ac.uk/ihd/laeme2/laeme2.html).
Laing, Margaret (2008). 'The Middle English scribe: sprach er wie er schrieb?', in M. Dossena, R. Dury and M. Gotti (eds), *English Historical Linguistics 2006, Vol. III: Geo-historical Variation in English*, Amsterdam: John Benjamins, pp. 1–44.
Laing, Margaret and Roger Lass (2009). 'Shape-shifting, sound-change and the genesis of prodigal writing systems', *English Language and Linguistics* 13(1): 1–31.

Laker, Stephen (2003). 'Review of Minkova (2003)', *LINGUIST List* 14.2625 (available at http://linguistlist.org/issues/14/14-2625.html).
Lass, Roger (1984). *Phonology: An Introduction to Basic Concepts*, Cambridge: Cambridge University Press.
Lass, Roger and Margaret Laing (2013). 'The Early Middle English reflexes of Germanic *ik 'I': Unpacking the changes', *Folia Linguistica Historica* 34(1): 93–114.
Lavoie, Lisa (2009). 'Testing consonant weakness phonetically', in Minkova (ed.), pp. 29–46.
Lleó, C. and M. Prinz (1997). 'Syllable structure parameters and the acquisition of affricates', in S. J. Hannahs and M. Young-Scholten (eds), *Focus on Phonological Acquisition*, Amsterdam: Benjamins, pp. 143–164.
MED: *Middle English Dictionary*. Electronic edition (available at http://quod.lib.umich.edu/m/med/).
Minkova, Donka (2003). *Alliteration and Sound Change in Early English*, Cambridge: Cambridge University Press.
Minkova, Donka (ed.) (2009). *Phonological Weakness in English: From Old to Present-Day English*, Houndmills: Palgrave Macmillan.
Minkova, Donka (2013). *A Historical Phonology of English*, Edinburgh: Edinburgh University Press.
Minkova, Donka (2016). 'From stop-fricative clusters to contour segments in Old English', in Don Chapman, Colette Moore and Miranda Wilcox (eds), *Studies in the History of the English Language VII*, Berlin: De Gruyter Mouton, pp. 29–60.
Minkova, Donka (2016a). 'Prosody-meter correspondences in late Old English and in the Middle English *Poema Morale*', in Leonard Neidorf, Rafael J. Pascual and Tom Shippey (eds), *Old English Philology: Studies in Honor of R. D. Fulk* [Anglo-Saxon Studies 31], Cambridge: D. S. Brewer, pp. 122–144.
Morris, Richard (ed.) (1874–93). *Cursor Mundi (The Cursur o the World). A Northumbrian Poem of the XIVth Century in Four Versions*. London: Trübner & Co. [EETS OS 57, 99, 101.]
Muthmann, G. (1999). *Reverse English Dictionary* [Topics in English Linguistics 29], Berlin: Mouton de Gruyter.
Oakden, J. P. (1968 repr. [1930, 1935]). *Alliterative Poetry in Middle English. The Dialectal and Metrical Survey*, New Haven: Archon Books.
Ohala, John J. (2005). 'Phonetic explanations for sound patterns', in William J. Hardcastle and Janet Mackenzie Beck (eds), *A Figure of Speech: A Festschrift for John Laver*, Mahwah, NJ and London: Erlbaum, pp. 23–38.
Phillips, Betty (2006). *Word Frequency and Lexical Diffusion*, Basingstoke: Palgrave Macmillan.
Pope, Mildred Katharine (1934). *From Latin to Modern French with Especial Consideration of Anglo-Norman: Phonology and Morphology*, Manchester: Manchester University Press.
Prinz, Michael and Richard Wiese (1991). 'Die Affrikaten des Deutschen und ihre Verschriftung', *Linguistische Berichte* 133: 165–189.
Rákosi, Csilla (2014). 'Inconsistency in two approaches to German affricates. Part 2:

The basic inconsistency of German affricates in Prinz & Wiese's approach', *Sprachtheorie und germanistische Linguistik* 24(2): 151–182.

Ritt, Nikolaus (1997). 'Now you see it, now you don't Middle English lengthening in closed syllables', *Studia Anglica Posnaniensia* 31: 249–270.

Roberts, Jane (2006). *A Guide to Scripts Used in English Writings up to 1500*, London and Boston Spa: British Library Publishing.

Sagey, E. (1986). *The Representation of Features and Relations in Non-linear Phonology*, Cambridge, MA: MIT Diss.

Schumacher, Karl (1914). *Studien über den Stabreim mittelenglischen Alliterationsdichtung*, Bonn: Peter Hanstein Verlagsbuchhandlung. [Bonner Studien zur englischen Philologie Heft XI.]

Stanley, Eric (ed.) (1972). *The Owl and the Nightingale*, Manchester: Manchester University Press.

van Langenhove, George (1930). 'The assibilation of palatal stops in Old English', in N. Bøgholm, A. Brusendorff and C. Bodelson (eds), *A Grammatical Miscellany Offered to Otto Jespersen on his 70th Birthday*, Copenhagen: Levin & Munksgaard, pp. 69–75.

Willis, David (2009). 'Old and Middle Welsh', in Martin Ball and Nicole Müller (eds), *The Celtic Languages*, London: Routledge, pp. 117–160.

Zuraw, Kie Ross (2009). 'Treatments of weakness in phonological theory', in Minkova (ed.), pp. 9–28.

Part III Placing Features in Context

9

The Predictability of {S} Abbreviation in Older Scots Manuscripts According to Stem-final *Littera*

Daisy Smith

1. Statistical modelling of diachronic corpus data

The recent availability of large-scale diachronic corpora has made it possible to investigate historical linguistic phenomena using sophisticated statistical methodology. Gries (2015: 97) describes corpus data in general as 'observational and, thus, usually unbalanced and messy/noisy'. He points out that techniques frequently employed in other areas of linguistics, particularly those which use experimental methods (such as sociolinguistics), can be applied to corpus linguistics. More than that, he suggests that these methods are actively necessitated by the very nature of corpus data. In particular, Gries suggests that mixed effects regression modelling is highly beneficial to corpus-based research due to the hierarchical nature of corpus data. For example, consider a corpus of 100 texts each containing 1,000 words. The corpus therefore contains a total of 100,000 words, each 'nested' within a particular text. An analysis using this corpus needs to account not only for the trends observable within the corpus as a whole, but for potential similarities between tokens drawn from the same text. Gries argues that this and similar sources of potential systematic variance (such as that between individual tokens of the same lexical item) are often overlooked in corpus studies, to the detriment of the conclusions drawn from them.

Historical corpus studies are no exception to this generalisation, but historical dialectology is a field in which the potential for access to the kind of 'big data' necessary for the kind of analyses Gries advocates has been understandably smaller than in others. Compare, for example, the following corpora:

1. The *Edinburgh Twitter Corpus* (Petrović, Osborne and Lavrenko 2010): a corpus of social media interactions containing 97 million tweets with a combined total of over 2 billion words.
2. A *Linguistic Atlas of Early Middle English* (LAEME) (Laing 2013): a corpus of Middle English (ME) texts containing approximately 300 transcribed medieval manuscripts with a combined total of approximately 650,000 words.

Petrović, Osborne and Lavrenko's (2013) corpus of tweets was extracted automatically over a period of two months using Twitter's streaming application programming interface (API). By contrast, LAEME was compiled over the course of twenty years by the manual sourcing, reading, deciphering and transcribing of manuscripts (Laing 2013). That the Twitter Corpus could be compiled in one-twentieth of the time it took to compile LAEME, and in doing so contain around 150 times as many words, illustrates, albeit with an extreme example, the potential difference in data accessibility between historical linguistics and other fields such as sociolinguistics. Studies which require medieval manuscripts, or transcriptions thereof, as their primary source material are particularly susceptible to issues like this, due to the large amount of variability in spelling and orthographic conventions. Therefore, manual transcription is a necessity, rather than machine transcription.

The techniques which Gries (2015: 97) suggests are beneficial and even vital to corpus research have long been out of reach for historical dialectology. However, the completion of projects such as a *Linguistic Atlas of Older Scots* (LAOS) (Williamson 2008), LAEME (Laing 2013), an *Electronic Version of A Linguistic Atlas of Late Mediaeval English* (eLALME) (Benskin et al. 2013) and a *Corpus of Narrative Etymologies* (CoNE) (Lass et al. 2013) has rendered possible large-scale investigations of trends in medieval manuscript data using statistical methods.

In this chapter, I present an analysis of an aspect of the orthography of the Older Scots (OSc) plural noun (npl) {S} morpheme, specifically, the realisation of this morpheme as the abbreviation symbol <ʃ>. In section 3 I provide some background to OSc and describe the orthographic realisation of {S} in OSc manuscripts. I outline the previous study of {S} in OSc, highlighting in particular the use of <is/ys> representations of {S} as a diagnostic feature of OSc manuscripts. In section 4, I introduce the data source for my investigation, (LAOS) (Williamson 2008), and present the distribution of orthographic variants of {S} contained therein. In particular, I note that 61 per cent of {S} tokens in LAOS are realised using the abbreviation symbol <ʃ>. In section 5, I give an account of the form and signification of this symbol as it is described in handbooks of English, Scottish and Latin palaeography (Johnson and Jenkinson 1915; Simpson 1973; Cappelli 1982 [1899]). Section 6 first outlines the structure of the dataset extracted from LAOS which I use in my investigation, and, second, provides a brief overview of the statistical methodology. This overview is intended to explain the relevance and purpose of the results I present in the subsequent sections, rather than as an account of the underlying theory behind the methodology. In the interest of communicating the statistical validity of my conclusions, but also remaining accessible to a non-statistical audience, section 7 presents traditional proportion graphs of the frequency data extracted from LAOS alongside an explanation of the statistical model output which confirms the trends shown by the frequency data.

2. A note on orthographic conventions

The investigation in this chapter uses as its source LAOS (Williamson 2008). Where examples are given from LAOS in this chapter, I retain the transcription conventions used in LAOS, as set out in section 4. Where examples are not directly from LAOS,

Figure 9.1 <(com)moditſ> *commodities*. LAOS text 36: liferent from Dirleton, East Lothian. May 1447. (Source: Edinburgh University Centre for Research Collections (CRC))

angle brackets denote orthographic forms. Within these, ordinary parentheses denote abbreviated letters, with the exception of the abbreviation symbol which is the subject of this study – this is represented as its own character <ſ>. Italics are used to represent lexical items. An example is shown in Figure 9.1 with the corresponding manuscript form for reference.

3. Older Scots and noun plural {S}

OSc is the label traditionally applied to the language spoken in Lowland Scotland in the period 1100 to 1700. This period is broken down by Aitken (1985: xiii) into further sub-periods: Pre-Literary Scots (1100–1375); Early Scots (1375–1450); Early Middle Scots (1450–1550); and Late Middle Scots (1550–1700). This chapter is concerned with the period covered by LAOS (Williamson 2008), 1380–1500. According to the periodisation employed by Aitken, this period falls between the Early and Early Middle periods of Scots; however, Williamson refers to the Scots exemplified by LAOS simply as 'Older Scots'. I will therefore adopt this label throughout this chapter, in which the term 'OSc' should be understood to refer to the period covered by LAOS.

The OSc period covered by LAOS is roughly concurrent with the ME period south of the Scottish-English border. The development of OSc itself is unclear due to the lack of documentary evidence prior to the late 1300s, but the main sources of OSc forms are the various dialects spoken by Germanic-speaking settlers from around the twelfth century, particularly Old Northumbrian (Aitken and Macafee 2002). OSc is, however, a language distinct from these input sources, with various marked diagnostic features identified as characteristic of OSc as distinct from ME. Kniezsa (1997: 41) identifies several features as diagnostic of the 'Scottishness' of a text. One of these features is the orthographic realisation of the npl {S} morpheme (henceforth '{S}') as <is> or <ys>, as shown in Example (1).

(1) <acct(i)onis causis & q(ua)rellis> (LAOS text 27 [Gordon Papers, 1491])
    'actions, causes and quarrels'

Npl {S} is derived from the Old English (OE) strong masculine –*as* inflection. The OE unstressed vowel system contained a variety of vowel qualities, but by early ME, the unstressed vowel system had undergone substantial neutralisation, and the {S} inflection was generally represented orthographically by <–es>. Later in ME, {S} began to be represented by <–is> as well as <–es> in Northern Middle English (NME), reflecting a raised vowel quality before coronal consonants (Minkova 1991; King 1997; Lass et al. 2013).

There is widespread agreement that the realisation <is>, and its graphic alternant <ys>, is the typical realisation of {S} in OSc (King 1997: 160; Aitken and Macafee 2002: 71; Smith 2012: 45; Bann and Corbett 2015: 5). However, there have been few empirical studies of OSc inflections, due to the lack of readily available corpora of OSc material prior to the recent publication of LAOS (Williamson 2008) (see section 1). There are, however, two notable studies by Kopaczyk, one which uses a *Linguistic Atlas of Late Mediaeval English* (LALME) (McIntosh, Samuels and Benskin 1986) to compare the realisation of {S} in Scots border texts to that in NME texts (Kopaczyk 2001); and an independent linguistic analysis of the *Wigtownshire Burgh Court Book*, a text from the county of Wigtownshire in South-West Scotland (as Bugaj 2004a, 2004b).

Kopaczyk (2001) finds that all of the OSc border texts use <is/ys> as their primary variant. Half of the OSc texts use <es>, though not as a primary variant. By contrast, approximately half of the NME texts use <es> as their main variant. Kopaczyk's (2001) data support King's (1997: 160) assertion that OSc used the form <is/ys> for npl {S} in the majority of cases. Because the texts with <es> in Kopaczyk's data are both dated before 1400, they also support King's (1997) statement that <es> was used in the earliest OSc texts. Kopaczyk (2001) concludes from her analysis that OSc texts were more homogenous in their representation of npl {S}, whereas NME texts were characterised by greater variety, particularly in their alternation between <es> and <is/ys>.

However, whilst Kopaczyk's (2001) conclusions are supported by her data, she acknowledges that there are only four OSc texts available in LALME for comparison against forty-three NME texts. There is no objective reason to assume that these texts are representative of OSc as a whole, especially as they are specifically selected from the areas of Scotland closest to England, Kopaczyk's (2001) main aim being cross-border comparison. In fact, there is reason to suppose that the texts may not be representative of OSc inflectional orthography. Simpson (1973: 44) discusses the plural abbreviation symbol which he describes as 'a looped vertical mark which usually indicates suspension of *–is* or *–es* [which was] especially common [. . .] in vernacular texts'. This <ꝛ> abbreviation symbol has traditionally been subsumed under one or other of the fully-realised inflectional forms, hence Aitken and Macafee's (2002: 71) characterisation of it as 'the manuscript abbreviation for *–is*'. The <ꝛ> abbreviation is discussed by Kopaczyk (2001), who found that it was most common in ME texts from Cumberland, but that the OSc manuscripts did not use it at all. Based on this finding, Kopaczyk (2001) speculates that the plural abbreviation symbol was not frequently used in Scotland and, on the evidence of the majority unabbreviated npl {S} form in Cumberland being <es>, that the abbreviation could be interpreted as standing for <es>. Having said this, Kopaczyk does acknowledge the impossibility of definitively assigning an equivalence relationship between the abbreviation and a particular orthographic representation of the inflection. Even if a scribe consistently used <es> whenever he did not abbreviate the inflection, it is not certain that he considered <ƒ> a direct abbreviation of <es>. If the scribe also occasionally used <is/ys> forms, which many NME scribes did (King 1997: 160), the uncertainty is even greater.

Kopaczyk (as Bugaj 2004a, 2004b) performed a study of the npl {S} forms found in the *Wigtownshire Burgh Court Book*, finding that the most common {S} realisation was <is/ys> (59 per cent), followed by <ƒ> (40 per cent). <ƒ> is represented in the LALME Linguistic Profile for the *Wigtownshire Burgh Court Book* as italicised '–es'. Kopaczyk acknowledges that it is possible to argue for the interpretation of <ƒ> as <is/ys>, and a consequent change in the usual LALME practice of expanding this symbol as –es; but ultimately comes to the same conclusion as in her previous (2001) study, that it is impossible to say whether a scribe intended one or other fully realised inflection when he wrote the abbreviated form. As stated in the LALME documentation (McIntosh, Samuels and Benskin 1986), the encoding of abbreviated forms of {S} as '–es' is intended to provide consistency across the corpus, rather than as a judgement indicating any particular underlying representation.

Kopaczyk's empirical studies present a mixed view of the role of abbreviation in the representation of {S} in OSc, with occurrence of abbreviation ranging from complete absence in the Scottish-English border manuscripts (Kopaczyk 2001) through occasional attestation in the first part of the manuscripts of the *Wigtownshire Burgh Court Book*, to accounting for 40 per cent of all {S} inflections in the latter half of the same group of texts (Kopaczyk, as Bugaj 2004a, 2004b). However, Kopaczyk's studies were constrained by lack of data, the only substantial source material being the OSc material from areas close enough to the Scottish-English border to be included in LALME, the primary focus of which is English texts. To more fully investigate the distribution of the orthographic forms of {S} in OSc prose, it is necessary to use a data source which represents OSc as a geographic whole.

4. A Linguistic Atlas of Older Scots

LAOS (Williamson 2008) is an online, lexico-grammatically tagged corpus containing transcriptions of approximately 1,250 OSc legal records. Each text in LAOS represents a diplomatic transcription of an OSc legal document dated between 1380 and 1500. Each token of each word or, in some cases, morpheme, is lexically and grammatically tagged. A LAOS tag is identified by an initial '$' symbol, followed by:

(a) a *lexel*, representing the Present-Day English (PDE) lexical item exemplified by the token;
(b) a *grammel*, preceded by '/' representing the word class and grammatical categorisation of the word form; and
(c) a transcription of the orthographic form of the token, preceded by '_'.

Figure 9.2 shows a manuscript image of an extract from LAOS text number 36. The text below the image shows the transcription of the words in LAOS, a transcription which

LAOS	$day/npl_DAI+S	$of/pr_OF	$/P23G_YAIRe	$life/npl_LIF+is
Manuscript	<dais>	<of>	<yair(e)>	<liſſ>
PDE	days	of	their	lives

Figure 9.2 Extract from LAOS text 36: liferent from Dirleton, East Lothian. May 1447. (Source: Edinburgh University Centre for Research Collections (CRC))

Table 9.1 The frequency of different orthographic forms of {S} attested in LAOS

Orthographic form of {S}		Number of tokens in LAOS	
<ſ>		7480	(61%)
<is>	(inc. <js>, <iß>, <iȝ>)	2517	(20%)
<es>	(inc. <ese>, <eß>, <eȝ>)	1314	(11%)
<ys>	(inc. <yß>)	558	(5%)
<s>	(inc. <ß> <ȝ>)	412	(3%)
Total		12281	100%

indicates (as far as possible) the actual manuscript letters and, finally, a PDE translation. The first token shown in Figure 9.2 is <dais>, a plural form of *day*. This token is represented in LAOS by an initial lexel 'day' followed by the grammel 'npl' denoting 'plural noun'.[1] The LAOS transcription of the manuscript form, <dais>, uses upper-case letters to represent lower-case manuscript forms, and indicates a morpheme boundary between the stem and the {S} suffix with '+'. The third and fourth words in the extract, <yair> *their* and <liſſ> *lives*, illustrate the LAOS convention of representing manuscript abbreviations using lower-case letters. In contrast to the Scottish border data in LALME (see section 3.1), <ſ> is indicated in LAOS by lower-case 'is', reflecting the characteristic fully-realised OSc variant of {S}.

To ascertain the distribution of orthographic variants of {S} in the LAOS data, I extracted all tokens of plural nouns inflected with {S}. Table 9.1 shows the frequency of each orthographic form of {S} attested in LAOS, with the percentage of the dataset of npl forms each realisation accounts for.

The most common realisation of {S} in LAOS is <ſ>, with 61 per cent of {S} tokens realised this way. The frequency of <ſ> to denote {S} is therefore higher than

---

[1] The full LAOS specification of this form, and all forms including a morpheme boundary, contains an additional tag which refers only to the affix. The full specification of <dais> is therefore $day/npl_DAI+S $/pln_+S. These additional tags serve a crucial purpose when searching for bound morphemes in LAOS, but are omitted here in the interest of clarity.

the frequency of all full realisations of {S} combined. Of the full realisation forms, the most common is <is/ys>. However, this form, which is widely accepted as a diagnostic of Scots texts (see section 3), accounts for only 25 per cent of the total {S} tokens in LAOS.

5. The abbreviation symbol

As mentioned in section 3, Simpson (1973: 44) describes this OSc abbreviation symbol as 'a looped vertical mark which usually indicates suspension of –is or –es [. . .]'. The focus of Simpson's (1973) book is the assistance of modern readers in the deciphering of OSc manuscripts. In editions in which the rendering of this level of palaeographic detail is unnecessary (for example, an edition focusing on the literary aspects of a text), the <ʄ> abbreviation symbol has traditionally been subsumed under one or other of the fully-realised inflectional forms. Some accounts of OSc morphology make no mention of manuscript abbreviation (Kuipers 1964; King 1997). Those who do, acknowledge it as a 'manuscript abbreviation for –is' (Aitken and Macafee 2002), with the implication that <ʄ> and <is> can be assumed to be equivalent and functionally identical.

The tendency in the transcription of medieval texts to treat manuscript abbreviations as irrelevant and to expand them silently is exemplified by Jenkinson's (1937) advice to transcribers of such texts. He advocates reproducing 'all the peculiarities of the original' without making judgements as to their 'value or interest'. The single exception he makes to this rule, however, is to sanction the expansion of abbreviations 'where there can be no doubt as to the way in which the original writer would have written them *in extenso*'. In published editions of medieval manuscripts intended to be read as prose texts, this procedure is likely to be both typographically necessary and reader-friendly. For palaeographic and linguistic analyses, however, silent expansion masks the manuscript reality.

The shape of the symbol itself is described with reference to ME manuscripts by Johnson and Jenkinson (1915: 63). They classify the abbreviation as a 'special sign [denoting] *–es* or *–is*', differentiating it from superscript letters and from mutually indistinguishable *sigla*. These *sigla* generally take the form of a horizontal stroke above a manuscript word to indicate the truncation of an internal letter or letters; or an upward- and backward-curving stroke extending from the final letter of a word to indicate the suspension of a final letter or letters. Johnson and Jenkinson's illustration of the form the abbreviation takes is reproduced in Figure 9.3. Though the shape of

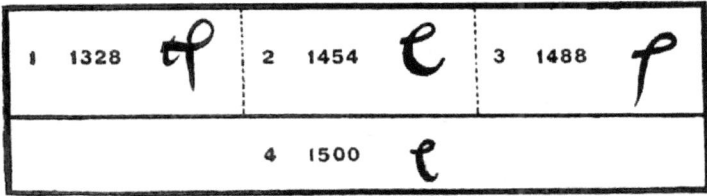

Figure 9.3 Illustration of palaeographic forms of the {S} abbreviation over time (Johnson and Jenkinson 1915: 63).

the abbreviation appears consistent, or, at least, recognisable, from the first illustration (1328) to the last (1500), Johnson and Jenkinson note its similarity to a stroke indicating suspension of final <g>, as well as other letters. The most reliable criterion for identifying this abbreviation shape where it stands for –*is* or –*es*, they suggest, is whether the stem it occurs with is clearly a plural noun.

Like Johnson and Jenkinson (1915: 63), Simpson (1973: 44) suggests that the abbreviation was 'especially common in plurals in vernacular texts'. The roots of the abbreviation are, as suggested by Simpson's example of its use to signal the omission of <is> in *multis*, in Medieval Latin orthography. Cappelli (1982 [1899]: 2) describes <ſ> as a 'truncation sign' used in Medieval Latin, stating that, though it could be used to signify the omission of any final letter or series of letters, it was most commonly used for –*is*.

6. Investigation

Section 5 described the tendency in the literature on OSc inflectional morphology to characterise <ſ> as a direct abbreviation of <is> and make no distinction between the two. My analysis seeks to determine whether the identification of <ſ> as a palaeographic device can be empirically verified. In particular, I aim to determine:

(a) whether scribes employed <ſ> for {S} as a 'shorthand', convenient abbreviation of what would otherwise have been written fully as <is/ys>; or
(b) whether there is evidence in LAOS to suggest that factors other than scribal convenience motivated the use of <ſ>.

6.1 Data

I extracted a dataset from LAOS consisting of all tokens containing an npl {S} inflection following a consonant-final stem (the reason for the exclusion of vowel-final stems is the difficulty of assigning with any certainty the boundary between a vowel-final stem and a vowel-initial suffix). This data extraction yielded a list of 12,281 tokens, with each individual token identified according to the text which contains it, the lexel it exemplifies, its grammatical category and manuscript form (see section 4). Using the text number, contextual information was added to the dataset using the LAOS *Index of Sources* (IoS) (Williamson 2008). This contextual information is further discussed in section 6.3.

Table 9.2 The structure of the dataset extracted from LAOS

Text	Lexical item	Form	Text date	Text location	Text type
36	life	lifſ	1447	British National Grid: 351 683 N	charter
	heir	airſ			
	portion	port(i)onis		Latitude and Longitude: 56.037365, 2.7879873	

6.2 Statistical methods

To investigate the potential conditioning factors for the realisation of {S} as <ʃ> in LAOS, I use a bipartite statistical methodology consisting of traditional proportion graphs as well as a more statistically robust regression modelling technique. As described in section 1, the field of historical dialectology has not, hitherto, been at the forefront of statistical innovation. However, I hope to bridge the gap here by showing how familiar and interpretable investigative output can be backed up by a solid statistical foundation. The technique I use to create this statistical foundation is generalised additive modelling (GAM). I do not offer an in-depth explanation of the theoretical background to this methodology, but instead refer the interested reader to several texts which do offer such background: Wood (2006); Baayen (2008); Zuur (2009); Wieling, Baayen and Nerbonne (2011); and Wieling and Nerbonne (2015).[2] The following section, however, provides a brief overview of GAM as it is used in this investigation.

GAM is a type of regression modelling. The most basic type of regression is simple linear regression, in which the effect of a change in an independent variable (IV) on a continuous dependent variable (DV) is measured. For example, we could fit a simple linear model of the effect of the IV date on the DV 'number of texts in LAOS'. The model's output would show how changing the value of date affected the value of 'number of texts in LAOS'. A model output suggesting that a higher value for DATE leads to a higher value for 'number of texts in LAOS' would mean that there existed a positive correlation between these two variables: as DATE increases, so does 'number of texts in LAOS'. The likely explanation for this would be that there are more extant records of OSc from later periods than from earlier ones.

The basic concept of GAM is the same as simple linear regression – measuring the effect of change in the value of an IV on the value of a DV. However, GAM differs from simple linear regression in several ways which make it especially suitable for the current investigation:

(a) GAM allows analysis of non-continuous DVs (such as binary ('yes-no') variables). The feature under investigation here is the realisation of {S} as <ʃ>, a binary variable with two levels: 'abbreviated' or 'not abbreviated'. Whereas a simple linear regression measures the change in the value of a continuous DV, a GAM fit with a binary DV measures the likelihood of one outcome as opposed to the other, in this case, the likelihood of 'abbreviated' as opposed to 'not abbreviated'.

(b) GAM enables mixed effects modelling. Recall Gries' argument, quoted in section 1, that corpus studies must account for the hierarchical structure of their data. Table 9.2 shows how LAOS tokens are nested both within texts and within lexels. IVs which are included to account for potential idiosyncrasies caused by nested data are known as random effects. Random effects are not part of the core focus of the investigation, but need to be controlled for because of the hierarchical structure of the data. The

---

[2] In particular, Wieling and Nerbonne (2015) demonstrate the advantages of GAM from a linguistic standpoint.

investigation is not particularly concerned with obtaining results for the effect of individual texts or lexels on the likelihood of abbreviation, but if these factors are not considered, systematic variation caused by them may be attributed to other factors. The inclusion of random effects therefore allows us to account for a source of systematic variation in the data and increases the confidence we can have that the results of our model accurately reflect the effects of the IVs we are interested in (known as fixed effects).

(c) GAM can produce results for IVs which are not linear in their correlation with the DV. The simple linear model discussed above of the effect of DATE on 'number of texts in LAOS' could reveal a correlation between these two factors, but would not be able to reveal a non-linear relationship between them. For example, if the number of texts in LAOS increased between 1380 and 1450, decreased between 1450 and 1480, and increased again between 1480 and 1500, the simple linear model would show only an overall trend across the period 1380–1500. A GAM, however, would capture the fluctuating trend across the period by fitting a 'smooth' function, that is a trend which allows for the correlation between the IV and DV to differ at different levels of the IV. As well as being able to capture temporally changing trends, GAM is able to model spatial trends in data, allowing the visualisation of trends in a DV over a geographic area.

In the following sections, I describe the IVs included in the GAM and present the tabulated results of the final model fit. I explain the results of the model with reference to this table and explain how the coefficient values can be interpreted. Alongside this explanation, I present traditional proportion graphs which reflect the results shown by the model. Whilst these two methods yield the same conclusions, the advantage of using a GAM model as opposed to simply presenting the percentage data is the increased certainty that the trends shown by the proportion graphs are indeed reflective of the correlation between the DV and the IV they represent, to the exclusion of other IVs as well as potential idiosyncratic effects of individual texts and lexels.

6.3 Independent variables

What follows is a description of each IV included in the model, details of its extraction from LAOS and an account of any changes or omission made for the purpose of this investigation.

6.3.1 Stem-final letter

As described in section 5, the abbreviation symbol is generally assumed to be a solely palaeographic feature and therefore functionally equivalent to a full realisation of {S}. The inclusion of stem-final letter (SFL) as an IV will indicate whether the immediate palaeographic environment of {S} has an effect on whether it is realised as <ꝼ> or not. To populate the values for this IV, each token is assigned a value according to the final letter of the transcription of its form, with the following exceptions:

1. tokens ending in scribal flourishes (*sigla*) are assigned a value reflecting the final fully-realised letter only. Where *sigla* are indicated in LAOS by ~ or ", the *siglum* is assumed to have no linguistic content. If a mark is judged to indicate the suspension of a final letter such as <e>, that letter is indicated in the transcription (see Figure 9.2, in which the upward- and backward-turning flourish on the <r> of <yair(e)> *their* is taken to represent the omission of a final <e>). For example, $sum/npl_SOM~+YS *sums* is assigned an SFL value of 'm'.
2. tokens ending in an indecipherable letter (denoted by '[]' in LAOS) are omitted from the dataset. For example, $pertinent/npl_PerTINEn[]+is *pertinents*.
3. tokens ending in a superscript letter (denoted by a preceding '^') are omitted due to low frequency. For example, $heir/npl_A^R+is *heirs*.

Table 9.3 shows the resultant categories of the SFL variable, and the frequency with which they occur in the dataset. In total, there are nineteen unique SFLs attested in the dataset. To avoid misleading results caused by SFLs with very few representative tokens, the SFLs with the lowest token frequency are omitted, with an essentially arbitrary threshold for inclusion of >50 tokens. The SFLs omitted are <b, ß, u, v, w> and <x>, leaving a total of thirteen unique SFLs.

Table 9.3 The original categories of the SFL variable, and the frequency with which they occur in the dataset. Items below the dotted line were omitted due to low frequency

SFL	Tokens
r	4222
d	2812
t	1726
n	988
m	730
l	497
g	440
h	264
c	153
k	147
f	77
s	60
p	52
w	45
v	28
u	25
b	10
x	4
ß	1
Total	12281

6.3.2 Text location

The IoS lists the location of origin for each manuscript where it is stated within the text itself. As the manuscripts are legal records, the place of issue or signature was often recorded, so most texts in the corpus have a location recorded in LAOS. These locations are given as British National Grid coordinates in the IoS, and converted into geographic coordinates for the purpose of my analysis. This conversion was completed using an online, public-access coordinate conversion tool (Ordnance Survey 2016). Some texts are not assigned coordinate values in the IoS. Where this is the case, the text and all tokens associated with it are retained in the dataset but given null values for latitude and longitude (LAT./LONG.).

6.3.3 Text date

As with text location, the legal status of most of the LAOS manuscripts meant that they were marked with the date of composition or issue within the text. Where it exists, this information is included in the IoS. I have included in my analysis the year of composition of each text, disregarding the day and month if mentioned. Where a period of years is specified, I take the earlier year as representative of the text (for example, a text with an entry in the IoS specifying a date range of 1477–1478 is assigned the date 1477).

6.3.4 Text type

The majority of texts are assigned a type in the IoS. This type classification contains information about the form as well as the purpose of the document. In Example (2), text number 960 is identified as a *transumpt* (transcript) of a signet letter, that is a document to which the king's official seal was appended (*notar*, n. 1, *Dictionary of the Scots Language* 2004). The text is further specified as relating to an *excambion*, or exchange of lands; as a result, this charter has as many as four text subtypes. Most texts have at least one subtype as in (3), while some texts have a single-category type, e.g. (4) and (5).

  (2) Text 960: Charter/ transumpt/ signet letter/ exchange/ excambion
  (3) Text 238: Cartulary/ copy/ lease
  (4) Text 1415: Cartulary
  (5) Text 93: Charter

Taking into account all the permutations of different text categories existing in the IoS, there are a total of 191 unique classifications. Clearly, it is not practical to retain all details of the original text type categorisation in a statistical analysis. The categories in first position ('first position' meaning that the category label is listed either alone or before the other categories of a text) in my dataset are listed in Table 9.4. Five categories together account for 1,000 texts of a total 1,098 in my dataset (91 per cent). Seventeen texts (1 per cent) are split between a further thirteen categories.

Table 9.4 Frequency of text types attested in LAOS

Category	Number of texts
Book	397
Charter	334
Cartulary	110
Notarial Protocol Book	106
Burgh Record	53
Summons (5), Letter (2), Assize, Bond, Court Book, Credence, Deed Poll, Law, Record, Record Book, Royal Letter, Signet Letter (1 each)	17
Total	1017

Eighty-one texts (7 per cent) are not assigned a type in the IoS. However, fifty-six of these are noted as being transcribed from a manuscript which is clearly a burgh record book,[3] and four are identified as Acts of Parliament.[4] Based on this information, I assigned the types 'Burgh Record' or 'Act of Parliament' to these texts. The remaining twenty-one texts and their tokens are retained in the dataset but assigned a null value for the variable of text type.

As well as assigning these new types, I reduced the list of text type categories by combining category names which suggest a high potential for textual similarity. For example, the separate categories 'Burgh Record' and 'Record Book' seem, *prima facie*, likely to have a great deal in common. This is not to say that a differentiation as it is presented in the IoS is unwarranted, but rather that, for the purposes of my analysis, there is no reason to suppose that such fine-tuned categorisation is necessary. In the case of 'Burgh Record' (three texts) and 'Record Book' (one text), consultation of the IoS shows that all four texts are extracts from the *Peebles Burgh Council Record Book*. This suggests that the categories of 'Burgh Record' and 'Record Book' can be combined, certainly for the purposes of my analysis, into one category, taking the title of the largest category, 'Burgh Record'. Having examined the text typology in the IoS together with the text content, I ultimately reduced the text type categorisation in my dataset to the groupings shown in Table 9.5.

All the text types used in this investigation are formed by merging smaller categories with larger categories, apart from State Document (STA). Rather, this text type grouping consists of texts which are identified as state documents in the IoS, including royal letters (given under a royal seal such as the signet or privy seal), summonses, petitions to parliament, Acts of Parliament, and diplomatic texts such as treaties and declarations of war.

---

[3] Fifty-five texts (1801 to 1861 and 3007): *Burgh Court Book of Dunfermline*; five texts (3001 to 3006): *Aberdeen Council Register*; one text (3008): *Ayr Burgh Court Book*; one text (1234): *Newburgh Court Book*.

[4] Texts 9502, 9516, 9517 and 9522.

Table 9.5 Reduced typology of LAOS texts

Type	Total texts
Burgh Record (BUR) This category contains record books and documents kept by local Burgh councils relating to the administration and law of the Burgh.	509
Cartulary (CAR) Most texts in this category are monastery copies of charters.	110
Charter (CHA) This is a somewhat 'catch-all' type, essentially covering any legal documents which do not belong to the other categories.	298
Notarial Protocol Book (NOT) Books used by a notary public to record details of legal transactions. A notary public was someone authorised to perform legal transactions.	106
State Document (STA) Texts which are identified as state documents in the IoS. This category includes royal letters (given under a royal seal such as the signet or privy seal), summonses, petitions to parliament, acts of parliament, and diplomatic texts such as treaties and declarations of war.	54
No type	21
Total	1098

7. GAM summary

Table 9.6 shows the results of the GAM model fit to the data extracted from LAOS.[5] DATE, LAT./LONG., TYPE and SFL are fixed effect IVs, so the model shows the effect of a change in these IVs on the DV. DATE is modelled as a smooth function, meaning that the relationship between DATE and ABBREVIATION is not assumed to be linear. Rather than generating a straight trend line to show a correlation of date with the likelihood of abbreviation, the GAM captures fluctuation of the likelihood of abbreviation over time. Latitude and longitude are combined in a smooth function (LAT./LONG.) to produce a geographic visualisation of the likelihood of abbreviation. SFL is modelled as a parametric term as it is a categorical variable. TEXT and LEXEL are random effect IVs. Random effects account for similarities between tokens which come from the same text, or exemplify the same lexical item. By including these predictors, I can be confident that, for example, an apparent effect of date is not an artefact of idiosyncrasies displayed by individual texts. The results of the GAM indicate that both of these random effects are significant, meaning that there is a significant amount of variation in the data which can be attributed to the idiosyncrasies of individual texts and lexical items.

The coefficient estimate ('Est.') for each category of these IVs indicates the difference between the log-likelihood of abbreviation at that level of the IV and the refer-

---

[5] GAM fit using R (R Core Team 2013) package mgcv (Wood 2006). Visualisations created using packages ggplot2 (Wickham 2009) and visreg (Breheny and Burchett 2016).

ence level. In other words, the relative likelihood of the DV ABBREVIATION having the value 'abbreviated' compared with the (arbitrary) reference level of the IV. For example, the IV TYPE consists of the categories 'Burgh Record' (BUR), 'Cartulary' (CAR), 'Charter' (CHA), 'Notarial Protocol Book' (NOT) and 'State Document' (STA), as specified in Table 9.5. The reference level is BUR. The GAM therefore provides coefficient values indicating the relative likelihood of {S} being realised as <ʃ> for each of the other types compared to BUR. A negative coefficient value indicates that the likelihood of <ʃ> for a text type is lower than for BUR, and a positive coefficient value indicates that the likelihood is higher. Table 9.6 also gives the corresponding standard error ('Std. Err.') and z-value ('z-val.') of each coefficient. The standard error value indicates the standard deviation within the category, or how much the individual coefficient estimates of tokens with that level of the IV differ from the mean on average. A lower value means we can have greater confidence in the coefficient estimate because there is less variation between individual data points – they behave more like a coherent category. The z-value indicates, for each coefficient value, how many standard deviations away from the overall mean for the IV that value is. This value is used to judge whether a coefficient is significantly different from the mean. In Table 9.6, z-values with stars following them represent coefficients which are significantly different from the mean at p<0.05. That is, the level of the IV corresponding to that significant coefficient value has a significant correlation with the likelihood of abbreviation.

Overall, the model explains approximately 68 per cent of the observed deviance in the data. This suggests that the model containing the combined effect of these IVs is a fairly good fit to the data, but that there is also a large amount of variance in the data which is not accounted for by the model. However good the fit of a model, there will always be some variation remaining in the data which the model does not fully capture. This may be due to the existence of another significantly correlated IV which has not been included into the model, or there may be sources of explained variation which are impossible to include in the model. When working with a corpus of transcribed manuscripts such as LAOS, there are many potential sources of this latter kind of variation, because a transcriber and compiler of a corpus is required to make decisions about the representation, inclusion and organisation of the data with the needs of all potential users of the resource in mind. The transcriber is also constrained by the limitations of the data available to them. For example, the numbering of texts in LAOS is done on the basis of individual manuscripts – each unique manuscript has a unique number. The feature which is under investigation here is palaeographic, and therefore more likely to vary between scribes than the texts they produce. Very few documents in LAOS are specific as to the identity of their scribe however, so this element of variation cannot be captured. The results of the fitted model show that individual text variation is a significant factor in predicting abbreviation, but it is likely that this is indicative of scribal variation, rather than actual textual variation. In the following sections, I interpret the model results for each IV using knowledge of the OSc period and, in the final section, I again address the limitations of this kind of data source, but show that the techniques demonstrated in this chapter are crucial in controlling for hierarchical data structure and revealing the significance and explanatory power of IVs.

Table 9.6 Summary of a generalised additive model (GAM) of the likelihood of npl {S} abbreviation. $R^2 = 0.72$; deviance explained = 68%; n = 10,886

Parametric coefficients

	Est.	Std. Err.	z-val.
(Int.)	3.00	0.27	11.12*
Type			
CAR	-1.25	0.26	-4.89*
CHA	-0.80	0.19	-4.12*
NOT	-0.83	0.30	-2.78*
STA	-2.24	0.33	-6.77*
SFL			
c	-0.05	0.49	-0.12
f	-0.14	0.57	-0.24
g	0.16	0.40	0.4
h	-4.14	0.47	-8.75*
k	0.73	0.50	1.46
l	-3.54	0.35	-10.06*
m	-8.55	0.87	-9.88*
n	-7.18	0.50	-14.49*
r	0.28	0.28	1.03
s	-5.59	0.88	-6.39*
t	0.32	0.28	1.14

Approximate Significance of Smooth Terms

	EDF†	Chi sq.
Random Effects		
Text	392.23	1,968.53*
Lexel	161.98	1,097.99*
Fixed Effects		
Date	4.08	67.35*
Lat./Long.	6.08	27.43*

†EDF = estimated degrees of freedom

7.1 Text date and location

Table 9.6 shows that DATE and LAT./LONG. are significant predictors of <ʃ> (both p<0.001). The GAM estimates the degrees of freedom (EDF) for the IV DATE to be 4.08, suggesting that the correlation with the DV is not linear (a linear correlation is suggested by an EDF of 1). Figure 9.4 shows the change in likelihood of {S} being realised as <ʃ> over the period 1380–1500. The likelihood of abbreviation increases initially up to approximately 1450, then remains fairly static to 1500. Figure 9.5 shows the likelihood of {S} tokens being realised as <ʃ> across the geographical

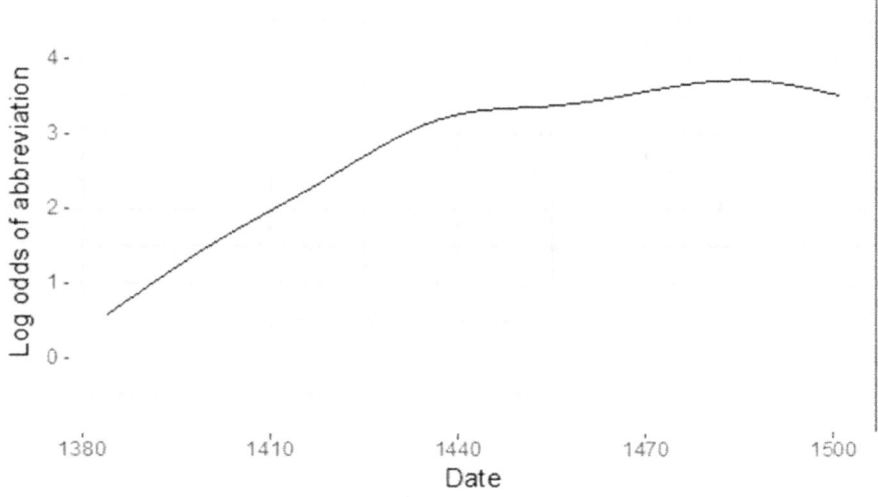

Figure 9.4 The likelihood of npl {S} token to be realised as <ʃ> over the period 1380–1500 (shading represents 95% confidence interval)

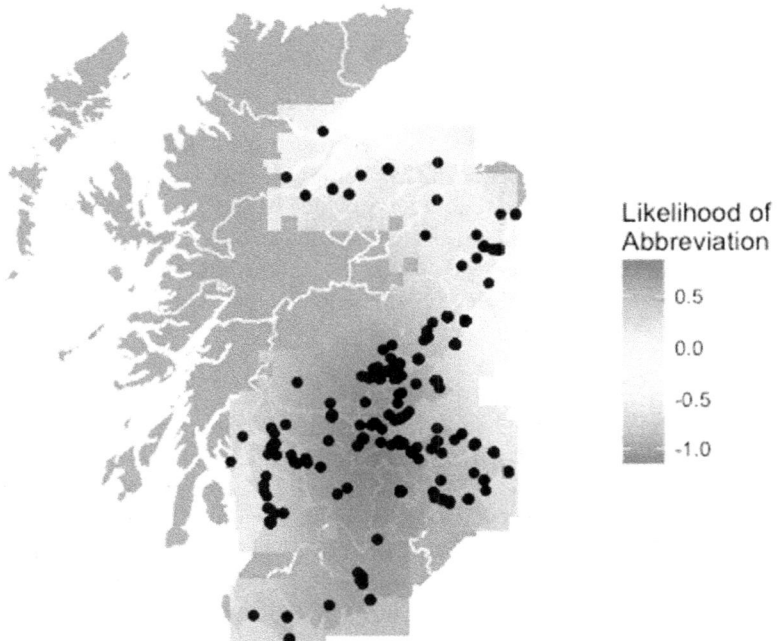

Figure 9.5 The likelihood of {S} being realised as <ʃ> over the geographical area represented by LAOS: black dots represent locations of individual texts, red shading represents a higher likelihood of <ʃ>, blue shading represents a lower likelihood of <ʃ>

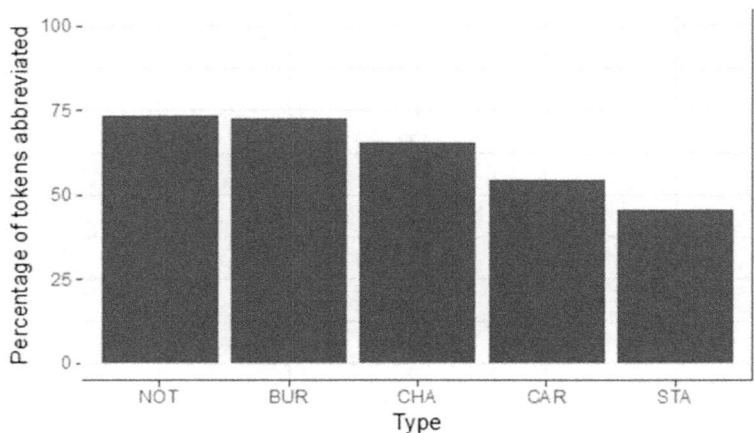

Figure 9.6 The percentage of {S} tokens belonging to each 'type' category realised as <ʃ> (tokens from texts with no type specified excluded)

area represented by the LAOS Corpus. The red shaded areas in the central belt and borders represent a higher likelihood of <ʃ> in these areas, whilst the yellow-blue shading in the peripheral areas indicates a lower likelihood of <ʃ>.

7.2 Text type

Figure 9.6 shows that texts of type CAR, CHA, NOT and STA are significantly less likely to contain <ʃ> as a realisation of npl {S} than those of the reference type, BUR, as all of these types have negative coefficient values with p-values <0.05. The text type which shows least similarity to BUR is STA, which has the lowest coefficient value of the four texts. Figure 9.6 shows the overall percentage of {S} tokens realised as <ʃ> for each of these types. In line with the GAM results, Burgh Records contain the highest proportion of <ʃ>, and State Documents the lowest.

7.3 Stem-final letter

The contextual IVs presented in the previous sections provide evidence of the trends in scribal usage of <ʃ>. However, the IV which is most informative about the potential reason for the use of <ʃ> specifically as opposed to a full form such as <is> is SFL. Table 9.7 lists comparative Akaike Information Criterion (AIC) scores for the full GAM shown in Table 9.6, as well as nested models, each with one IV removed. AIC is a statistic which measures the quality of regression models fit to the same dataset relative to one another. The 'quality' of each model is assessed according to the variation in the dataset which it accounts for, traded off against its complexity. The larger the difference between the AIC score of the full GAM and the AIC score of a nested GAM, the larger the improvement in the accuracy of the GAM caused by the predictor which has been removed. Removing SFL from the

Table 9.7 AIC scores for the full GAM model and nested models (a larger difference in AIC indicates more model improvement contributed by an IV)

	IV removed	df*	AIC	AIC Difference
Full GAM fit by fREML:	-	583	5777	-
	LAT./LONG.	613	6172	395
	DATE	606	5819	41
Full GAM fit by ML:	-	577	5782	-
	TYPE	620	6044	262
	SFL	814	6375	593

*degrees of freedom

GAM causes the largest AIC difference, suggesting that this factor makes the biggest improvement to the model in terms of how much of the variation in the data it accounts for.

Table 9.7 shows the coefficient values estimated by the GAM for each level of the IV SFL (each individual letter). These values represent, for each letter, the log-likelihood that any given token of {S} attached to a stem ending in that letter will be realised as <ʃ>, relative to the likelihood value corresponding to the letter used as the baseline for these estimates. The baseline (or 'default') level of SFL is arbitrarily set as <d>, so the coefficient values for individual SFL represent how much more likely (positive values) or less likely (negative values) a token of {S} following that particular letter in stem-final position is to be realised as <ʃ>. For example, the model estimates the coefficient value for <c> to be -0.05. As this is a negative number, we can state that a token of {S} following stem-final <c> is less likely to be realised as <ʃ> than a token following stem-final <d>. The p-value for <c> is 0.903. Assuming a significance threshold of $p < 0.05$, this p-value shows that the difference in likelihood of <ʃ> represented by the coefficient value for <c> is not significant. This means that a token of {S} following stem-final <c> is slightly less likely to be realised as <ʃ> than a token of {S} following stem-final <d>, but not significantly so. The letters <h, l, m, n> and <s> all have values of $p < 0.05$. The corresponding coefficient values, which are all negative, show that all of these letters are significantly *less* likely than <d> to be followed by <ʃ>. The letters <c, f, g, k, r> and <t>, on the other hand, all have values of $p > 0.05$, indicating that they are not significantly more or less likely than <d> to be followed by <ʃ>.

Two clear groups of SFL are evident in these results, those which correlate with likelihood of <ʃ> in the same way as <d>, and those which do not. Those which do not are all significantly less likely to be followed by <ʃ> than <d>. The two groups of SFL, then, correspond to the likelihood of <ʃ>, with one group containing SFL which are much more likely than those in the other group to be followed by <ʃ>. This category division is clearly shown by the percentage plot in Figure 9.7. The SFL <c, f, g, k, r> and <t> are followed by <ʃ> in 65–85 per cent of tokens whereas the letters <h, l, m, n> and <s> are followed by <ʃ> in fewer than 23 per cent of tokens. This visualisation shows the reality of the dichotomy observed in the GAM results, which is that <c, f, g, k, r> and <t> are followed by <ʃ> in the majority of

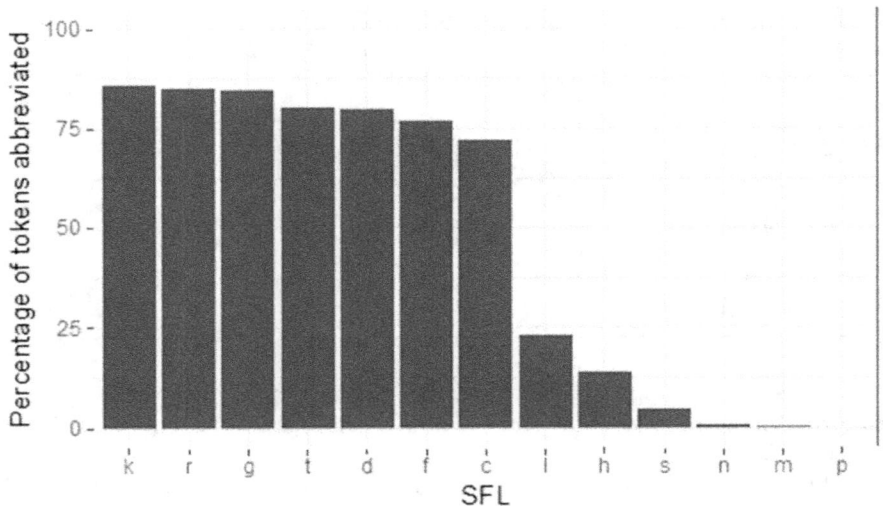

Figure 9.7 The percentage of {S} tokens realised as <ʃ> following each SFL

cases, and <h, l, m, n> and <s>, especially <m, n> and <s>, are rarely followed by <ʃ>.

The reason for this can be found in the respective orthographic forms of these SFL. Table 9.8 gives an example of each SFL taken from a LAOS manuscript. Each SFL is shown in word-final position and preceding {S}. The letters which are often followed by <ʃ> are those which terminate in a horizontal stroke. These horizontal strokes proceed from different parts of the anatomy of each letter, but all the letters which are commonly followed by <ʃ> have this in common. Conversely, all the letters which are seldom followed by <ʃ> culminate in a downstroke (<m, n, h>), a curve (<s>) or a hook (<l>). The <ʃ> symbol consistently begins with a horizontal stroke before looping backwards into a descender.

Figure 9.8 illustrates how easily a letter ending in a horizontal stroke flows into <ʃ>, compared with a letter ending in a downstroke.

8. Generalised additive modelling for diachronic corpus data

In section 1, I introduced the concept of statistical modelling of diachronic corpus data and commented on the recent increase in data sources which are suitable for detailed quantitative analysis. Putting this into practice, a GAM showed that <ʃ> was correlated with stem-final letter as well as with some contextual factors: the date, location and register of a text. In particular, fitting a GAM with a random effects structure as advocated by Gries (2015: 97) allowed me to take into account the hierarchical structure of the LAOS Corpus data. The model results showed that there was significant variation in the data due to the individual differences between texts and between lexels, but that even accounting for these differences, the main effects in the model remained significant.

Table 9.8 Illustrations of SFL from LAOS manuscripts in word-final position and preceding {S}. (Sources: Scotland's Places (Historic Environment Scotland 2017); Edinburgh University CRC)

SFL	<ʃ> (%)	Word-final		Preceding {S}	
t	86		<grauntt> grant		<settʃ> sets
k	85		<qwilk> [the -]-which		<likʃ> likes
g	83		<thyng> thing		<schillingʃ> shillings
d	78		<said> '[afore -]said [thing]'		<saidʃ> '[afore -]said [things]'
f	78		<y(air)of> thereof		<wyffʃ> wives
r	71		<ʒher> year		<airʃ> heirs
c	65		<sic> such		<placʃ> places
l	22		<sal> shall		<malis> mails
h	13		<worth>		<scathis> scathes ('damage')
s	3		<hors> horse		<causeʒ> causes
n	1		<reuocation> 'revocation'		<port(i)onis> portions
m	1		<tym> time		<fredomis> freedoms

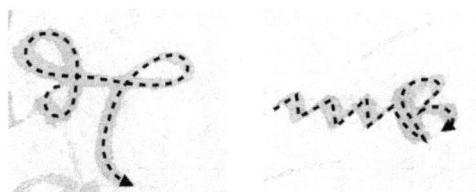

Figure 9.8 The path of a pen-stroke for stem-final <dʃ> and <nis>

Having said that, it should be noted that the model itself did not fully get to the root of the research question. The model revealed the significance of SFL in the likelihood of abbreviation, and that the likelihood of <ʃ> following particular SFL follows a clear-cut distribution into a group with high likelihood of <ʃ> and a group with low likelihood of <ʃ>. However, the link between the SFL which make up these two groups is clear only on inspection of the manuscript forms themselves. To make sense of the fact that, for example, <m> is far less likely to be followed by <ʃ> than <d>, it is necessary to see the palaeographic forms of the letters and make a logical deduction about the physical formation of them by a scribe. This is an aspect of analysing medieval manuscripts which does not apply to studies in which the primary data source is digital, and which have led the way in the application of regression modelling techniques to corpus data. Nonetheless, the techniques used in this chapter allow the researcher of medieval manuscripts to simultaneously examine the correlation of many contextual and lexical factors with transcribed manuscript forms. This has the advantage, not only of revealing whether specific predictor variables significantly correlate with particular features when all predictors are taken into account, but also of controlling for the variance that idiosyncratic features of particular texts or words cause in such a dataset.

9. Conclusions

The main conclusion arising from the results presented here is that the realisation of the npl {-S} inflection as the abbreviation sign <ʃ> in OSc legal texts is primarily conditioned by SFL. This suggests that the representation of {S} as <ʃ> as opposed to one of the available fully-realised orthographic forms of {S} is motivated by palaeographic convenience, rather than an intention on the part of the scribe to represent any functional difference.

There are also contextual factors which show a significant correlation with the likelihood of <ʃ>. <ʃ> becomes more likely over time, perhaps suggesting that as vernacular writing became more common, scribes began to use more 'shorthand' features. However, this increase in likelihood plateaus in the mid-fifteenth century. Given the strong predictive capacity of SFL, this 'ceiling' effect may be due to the restriction of <ʃ> to certain SFL. <ʃ> is never completely dominant because certain letter shapes are incompatible with it.

The location (LAT./LONG.) of a text correlates significantly with the likelihood of abbreviation. Abbreviation is more likely in the central and southern counties than the northern, peripheral areas. These areas are historically less densely populated than

Central and Southern Scotland, so this trend may suggest a spreading of the scribal practice of abbreviation from central areas, though this hypothesis would require a model containing an interaction between date and location to confirm.

As well as temporal and spatial effects, the type of text in which a token occurs also emerges as a significant predictor of the occurrence of <ʃ>. <ʃ> is significantly more likely in Burgh Records and Notarial Protocol Books than in Acts of Parliament and Cartularies, suggesting that register influenced use of <ʃ>. As noted in Table 9.5, the type label 'Burgh Record' denotes day-to-day administrative and judicial records of local Burgh councils. This type of text may well be expected to contain more palaeographically-convenient features than, for example, a state document such as an Act of Parliament. There is the potential for a register difference between these two text types, with State Documents requiring a higher level of formality than Burgh Records; State Documents may have been written with the idea of preserving their contents for posterity, particularly in the case of Acts of Parliament or diplomatic treaties. Furthermore, the time period covered by LAOS saw the evolution of script styles, from the formal and regular charter hands to secretary hands, which employed more cursive and speed-motivated features such as abbreviation (Simpson 1973: 43). The scribes of Burgh Records are less likely to have undertaken such training in formal script styles, and in any case are more likely to have utilised a script which facilitated faster copying (Williamson 2017, personal communication). State Documents, however, are more likely to have been written by professional scribes, trained in the penmanship appropriate for courtly records, and may exhibit a more formal (less cursive) style of script as a result.

References

Aitken, Adam J. (1985). 'Introduction: A history of Scots', in Mairi Robinson (ed.), *The Concise Scots Dictionary*, Aberdeen: Aberdeen University Press, pp. ix–xvi.

Aitken, Adam J. and Caroline Macafee (2002). *The Older Scots Vowels: A History of the Stressed Vowels of Older Scots from the Beginnings to the Eighteenth Century*, Edinburgh: Scottish Text Society.

Baayen, R. Harald (2008). *Analyzing Linguistic Data: A Practical Introduction to Statistics Using R*, Cambridge: Cambridge University Press.

Bann, Jennifer and John Corbett (2015). *Spelling Scots: The Orthography of Literary Scots, 1700–2000*, Edinburgh: Edinburgh University Press.

Benskin, M., Laing, M., Karaiskos, V. and Williamson, K. (2013). *An Electronic Version of A Linguistic Atlas of Late Mediaeval English*, Edinburgh (available at http://www.lel.ed.ac.uk/ihd/elalme/elalme.html).

Breheny, Patrick and Woodrow Burchett (2016). *visreg: Visualization of Regression Models*, R package version 2.3–0.

Bugaj, Joanna (2004a). '"For ye vrangus haldyn of thre bollis of beire fra hyre": Nominal plurals in south-western Middle Scots', *Linguistica e Filologia* 19: 53–74.

Bugaj, Joanna (2004b). *Middle Scots Inflectional System in the South-West of Scotland*, Frankfurt am Main: Peter Lang.

Cappelli, Adriano (1982 [1899]). *The Elements of Abbreviation in Medieval Latin*

Paleography [translated by David Heimann and Richard Kay], Lawrence: University of Kansas Libraries.

Dictionary of the Scots Language (2004). Scottish Language Dictionaries Ltd (available at http://www.dsl.ac.uk/entry/dost/notar_n_1 (accessed 7 September 2017)).

Gries, Stefan Th. (2015). 'The most under-used statistical method in corpus linguistics: Multi-level (and mixed-effects) models', *Corpora* 10(1): 95–125.

Historic Environment Scotland (2017). *Scotlands Places* (available at http://www.scotlandsplaces.gov.uk).

Iosad, Pavel (2016). *scotmappR: Map of pre-1890 Scottish Counties for Use with ggplot2*, R package version 0.0.0.9000.

Jenkinson, Hilary (1937). *A Manual of Archive Administration*, London: P. Lund, Humphries & Co. Ltd.

Johnson, Charles and Hilary Jenkinson (1915). *English Court Hand, A.D. 1066 to 1500, Illustrated Chiefly from the Public Records. Vol. 2*, Oxford: Clarendon.

King, Anne (1997). 'The inflectional morphology of Older Scots', in Charles Jones (ed.), *The Edinburgh History of the Scots Language*, Edinburgh: Edinburgh University Press, pp. 156–181.

Kniezsa, Veronika (1997). 'The origins of Scots orthography', in Charles Jones (ed.), *The Edinburgh History of the Scots Language*, Edinburgh: Edinburgh University Press, pp. 24–46.

Kopaczyk, Joanna (2001). 'The Scots-Northern English continuum of marking noun plurality', *Studia Anglica Posnaniensia* 36: 131–140.

Kuipers, Cornelius (1964). *Quintin Kennedy, 1520–1564: Two Eucharistic Tracts*, Nijmegen: Drukkerij Gebr. Janssen.

Laing, Margaret (2013). *A Linguistic Atlas of Early Middle English, 1150–1325* (available at http://www.lel.ed.ac.uk/ihd/laeme2/laeme2.html).

Lass, Roger, Margaret Laing, Rhona Alcorn and Keith Williamson (2013). A Corpus of Narrative Etymologies from Proto-Old English to Early Middle English and Accompanying Corpus of Changes, The University of Edinburgh (available at http://www.lel.ed.ac.uk/ihd/CoNE/CoNE.html).

McIntosh, Angus, M. L. Samuels and Michael Benskin (1986). *A Linguistic Atlas of Late Mediaeval English*, Aberdeen: Aberdeen University Press.

Minkova, Donka (1991). *The History of Final Vowels in English: The Sound of Muting*, Berlin: Mouton de Gruyter.

Ordnance Survey Ltd (2016). *Batch Coordinate Transformation Tool* (available at https://www.ordnancesurvey.co.uk/gps/transformation/batch).

Petrović, Saša, Miles Osborne and Victor Lavrenko (2010). 'The Edinburgh Twitter corpus', in *Proceedings of the NAACL HLT 2010 Workshop on Computational Linguistics in a World of Social Media* [WSA 10], Stroudsburg, PA: Association for Computational Linguistics, pp. 25–26.

R Core Team (2013). *R: A Language and Environment for Statistical Computing*, Vienna: R Foundation for Statistical Computing (available at http://www.R-project.org/).

Simpson, Grant (1973). *Scottish Handwriting, 1150–1650: An Introduction to the Reading of Documents*, Aberdeen: Aberdeen University Press.

Smith, Jeremy (2012). *Older Scots: A Linguistic Reader*, Woodbridge: Boydell Press.
Wickham, Hadley (2009). *Ggplot2: Elegant Graphics for Data Analysis*, New York: Springer-Verlag.
Wieling, Martijn and John Nerbonne (2015). 'Advances in dialectometry', *Annual Review of Linguistics* 1(1): 243–264.
Wieling, Martin, Harald Baayen and John Nerbonne (2011). 'Quantitative social dialectology: Explaining linguistic variation geographically and socially', *PLOS ONE* 6(9): 1–14.
Williamson, Keith (2008). *A Linguistic Atlas of Older Scots* (available at http://www.lel.ed.ac.uk/ihd/laos1/laos1Z.html).
Wood, Simon N. (2006). *Generalized Additive Models: An Introduction with R*, Boca Raton, FL: Chapman & Hall/CRC.
Zuur, Alain F. (2009). *Mixed Effects Models and Extensions in Ecology with R*, New York: Springer.

10

An East Anglian Poem in a London Manuscript? The Date and Dialect of *The Court of Love* in Cambridge, Trinity College, MS R.3.19*

Ad Putter

1. Introduction

The Court of Love (henceforth *CL*) has come down to us in a single manuscript: Cambridge, Trinity College, MS R.3.19, folios 217r–234r. This manuscript is well known, especially to students of Chaucer. In the sixteenth century it was owned by the London antiquarian John Stow (c.1525–1605). The manuscript contains various annotations and a Lydgate fable (fols 235r–236r) in his hand, and it provided the basis for some of the spurious additions to the Chaucerian canon as assembled by Stow himself in his 1561 edition of *The Workes of Geffrey Chaucer* (Forni 2001: 36–38). *CL* was one of the works printed in this edition, its text based directly on that of the Trinity manuscript (Fletcher 1978), and for a long time it passed as a poem by Chaucer. The significance of the manuscript is reflected by its accessibility: it was included in the Facsimile Series of the Works of Geoffrey Chaucer (Fletcher 1987) and is now available online.[1] There are published editions of the poem itself by Skeat (1897) and Forni (2005), neither of which is wholly satisfactory. In the case of Skeat, this is because he airbrushed the text as he found it in the manuscript, deleting unhistorical final -*es*, standardising spellings and emending to restore sense, rhyme and metre. I have no problem with emendation *metri causa*, but because Skeat's idea of correct English was Chaucerian English he often restored rhyme in ways that take the text further away from rather than closer to the original (see below, p. 229). Forni's more recent edition, on the other hand, presents the text, 'warts and all, as it appears in the manuscript, only correcting what seem to me to be obvious scribal errors that interfere with sense' (Forni 2005: 9). The edition thus makes no attempt to recover what the poet actually wrote, but it is not a wholly reliable

---

* This chapter has benefited substantially from corrections and comments by a number of readers. I would particularly like to thank Richard Beadle, Richard Dance, Judith Jefferson, Myra Stokes, the editors and the two anonymous peer reviewers for various suggestions for improvement.

[1] See http://trin-sites-pub.trin.cam.ac.uk/james/viewpage.php?index=1370.

transcription of the manuscript either. A particularly persistent problem is confusion of <y> with <g> (or perhaps with yogh, which the editor modernises to <g>). Given the resulting mistranscriptions – for instance, Forni consistently reads *gove* and *gove(n)* ('gave' and 'given') for MS *yove(n)* (278, 531, 547, 642, 668, 688, 742, 770) – the edition should be used with caution. In the text below citations from the poem are from Forni's edition, but I have checked these against the digitised manuscript and have flagged up corrections in footnotes.

In this chapter I would like to discuss *CL*'s date of composition and the date of the manuscript copy, and to analyse and account for some of the text's linguistic peculiarities. These topics have received a certain amount of attention before. Walter Skeat when editing the poem in *Chaucerian and Other Pieces* effectively dismissed the idea that Chaucer could have written it, though in doing so he went from one extreme to the other, arguing that the poem was a neo-medieval fabrication dating from the fourth decade of the sixteenth century at the earliest. While he accepted that the hands of the two main scribes of Trinity College, MS R.3.19 belong to the late fifteenth century, he thought that the *CL* scribe's hand was mid-sixteenth century. This gave him scope to maintain that the language of *CL* was deliberately archaic: 'I have no space to discuss the matter at length; so shall content myself with saying that the impression produced upon me is that we have here the work of one of the heralds of the Elizabethan poetry' (Skeat 1897: lxxvi). As we shall see, Skeat did in fact pursue the matter at some length. In his edition, various notes on language and metre reinforce his 'impression', and he returned to the matter in his book on the Chaucer canon (1900).

Because generations of scholars read the poem in Skeat's edition, his views have continued to be influential. C. S. Lewis's statements about *CL* in *The Allegory of Love* (1936: 256–257) and in *English Literature in the Sixteenth Century* (1954: 239–241) repeat Skeat's view of it being a sixteenth-century exercise in medievalism, and from Skeat and Lewis the idea has passed uncritically into modern criticism (e.g. Miskimin 1975: 23; Windeatt 1990: 11). The most significant consequence of this for our knowledge of Middle English (ME) is that *CL* was excluded from the corpus of sources for the *Middle English Dictionary* (*MED*). On what I can only assume to be Skeat's authority, all texts copied by the two main scribes of Trinity R.3.19 were mined for *MED* entries (these dated to c.1500), while the texts copied by the *CL* scribe were set aside. Again on Skeat's authority, citations from the poem were assigned a date of c.1530 in all printed volumes of the *New English Dictionary* (as *OED* was then known) that were published after Skeat's 1897 edition. The fascicles published before 1897, covering A to mid-F, had a date of c.1450. The conflicting dates for *CL* in the current online edition of *OED*, where some citations are dated c.1450 and others c.1530 (with some further dates in between) reflect this curious history of scholarly 'progress'.[2]

In the light of new findings about this manuscript and about the scribe who copied *CL* in Trinity College, MS R.3.19, Skeat's late dating of the poem has become untenable, however, and so his view of the poem's language and prosody as

---

[2] I owe this explanation for the *OED* datings to Nicolay Yakovlev (personal communication).

a pseudo-medieval fabrication is in urgent need of revision. My aim is to show that the text of the poem as it stands reflects a compromise between the language of the original poet and that of the scribe (with intermediate stages of copying being highly likely). Although the complications resulting from this scribal layering make it difficult to date and localise the original poem, I hope to show that the poet's language was both earlier and more northerly – probably East Anglian – than that of the Trinity scribe, who was a professional scribe from London. Although this scribe set about translating the poem into his own language, various traces of the poet's original dialect remain.

The result is what, following Benskin and Laing (1981), we may call a *Mischsprache*. A *Mischsprache* is

> what the late Professor Tolkien aptly described as a 'nonce-language', 'an "accidental"' form of language, occurring in all its details only in one text (Tolkien 1929, p. 105). Its defining characteristic is the persistent co-occurrence of dialect forms whose regional distributions are such that their geographical overlap cannot reasonably be supposed.[3]

The Introduction to eLALME, from which this definition is taken, makes two further points that inform my methodology. The first is that if a *Mischsprache* is in rhymed verse, as is the case with *CL*, rhyme words are often of special diagnostic value (Introduction, 3.3.5). As is well known, scribes who converted the language of the original into their own dialect often felt constrained by rhyme to retain original forms. If they disregarded rhyme constraints, this will be evident in spoiled rhymes. Since scribes were at least as likely to take over the whole rhyme word as to reproduce only the rhyming element (Introduction, 3.3.6), attention should be paid not merely to the rhyme sound but to the rhyme word in its entirety. The second point is that scribes who translated the language of their exemplar into their own dialect were nevertheless prone to perpetuate some 'relicts' from their copy-text (Introduction, 3.2.1). Such relicts can consist either of exotic dialect words which were not used in the scribe's own language or of common words which the scribe frequently used, but not in the form in which he imported them from his exemplar. In a text that has been 'translated' very thoroughly, we would expect relicts of the second type to be few in number and to stand out in sharp relief against the majority form(s) of the same word that represent(s) the copyist's own dialect and scribal practice.

Of course, Skeat had at his disposal neither the methodological insights nor the research tools that exist today. The norm against which he measured *CL* was Chaucerian English, and deviations from this norm he described as 'blunders', 'bad mistakes', 'false grammar', 'misspellings', 'utterly disgraceful specimens', and so on. Imperfections of rhyme he tended to regard as failures on the part of the poet. That said, his notes on linguistic details almost always draw attention to things that need explaining, and his theory that the poem was written in a fake form of ME has the

---

[3] Cited from M. Benskin, M. Laing, V. Karaiskos and K. Williamson, *An Electronic Version of A Linguistic Atlas of Late Mediaeval English* (2013), at http://www.lel.ed.ac.uk/ihd/eLALME/eLALME.html, 'General Introduction', 3.5.1.

considerable merit of recognising that the language of *CL* is indeed a peculiar 'nonce language', even if the reason for this may not be the one Skeat proposed. Skeat also observed that some forms (the verbal inflections *-in* and *-yn* in infinitives and plural presents) are 'consistent with East Anglian spellings' (Skeat 1897: lxxvii), though he variously ascribed these non-standard forms to the scribe (Skeat 1897: lxxvii) and to the poet (Skeat 1900: 135).

My own position is that *CL* is a mid-fifteenth-century East Anglian poem, which in the course of scribal transmission was thoroughly but not completely translated into the language of London, c.1480. I have organised my argument in four main sections. Since the definitive *terminus ad quem* for *CL*'s original date of composition is provided by the manuscript copy of the poem, I begin with a discussion of Trinity R.3.19, drawing on the latest research and on my own findings about one of the items copied by the scribe of *CL* (section 1). I then examine critically the linguistic and metrical evidence on which the theory that the poem is from the sixteenth century has been based (section 2). After arguing that this evidence is faulty, I hope to show that some of the peculiarities and errors in the text are not the result of a poet failing to produce 'proper' ME, but rather due to the fact that the poet's language and dialect differed in numerous minor but significant ways from the scribe's. To reveal the mixture of dialectal forms in the resulting *Mischsprache*, I focus on rhyme words and on apparently faulty rhymes, which indicate that the scribe frequently imposed his own forms on those of the original (section 3). The rhyme evidence will be supplemented with consideration of relicts outside of rhyme that similarly seem to point to an East Anglian provenance for the poet (section 4). The findings will be summarised in a brief conclusion.

2. The manuscript and the scribe of *CL*

Cambridge, Trinity College, MS R.3.19, the manuscript that Stow used to augment the Chaucer Corpus in his printed Chaucer edition, can itself be described as a commercial anthology of Chaucerian pieces. It consists of a series of booklets, mostly containing poems, but it ends with a booklet containing a prose chronicle entitled *The Petigrew* [i.e. pedigree] *of Englond* (folios 247r–251r). In line with his argument that *CL* is a Renaissance poem, Skeat claimed that the *CL* scribe was a contemporary of John Stow's and wrote in 'a hand of his [i.e Stow's] own period' (Skeat 1900: 132). This is simply not the case. Stowe's script is a mid-sixteenth-century italic; the *CL* scribe's is a late-fifteenth-century secretary.

Thanks to Linne Mooney's work (2001; 2011: 207–210), the activities of the professional scribes who produced the manuscript, all of them London based, can be documented more precisely. One of the main scribes of the Trinity manuscript – scribe A, known as 'Trinity Anthologies scribe' – also produced booklets for other manuscripts that have survived; in one of these, Trinity College, MS R.3.21, he added a prayer (in different ink) for Edward IV to Lydgate's poem 'A Prayer for King, Queen and People', where the 'King' in question was Henry VI. The addition must have been made to bring the poem up to date with the political situation after the deposition of Henry VI in 1461, and before the death of his successor, King Edward IV, who died in 1483. The scribe of *CL*, also known as scribe C, can also be located in time and space, for his hand has been identified in another manuscript, now Oxford, St John's College, MS 266, containing Lydgate's *Siege of Thebes*. The peculiarity of this manuscript is that it was formatted and ruled to accompany Caxton's 1483 printed editions of Chaucer's *Troilus*, *The Canterbury Tales* (henceforth *CT*) and John Mirk's *Quattor Sermones*, with which it was then bound (Bone 1931–2: 286–291). To make this printed book (ESTC S108840[4]) look even more like a manuscript the first printed page was replaced by a full-page illumination on vellum, probably executed by the same artist as that of Cambridge, Trinity MS R.3.21 (Hanna 2002: 329–331). The connections between the producers of Trinity MS R.3.19, R.3.21 and the early printed book trade are further apparent from the fact that the exemplar for the excerpt from Chaucer's Monk's Tale in Trinity MS R.3.19 was Caxton's 1478 edition of the *Canterbury Tales* (Fletcher 1987: xxix).

Scribe C, the copyist of *CL*, was active around the same time as scribe A, and, as Bradford Fletcher's analysis of the watermarks has shown, they used the same paper stock (Fletcher 1987: xxii–xxiii). Although the manuscript was not actually bound until the late sixteenth century and the copying of the individual booklets was parcelled out to different professional scribes, there is every indication that the manuscript was conceived of as a unit and 'was together in generally its present form by ca. 1480' (Fletcher 1987: xxii). The booklets were ruled to the same specifications; the different scribes all left gaps for decorated initials (which, unlike those of its sister manuscript, Trinity MS R.3.21, were never completed). The booklets were then foliated by the same hand that also foliated MS R.3.21. That hand is 'pretty certainly fifteenth century' (Greg 1913: 540).

The Petigrew of Englond (*P*), the only other item in this manuscript copied by the *CL* scribe, offers some further evidence about dating. The purpose of *P* is to make the case that the English monarchy has a just entitlement to the crowns of France and Castile. Since the title claims asserted in *P* are those of Edward IV, it must have been copied before 1483, since it 'would not have been worth the copying after his death' (Fletcher 1987: xxix). Fletcher was unaware that *P* is substantially the same text as *The Chronicle from Rollo to Edward IV*, edited by Raluca Radulescu (2003) on the basis of the only two manuscripts then known to her, BL, MS Harley 116 and MS Harley 326. Michael Hicks (2009) was able to add three other known manuscripts to the list, including Trinity MS R.3.19, and further noticed that versions of this chronicle were different because scribes adapted the text to their individual purposes and kept dynastic genealogies up to date. These revisions do not obscure the fact that the original version was written in 1461 or 1462. Both in *P* and in the two Harley versions edited by Radulescu, the last of the kings who is mentioned in a series of sections rubricated 'The xiii[th] kyng', 'The xiiij king', and 'The xv. king' (fol. 249v; cf. Radulescu 2003: 420–421) is Henry VI, and this section ends 'Thise iij heires haue occupied and kepte the seid Crowne of Englond ffrom the Rightfull heires this iij score yeres and iij and Blessed be god it is for the moste parte knowen' (fol. 250r).[5] 'Thise iij heires' who

---

[4] ESTC refers to the English Short Title Catalogue, at http://estc.bl.uk/.
[5] Quotations are based on my transcriptions of *P* from Trinity College, MS R.3.19. To my knowledge there is no published edition of this version.

have kept the crown of England from the 'Rightfull heires' are presumably Henry IV, V and VI (the Harley versions read 'Thies thre Harryes', p. 421). This seems to have been written by a Yorkist sympathiser awaiting Edward IV's accession, though it should be said that the 'iij score yeres and iij' (i.e. sixty-three years) after the usurpation of Henry IV (1399) would take us to 1462, one year into the reign of Edward IV. Edward IV is subsequently mentioned in a section on the sons of Edward III and their descendants. These include Richard, Duke of York, who 'begatte kyng Edward the iiij[th] nowe beyng the most Rightfull kyng of Englond' (250r; Radulescu 2003: 421).

The text of *P*, however, contains some interesting evidence of revision. In the base text edited by Radulescu from MS Harley 116, Margaret of York is referred to as 'Margaret that is vnmaried' (422); MS Harley 326 instead has 'Margaret þe duches of Burgoyn' and thus brings Margaret's marital status up to date: Margaret had married Charles the Bold to become Duchess of Burgundy in 1468. However, Margaret was widowed nine years later, which probably explains why *P* has yet another reading: 'Margaret whiche was maryed vnto Charles Duc of Burgoyne' (f. 250r). The past tense appears to acknowledge Charles's death in 1477. If this is indeed the implication of 'was maryed', *P* can be tentatively dated to between 1477 and 1483 (when Edward IV died). This is consistent with Fletcher's conclusion that the manuscript in its entirety (barring Stow's later additions) was complete around 1480. Since the scribe of *P* also copied *CL*, and in the 1480s, Lydgate's *Siege* in Oxford, St John's, MS 266, *CL* can hardly have been composed in the sixteenth century: it must pre-date the date of the manuscript copy, which is c.1480.

Moreover, the Trinity scribe of *CL* was evidently copying a poem with a tangled pre-history of textual transmission. The clearest signs of this are apparent lacunae in the narrative. It is doubtful, for instance, that the lines numbered 1093–1176 in modern editions of *CL* are actually in the right place: the passage is oddly sandwiched between the poet's encounter with allegorical vices and virtues (1023–1092 and 1176–1316) and seems to belong to an earlier part of the poem. William Neilson argued that this problem can be solved by inserting lines 1093–1176 after line 266 (Neilson 1899: 6–7), but if we do this we notice some suspicious repetition:

'Ye than,' quod I, 'whate done thise prestes here,
Nonnes, and hermytes, freres, and all thoo
That sit in white, in russet, and in grene?'
'For soth,' quod she, 'thay waylen of theire woo . . .' (253–256)

'O why be som so sory and so sadde,
Complaynyng thus in blak and white and gray?'
'Freres thay ben, and monkes, in gode fay.
Alas, for rewth, grete dole it is to sene,
To se thaim thus bewaile and sory bene . . .' (1095–1099)

This repetition and the breakdown of the rhyme scheme at one of the fault lines (*here*: *grene* at 253–255) show that the textual problem is more intractable than Neilson thought, and suggest that the displacement of the passage in the transmission of the poem in turn prompted further scribal revision. There is another lacuna after line 1316, when, just after the poet has introduced two allegorical 'officers of love', the text launches straight into a passage of direct speech. No speaker has been introduced, and there is no *inquit* formula to prepare us for this abrupt shift.

We are therefore clearly dealing with a poem that had undergone several stages of copying before it was copied again by a professional London scribe around 1480.

3. Vocabulary and metre

In the light of the manuscript evidence, we need to look again at the arguments that persuaded earlier scholars to date the poem to the sixteenth century. One of these arguments has no bearing on ME language, and can be dealt with quickly. The *CL* poet had read widely in the works of Chaucer and his followers, and Skeat conjectured that he had access to Thynne's 1532 edition. According to Skeat, 'suspicion becomes almost a certainty if it be true that ll. 495–496 are borrowed from Rom. Rose, 2819–20 (Skeat 1897: lxxvi–lxxvii). The lines in question – 'and all the chere / That thee hath made thy lives lady dere' – do indeed recall the *Romaunt of the Rose* – 'or of hir chere / That to thee made thi lady dere' (Benson 1987), and there is plenty of other evidence that the poet knew the *Romaunt* (Neilson 1899: 52–55, 186–187, 205, 228), but it hardly follows that he knew it from Thynne's edition. He could surely have read it in manuscript. Admittedly, only one manuscript of this poem was known to Skeat (University of Glasgow, MS Hunter 409 (V.3.7)), and this manuscript itself served as the copy-text for Thynne's edition, but given the extent of scribal error and dialect layering in this manuscript (Dahlberg 1999) it was always a reasonable assumption that there were others. The recent discovery of a new manuscript fragment of the *Romaunt* (Horobin 2006) puts this beyond doubt.

Of greater linguistic interest are Skeat's editorial notes on items of vocabulary, where the supposed lateness of the poem is the dominant theme:

> 30. *metriciens* . . . a word which has a remarkably late air about it. Richardson gives an example of it from Hall's chronicle.

> 170. This is the first quotation in the New E. Dictionary s.v. Assumon; and the next is from the poet Daniel.

> 913. *Cambridge*; this form is not found till after 1400. Chaucer has *Cant-e-brigg-e* (C.T., A 3921) in four syllables, which appears as *Cambrugge* in the late Landsdowne MS., after 1420.

> 1087. *goth on patens* . . . a very early example of the word *paten*. It occurs in Palsgrave (1530).

Skeat 1900 adds further ammunition (134):

> I note, for example, the earliest dates which the Dictionary gives as other examples of a word's appearance: *demene*, demeanour, 734, and in More (A.D. 1534); *dulled*, 478, known in A.D. 1514; *bedreint*, 577, known in 1563; *flawe* = *flave*, yellow, 782, known in 1657; *directed*,

785 (instead of Chaucer's *direct*), known in 1598 [. . .]; *bass* 797, known in 1529; *aureat*, 817, known in 1599 [. . .] *acroke*, 378, used by Caxton; *cocold* (for Ch. *cok-e-wold*), 410, ab. 1530; *celsitude*, 611, found in Dunbar; *deformity*, 1169, used by Caxton, &c.

None of these notes stands up to scrutiny. *Metricien* is not 'remarkably late': Hall's chronicle is actually the latest attestation of 'metrician' in the now-obsolete sense of 'poet' cited in *OED*; the earliest is from an anonymous translation, c.1425, of Higden's *Polychronicon*. With regard to the verb *assummon*, *OED* overlooks the fact that Malory uses it repeatedly in his *Morte D'Arthur* (see *MED* s.v. assomonen). Spellings of *Cambridge* with <Cam> (or variants thereof) as the first syllable had become widespread much earlier than Skeat claims. Below is a list of forms taken from *The Historical Gazetteer of English Placenames*:[6]

Caumbrig(g)e 1348 Works, 1458 Paston
Caumbrygge, Caumbrege 1348 Works, 1458 Paston
Cawmbregge 1406 Cl
Kawmbrege 1449 Paston
Cambrugge 1378 Cl
Cambregge 1412 Pat, 1552 Pat
Cambrig(g)e, Cambryg(g)e, Cambrydge, Cambredge 1412 Pat, 1552 Pat
Camberage 1473 Paston
Camebrygge 1478 Paston
Caunbrigg(e) 1386 Cl, 1396 Pat
Cawnbrygg 1461 Paston

It is clear from this list that the spelling 'Cam' (or variants thereof) dates back to the second half of the fourteenth century. This is also true for spellings of 'bridge' with <dg>. LALME attests <dg> spellings for BRIDGE (item 95) in only one linguistic profile (LP) (7420, CUL Kk.1.12, Herefordshire, c.1450), while *MED* omits all such spellings in its list of variant forms (see brigge n.), but a search of its quotations and its text corpus shows they are not uncommon: the spelling first occurs c.1390 in Trevisa's translation of Higden's *Polychronicon* (Cambridge, St John's College, MS H.1 (204)), and later <dg> forms occur in the Paston Letters, the Winchester Malory, and elsewhere. The form 'brydge' in *The Treatise of Fishing* in Yale University Library, Beinecke MS 171 (Leicestershire, c.1450) is worth noting, because it has not been picked up by LALME in its relevant LP (464). *Paten* is not 'very early': *OED* (s.v. patten) and *MED* (s.v. patin) give a string of earlier attestations from 1390 onwards. *Demene* is attested in *MED* c.1450 (s.v. demeine n. 2) and *dulled* c.1425 (s.v. dullen v.); *bedreint*, is not attested in *MED* but cf. *adreinte* a1450 (s.v. drenchen v.). *Flawe* is a *hapax legomenon* (*OED* s.v. flaw); *directed* is recorded in *OED* a1400 (s.v. direct v. 2b); *bas* 'kiss' is first attested in *MED* c.1400; *aureate* is

---

[6] See http://placenames.org.uk/. The list has been generated by a search (by 'modern place-name form') for 'Cambridge'. Abbreviations can be expanded on this website tool by hovering over the abbreviation.

Lydgate's coinage (see *OED* and *MED*); *acroke* first occurs a1387 (*MED* s.v. acroke and *OED* s.v. acrook); the spelling *cokolde* a1440 (*MED* s.v. cokewold); the word *celsitude* a1460, and *deformity* in 1413 (*OED* and *MED* s.v. deformite). The only word in the poem that really is late is one that Skeat does not pick up on: it is the word 'stirp' ('lineage', from Latin *stirps*), which appears in the metathesised spelling *stripe* in line 16: 'So is she sprong of noble stripe and high'. *OED* dates the first occurrence of the word to 1503; *MED* does not record it at all. Given the date of the manuscript booklet of *CL* (c.1480), we have here the earliest attestation of the word in the English language

The poet's metre, too, gave Skeat the idea that the poem must be late. The poet writes fluent iambic pentameter verse, but inflectional and etymological final *e* is for the most part silent. Skeat (1897: lxxvii) observed only four examples of pronounced final *e* ('to dredë vice', 603, 'in thilkë place', 642, 'to servë me', 909, 'his lenë body', 1257), and writes about one of them in his note to 642: 'Here, for a wonder, is an example of final *e*. The author took the whole phrase, "In thilk-ë place", from some previous author. Cf. in thilke places (*sic*); *Rom. Rose*, 660 (Thynne).' Again Skeat's note is misleading. The citation from Thynne suited Skeat's theory that the poet had read the *Romaunt* in Thynne's 1532 Chaucer edition, but there are exact matches in other places (e.g. 'in thilkë place', *CT* V.160, VII.601), and the idea that this is a literary borrowing is in any case unnecessary. The tenacity of disyllabic 'thilke' and 'ilke' in late-fifteenth-century poetry probably has a linguistic explanation (Horobin 2003: 101): these adjectives only ever occurred in weak position and so would not have been encountered in forms with and without grammatical final -*e*, as other adjectives were. Moreover, there are several other instances where final *e* is needed to avoid clashing stress, e.g.: 'where thay hadë woned' (241); 'to lyve and dyë same' (317); 'that may her hartë pease' (397); 'Enrolle it thyn hartë privité' (492);[7] 'a millë milion' (589); 'In wofull ourë [=hour] fostered' (975); 'and then myn hartë brak' (1327). Certainly, pronounced final *e* is uncommon, but the examples show that the poet used it correctly, where grammar and etymology justify it, and not just in set phrases conceivably borrowed from other poets. It is possible that some further cases of final *e* were lost in scribal transmission, for some of the short lines that occur in this poem are easily fixed by adding historical final *e*.[8] The scribe's copy of Lydgate's *Siege* certainly shows that he omitted final *e*s where metre requires them and where Lydgate continued to write and pronounce them (Horobin 2003: 129–130),[9] just as he wrote them in places where they do not grammatically belong.[10]

In infinitives, plurals and in past participles of strong verbs, the metrical need for an unstressed syllable is usually met by inflectional -*en*. The extent to which -*n*

---

[7] *Privité* is not the adverb 'secretly' (Forni 2005) but the noun 'secret hiding place', with preceding uninflected genitive ('of your heart').

[8] For instance, 'Whose harte is yet yoven to no wight' (742) can plausibly be emended to 'Whose hartë yet is ...'.

[9] E.g. (with metrical emendations in square brackets): 'Whan bright[e] Phebus passed was the Ram' (fol. 263r), 'He seid[e] playnly / wening for the best' (285r).

[10] As in 'Satorn olde' and 'Complet and tolde' (fol. 263r).

is retained in these contexts is striking (see Skeat 1900: 130), especially when compared with the scribe's usage in *P*, where inflectional *-n* never occurs except in two past participles (*begotten* and *knowen*). In *CL* 784, 'From every browe, to shewe a distaunce', the scribe probably omitted *-n* in line with his own usage (Skeat judiciously emends to 'schewen'). According to Skeat, *-n* retention is an 'anachronism' showing the inauthenticity of the poet's language (Skeat 1897: n. to 628), but the use of of *-n* in verbal inflections was subject to local variation. It is known to be a feature of late ME texts in East Anglian dialects (Seymour 1968: 167; Parkes and Beadle 1979–80: III, 55) and is unlikely to have struck audiences in these parts as 'anachronistic'.

A remarkable peculiarity of the poem is that the *-n* inflection also appears where it is not grammatically justified:

1. That thowe be trewe from hensforth to thy myght
   And *serven* love in thyne entencion. (289–290)
2. Wheder that she me *helden* lefe or loth (347)
3. Sojorne to tyme thow *sene* thy lady eft (499)
4. In secrete wise thay *kepten* ben full close (526)
5. That goddess chaste I *kepen* in no wise (684) (I kepen] MS in kepen)
6. For yf, by me, this mater *spryngen* oute (725)
7. For yf the basse *ben* full, there is delite (797)
8. Subjecte to ben, and *serven* you mekely (850)
9. And yf that I offend, or wilfully,
   Be pompe of harte, your precepte disobey
   Or *done* agayn youre wille unskilfully,
   Or *greven* you, for ernest or for play . . . (925–928) (greven] MS growen)
10. Many a stripe and a many a grevouse lasshe
    She *gaven* to thaym that wolden lovers be (1207–1208)

The conclusion Skeat drew from this is that inflectional *-en* had died out in the poet's language and that he was writing it randomly, wherever he needed an offbeat. This conclusion is far from inevitable. First, nunnation, the addition of ungrammatical *-n*, is well attested in ME poems (e.g. *Genesis and Exodus* and Layamon's *Brut*) from an earlier period when inflectional *-en* was alive and well (Arngart 1968: 18; Minkova 2003: 173–174). Second, we cannot tell from these examples whether we are dealing with an authorial practice or with scribal error. At 850 and 1208 the final *-en* is hypermetrical and looks to be scribal; at 374 'held' for *helden* would restore grammar and metre (a headless line, common enough in this poem); 684 and 928 already contain corruption, so it is reasonable to suspect scribal tampering (did the poet write 'ne kepe I in no wise' and 'grevë you'?); at 526 the poet may have used the disyllabic form 'keped'; at 797 we are probably dealing with an uninflected plural (common in Romance words ending in *-s*), particularly as the source for the line, Maximian's first elegy, also has the plural (*basia plena*).[11] The remaining lines are easy to emend ('this mater spryng[eth]', 'and

---

[11] The Latin source is cited by Forni 2005, n. to 798.

servë love'). I am not convinced that we have evidence here of a poet who was making up ME grammar as he went along. An alternative hypothesis is that the retention of historically justified -*n* was common in the poet's language but not in the scribe's, and that the latter was confused about where it should and should not be written.

The situation is more complex than Skeat allowed, and he and his followers overstated the artificiality of the poem's prosody. According to C. S. Lewis, the poem 'scans perfectly provided you make every final -e mute and also sound the -e in every plural and genitive in -es' (Lewis 1936: 256), but just as it is untrue that every final *e* is mute, so it is untrue that *e* in inflectional endings (*-es*, *-eth*, *-est* and *-ed*) is always sounded. For instance, *woneth* (143), *billes* (577), *Throwest* [=Trowest] (1039), *nonnes* (1102), *loved* (1197) are all monosyllabic. As far as metre is concerned, *CL* is not very different from, for example, Richard Roos's mid-fifteenth-century *La Belle Dame Sans Mercy* (also in Skeat 1897), a poem where metrical regularity also rarely depends either on the pronunciation of final *-e* or on apocope in final inflections.

4. The linguistic evidence of rhymes and rhyme words

In *Mischsprache* defective rhymes can reveal linguistic differences between the poet and the scribe, if (and this is an important caveat: see Cartlidge 1998) it can be assumed the poet was exact in his rhymes. In the case of *CL* this is a reasonable assumption. That the poet was particular about his rhymes is shown by his intolerance for the kinds of imperfect rhyme found in other ME verse, such as 'feature rhyme' and 'subsequence rhyme' (Jefferson, Putter and Minkova 2014).[12] The only apparent example of feature rhyme (involving consonants that are similar but not identical) occurs in the following lines:

> The secund statute: Secretely to kepe
> Councell of love, nat blowing everywhere
> All that I knowe, and let it synk and flete.
> It may not sowne in every wightes ere. (309–312)

Skeat's note to 311 reads: 'this must of course be emended to "synk or flete", as in Anelida, 182; C.T., A 2397', but the idiomatic expression Skeat refers to (not caring

---

[12] The feature rhyme reported by Dibelius (*rt*; *rd* at lines 147–148) is based on misreading of the rhyme scheme (Dibelius 1901: 167). Most of the so-called imperfect rhymes cited by Skeat (1897: lxxviii) have their origin in scribal translation, and are discussed in section 2; I do not discuss there the rhyme *playnt : talent : consent* (716–719), which is perfectly acceptable as it stands. The spelling *playnt* conceals the monophthong pronunciation [plɛnt]. The pronunciation [ɛ] for Old French /ei/ is indicated by spelling in various Chaucer manuscripts, such as Ha³ (from Leicestershire: Shonk 1988), 'And right as Alen in the plente of kynde', *Parliament of Fowls*, 316 (Furnivall 1871) and Gg (from East Anglia), 'How with hise blod hir selve gan she pente', rhyming with compleynt', in *Legend of Good Women*, 875 (Parkes and Beadle 1979–80, with discussion of MS provenance in 'Commentary', III, 1–67). Here and elsewhere, Chaucer manuscripts are referred to by their standard sigla (see Benson 1987: 1119–1120).

whether someone 'sinks or swims') makes no sense here and is probably precisely what led the scribe astray. The poet's point is that the secrets of love should be securely committed to one's mind and not divulged. Sense and rhyme are restored by emending *synk and flete* to 'synken depe', with 'sink' in the sense of 'commit to one's mind' (*MED* sinken s.v. 3(c)). Pertinent examples can be found in John Gower's *Confessio Amantis* II, 2068–2070: 'His tales with myn Ere I herde, / Bot to myn herte cam it noght / Ne sank no deppere in my thoght' (Macaulay 1900–1901) and in *CL* itself: 'And in thyne hartes botom let it synke ...' (395). Of subsequence rhyme (where one of the rhyme fellows has a subsequent phoneme or syllable not present in the other), I also find a lone example, and this one, too, is more apparent than real: the rhyme *array* and *always* (478–480) has been created by the editor; the manuscript clearly reads *alway*.

Given the complicated rhyme scheme, that of the rhyme royal stanza (ababbcc), another sign of the poet's high standards is that auto-rhymes are strictly avoided. Again there is one apparent exception:

And frayned hym question full hard:
'Whate is,' quod I, 'the thyng thou lovest beste?
Or whate is bote unto thi paynes hard?' (1275–1277)

However, given the poet's general avoidance of auto-rhymes, it seems likely that the first *hard* is not the adjective, as Forni appears to construe it, but the adverb ('insistently, earnestly'). In other words, we are not dealing with auto-rhyme but with *rime riche*, here involving the same words in different parts of speech. Medieval readers admired this type of rhyme as displaying skilful artistry (Yeager 1990: 34–36): it is not sloppy rhyming.

The scribe, on the other hand, was clearly not a poet, and his work (or his predecessor's) results in a number of short verses and deficient rhymes. Some of these simply involve carelessness. For instance, instead of the rare 'adversaire' (rhyming with *dispaire*), for which *MED* has only five entries, the scribe wrote the more common word 'adversary' (1035), and instead of the verb 'sojoure' (rhyming with *dishonoure*), he wrote *sojorne* (1253). Skeat did not approve of 'sojoure' as a verb, calling it a 'bad mistake' in his note to the line, but, although much less common than 'sojourn', it is securely attested, especially in East Anglia from where I argue the poet originated.[13] Potentially difficult proper names are miswritten: thus 'Metamorphoseos' (cf. Chaucer *Metamorphosios*, *CT* II.93, and n. to this line in Benson 1987) erroneously appears as *Metamorphosees*, wrecking the rhyme with *gloose* (1259–1260). Skeat tidied up most of

---

[13] See *MED* s.v. sojouren (v.). With the exception of occurrences in Charles D'Orléans and a Wycclifite tract in Cambridge, Corpus Christi College, MS 296 (localised by *eLALME* to Buckinghamshire), the attestations are East Anglian and North-East Midland, from Lydgate (Suffolk), Margery Kempe, Capgrave and *Promptorium Parvulorum* (all Norfolk) and Mannyng (Lincolnshire). All attestations are fifteenth-century: the earliest *MED* entry 'soioiuringe' from *Arthour and Merlin* in the Auchinleck MS is more likely to be an error for *soiourninge*.

these scribal errors, and his emendations are convincing, with some exceptions. Lines 820–821 appear in his edition (with Skeat's additions in square brackets) as 'For yf that Jove had [but] this lady seyn / Tho Calixto ne [yet] Alcmenia', but they are more plausibly emended by assuming that the poet, unlike the scribe, picked the correct metrical variant of the Latin names: 'For yf that Jov[es] had this ladys seyn / Tho Cali[stopee] ne Alc[ume]na'.[14]

As one would expect in a *Mischsprache*, some faulty rhymes are symptoms of scribal translation, with the scribe substituting familiar forms and spellings for ones outside his normal usage. To give us a fix on what 'normal' usage was in London c.1480 and on the likely provenance of the poet, we need comparative data and I should say briefly what data I have used. Needless to say eLALME is foundational, but for various reasons I have also fallen back on other and older sources. The main issues are that eLALME is based on earlier manuscript sources, c.1325–1450, and that, even in the case of the original poem, which may just about antedate 1450, linguistic forms have to be reconstructed on the basis of rhyme and suspected relicts: such reconstructed forms are blunt instruments compared with the fine-grained data of actual LPs. In the case of the scribe, we have at our disposal other texts he copied. There is also, in addition to *MED* and *OED* data, a wealth of earlier scholarship about London English as it appears in documents, letters and literary texts from across the fifteenth century. Some of this scholarship – notably Dibelius (1901) (dealing more fully with the fifteenth century than Jordan 1974) and Kihlbom (1926) – also contains useful comparative data about provincial usage.[15] Other scholarship on fifteenth-century English that I have found valuable are studies of how Chaucerian English was transmitted in later manuscripts from different geographical areas (Wild 1915; Horobin 2003).

With the help of these resources, let us examine some instances of rhymes in *CL* that are symptomatic of scribal translation:

(1) *harte* ('heart') : *smert* (n.) : *oute sterte* (856–859)
(2) *harde* ('heard') : *harde* ('hard') : *ferde* (149–152)
(3) *pray* (1pl.) : *dye* ('die' inf.) (582–584); *pray* (1sg.) : *dye* (inf.) (1373–1375)
(4) *sawe* (1sg. pret.) : *felowe* (1030–1032)
(5) *dede* (adj.) : *womanhode* (713–714)

---

[14] The poet had read Chaucer carefully and is sure to have noticed Chaucer deploy the variants 'Jove' (*CT* I.2222) and 'Joves' (*Troilus* I.878), 'Calyxte' (*PF* 286) and 'Calistopee' (*CT* I.2056). The story of how Jove slept with Alcmene (*Alcumena* in Latin) is told in Plautus' *Amphytrion*. Perhaps the poet derived it indirectly from Geoffrey de Vinsauf's *Poetria Nova* (as suggested by Forni 2005, n. to 821–824), but the wording of this passage suggests another intermediary: John Lydgate. Cf. *CL* 820–824 with *The Temple of Glas*, 115–123 (Schick 1891). Both poets mention Jove, Diana, Alcmene ('Almen' or 'Alcumena' in the Lydgate texts) and 'Europa' (spelt 'Eurosa' by the Trinity scribe!), who receives the epithet 'the faire' from both poets.

[15] It should be noted that neither Dibelius nor Kihlbom contain materials about North Midland and northern usage.

(6)   *well* (adv.) : *dele* (n.) (811–812)
(7)   *yet* : *fitte* (n.) (982–984)
(8)   *cheryssh* (inf.) : *devise* (inf.) (893–894)
(9)   *hold* : *cockold* : *shuld* (408–411)
(10) *clere* : *stirre* : *there* (1066–1069)
(11) *discrive* : *high* (97–98)
(12) *dere* (adj.) : *require* (852–853)
(13) *dede* (n.) : *rede* (1sg) : *forbidde* (inf.) (430–432)

In (1) the scribe has modernised 'herte' to *harte*. The characteristically late ME development [ɛr] > [ar] (Jordan 1974: 234) is writ large over the Trinity scribe's language elsewhere: cf. *harde* ('heard') in *P* (fol. 249v) and *harte* ('heart') in his copy of Lydgate's *Siege* (Oxford, St John's, MS 266, fol. 285r), where it similarly intrudes at the expense of rhyme: *adverte* : *harte*, *Siege* 251–252, fol. 466r; *sterte* : *harte*, *Siege* 2519–2520, fol. 495v; *swerde* : *harde*, *Siege* 2535–2536, fol. 495v.[16] There is reason to think that this development was less advanced in the poet's language, and that scribal intrusion in *CL* has here spoilt the poet's rhyme with *smert* and *sterte*. While 'heart' appears numerous times as *hart(e)*, there are three instances of *hert*, all at the start of the poem (1, 205, 398). The pattern is consistent with 'progressive translation' (eLALME, Introduction, 3.3.3): scribes are usually more faithful to the original at the start, resorting progressively to forms from their own repertoire as they warm to the task. The development [ɛr] > [ar] in the scribe's language would also account for the faulty rhymes in example (2), which can be fixed by emending both *harde* ('heard') and *harde* ('hard') to 'herde'.[17] The form *herd(e)* ('hard') is predominantly West- and East-Midland, with attestations from Norfolk and Leicestershire in *MED* s.v. hard (adj.) and harde (adv.).

Example (3) shows the scribe's preferred vowel in 'die' – cf. pret. *dyed/died* in *P* 247r and 247v and *dye* in Oxford, St John's, MS 266 (507v) – but the rhymes indicate that the poet here had the diphthong [aɪ] or [ɛɪ]. Since other rhymes in *CL* point to [i:] (*dye* : *piteously*, 704–705; *remedy* : *dye* : *company*, 1052–1055), the poet, like Chaucer and Lydgate before him (Dibelius 1901: 344), must have had both monophthongal and diphthongal forms at his disposal. The spellings of the earliest English official documents from London also indicate both forms, but *dye* steadily displaces its rival *deye* until, in the period 1430–1500, it is the only form left (Lekebush 1906: 129; Fisher, Richardson and Fisher: 1984, glossary s.v. died). According to Asta Kihlbom, 'the diphthongic form must have been distinctly old-fashioned by now', though, as she also shows, both forms, *deye* alongside *dye*, however old-fashioned in London, continued to be current in the provinces: the Norfolk letters of John Paston III (1444–1504) show both forms (Kihlbom 1926: 39; Davis, Beadle and Richmond 2004–5: III, 535, 616).

---

[16] Line references are to the edition of Lydgate's *Siege* by Edwards 2001.
[17] The alternative would be to assume *farde* for 'ferde': *MED* s.v. faren has two attestations for the form (both North-East Midlands), but assumes the vowel is long (*fārde*).

In (4) the rhyme suggests that the poet's form was 'felawe' (< Old Norse (ON) *felagi*), with the scribe imposing the modern form. While noting the persistence of *felawe* in official London documents, Kihlbom shows that *felowe* is the form in the fifteenth-century letter collections she examined. Only the Pastons still write *fellaw(e)*. In their general preference for *felowe* 'the private letters are apparently more modern than the official language' (Kihlbom 1926: 136).

Example (5) suggests that the poet wrote 'womanhede', not *womanhode*. The suffix *-hede* is also invariably indicated by other rhymes in the poem (3, 805, 930), but the scribe was apparently more comfortable with *-hod*. The imposition of *-hod* on original *-hed* can be paralleled in Chaucer manuscripts. Judging by his rhymes, Chaucer's normal form was *-hede* (*-hod* occurs only once in rhyme); but his fifteenth-century scribes steadily introduced *-hod*. As Wild argues, in Chaucer manuscripts *-hod* is 'probably the more progressive form, which only gained such wide currency because of later scribes' (Wild 1915: 71–72; my translation). On the gradual attrition of *-hed*, see also *OED* (s.v. -head, *suffix*), which notes that this form of the suffix ceased to be productive in southern dialects by c.1650.

Example (6) shows that for the adverb 'well' the poet had, alongside *wel(l)* (indicated by rhyme at 895 and 1350), the form 'wele' – apparently from the Old English (OE) by-form *wēl* (Kihlbom 1926: 55). This form also occurs in rhyme at, e.g. 772 (*wele : knele*) and 1073 (*wele : fele*). Judging by spellings, forms with [e:] were especially common in East Anglia;[18] there are occurrences also in London (LP item 281–220; Fisher, Richardson and Fisher 1984, glossary s.v. well), but *wel(l)* is standard in the London letter writers, while *weel/wele*, or the coexistence of spellings suggesting [e:] and [ɛ], is East Anglian (Kihlbom 1926: 41–55). The possibility that the scribe spoiled the rhyme by writing *well* for 'wele' is strengthened by what we see in his copy of Lydgate's *Siege*, where East Anglian [e:] forms are indicated by rhymes at lines 1133–1134 and 1449–1450, which again appear as defective rhymes in the scribe's copy: *well : whele* (fol. 477v) and *well : stele* 'steel' (fol. 490v).

In (7), the only instance of 'yet' in rhyme position, the poet obviously wrote *yit* (or *ʒit*), showing the change of [ɛ] to [ɪ] before dentals associated with the North and East and spreading from there to London (Luick 1921: 375–376). The scribe has modernised the word to the form that came naturally to him. The situation here again parallels that of Chaucer. Chaucer's form was *ʒit* (*yet/ʒet* does not occur in rhyme), but later London manuscripts introduce *yet*, even in places where it spoils the rhyme (Wild 1915: 82; Horobin 2003: 154, 161, who also notes the reintroduction of *yit* by the northern scribe of Ld²). The London records have both *e* and *i* (Samuels 1988a: 27), with the former dominating (Morsbach 1888: 59; Lekebush 1906: 27; Wild 1915: 7). Among the fifteenth-century correspondents examined by Kihlbom, the Londoners typically use *e*, while *i* is more common in the letters of John Paston II (Kihlbom 1926: 41–52). Lydgate's *Siege* invariably has *yit* (e.g. 192,

---

[18] See eLALME dot map 281 and Samuels (1988b: 95, n. 14). The pronunciation with [e:] is borne out by the rhyme of *wele* (well adv.) with *wheel* (wheel) in Capgrave, *Life of Saint Katherine*, I, 867–868 (Winstead 1999). See also Dobson (1957: 640).

293, 1335, etc.),[19] but in the *CL* scribe's copy the form is *yet* (fols 465v, 467r, 479v, etc.).

In (8) the scribe has updated the poet's 'cherise' (< Old French *cherisser*) to *cheryssh*. As noted by *OED* (s.v. -ish, *suffix*²), at their first adoption French verbs in *-isse* retained their original suffix, 'which before 1400 changed to *-isshe*'. On the evidence of London documents of 1430–1480, the new suffix had become prevalent in the capital (Lekebush 1906: 93–94). Outside London, Dibelius (1901: 455) reports the older suffix in Bokenham (*acomplysyd*) and the Pastons (*cherysyd*).[20] Chaucer, as far as we can tell from rhymes, only had *-s* in *cherice*, *punyce*, *accomplyce*, etc., but the fifteenth-century manuscripts similarly bear witness to the encroachment of modern [ʃ] (Wild 1915: 248).

In (9) the scribe's substitution of *shold* (or *schold*) by *shuld* again shows the imposition of the standard on a non-standard form. In early fifteenth-century London documents both *shold(e)* and *shuld(e)* are common; the later ones, however, have *shuld(e)* with only two exceptions (Lekebusch 1906: 126; Samuels 1988a: 27). *Shuld* is also the form the scribe uses elsewhere (e.g. Oxford, St John's, MS 266r, 285r, etc.).

In (10), *stirre* (< OE *styrian*, *stirian*) has evidently ousted the poet's original *stere*, and in (11) *discryve* has replaced 'discrye'. According to *OED* (s.v. stir v.), *stere* is 'chiefly northern'. The distribution of *discrye* ('describe') and *discryve* shows the same geographical pattern. As *MED* attestations show (s.v. *descriven* v.1 and *descrien*), *discrye* is predominantly northern.

Finally (12) and (13) both suggest the introduction of more modern forms. In (12) the rhyme implies original *requere*, but the scribe opted for the Latinate form that was becoming standard in London English: it is the only form encountered in the official documents from 1430–1480 (Lekebush 1906: 29–30). As in many Chaucer manuscripts, where later scribes likewise foist *require* on Chaucer's original *requere* (Wild 1915: 208), the modernisation of the form has spoiled the rhyme. In (13) the rhyme points to the older form *forbede* (< OE *forbēodan*). The scribal alteration is to the modern form, based on ME *bidden*, first attested c.1425 (*MED* s.v. *forbeden*).

These examples give the impression of a scribe whose language was more modern and/or less strongly regional than the poet's. This impression can be confirmed by two more persistent patterns that emerge from defective rhymes. One of these is that the poet, more frequently than the scribe, rounded [a] to [o] before nasals; the other is that there is evidence for the lowering of the front vowels [iː] and [ɪ] to [eː] and [ɛ] in the poet's dialect.

Let us begin with rounding of [a] to [o] before nasals. This feature has traditionally been ascribed to the West Midlands, but eLALME data show that it was also characteristic of East Anglian dialects. Dot map 423–480 below shows the spread of <o> spellings in MAN, BEGAN, CAN:

---

[19] The two instances of *yet* (*Siege* 1222, 3086) are the product of editorial emendations by Edwards.

[20] Note also *cherse*, alongside spellings with the newer suffix (Davis, Beadle and Richmond 2004–5: III, glossary s.v. cherysche).

Figure 10.1 *eLALME* dot map for <o> spellings in MAN, CAN, BEGAN

In *CL*, rounding of [a] to [o] is found in closed syllables before *n*, *ng* and *nd*. However, it must have been more common in the poet's language than in that of the scribe, who preferred [a] in these contexts. Below are the relevant rhymes:

(14) *mencion* : *offencion* : *beganne* (1sg. pret.) (919–922); *opynyon* : *begonne* (p.p.) (1063–1064)
(15) *sang* (3rd person sg. pret.) : *sprong* (3sg. pret.) (1380–1382)
(16) *stand* (3pl.) : *found* (1sg.) : *hond* (800–803)
(17) *Holand* : *lond* : *withstond* (inf.) (1227–1230)

Knowing which of these rhyme words was authorial and which one scribal is not straightforward in all cases. Moreover, variation between *o* and *a* in some of these words ('hand', 'stand', 'land') was common throughout the south, and some of the rhymes are emendable either way.

In (14) the rhyme unambiguously indicates *begonne*: the form is to be expected in West Midland dialects but is otherwise unusual: Dibelius (1901: 178) reports it in Norfolk records and the eLALME dot map above shows clusterings in East Anglia; I have otherwise found it (in rhyme) in *Bevis of Hamtoun* ('In bataile wo begon / And al to-heve, flesch and bon', 4043–4044) in the Auchinleck manuscript (London) and in *Lybeaus Desconus* in Lambeth Palace, MS 306 (North-East Midlands?: see Mills 1969: 28–41): 'The fourthe begon to flee' (1180).[21]

In (15) Skeat restored the rhyme by emending *sprong* to 'sprang', but scribal error is more likely to be responsible for *sang*. The fifteenth-century Chaucer manuscripts that give us an insight into London English of the period show the steady imposition of *sang* on Chaucer's own form *song* (Wild 1915: 98–99), and the *CL* scribe made the same change in Lydgate's *Siege*, lines 2259–2260, wrecking Lydgate's original rhyme, *among* : *song* (3sg. pret.), with *among* : *sang* (fol. 492v).

In (16) the scribe garbled the original rhymes by writing *stand* for 'stond' and *found* for 'fond', while in (17) he imposed *Holand* (cf. *Holand* in P, fol. 248v) on the original *Holond*. Skeat's emendation of the rhymes in (4) to *Holand* : *land* : *withstand* takes further license with the poet's original. Spellings with <a> in 'stand' and 'land' gained the ascendancy in fifteenth-century London letters and documents (Lekebush 1906: 52; Kihlbom 1926: 123;), and the scribe participated in this trend by introducing such forms in his copy of Lydgate's *Siege of Thebes*, irrespective of rhyme. Thus *understond* : *hond* (lines 1909–1910) becomes *understand* : *hond* and *bond* : *londe* (2005–2006) becomes *bond* : *land* (fol. 487v). The long vowel suggested by spellings such as *bound* and *found* is regular in the London letter writers, and the scribe similarly writes *found* for *fond* in his copy of Lydgate's *Siege* (line 2198, fol. 491r). Spellings with <o> persist, however, in the Paston and Stonor letters (Oxfordshire), and 'probably indicate a provincial pronunciation' (Kihlbom 1926: 185, and see also Dibelius 1901: 179, 359). The same rhyme – *lond* : *fond* : *stond* – can be found in Capgrave's *Life of Saint Katherine*, prologue 121–124 (Winstead 1999).

It is possible that the scribe obscured another original rhyme showing pre-nasal [a] > [o] at line 379:

> The eleventh statute: Thy signes forto *knowe*,
> With ie, and fynger, and with smyles soft,
> And lowe to kowigh, and alway[22] forto *shon*,
> For dred of spies, forto wynken ofte . . . (379–382)

As Skeat observed, behind *knowe* probably lies 'con' (in the sense of 'know'). *Con* is not common in London and the South-East Midlands, but Dibelius (1901: 178) lists examples in the Paston letters and in Lydgate.

---

[21] Citations are from the TEAMS digital corpus (http://d.lib.rochester.edu/teams), which I searched for 'begon'/'bigon' (I report only 1/3 sg, not 2sg., plural and p.p., where the historical vowel was [u], which often appears as <o> before minims for purely orthographic reasons).

[22] Forni (2005) again reads 'always'.

With regard to the lowering of [iː] and [ɪ], the following rhymes deserve consideration:

(18) *eke* : *like* (561–563)
(19) *here* (adv.) : *desire* (1301–1302)
(20) *strength* : *thynketh* (1061–1062)
(21) *frande* ('friend') : *mynde* (1056–1057)

The rhyme in (18) was taken by Skeat as evidence for the raising of ME [eː] to [iː] (Skeat 1897: n. to 561–563), but the integrity of the rhyme scheme (ababbcc) depends on the two remaining distinct.[23] For instance, the a- and b-verses of the stanzas beginning at 211 and 1345 rhyme alternately on [eː] and [iː]. It is therefore more likely that *like* (< OE *līcian*) should read 'leke'. Other rhymes in *CL* support this hypothesis. In (19) the rhyming of *here* and *desire* again points to the lowering of [iː] to [eː] in the poet's dialect (read 'desere').[24] The verb 'shine' (< OE *scīnan*) appears as *shene* (*CL* 81), rhyming with *grene* and *bene* (3pl. of 'to be').[25] The distribution of these forms is clearly dialectal, as eLALME's dot map for item 369 ('e' for ME ī in LIKE, RICH, SHINE) shows.

The dot map explains why rhymes based on this feature are encountered in fifteenth-century poets from Suffolk and Norfolk. The rhyme *eke* : *leke* is a popular one in Capgrave's *Life of Saint Katherine* (Winstead 1999): 'And we wyll thank and rewarde yow eke / With swech plenté that it schall yow leke!' (III.503–504; see also III.603–605 and IV.1748–1749). Capgrave also rhymes on 'desere': 'Al here lokyng and here goostly desere / Is sette his lernyng and doctryne to here' (*Life of St. Norbert*, 1245–1246). The citation is from Capgrave's autograph manuscript, San Marino, Huntington Library HM 55 (Smetana 1977). In Capgrave's *Life of Saint Katherine*, not an autograph, the same rhyme must be assumed, though the scribe has obscured it: 'But be commaundment of hir Lord and hir desire / Swech is hir might and alsso hir powere' (III, 510–511). Also of interest is the rhyme *deseres* : *reveres* in Lydgate's *Siege of Thebes*, 1617–1618,[26] which in the *CL* scribe copy appears as *desirs* : *revers* (fol. 484r).

---

[23] The rhyme *eke* : *syke* ('sick') (946–948) does not support Skeat: for *syke* read 'seke'. The variant form with [iː] imposed by the scribe became the standard one in London, as official documents and Chaucer manuscripts show (Morsbach 1888: 59; Wild 1915: 139).

[24] Kihlbom (1926: 37) notes the development in Devon, East Anglia and northern dialects, and writes: 'These forms are not altogether easy to explain. It appears, as if in most dialects *ī* was occasionally levelled under ME *ē*, probably in late ME (the earliest spellings with *e*, *ee* appear all to be from the fifteenth century, cf. NED like a.: 5 lek(e), like vb.: 5 leke, 6–7 leeke; also in French words, desire sb.: 5 desere; guide v.: 5 gede).'

[25] *MED* and *OED*, unlike eLALME, attribute instances of *shene* to a different verb (*MED* s.v. shenen; *OED*, s.v. sheen (v.)), from the adjective 'shene'. If it is a different verb, it is (outside of Scotland) of very restricted currency (West Midlands and East Anglia). In the East Midlands, 'shene' occurs in Hilton's *Scale of Perfection* (London, British Library, MS Harley 6579, Ely or S Lincs) and Skelton's *Garland of Laurell*, 1358.

[26] Edwards (2001) follows his base manuscript (Arundel 119, from Essex), where the rhyme has also been spoiled (*desyres* : *ryveris*).

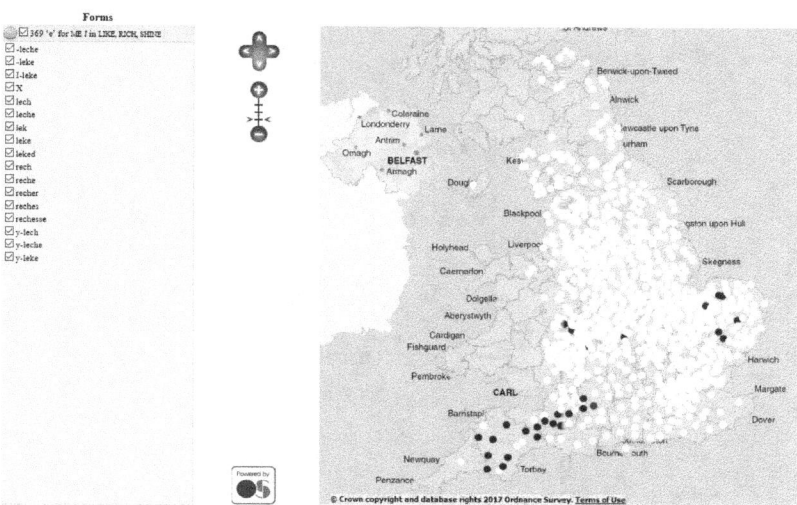

Figure 10.2 eLALME dot map for <e> spellings in LIKE, RICH, SHINE

The lowering of *i* to *e* is also evident in French-derived words with short *i*. It is notable, for instance, that *CL* alternates between spellings of 'distress' (*distresse* at 861, but *destresse* at 706), 'pity' (*pite(e)* at 369, 701, etc., but *petiously* at 1136) and 'privy' (*prively* at 1325, but *previty* at 1304). Given that scribes tended to copy not just the rhyming element but the whole rhyme word more faithfully, it is probably significant that the <e> spellings in the above-listed words all occur in words that are in rhyme position.

In (20) the original rhyme was probably *strength* : *thenkth*, as Skeat surmised (1887: lxxix). The rhyme not only provides further evidence of apocope of *e* in inflections, but also suggests that the poet used *thenk* alongside *think* (the latter confirmed by rhyme at 393–395). The ME variants *think* and *thenk* ultimately go back to two different etymons with different senses (OE *þencan* 'to think' and impersonal *þyncan* 'to seem'), but by the fifteenth century they had fallen together, and the choice between the two becomes revealing of dialect and scribal practice. In the fifteenth-century private letters examined by Kihlbom, <i/y> spellings dominate except in the letters of Edmund de la Pole (Suffolk) who writes 'thenk' (Kihlbom 1926: 23). In transmitting Chaucer, who used both forms, the early printed editions (Caxton, Thynne) regularise to <i/y> spellings while manuscripts of northern provenance (Pt, Ln) opt for <e> (Wild 1915: 51).

In (21) the spelling *frand* for 'friend' is unattested in *MED*, and the rhyme shows it is not what the poet wrote. Conceivably, the poet wrote the unusual 'frynd',[27] but more likely is 'frend' : 'mend' (< OE *gemȳnd*), for there are traces of *e* < OE *y* elsewhere in the poem. Thus 'fire', which is always *fire* mid-line (457, 645, etc.) appears as *fere* (623) in

---

[27] The form is sporadically found in the West Midlands and in East Anglia (see Davis 1955: 24 for examples in William Paston II and eLALME, dot map for item 146 (FRIEND: 'frind' and 'frynd' forms)).

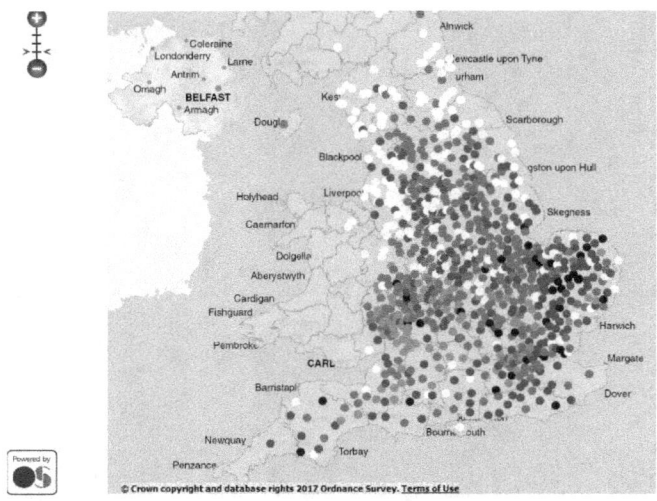

Figure 10.3 eLALME dot map for <e> spellings in FIRE, DID, MIND

rhyme with *i-fere*, and while 'did' normally appears as *did(e) / dyde* it appears as *ded* on the two occasions where it immediately precedes the rhyme word (*ded rave*, 1187, *ded wowe*, 1202).[28] Forms of this kind with *e* for OE *y* are usually associated with the south-east in handbooks of ME (Brunner 1970: 14) and they continue to occur sporadically in London English of the fifteenth century. However, they are common in the dialects of the south-west (Wakelin 1988: 613–614) and East Anglia. A combined mapping of 'fere', 'fer*e*', 'feer', 'feer*e*' (item 137: FIRE), 'ded', 'ded-', 'dede' (item 115–150: DID sg), 'mend', 'mend-' and 'mende' (item 179: KIND, MIND, DINT, STINT / KIND etc) in eLALME shows the distribution of these features in Figure 10.3.

In interpreting maps produced by the 'fitting' tool in eLALME it should be borne in mind not only that darker shades indicate likelier areas of localisation, but also that dots go dark even if there is a positive match for only one of the selected items.

The eLALME map broadly confirms what has long been known about East Anglian dialect characteristics. Beadle (1977: I, 64–65) discusses the 'appearance of OE *y* as *e*' in his study of late medieval English texts from East Anglia and notes the frequent use of *mende* ('mind') and *kende* ('kind') in late medieval literary and non-literary sources from the area. Lydgate and Capgrave both exploit this dialectal feature in their rhyming practice (Dibelius 1901: 375), and in his *English School-Master* (1596), written from Bury St Edmunds in Suffolk, Edmund Coote still records [ɛ] for [ɪ] in words with OE *y* as part of the 'barbarous speech of your country people' (Dobson 1957: 566–567, and see also Lodge 2001: 210 for a possible reflex of this same feature in

---

[28] The poet's remarkably frequent use of auxiliary 'did' is itself worth noting. Skeat presents it as another archaising mannerism (Skeat 1900: 128–129), but Norman Davis (1972) observes the same peculiarity in the letters of Margaret Paston (where incidentally *ded* is also a common spelling).

modern Norfolk speech). The form *ded(e)* for 'did' was noted by Kihlbom (1926: 23) as occurring in letter collections only in the Paston letters and Edmund de la Pole (alongside *dyd/did*); it was flagged up as an East Anglian dialect characteristic by Seymour (1968: 166). It also occurs in Lydgate's *Siege of Thebes*, but predictably the *CL* scribe in his copy overrides it with his own form *dide* (e.g. line 55, fol. 463v).

Two final dialect features should be mentioned in the context of rhyme constraints. The first involves *everywhare*, rhyming with *stare* at line 423. In late ME, the form is characteristically northern; eLALME shows further pockets of *a* forms in the West Midlands, Norfolk and London (dot map for item 53, WHERE: all forms with unabbr[eviated] medial *a*). Morsbach (1888: 46) interprets their rare appearance in official documents from London (cf. Lekebusch 1906: 35–36; Fisher, Richardson and Fisher 1984: 399) as northern imports. Such forms do not occur in the letters collections from London, but are met with in the Paston letters (e.g. *nowhar*, *wharfor*) and 'must have had a dialectal flavour' (Kihlbom 1926: 76). Beadle comments on their appearance in localised texts and documents from Norfolk (Beadle 1977: 71). The second feature is the poet's frequent rhyming of <-ight> and <-ite>, e.g.: *write : aright* (13–14), *white : plight* (1100–1102). These are precise rhymes, predicated on the loss of the fricative with compensatory vowel lengthening in late ME. The pronunciation [iːt] for [içt] is predominantly Eastern (Dobson 1957: 667), and is evident from spellings such as *mite* and *myte* for 'might', which are found predominantly in East Anglia, as suggested by *eLALME*, dot map 54, MIGHT vb: forms in *V[owel]'t(t)(e)*, in Figure 10.4.

The dot map explains why neither Chaucer nor the later London poets Hoccleve and Lovelich practised these rhymes, and why they are frequent in Lydgate, Capgrave and Bokenham (Dibelius 1901: 465–466). Their occurrence in Gower, possibly the earliest poet to use them, is perhaps best explained as one of the features of the Suffolk stratum in Gower's language (cf. Samuels and Smith 1988).[29] The *CL* scribe's spelling <ght> is regular in *CL*, *P* and his copy of Lydgate's *Siege*, but it is not likely that the poet's rhymes may have been reflected in alternative spellings, as they are in Capgrave (and other writers from East Anglia) who did not write <gh> or yogh in reflexes of OE *-ht* (Davis 1955; Lucas 1973: 349; Beadle 1977: II, 56–57). Rhyme words in *CL* provide a trace of such spellings: 'night(-)' is always *nyght(-)* except in the words *nytirtale* ('night-time') and *nithingale* (1353), both of them occurring in rhyme position.

5. Diagnostic features outside of rhyme

When the language of a poem has been thoroughly translated by scribe, the rhyme constraints allow us a way back to the original phonology. But even without the help of rhyme, it is often possible to detect linguistic composites on the basis of significant 'relicts' (Benskin and Laing 1981; Laing 1989). In the case of *CL*, there are some unusual forms or words that look out of place in the language of London, c.1480.

Some cases present phonological features that we have already seen in the previous section. The development of [içt] > [iːt], evident from rhymes and from the spellings

---

[29] Dobson (1957: 667) suggested, without evidence, that it could be a Kenticism.

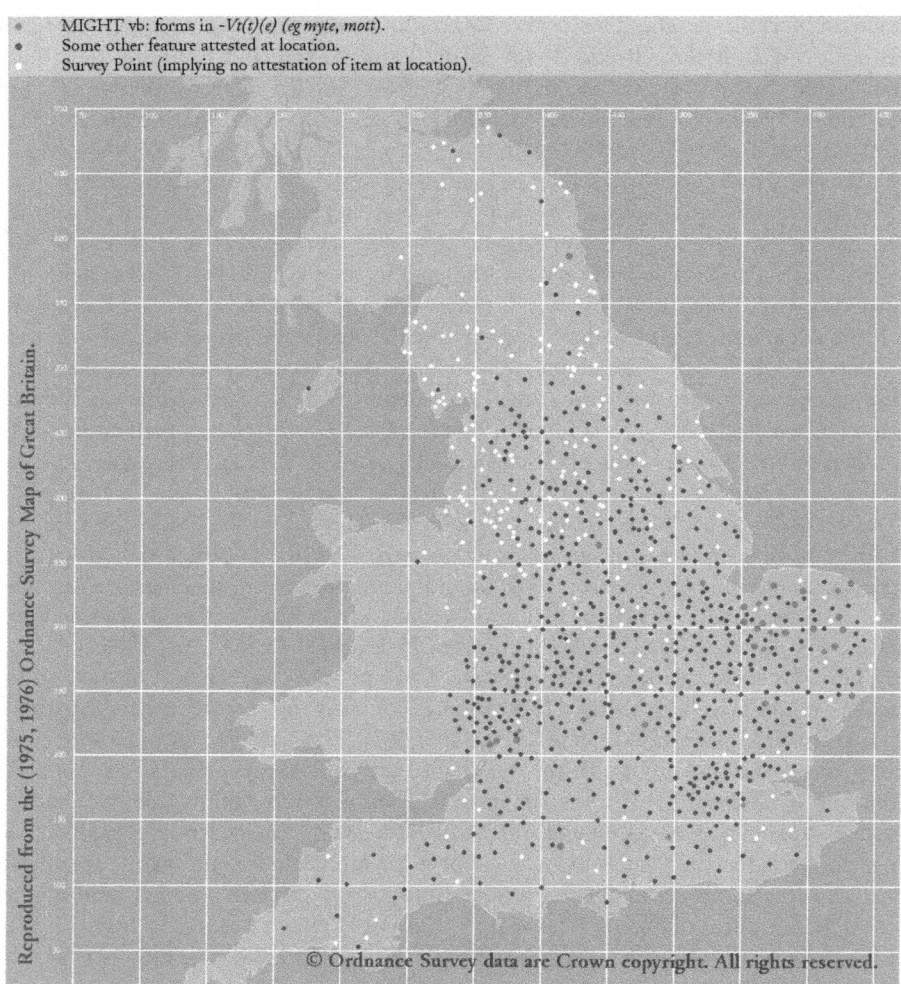

Figure 10.4 eLALME dot map for spellings of MIGHT indicating loss of fricative

nyt- and *nith-* in rhyming words, is also indicated by the curious reverse spelling *kiʒt* ('kite') in 1416 (see Beadle 1977: I, 56–57 for comparable spellings in fifteenth-century East Anglian texts). The lowering of ME *i* is visible in the spelling *prevey* ('privy') at 1295. The anomalous *a* in *everywhare* also appears in forms of 'ere' ('before' < OE *ǣr*, ON *ār*). Spellings with <e>, to be expected in the language of the scribe, occur at 167 and 1309, but at 983 we encounter *arst* and at 994 *ar*. These *a* forms, probably influenced by the ON etymon, are typically northern and North Midland (Jordan 1974: 77). In the fifteenth-century southern writers examined by Dibelius they occur only in Norfolk (Dibelius 1901: 326).

An orthographic peculiarity that has previously been noticed as an East Anglian characteristic is the use of possessive adjectives with *-n* not just before a vowel or *h-*, but before a consonant (Seymour 1968: 168; Parkes and Beadle 1979–80: III, 55). The *CL* scribe mostly uses *my* and *thy* before consonants but there are three exceptions in *CL*: *myne commaundement*, 1231; *myne protestacioun*, 1338; *myne power*, 1339.

The pret. and p.p. of 'give' also reveal some interesting variations: besides *gave* (447, 1123) we find 1sg. *yove* (688) and p.p. *yove(n)* (278, 531, 547, 642, 742, 770).[30] The vowel, influenced by ON *gāfu*, is especially common in the North-East Midlands (Jordan 1974: 78). Although p.p. *yove(n)* is sporadically found in London (Dibelius 1901: 238),[31] singular past tense *yove* is not: eLALME records *o* forms only in Norfolk (*ʒoue*) and Leicestershire (*goffe*). The scribe's unfamiliarity with *yove* is further suggested by the fact that he miscopies it as 'you' at 770, and that his own form was 'gave' is shown by another curious scribal error at line 690:

And thus gan fynyssh preyer [Forni 2005: prerer], lawde, and preice
Which that I yove[32] to Venus on my kne;
And in myne harte to ponder and to peice,
I gave anon hir ymage fressh bewtie ... (687–690)

As Skeat observed, the scribe here wrote probably *gaue* for original *gan*, with 'hir ymage fresh bewtie' meaning 'the fresh beauty of her statue'. Such uninflected genitives are unusual (except in the case of nouns of relationship in *-r*) but occur commonly in northern dialects and in Norfolk (Dibelius 1901: 331–332; Mustanoja 1960: 71–72; Blake 1977).[33]

A few words and idioms also seem to be inconsistent with a London dialect. Skeat himself commented on a few northernisms. His examples turn out to be inconclusive,[34] but there are some dialect words that escaped his attention. In addition to the adjective and pronoun *yonder* (246, 249, etc.), *CL* has three instances of *yon(ne)* (1236, 1239, 1260). That the latter form is northern is evident both from citations in *MED* s.v. yon (pron.) and (adj.) and from the fact that Chaucer (who used *yond* and *yonder*) resorts to *yon* only once, to mark the northern dialect of the clerics in *The Reeve's Tale* ('yon wenche wil I swyve', *CT* I.4177) (Horobin

---

[30] All of these are mistranscribed by Forni (2005) as *gove(n)*.
[31] In the past participle (and past plural) the vowel could be explained by the influence of class IV strong verbs (cf. Dibelius 1901: 238). The past participle *yove(n)* (pret. *yaf*) is also found in Gower; Samuels and Smith (1988: 16) attribute this to the Suffolk stratum in his language.
[32] Forni (2005) misreads *gove*.
[33] For another example in *CL* see n. 7 above.
[34] The single example of a northern inflection, *me thynkes* (874) (Skeat 1897: lxxvi), is of doubtful significance; this also occurs exceptionally in Chaucer (ten Brink 1901: 133) and in official London records (Fisher, Richardson and Fisher 1984: 45); occasional verbal inflections in *-in/-yn* (Skeat 1897: lxxvii) are also common enough in London texts (see e.g. Fisher, Richardson and Fisher 1984: 213); the word *ure* (*CL* 862) no longer had restricted currency by the second half of the fifteenth century, as shown by attestations from other texts in Trinity R.3.19 and its sister manuscript, Trinity R.3.21, cited in *MED* s.v. ure (n); *boun* ('ready') is in Chaucer, Gower, and *Roland and Vernagu* (Auchinleck MS), which Purdie localises in the London area (Purdie 2008: 226–227).

2013: 97). Another clear case is the preposition *intill*. *Into* is what we would expect to find, and do find (*CL* 114 and 637), but on two other occasions the preposition is *intill* (219, 766). The word is chiefly northern and north-eastern (Mustanoja 1960: 391; *MED* s.v. in-til (prep.)). Even more restricted in currency is the word *prang*, meaning 'agony, throes': 'The prange of love so strayneth thaym to crye' (1150). The word, probably from medieval Dutch *prang* ('strife, turmoil'), is securely attested, but only in texts from Suffolk and Norfolk.[35] A final word unattested in the South is *blome*, which is presumably the word the scribe should have written at lines 1432–1433:

> To feche the floures fressh, and braunche, and blome; [MS bleme]
> And namly hawthorn brought both page and grome . . .

The word is an ON borrowing (cf. Old Icelandic *blōm*), which could explain why in ME it is never found further south than Suffolk (Lydgate), though it entered common parlance in the course of the sixteenth century.

6. Conclusion

CL has always seemed to modern readers something of an enigma. In C. S. Lewis's classic formulation:

> few poems are so deeply anonymous as the *Court of Love*. Its style and metre are not those of any known period in our literature; and it is difficult to guess who this author was when he wrote a poem which scans perfectly provided you make every final -e mute and also sound the -e in every plural and genitive in -es. (Lewis 1936: 256)

Lewis's guess, following Skeat's, is that he was a sixteenth-century poet trying to reinvent a medieval language and literary mode.

As we have seen, Lewis overstated the eccentricity of the poet's metre. He also exaggerated his anonymity. Towards the end of the poem, the poet reveals something about his identity:

> 'My name, alas, my hart, why make it straunge?
> Philogenet I cald am, fer and nere,
> Of Cambridge clerk' (911–913)

'Philogenet' is Greek code for 'born-to-love' or perhaps 'woman-lover' and not the poet's real name, but there is no reason to doubt he was indeed a 'Cambridge clerk'. This 'Cambridge clerk' was writing sometime before c.1480, when his poem appears, much garbled in transmission, in the manuscript that is now Cambridge, Trinity College, MS R.3.19. Of course, Cambridge students were not necessarily from the

---

[35] See *MED* s.v. pronge. The final entry under this item (from a Warwickshire MS), assigned by *MED* to a different sense – (b) a pointed instrument, a pitchfork – probably does not belong here. See *OED*, which assigns these senses to different words, *prong* n. 1 and 2.

vicinity of Cambridge, but in this case we have strong linguistic evidence to link him with East Anglia.

It is fortunate that we also know something about the Trinity scribe: he was a professional scribe involved in the London book trade. In the same manuscript he also copied *The Petigrew of Englond*, which he updated to take account of Margaret of York's marital status. He also copied Lydgate's *Siege of Thebes* in Oxford, St John's, MS 266. The likelihood that he was from London, while the poet was from further north and writing earlier, is indicated by frequent failures of rhyme. Some of these same failures occur in his copy of Lydgate's *Siege*. The linguistic differences between the poet and the scribe, as reconstructed from rhyme, metre and possible relicts, are set out in Table 10.1 in the order in which they have been discussed.

Before we draw conclusions from Table 10.1, some caveats are in order. First, because the poem was 'translated' by scribes we cannot be confident about original spellings. Rhymes enable us to reconstruct phonology, not orthography – which is why for the purposes of localising our poet the eLALME dot maps based on broad phonological criteria have proved to be more useful than eLALME's 'fitting' facility, which brings detailed spelling variations into play.[36] Second, while rhymes are revealing because they provide a check on scribal translation, the need to rhyme may also have constrained the poet. The forms found in rhyme were presumably available in the poet's dialect, but that does not mean they were his normal ones. Occasionally, other rhymes show that the poet had more than one form at his disposal. In Table 10.1 all alternative forms that can be confirmed by rhyme have been added, but the poet will have had many others. Thus, while the table indicates that *desere* ('desire) and *myne* before consonant-initial words probably featured in the poet's language, it should not be read as suggesting that they invariably or frequently did. For all these reasons, it is not to be confused with an actual LP.

Second, in the case of some of the forms which I have attributed to the poet, it is difficult to be certain that they were not (or were not also) minority forms in the scribe's own language. For instance, *whar* ('where'), *ded* ('did'), *fere* 'fire', *pete* are all occasionally found in London texts. This quandary is really part of a much larger issue, which is that the language of East Anglia cannot neatly be separated from that of London since speakers of the former (such as Chaucer's grandfather, from Ipswich) migrated to London, and since it was the conduit for many linguistic imports from the north. Thus the ON pronouns *theire* and *thaim* that we find in *CL* were North-East Midland in the fourteenth century, but by 1480 they were normal in the scribe's own language (cf. 'thaim' in *Petigrew*, fol. 249v) and in London documents more generally (Lekebush 1906: 106; Fisher, Richardson and Fisher 1984: 44). Some infiltration of East Anglian forms into London English is to be expected (Samuels 1988a: 36, n. 27), and phonological differences between London and East Anglian writers are therefore usually measured not by the complete absence or presence of a particular form

---

[36] To give but one example, anyone trying to 'fit' the form *yove* ('gave') 1/3 sg (item 153-20) in *eLALME* will find it precisely nowhere: the closest match is *ȝoue*, apparently attested in two LPs (776, 4057) from King's Lynn in Norfolk. I say 'apparently' because *ȝoue* is not actually returned in LP 776, and also shows up only in LP 4057 in the item list for *gave* (153-20).

Table 10.1 Authorial versus scribal forms

Poet	Scribe
adversaire	adversary
sojoure / sojorne	sojorne
-n / -e / Ø in verbal inflections (inf. and plural)	-e / Ø
herte	harte
herde ('hard')	harde
day (die') / dye	dye
felawe	felowe
-hede	-hode
wele / well	well
yit	yet
cherryse	cherrysh
shold	shuld
stere	stirre
discrye	discrive
requere	require
forbede	forbidde
begon(ne) / beganne[1]	beganne
song	sang
stond	stand
fond	found
Holond	Holand
con ('know') / can	knowe
leke / like	like
fere / fire	fire
desere	desire
thenk / thynk	think
mende / mynde	mynde
pete, prevy, destresse	pite(e), privy, distresse
ded	dyd(e)/did(e)
-whare	-where
nyt / nith	nyght
kiȝt	kite
ar ('ere')	er
myne + consonant	my + consonant
yove (1/3 pret.)	gave
yonne / yonder	yonder
intill	into

1 The rhyme itself (*beganne : can*, 459–460) is not decisive, but these are the c-verses of a rhyme-royal stanza that already rhymes on *-on* in the a-verses.

but rather by the 'marked predominance of a certain spelling' (Kihlbom 1926: 22). Without access to the poet's autograph this is not something we are able to do. We can be more certain, however, that the forms attributed to the poet were not standard ones for the scribe. His preferred forms, which correspond closely with those of London letter writers and London documents of the period, and which can be confirmed with reference to other texts in his hand, are those in the right-hand column; and it is because he wrote these, and not the ones in the left-hand column, that we are now left with a poem that seems to rhyme so loosely.

Comparing the poet's forms with the scribe's, it is clear he has almost invariably introduced forms closer to Present-Day English. The fact that he was probably writing a few decades after the poet is relevant here, but so is the fact that he was a professional London scribe, who wrote a style of written English that resembles what Samuels termed the 'Chancery standard' (Samuels 1988a: 24), which developed in London from the 1430s onwards. As demonstrated by Benskin (2004), there was more variation in the writings of London government clerks than the word 'standard' might suggest, and they certainly were not engaged on a conscious programme to standardise English, as argued by Fisher (1996). In preferring certain forms to others (e.g. *shuld* rather than *shold*, *found* rather than *fond*), they drifted closer towards Modern English, but that sense of direction is the product of our hindsight rather than their foresight. The scribal usage of the *CL* scribe shows this same drift. In defiance of rhyme constraints, he introduced the forms that were the common currency of London correspondents and administrators of the period.

The poet's language, on the other hand, is marked by a number of regional forms and dialect words. Some cannot be characterised very precisely beyond the fact that they are northern (*intill*, *stere*, *ar*, *yon*, *discrye*), but others point more firmly to East Anglia. The lowering of [iː] and [ɪ] in 'leke' ('like'), 'desere', 'mende' implied by rhymes and by non-standard spellings is strongly associated with this area, as is the combination of the rounding of [a] to [o] before nasals and the loss of the fricative in words like *bright* and *night*, which is indicated by rhymes and occasional spellings. The pret. sg. *yove* is only attested by eLALME in Norfolk (in the spelling *ʒove*). The word *prang* is restricted to East Anglia. It is therefore likely that our 'Cambridge clerk' came from East Anglia, probably from Norfolk. However, since many Cambridge school and university teachers and students were recruited from this county, and since writing was acquired by education, Norfolk features need not necessarily be inconsistent with a Cambridge origin (Samuels 1988b).

CL is thus not a Renaissance fabrication containing false ME, but a late medieval poem from East Anglia. Since the poet relies heavily on Lydgate, and uses aureate diction (*celsitude*, *metricien*) and other words (*courtly*, *assummon*, *demene*) that are late ME, I would tentatively date it to the middle of the fifteenth century. This East Anglian poem was subsequently filtered through the language of London of c.1480. The accusations of 'false English' that Skeat levels against the poet miss the point if, as I have argued, the language of *CL* was a *Mischsprache* of standard London English overlaid on a strongly regional substratum.

My hypothesis offers an alternative perspective on *CL*'s linguistic peculiarities, and to show how this can alter our understanding of the poem, I would like to end by returning, for a moment, to Skeat's perspective:

167.   *non erst* ; false grammar for *non er* 'no sooner'; 'no soonest' is nonsense.
1045. *thou wot* ; false grammar for *thou wost*.

Skeat was a brilliant editor, and understood better than most modern editors that medieval poets cared about their rhymes and rhythms being right, but his linguistic prescriptivism has fortunately had its day. With regard to *non erst*, the sense 'earlier' for *erst* is a logical development of one of its main senses, 'the earlier of the two' (*MED* s.v. erest, sense 4), and even Chaucer used it 'falsely' ('Nevere erst er now', *CT* III.2220). It is only the combination with preceding *non* that is unusual, though not, interestingly enough, in the Paston letters, which is the only other place where it can be found: 'I thank God that John Paston yed non erst forthe'; 'I sent to yowe non erste no wrythgtyng'; and 'non erst but on Wednysday' (Davis, Beadle and Richmond 2004–5: II, 282, 390, 477).

With regard to *thou wot*, the key point is that in northern dialects the 1/3sg. past tense form of strong verbs was often extended to the 2sg. This affects the present tense of preterite-present verbs (Mossé 1952: 83) and explains *thou wot*. With the help of digital databases parallels are easy to find. Cf. Richard Rolle's *Commentary on the Psalter*, 'thou wot holly all' (cited from the Corpus of Middle English Prose and Verse: http://quod.lib.umich.edu/c/cme/). The lack of inflection in 2sg preterite-present verbs in *CL* is confirmed by rhyme at 462–463 (*beganne* : *[thowe] can*, 461–462) and appears to be typical of East Anglia. Dibelius (1901: 246–247) cites comparable rhymes by Bokenham (*thou shal* : *al*) and Capgrave (*thou can* : *man*).

The hypothesis that the poet was from East Anglia and the scribe from London thus makes it possible to understand that what Skeat called 'false grammar' is syntax that is true to the poet's own dialect, and that the 'imperfect rhymes' in *CL* are epiphenomena reflecting the compromise between the poet's language and that of the scribe.

References

Arngart, Olof (1968). *The Middle English Genesis and Exodus, Re-edited from Ms. C.C.C.C. 444 with Introduction, Notes and Glossary*, Lund: Gleerup.

Beadle, Richard (1977). 'The medieval drama of East Anglia: Studies in dialect, documentary records and stagecraft', 2 vols, unpublished PhD dissertation, York: York University.

Benskin, Michael (2004). 'Chancery standard', in Christian Kay, Carole Hough and Irené Wotherspoon (eds), *New Perspectives in Historical Linguistics: II: Lexis and Transmission*, Amsterdam: Benjamins, pp. 1–40.

Benskin, Michael and Margaret Laing (1981). 'Translations and mischsprachen in Middle English manuscripts', in Michael Benskin and M. L. Samuels (eds), *So Meny People Longages and Tonges: Philological Essays in Scots and Mediaeval English Presented to Angus McIntosh*, Edinburgh: The Editors, pp. 55–106.

Benson, Larry D. (gen. ed.) (1987). *The Riverside Chaucer*, Boston: Houghton Mifflin.

Blake, Norman F. (1977). 'Another northernism in "The Reeve's Tale"?', *Notes and Queries* n.s. 24: 400–401.

Bone, Gavin (1931–2). 'Extant manuscripts printed from by W. De Worde with notes on the owner, Roger Thorney', *The Library*, 4th ser., 12: 248–309.

ten Brink, Bernhard (1901). *The Language and Metre of Chaucer* [revised by Friedrich Kluge and translated by M. Bentinck Smith], London: Macmillan.
Brunner, Karl (1970). *An Outline of Middle English Grammar* [translated by G. K. W. Johnston], Oxford: Blackwell.
Cartlidge, Neil (1998). 'The linguistic evidence for the provenance of *The Owl and the Nightingale*', *Neuphilologische Mitteilungen* 99: 249–268.
Dahlberg, Charles (ed.) (1999). *The Romaunt of the Rose*, Variorum Edition of the Works of Geoffrey Chaucer, Norman: University of Oklahoma Press.
Davis, Norman (1955). 'The language of the Pastons', *Proceedings of the British Academy* 40: 119–144.
Davis, Norman (1972). 'Margaret Paston's uses of DO', *Neuphilologische Mitteilungen* 73: 55–62.
Davis, Norman, Richard Beadle and Colin Richmond (eds) (2004–5). *Paston Letters and Papers of the Fifteenth Century*, 3 vols, EETS s.s. 20, 21, 23, Oxford: Oxford University Press.
Dibelius, Wilhelm (1901). 'John Capgrave und die englische Schriftsprache', *Anglia* 23: 153–194, 323–375, 427–472; *Anglia* 24: 211–263, 269–308.
Dobson, E. J. (1957). *English Pronunciation, 1500–1700*, 2 vols, Oxford: Clarendon Press.
Edwards, Robert R. (ed.) (2001). *John Lydgate: The Siege of Thebes*, TEAMS, Kalamazoo, MI: Medieval Institute.
Fisher, John H. (1996). *The Emergence of Standard English*, Lexington: University of Kentucky Press.
Fisher, John H., Macolm Richardson and Jane L. Fisher (1984). *An Anthology of Chancery English*, Knoxville: University of Tennessee Press.
Fletcher, Bradford Y. (1978). 'Printer's copy of Stow's *Chaucer*', *Studies in Bibliography* 31: 184–201.
Fletcher, Bradford Y. (1987). *Manuscript Trinity R.3.19: A Facsimile*, Norman, OK: Pilgrim Books.
Forni, Kathleen (2001). *The Chaucerian Apocrypha: A Counterfeit Canon*, Gainesville: University Press of Florida.
Forni, Kathleen (ed.) (2005). *The Chaucerian Apocrypha: A Selection*, TEAMS, Kalamazoo, MI: Medieval Institute.
Furnivall, Frederick J. (ed.) (1871). *A Parallel-Text Edition of Chaucer's Minor Poems*, part 1, Chaucer Society Publications, 1st ser., vol. 21.
Greg, W. W. (1913). 'Chaucer attributions in MS R.3.19', *Modern Language Review* 8: 539–540.
Hanna, Ralph (2002). *A Descriptive Catalogue of the Western Medieval Manuscripts of St John's College*, Oxford: Oxford University Press.
Hicks, Michael A. (2009). 'Edward IV's *Brief Treatise* and the Treaty of Picquigny of 1475', *Historical Research* 83: 253–265.
Horobin, Simon (2003). *The Language of the Chaucer Tradition*, Woodbridge: Boydell and Brewer.
Horobin, Simon (2006). 'A new fragment of the *Romaunt of the Rose*', *Studies in the Age of Chaucer* 28: 205–215.

Horobin, Simon (2013). *Chaucer's Language*, 2nd edition, London: Palgrave Macmillan.
Jefferson, Judith, Ad Putter and Donka Minkova (2014). 'Perfect and imperfect rhyme: Romances in the abab tradition', *Studies in Philology* 111: 631–651.
Jordan, Richard (1974). *Handbook of Middle English Grammar: Phonology* [translated and revised by Eugene J. Crook], The Hague: Mouton.
Kihlbom, Asta (1926). *A Contribution to the Study of Fifteenth-Century English*, Uppsala: Lundequista Bokhandeln.
Laing, Margaret (1989). 'Dialectal analysis and linguistically composite texts in Middle English', in Margaret Laing (ed.), *Middle English Dialectology: Essays on Some Principles and Problems*, Aberdeen: Aberdeen University Press, pp. 150–169.
Lekebush, Julius (1906). *Die Londoner Urkundensprache von 1430 bis 1500*, Halle: Niemeyer.
Lewis, C. S. (1936). *The Allegory of Love*, Oxford: Oxford University Press.
Lewis, C. S. (1954). *English Literature in the Sixteenth Century Excluding Drama*, Oxford: Clarendon Press.
Lodge, Kenneth (2001). 'The modern reflexes of some Middle English vowel contrasts in Norfolk and Norwich', in Jacek Fisiak and Peter Trudgill (eds), *East Anglian English*, Woodbridge: Boydell and Brewer, pp. 205–217.
Lucas, Peter J. (1973). 'Consistency and correctness in the orthographic usage of John Capgrave's *Chronicle*', *Studia Neophilologica* 45: 323–355.
Luick, Karl (1921). *Historische Grammatik der englischen Sprache*, vol. 1, Leipzig: Tauchnitz.
Macaulay, G. C. (1900–1901). *John Gower's English Works*, 2 vols, EETS e.s. 81–82, London: Oxford University Press.
Mills, Maldwyn (ed.) (1969). *Lybeaus Desconus*, EETS o.s. 261, London: Oxford University Press.
Minkova, Donka (2003). *Alliteration and Sound Change in Early English*, Cambridge: Cambridge University Press.
Miskimin, Alice (1975). *The Renaissance Chaucer*, New Haven: Yale University Press.
Mooney, Linne R. (2001). 'The scribes and booklets of Trinity College, Cambridge, Manuscripts R.3.19 and R.3.21', in Alastair J. Minnis (ed.), *Middle English Poetry: Texts and Traditions*, Woodbridge: Boydell and Brewer, pp. 241–266.
Mooney, Linne R. (2011). 'Vernacular literary manuscripts and their scribes', in Alexandra Gillespie and Daniel Wakelin (eds), *The Production of Books in England 1350-1500*, Cambridge: Cambridge University Press, pp. 192–211.
Morsbach, Lorenz (1888). *Ueber den Ursprung der neuenglishen Schriftsprache*, Heilbronn: Henniger.
Mossé, Fernand (1952). *A Handbook of Middle English Grammar* [translated by James A. Walker], Baltimore: Johns Hopkins University Press.
Mustanoja, Tauno F. (1960). *A Middle English Syntax: Parts of Speech*, Helsinki: Société néophilologique.
Neilson, William A. (1899). *The Origins and Sources of* The Court of Love, Boston: Ginn.

Parkes, Malcolm and Richard Beadle (1979–80). *The Poetical Works of Geoffrey Chaucer: A Facsimile of Cambridge University Library MS GG.4.27*, 3 vols, Norman, OK: Pilgrim Books.
Purdie, Rhiannon (2008). *Anglicising Romance: Tail-Rhyme and Genre in Medieval English Literature*, Woodbridge: Boydell and Brewer.
Radulescu, Raluca (2003). 'Yorkist propaganda and *The Chronicle from Rollo to Edward IV*', *Studies in Philology* 100: 401–424.
Samuels, M. L. (1988a). 'Chaucer's spelling', in Jeremy J. Smith (ed.), *The English of Chaucer and his Contemporaries, Essays by Michael Samuels and J. J. Smith*, Aberdeen: Aberdeen University Press, pp. 23–37.
Samuels, M. L. (1988b). 'Spelling and dialect in the late and post-Middle English periods', in Jeremy J. Smith (ed.), *The English of Chaucer and his Contemporaries, Essays by Michael Samuels and J. J. Smith*, Aberdeen: Aberdeen University Press, pp. 86–95.
Samuels, M. L. and J. J. Smith (1988). 'The language of Gower', in Jeremy J. Smith (ed.), *The English of Chaucer and his Contemporaries, Essays by Michael Samuels and J. J. Smith*, Aberdeen: Aberdeen University Press, pp. 13–22.
Schick, Josef (1891). *Lydgate's Temple of Glas*, EETS e.s. 60, London: Trübner.
Seymour, M. C. (1968). 'A fifteenth-century East Anglian scribe', *Medium Aevum* 37: 166–173.
Shonk, Timothy A. (1988). 'B. L. Harley MS 7333: The "publication" of Chaucer in the rural areas', in *Essays in Medieval Studies: Proceedings of the Illinois Medieval Association* 15: 81–91.
Skeat, Walter W. (ed.) (1897). *Chaucerian and Other Pieces*, vol. 7 of *The Complete Works of Geoffrey Chaucer*, Oxford: Clarendon Press.
Skeat, Walter W. (1900). *The Chaucer Canon*, Oxford: Clarendon Press.
Smetana, Cyril Lawrence (ed.) (1977). *The Life of St. Norbert by John Capgrave*, Toronto: Pontifical Institute.
Tolkien, J. R. R. (1929). '*Ancrene Wisse* and *Hali Meiðhad*', *Essays and Studies by Members of the English Association* 14: 104–126.
Wakelin, Martyn F. (1988). 'The phonology of South-Western English', in Jacek Fisiak (ed.), *Historical Dialectology: Regional and Social*, Berlin: Mouton de Gruyter, pp. 609–644.
Wild, Friedrich (1915). *Die sprachlichen Eigentümlichkeiten der wichtigeren Chaucer-Handschriften und die Sprache Chaucers*, Vienna: Braumüller.
Windeatt, Barry (1990). 'Chaucer traditions', in Barry Windeatt and Ruth Morse (eds), *Chaucer Traditions: Studies in Honour of Derek Brewer*, Cambridge: Cambridge University Press, pp. 1–20.
Winstead. Karen A. (ed.) (1999). *John Capgrave: The Life of Saint Katherine*, TEAMS, Kalamazoo, MI: Medieval Institute.
Yeager, Robert (1990). *John Gower's Poetic: The Search for a New Arion*, Woodbridge: Boydell and Brewer.

11

'He was a good hammer, was he': Gender as Marker for South-Western Dialects of English. A Corpus-based Study from a Diachronic Perspective

Trinidad Guzmán-González

1. Introduction

This study explores the possibility that the gender system peculiar to the South-West (SW) English dialectal areas (masculine pronouns as the general reference for most nouns denoting inanimate – count – nouns), might be the result of early trends in the language, namely that similar patterns, or at least the seeds of the system (including the concurrence of feminine Middle English (ME) *he* from Old English (OE) *heo*) might already have been present in the ME ancestors of those dialects.

1.1 The grammatical category of gender in English

The received wisdom about the grammatical category of gender in Present-Day English (PDE) is that the pronouns employed in anaphora are 'he' for human males, 'she' for human females and 'it' for everything else ('he', 'she' and 'it' stand for the whole sets of personal pronouns). Nouns denoting male/female animals are included within the relevant gender by some authors (for example, Trudgill 1990: 88), and a certain degree of variation is usually acknowledged for some objects and entities (ships, countries, etc.). The case of 'it' for 'child' tends to be either ignored or otherwise considered a peculiar usage. In fact, the idea of peculiarity is what pervades a good deal of enquiries on gender assignment, as deviations from the usage described above (and which I have called 'assigned gender', Guzmán-González 2013a: 145) are assumed to be either exceptions or, in the best of cases, indicators of some kind of patterned variation, which is generally left uncharacterised.

The distinction made by Dahl (2000) between 'referential' (a property of the noun phrase as an occurrence) and 'lexical gender' (a property of the noun as a lexical item) is blurred in English by the fact that its gender system is covert, that is to say, it is expressed almost exclusively by third person singular pronouns in anaphora and, possibly, by sex-sensitive collocations and/or proper nouns. These may, or may not, trigger the use of 'he' or 'she', generally depending on the text type they appear: they often trigger them in poetry, or affectionate discourse, but not in scientific registers (cf. Guzmán-González 2013a), as shown in the three quotes below:

Our mother the earth is weary; through the night
I heard her laboured breathing, deep with pain
(Rupert Brooke, 'The earth', as quoted in Guzmán-González 1989: 373)

old nell's ribs stick out in spite of me. beside she hurt me this morning but hurt herself as bad while she was doing it. I took her out of the stable to exercise a little and Started acroos the prairie riding her with a halter . . .
(Letter from American settler Uriah Oblinger to his wife and their baby, 1872, as quoted in Guzmán-González 2015: 206)

During its last weeks of life, the *Antechinus* male shows changes associated with a severe stress response, including increased corticosteroid levels, hypertrophy of the adrenal glands, anaemia, marked lymphopenias and neytrophilias, and suppressed immune response.
(Baker, Gemmel and Gemmel's research article from *Journal of Experimental Zoology* 1998, as quoted in Guzmán-González 2013a: 158, 163)

English referential gender is thoroughly semantic, as the pronoun choices depend on extralinguistic criteria. 'Semantic' is here preferred to 'natural'[1] (Guzmán-González 2015: 200) in order to emphasise the idea of 'classification' implied by the Latin etymon (*genus* = class): whatever extralinguistic criterion they are based upon (and sexual differences are just one among other possibilities),[2] classifications are the result of the human primary instinct to apprehend reality in terms of hierarchised classes, and hence, involve formalisation, impositions of artificial conceptualisations on what lacks it: the outside world.

The English system shares with other gender systems the fact that it performs 'important communicative functions, both as to the referent of the noun and as to the speech community and type of discourse' (Guzmán-González 2015: 201). The use of 'it' for every noun except those denoting human males or females (with neuter as the default gender, as in Siemund 2008: 1) is generally considered a feature of unmarked registers in the PDE standard usage (Guzmán-González 2012b: 272). In consequence, assigned gender (which is widespread in English, see Guzmán-González 1989, 2012a, 2012b, 2013b, 2015) acts as a frequent indicator of all types of varieties: register ('he' for the sun in poetry, Guzmán-González 2013b), in-group usage ('she' for ships, Guzmán-González 2002), attitude ('he' or 'she' for pets) and dialect, the role with which this study is concerned.

---

[1] An adjective employed by many authors, for example: Classen 1919; Moore 1921; Ibrahim 1973; Hogg 1992; Lass 1992; Denison 2007 [1998]; Curzan 2003; Baugh and Cable 2005.
[2] Besides, 'natural' still tends to be associated with other adjectives like 'acceptable', and even with 'prescriptible', which makes its use, to say the least, slippery.

1.2 Gender as a diatopic marker: the South-Western traditional dialects

I will follow Trudgill's characterisation of traditional dialects, as those spoken by a probably shrinking minority of the English-speaking population of the world, almost all of them in England, Scotland and Northern Ireland. They are most easily found, as far as England is concerned, in the more remote and peripheral rural areas of the country, although some urban areas of northern and western England still have many traditional dialect speakers (Trudgill 1990: 5).

One of the features in which traditional dialects differ from the standard is precisely in that 'it' is not the default gender in some of them: thus, in the northern dialects 'she' has been identified as the typical anaphoric reference for non-living things (Upton, Parry and Widdowson 1994: 487); similarly, 'he' in the SW dialect area of England, an area that originates in southern ME and West Saxon (WS) OE.

From the end of the eighteenth century onwards, the West Country usage of masculine personal pronouns for nouns other than human males has been mentioned by many authors: by dialectologists but also by non-professional linguists interested in the subject. The description has remained basically the same from the very first recorded account (William Marshall in 1789 on Gloucester, as quoted by Wagner 2002–3: 16): 'it' is used for non-count lifeless things and for abstract nouns, while 'he' is the general pronoun for all kinds of count inanimate nouns. It is unclear whether 'he' is also the general usage for animals: Elworthy (1886: 328, as quoted by Wagner 2002–3: 17 and by Siemund 2008: 30, 41) stated that this was the case in West Somerset when the sex of the animal was not known, and even for 'a cow or a woman'. 'He' for 'cow' is also mentioned in the *Survey of English Dialects* (SED) (Upton, Parry and Widdowson 1994: 486). As to the forms themselves, apart from the standard ones ('he', 'him', 'his', 'it', 'its', 'she', 'her'), those specific from the SW are the following:

1. <en>, <'en>, <un>:

<'en> is mentioned by Barnes in 1886 (as quoted by Wagner 2002–3: 18); SED (Upton, Parry and Widdowson 1994: 486) lists various pronunciations ([ən], [n], [ŋ] [ɪn])[3] for the objective singular masculine case. It has been explained as deriving from OE *hine* (cf. also Wakelin 1972: 113–114). Dartnell and Goddard (1893: 124, as quoted by Wagner 2002–3: 19) record the spelling <un> for Wiltshire, which, they claim, could be used both for 'him' or 'it' (in instances like 'keyhole', 'bed' and 'table' (also referred to with 'he'). Wakelin (1972: 113) has claimed that though <en> is mainly objective, it may also be subjective in what he calls 'unemphatic contexts', i.e. tag-questions such as 'isn't he?' His examples come from Wiltshire and Somerset.

2. [əɹ] // [əʳː]:

---

[3] [ən] in Gloucester, Somerset, Wiltshire, Cornwall, Devon and Hampshire; [n] in Somerset, Wiltshire, Berkshire, Cornwall, Dorset, Hampshire, Sussex; [ŋ] in Cornwall, Hampshire, Sussex; [ɪn] in Somerset and Wiltshire.

Wagner (2002–3: 59) calls it 'a kind of "universal" pronominal form in West Country dialects', which 'can substitute all personal pronouns, regardless of person and gender, but is most frequently found in third person singular context'. The majority of authors in the relevant literature interpret this rhotic pronunciation of [ə] as a masculine form. Although this may be the case 'when the context or neighbouring forms suggest this interpretation' (Wagner 2002–3: 59), I concur with Paddock (1991: 36) that the clear homophony with the distinctively feminine forms <her>, <'er> used in more standard Wessex varieties cannot be completely disregarded.

According to certain surveys (Ihalainen 1985; Wagner 2002–3; Siemund 2008), the second half of the twentieth century has witnessed changes in the frequency of this feature. Although the English variety employed by elderly rural speakers (who were the typical informants in SED) is '(still) surprisingly close to the traditional West Country vernacular described by Barnes, Elworthy and other 19th-century authors' (Wagner 2005: 316) and their pronoun usage, at least for man-made objects, has 'remained largely intact to the present day' (338). However, 'he' for count nouns denoting things seems to be losing ground to the standard among speakers who, judging from the corpora researched by the above authors,[4] might belong to younger groups of the population. Apparently, this shift is grammar sensitive ('standard *it* forms first invaded the territory of personal forms in object position, later spreading to the more prominent subject contexts as well' (Ihalainen, as quoted by Wagner 2002–3: 26)) and extends from east to west (Wagner 2005: 315–318), with Somerset as the county most clearly open to the standard usage, with Devon, Dorset and Wiltshire gradually following, and (West) Cornwall as the most resilient area: 'The further westward we move, the more non-standard pronouns we encounter' (Wagner 2005: 336).

2. Text work

2.1 Aims and scope

The defining feature of traditional dialects is precisely to have kept away from the various standardisation processes undergone by the English language; they stem from medieval varieties which have resisted the levelling results of such processes (cf. Wakelin 1972: 3). Whether they have remained distinct either by keeping ancient features, or by innovating patterns of their own, or by a combination of both possibilities, these varieties are likelier to be found in 'remote and more peripheral rural areas' (Trudgill 1990: 5) of the country.

---

[4] Ihalainen's informants were born 'around the turn of the 20th century' (Siemund 2008: 57) and so were Wagner's speakers in her materials of oral provenance (2005: 242–246); Siemund did not find age a relevant factor in his research on the demographic part of the BNC (cf. 2008: 253, endnote 53) and hence does not specify the participants' ages; but given the project's closing date (1994) and the sampling procedure (cf. Burnard 2007) that even the older respondents in the study might have been some twenty years younger seems a reasonable estimation.

The general assumption tends to be that southern traditional dialects evolved from WS OE; and that, therefore, many of their linguistic traits (voicing of initial fricatives as in *zay*, *vinger*, *zhilling* ('say, finger, shilling'), universal present indicative <-th> as in *He go'th* (Ihalainen 1994: 214)) have been inherited from the medieval period, basically from southern ME coming from WS OE, and have survived through the Early Modern English (EModE) and the Late Modern English (LModE) periods. The hypothesis this study investigates, then, is that the SW masculine default gender system might be part of that medieval inheritance.

The tendency to ascribe a medieval origin to the SW system probably stems from comments on supposed developments towards the masculine as the default gender in ME once OE grammatical gender had collapsed, like those by Clark (1957: 109–115), by Mustanoja (1960) and by Jones (1988), presumably on account of the weight of masculine nouns in the OE lexicon: the General Masculine Declension (GMD)[5] alone contains 35 per cent of total amount of OE nouns, to which the masculine nouns in the rest of declensions must be added. Clark's and Mustanoja's statements are much questioned today, the former because her sources consist of just part of one text (the second period of the *Peterborough Chronicle*); Mustanoja lacks sufficiently reliable data to support what seem little more than general impressions. As for Jones, his work concerns just the noun phrase, without considering anaphora. Nevertheless, all three are symptomatic, as far as the grammatical category of gender in ME is concerned, of a perceived state of affairs where any outcome in gender assignment changes might have been possible, including exaptation of the most frequent gender class (masculine) in OE to the rest of the lexicon or to just part of it, as in the kind of gender system in the SW of England.

There seems to be no complete agreement on the geographical extent of the SW dialectal area: thus, Alexander Ellis's district 4 (1889, as quoted by Wagner 2002–3: 19) comprises Somerset, parts of Dorset, Hampshire and Gloucester; while Wakelin (1986) lists Cornwall, Devon, Somerset, South Avon, Wiltshire, Dorset and West Hampshire. My study's geographical scope is the same employed in Wagner's research on modern gender usage: Cornwall, Devon, Somerset, Dorset and Wiltshire; in her words, 'the core of what is called Southwest' (Wagner 2002–3: 52). The reason for my choice is that Wagner's work is the only recent one combining materials from the SED (Wagner 2002–3: 235) with others from 'interviews from various oral-history projects all over the Southwest of England' (Wagner 2002–3: 242).

2.2 Gender in ME

My own data (Guzmán-González 2002, 2012a) had contributed to supporting Moore's (1921: 45) idea that 'natural gender did not replace grammatical gender in Old English but survived it'. I kept the crux of Moore's argument (survival and extension of an already existing linguistic behaviour in anaphora), but I updated terms and framework: I characterised the OE gender system as overt (with gender markers on nouns and adjectives), and formal (based on linguistic assignment criteria), *cum* some semantic

---

[5] For declension names and the percentages I follow Hogg (2002).

criteria applied in anaphora for some nouns whose grammatical and notional genders do not coincide. More often, this is the case of nouns like *wif* 'woman', localised in high positions in animacy hierarchies like those proposed by Quirk et al. (1985: 314–318), where the various gender groups are distributed in scales of the type animate/inanimate > personal/non-personal > higher (male/female)/lower animals; but neuter pronouns for *nama* 'name' have also been found. These semantic criteria are the key to the subsequent process: once reduced morphology in the noun phrases proved unable to help speakers deduce the old formal classes, they were the only points of reference in pronoun selection, and, hence, they have prevailed since ME times. The gender systems built upon them, nevertheless, have been subject to variation along the usual parameters affecting the history of English.[6]

2.3 Methodological tools

2.3.1 Corpora

The texts for this study were retrieved from the digital corpora mentioned below: while it is not essential for these textual sources to have been digitised, the digital age has brought about, apart from the obvious practicalities (e.g. ready availability, automatic word count, etc.), theoretical and methodological advantages, including philological reliability (different researchers providing a multiplicity of complementary approaches, exhaustive editorial information, rationales behind the decisions taken in the editorial processes, etc.) plus, in the case of a *Linguistic Atlas of Early Middle English* 1150–1325 (LAEME) (Laing 2013–), tools for prospective further work on other related aspects of the topic under research.

My sources[7] were all the textual files specifically localised as SW in the relevant subsections of LAEME ({D1},{D2}, {Do1}, {So1}, {So2}, {So3}, {W1}, {W2}, {W3}, {W4}), the *Helsinki Corpus of English Texts* (HC) (Rissanen et al. 1991) ({D4}), and the *Middle English Grammar Corpus* (MEG-C) (Stenroos et al. 2011) ({D3}, {Do2}, {So4}, {W5}, {C}). A *Linguistic Atlas of Late Middle English* (LALME) (electronic version, Benskin et al. 2013–) has not been employed because it 'was never made by means of transcribing the materials in their entirety' but merely by subjecting 'each text to an analysis by questionnaire like a modern dialect survey' (Laing, personal communication); but it must be noted that {D3}, {Do2}, {So4}, {W5} and {D4} are localised in LALME; {W6} is a textual file on horse husbandry, also localised in LALME, and transcribed by Laing (2012).[8]

Once editorial comments within the running texts, Latin quotes, and so on, were excluded, the total word count of the corpus is 30,362, within Aston's (1997: 54) lower limit for small corpora (20,000 words). Given that it focuses on clearly localised

---

[6] Cf. further discussion, in section 4 (Conclusions).
[7] Details in Appendix; braced capitals (C = Cornwall, D = Devon, Do = Dorset, S = Somerset, W = Wiltshire) plus a number will be used for cross-reference in the examples.
[8] The article includes a partial transcription of the text; I am grateful to Margaret Laing for having made the complete text available to me for this and previous (unpublished) research.

dialectal specimens from a restricted geographical area, it is representative enough, especially as medieval extant written records cannot yield the large corpora obtained from materials dating from subsequent centuries when new demographic, economic and socio-historical circumstances brought about substantial increases in the numbers or readers and writers.

2.3.2 Units of Anaphoric Reference (UARs)

The concept was devised specifically for research on gender assignment (Guzmán-González 2012a, 2012b, 2013a, 2013b, 2015), and provides the kind of 'context-rich discourse data' which authors like Singer (2010) have called for in studies in nominal classifications. Since UARs are pragmatic units, they can be envisaged as a type of referential chain (a single referent which is tracked through the discourse by a range of anaphoric elements):[9] a UAR may express an idea, a wish, an opinion, etc., concerning the referent, may contain (part of) a description of or (a sequence of) actions performed by that referent, or be part of an account of events in which that referent plays a part, etc.

UARs are defined depending on whether a referent appears (either overtly or unambiguously identifiable by the context) more than once in a text section; the clause is the (loose) limit for each UAR; and, since what is crucial in research on referential gender is what could be termed as the 'referential anaphoric act', the length of the quote and the number of anaphoric references in it are irrelevant, as shown by the two UARs in examples (1) and (2):[10]

(1) Take an **aylewand**~ and make **hit** crokyd~ {W6}
 'Take a nail-rod[11] and bend it'

(2) For to make a **hors** Fatte Take newe draff and newe branne and xx rostyd~ eggis & pille then [sic] clene & breyse them smalle and put þer-to a quantite of salt and melle al thes to-gedire and lete **hym** ete this \ at morow and ʒeve **hym**~ drynke at none als meche gode ale as **he** wolle drynke wyth \ a horn and ʒeve **hym**~ drye otis and barley malt & als many hard~ eggis therin and thus \ diete **hym** iij daies but kepe **hym**~ warme and then after ʒeve **hym**~ other mete and drynke I-nowe and in xiiij daies **he** schalle be fatte. \ {W6}

 'To make a horse fat. Take fresh malt waste[12] and bran and twenty cooked eggs and peel them clean and smash them small and put a certain quantity of salt in it and mix

---

[9] I am grateful to Bettelou Los for having called my attention to referential chains as a framework for UARs; the definition is her personal communication. See also Komen et al. 2014: 95ff.

[10] UARs have been specially edited for this chapter: the relevant pronouns and referents have been highlighted with **bold type** and underlining. The tag assigned to each text in the list in section 2.3.1 appears in braces – {} – at the end of each UAR. Translations (mine for all examples) are as literal as possible without incurring in un-grammaticality.

[11] After Laing 2012: 31.

[12] After Laing 2012: 63.

all this together and let him eat this in the morning and give him to drink at noon as much good ale as he will drink with a horn and give him dried oats and barley malt and also many hard boiled eggs therein and diet him thus three days but keep him warm and afterwards give him right away another (kind of?) meal and drink and in fourteen days he shall be fat.'

Similarly we may find more than one referent and the corresponding anaphors syntactically intertwined in a passage in such a way that it is not possible to separate that pragmatic unit into different quotes. In that case, as every referent spawns its own UAR, the same quote may be counted as many times as referents appear in it, as in (3) and (4):

(3) Also þᵉ **poudr**~ of þ[ⁱˢ] herb be blow in-to a ma*n*nys nose **it** clenseth it fro rennyng~ {W5}
(4) Also þᵉ poudr~ of þ[ⁱˢ] herb be blow in-to a ma*n*nys **nose** it clenseth **it** fro rennyng~ {W5}

'Also, if the powder of this herb is blown into a man's nose, it cleanses it from congestion'

UARs are retrieved by means of manually scanning rather than by using a concordancer or search engine. Search engines cannot efficiently handle the very long strings needed for this specific type of research or distinguish between pronouns in the same passage referring to different referents, or to referents mentioned much earlier in the previous discourse. Annotating the whole corpus with referential information would have been more time-consuming than collecting the UARs needed for this study manually. Moreover, the risk that many potentially interesting collocations (for example 'Father Time'), impossible to predict beforehand, might be left unnoticed is thus avoided. The preliminary list of UARs was double-checked, using, first, the forms from SW texts under the LAEME grammels[13] for the third person singular pronouns, and, second, the forms of the third person singular pronouns in the LALME Linguistic Profiles[14] (LPs) of all the texts from Cornwall, Devon, Dorset, Somerset and Wiltshire.

Since this study focuses on the use of masculine pronouns as an almost-default gender in anaphora with the exception of human beings, UARs containing anaphoric reference for adult human beings were excluded, and also all those instances where it referred to complete clauses, existential *it*, and the like. Pronouns in fragmentary texts

---

[13] In the tagging system of LAEME, the nonce-term 'grammel' refers to the grammatical element indicating the function of the tagged item plus, for personal pronouns, number, person, case, gender and additional relevant information (spelling, adposition, etc.) (Laing and Lass 2013).

[14] An LP is 'an inventory, for some specified sample of text, of the forms observed which correspond to the test-items on the questionnaire' (McIntosh, Samuels and Benskin, Introduction to Volume 3 of LALME, available at http://www.lel.ed.ac.uk/ihd/elalme/intros/atlas_intro_lps.html). Questionnaires are the examining texts devised in LALME for the occurrence of a set of predetermined linguistic criteria.

where referents could not be unambiguously identified were excluded. Quotes containing only *his* were also excluded, as at the time no distinct neuter genitive adjective/pronoun existed; those containing *him/hym* references alone, however, were included, whenever object *it/hit* appeared in the same text in a way consistent enough to allow an interpretation of the former as masculine. Although 'child' and nouns denoting animals are not particularly mentioned in the literature as referred to by 'he' in the SW dialects,[15] they have also been considered because any potential deviation or preservation from OE usages were deemed significant.

3. Results

The corpus yielded 265 UARs in all. Table 11.1 summarises the distribution of nouns (for which, given the high spelling variability in ME, modern equivalents have been used for the sake of brevity) and of UARs in the corpus.

Table 11.1 UARs and nouns in the corpus

265 UARs	117 individual nouns + 'concoctions'
55	1 (horse)
24	1 (herb)
15	1 (land)
9	1 ('concoctions')
5	2 (borough, onion)
4	3 (city, lancet, sacrament)
3	5 (blood; book; child, plaster; vein)
2	21
1	83

Nine UARs (labelled as 'concoctions' in the table) are potions and salves to which no specific name is given, as in (5):

(5) Take þer-fore half a poynte of hony and a quarter of a libra of blak sope & \ melle them same & þerto take a sponefulle of venegre and als meche of Alym~ as a egge \ and brenne **hit** and sponefulle of rye floure or els of bene floure & medle hem same and \ leye **hit** to the sore as ferre as the melette rechis and lette **it** lye to the sore v. daies \ and then take **hit** a-wey {W6}

'Therefore take half a pint of honey and a quarter of a pound of black soap and mix them and then take a spoonful of vinegar and also as much alum as an egg and burn it and a spoonful of rye flour or else of bean flour and mix them together and lay it to the sore covering the whole mellit[16] and let it lay on the sore for five days and then take it away'

---

[15] Except for certain cases mentioned by Elworthy (1886) for West Somerset and by the SED for Somerset and Devon, see section 1.2 for details.

[16] *OED*: 'A skin lesion or disease affecting the heels of a horse'.

The remaining UARs refer to 117 different nouns, of which 104 appear with one or two UARs, something to be expected given the heterogeneous nature of the corpus, with a good number of short texts dealing with many different things; the few nouns with high numbers of UARs are explained by the presence in the corpus of works concerned with herbology, horse husbandry ({W5} and {W6}) and travels ({D3} and ({W4}) (cf. Guzmán-González 2012b: 277, 2015: 206). The nouns appear in parentheses after each figure in the relevant column, except for the last two rows.

My figures render a large predominance of neuter gender assignment: 180 UARs containing 'it' anaphors, around 68 per cent of the total amount of UARs. This predominance is strengthened by the rest of data:

1. One hundred and seven nouns ('concoctions' excluded) are referred exclusively by 'it' in 175 UARs.
2. Nouns referred by animate pronouns constitute a very small percentage of the total: 10 out of 117 ('borough', 'child', 'colt', 'herb', 'horse', 'knife', 'lantern', 'spice', 'sun', 'worm'); but these figures are nuanced by the following:
   (i) The UARs for 'horse' (55 UARs with 'he') and for 'herb' (22 UARs with 'she' + 2 UARs with 'it') appear in just two texts ({W6} and {W5} respectively).
   (ii) Four nouns are gender-fluid, i.e. nouns for which masculine/feminine and neuter anaphors have been found in 33 UARs:
   'borough': 5 UARs: 2 'he' + 2 'she' + 1 'it'
   'child': 3 UARs: 2 'he' + 1 'it'
   'herb': 24 UARs: 22 'she' + 2 'it'
   'worm': 1 UAR with both 'he' and 'it' anaphors

The analysis of the results shows that 'it' is the anaphor employed for all kinds of nouns: mass (example (6)) or abstract nouns (example (7)), or those for which, as described in section 1.2 above, traditional SW dialects would have had 'he', at least until the second half of the twentieth century, i.e. count nouns like those denoting plants and vegetables (8), place-names (9), body parts (10), objects (11), etc.:

(6) If thu haue **water** & no wyn
    anon right thu do **it** yn {C}
    'If you have water and no wine // pour it in immediately'

(7) Alle **wikkedhede** boe wat **hit** euere boe {W1}
    'all sinfulness, be it whatever be'

(8) and then rost the **onyon**~ and bray **hit** and ley **hit** to the serewe but kyt notte \ the skyn \ {W6}
    'and then rost the onion and chop it and lay it to the serew[17] but do not cut the skin'

---

[17] *OED*: 'a bony excrescence on the leg of a horse'.

(9) and ye schall onderstond þᵗ Constantynople ys a Fayr~ **cyte** & good & well wallyd & **hyt** ys. iij. cornede [. . .] {D3}
'And you shall understand that Constantinople is a fair city and good and well walled and it is three cornered'

(10) for \ the colt is **legge** is as longe wyth-in a monthe aftyr þt he is folyd~ as eu*er* **hit** wille \ be {W6}
'for the colt's leg is as long within a month after he is born as it will ever be'

(11) take þ*er*-fore a **launcette** and putte **it** thorowe the skyn~ \be-fore the shulder be-twene the spaude and þe mary-bon~ [. . .]{W6}
'therefore take a lancet and put it through the skin between the joint and the marrowbone'

The nouns denoting inanimate things in this study (115) come from originally masculine, feminine and neuter words from OE, Old Norse and Romance words. That only six of them get (unambiguously identified) anaphors other than 'it' is clearly compatible with the state of affairs described in section 2.2 above for ME, when gender had almost completed the transition from a grammatical to a semantic system, with 'it' as the most frequent pronoun for things. 'Almost' and 'transition' are key words in the basis of the explanations for the nouns labelled as 'gender-fluid' above. Interesting cases in this respect are 'borough' and 'worm': the five UARs identified for the former contain masculine, feminine (the OE gender) and neuter anaphors. All of them appear in {W4}, the London BL Cotton Otho C copy of Layamon's *Brut*, generally known in the literature for its mixed language (Anglo-Norman and intentionally archaic OE). 'Worm' in {W6} is described as the cause for a non-healing ulcer, the usual meaning of 'cancer' in ME (cf. Laing 2012: 62): the proximity of *kankere* may have triggered the mixed anaphors, but what is relevant in this UAR is, first, that both words come from OE masculine nouns (the latter is a borrowing from Latin masculine *cancer*) and, second, that in {W6} (see below) UARs referring to complaints contain 'it', and those for the other two nouns of animals in the corpus ('horse' and 'colt'), contain 'he'.

(12) For the ka*n*kere in the Eye \ Hit comys of a wikkyd blood in the hede þt fallyth downe in the eye & þ*er* it congeleth a **worme** \ as it **hit** [sic dittography] were the hede of a pismere and **hit** grouteh in the neþ*er* ende of the eye to the \ noseward~ and **hit** holdeth in-to the nostrell of the nose and if **he** go thorowe the grestill \ **he** wolle go in-to the heed and then~ the hors wolle deye [. . .] {W6}

'For the cancer in the eye. It comes of bad blood in the head that falls down into the eye and there it congeals into a worm as if it were the head of an ant, and it grows nosewards from the back end of the eye and it affects the nostril and if it goes through the gristle it will go into the head and then the horse will die'[18]

---

[18] Checked against Laing (2012: 56).

In individual texts like {Do2}, and {W5}, although I am generally inclined to agree with Jones in his argumentation against the influence of foreign genders,[19] direct contact with foreign languages (mainly Latin and French) probably explains the choice of other-than-'it' anaphors. The former is an early poem 'On the instruments of the Passion', or 'Arma Christi', very well-known elements in medieval religious iconography; the verses dedicated to each instrument are introduced by the corresponding Latin term, except 'lantern' (examples (13) and (14)).

(13)   <lat>cuttellus<lat> (sic)
       the **knyf** tokeneth the circumcision
       he distryed synne al & som
       Of oure forme fader adam
       wher-þurw we toke kynde of man
       Fro temptacioun and lechorie
       he be myn socour whanne y schal die {Do2}
       'the knife symbolises the circumcision // it destroyed every sin // from our first father, Adam, // by means of whom we received our human nature. // From temptation and lechery // let it be my protector when I die'

(14)   the **lanterne** þat men bare in þe liȝt
       whan cryst was y-take in þe niȝt
       he ke-pe me fram dedely sinne
       that y neuer deye þere-ynne {Do2}
       'the light-lantern that men carried // the night Christ was captured // let it keep me from deadly sin // that I never die in it'

The other three UARs identified in {Do2}, however, contain 'it' anaphors, despite the animate genders of two of the introductory Latin nouns ('sponge', *spongea* feminine, 'hammer', *malleus*, masculine; interestingly the corresponding OE words *sponge* (obviously a loanword from Latin) and *hamor* are also feminine and masculine). Even if personification is invoked as an explanation for (12) and (13) above, the question why some items have been personified and others have not remains. In {W5}, a SW copy of the translation (however imperfect) from the Latin herbal *Agnus Castus*, we find a majority of feminine anaphors for 'herb' (*herba*, in Latin, feminine): twenty-two out of twenty-four UARs; similarly for 'spice' (Latin *species*, feminine) (examples (15) and (16)):

(15)   The vertu of þ[is] **herb** is þᵗ the more of **hure** is good to hele the feu*er* cotidian@ & **he** be droncke wᵗ wyn@ **he** groweth in many plac*es*{W5}
       'The medicinal property of this herb is that its root is good to heal quotidian fever and he must be drunk with wine; it grows in many places'

[19] 'How it could be demonstrated that individual scribes actually "knew" the non-English items (far less what their native language gender classification might have been) is never discussed by the proponents of this theoretical viewpoint nor are any convincing reasons provided as to why non-native items should have such an influencing role in the first place' (Jones 1988: 15).

(16) þis is a **spice** of confirie & **he** growth in feldes {W5}
'This is a spice of comfrey and it grows in fields'

The rest of UARs with nouns denoting inanimate things ('powder', 'nose', 'skin', 'seed') identified in {W5} contain 'it' references; however, of all the Latin equivalents to these nouns, only *semen* is neuter.

The masculine anaphors for 'horse' and 'colt' in the fifty-seven UARs found in this research also deserve consideration. OE *colt* belongs to the GMD; and the *OED* states that, like other 'originally neuter' names of animals ('sheep, swin, neat, deer'), OE General Neuter Declension (GND) *hors* was 'applicable to the male or the female alike'; the name for the male was the GMD name *hengest*. It is true that animals in high positions in animacy hierarchies, like horses and their young, have long been considered typical referents for animate pronouns in unmarked discourse, as statements from grammarians like Alexander Hume (1612) or Robert Lowth (1762) show:

> Sex is a distinction of a noun be male and female, and these are distinguished the one from the other, or both from things without sex. The one is distinguished from the other be he and she. He is the noat of the male; as he is a good judge . . . he is a speedie horse . . . she is a cowe (Hume, as quoted by Guzmán-González 1989: 94)
>
> The English language, with singular propriety, following nature alone, applies the distinction of Masculine and Feminine only to the Animals; all the rest are neuter (Lowth, as quoted by Guzmán-González and González 2005: 34)

Pronoun choice ('he'/'she') for animal referents has been a frequent resource to convey 'personal feelings of attachment, in-group bonds, etc.' (Guzmán-González 2013a: 147), attitudes undoubtedly expected in the authors of the several short texts about horse husbandry in {W6}, the source for the fifty-seven UARs cited. A knowledge of the particulars in animal sexual differentiation might have always existed in the language as a kind of universal default criterion and, together with associated individuation strategies, would certainly account for these and for similar usages, even in scientific registers in subsequent centuries.[20] Hence, the shift to the masculine of OE GND *hors* and the preservation of the masculine gender of *colt* are clearly compatible with the criteria underlying the historical shift to semantic gender, and no further consideration would be needed for cases with male animals as referents. As far as the anaphor for the species, the selection of pronouns other than 'it' is also related with animacy hierarchy strategies; but 'he' need not be the first, or the most frequent choice for all animals:

> as when we call them Horses and Dogges, in the Masculine, though there be Bitches, and mares amongst them. So to the Fowles, for the most part, we use the Feminine, as of Eagles,

---

[20] Cf., for instance, Hooke's use of 'he' for a flea he was observing with his microscope (quoted in Nevalainen and Raumolin-Brunberg 1994: 183) and the use of 'he' and 'she' for individuals in a group of animals being reported about in zoology research articles (Guzmán-González 2013a).

hawkes; we say 'Shee flies well'[.] (Ben Jonson, 1750 [1640], as quoted by Guzmán-González 1989: 96)

Nevalainen and Raumolin-Brunberg (1994: 183) have found evidence for this masculine epicene for horses in their corpus data from the 1500–1710 parts of the HC and from six grammars composed between 1586–1652, including Jonson's grammar quoted above. Interestingly, the style of {W6} strongly suggests that in almost all of the UARs identified in it, the name of the species is meant, rather than individual animals.[21]

My point is that the choice between 'he' or 'she' in these cases (as any other where sex is unknown or felt as irrelevant) is not random. It is generally prompted by linguistic habits (Guzmán-González 1999: 38) shaped, among other factors, 'by the original grammatical gender from OE or from the language of provenance in the case of borrowings' (Guzmán-González 2012b: 285). This particular linguistic habit may certainly have native OE roots (a very early association of *hors* with the male of the species), but a fact that should not be overlooked is that the association with Latin *equus* is extremely frequent already in OE[22] and that the texts in {W6}, possibly 'put together originally from a number of different sources' (Laing 2012: 11) belong to a long-timed Anglo-Norman tradition (Laing 2012: 9) which included works in Latin, and their translations into Old French (OF) and ME; together with other practical texts (herbals, veterinary medicine, etc.). This kind of equine treatises were customary in the libraries of medieval English manors and states and foreign genders might have contributed to reinforce this habit, as readers and translators would have very often encountered noun phrases including Latin *equus* and *pultellus* and OF *cheval* and *poutrel* (all masculine).[23]

Like Bourdieu's *habitus* (1990: 53), these linguistic habits constitute interfaces between linguistic facts and social frameworks. The use of 'he' in example (17) can be interpreted in this same light, especially if we consider the literary tradition that, starting in ME times, has generally preferred the Latin and Greek models in the assigned genders for 'sun' ('he') and 'moon' ('she') to the OE original genders.

---

[21] No specific matter concerning females, which could perhaps have triggered feminine pronouns, is mentioned. As for the young of the species, 'filly' is very scarcely attested before the manuscript's date (late fifteenth century, Laing 2012: 10): the first quotation in the *OED*, the only one before 1525, dates from around 1400; the *MED* contains only two in the fifteenth century, in 1404 and 1408.

[22] The specification for *hors* as the male of the species does not appear in the main dictionary but in *The Supplement* (1921) to Bosworth and Toller: 'II. II. *a male of the horse kind*. (1) as distinguished from *mare:*--Hors *equus*, myre *equa*, Wrt. Voc. i. 78, 5: 287, 42. Hors mon sceal gyldan mid. xxx. scill ... myran mid. xx. scill; Ll. Th. i. 356, 2. (2) as distinguished from *hengest:*--Hors *equus*, hengest *cabullus*, Wrt. Voc. :. 287, 42. Án hundred wildra horsa and . xvi. tame hencgestas, Cht. Th. 548, 11.'; cf. also the *Dictionary of Old English* (*DOE*): 'Lat. equiv. in MS: caballus, cornipes, +equus, sonipes, subjugalis' plus relevant quotes.

[23] Cf. above comments on 'knife', 'lantern', 'herb' and 'spice'; additionally, Nevalainen and Raumolin-Brunberg (1994: 184) and Stenroos (2008: 450).

(17) For þᵉ **sonne** whane **he** ys ryth southe **he** castyth hys bemys vppon þᵗ contrye & yeveth ryght grett hette on þᵗ contye {D3}
'Because the sun when it is right south it casts its beams upon the country and gives great heat on that county'

As for the three UARs for 'child' in the corpus (all in {W4}), the presence of 'son' and masculine proper nouns in the nearby text may have triggered 'he' in examples (18) and (19); gender assignment in these UARs should then be analysed as based upon semantic criteria, in line with the shift discussed in section 2.2 above. As for the neuter reference in example (20), it has already been pointed out above that {W4} contains much intentionally archaic language; OE *cild* is neuter, and, as a preference for 'it' as the anaphor for newborns has been preserved to this day, this UAR might additionally be interpreted within the linguistic habits framework.

(18) One **sone** afde aschani(us þat wa sihote **Silui(us)**. þis **child** afde his hemes name ac lutele wile **he** liuede. {W4}
'Aschanius had a son who was named Silvius. This child had his uncle's name and was short lived'

(19) þis **child** leuede and wel iþeh and þeuwes **he** louede þo **he** was fiftene ʒer to þe wode **he** verde. an[d] his fader mid **him** {W4}
'This child lived and thrived and he loved virtues; when he was fifteen he went into the woods, and his father with him'

(20) þo þe time Icome was þat þe **childe** hi-bore weas. Þe Moder þorh **him** iwarþ dead alse ibore was þe **child**. **hit** was ihote Brut(us) {W4}
'When the time was come when the child was born, the mother died because of him when the child was born. He was named Brutus'

4. Conclusions

The ME abandonment of the former grammatical criteria in noun classification, however, does not imply that the gender systems resulting from the prevalence of semantic criteria were, first, strictly corresponding to sexual differences, and, second, more or less uniform across varieties. The tendency to the masculine as the default gender in ME had already been discussed in 2.2 above; recent surveys like Stenroos's (2008: 468–469) propose a semantic gender system emerging in the thirteenth-century West Midlands along the following parameters:

Masculine: human males (post-babies), human generic, 'superhuman' beings, some animals (post-babies)
Feminine: human females (post-babies), some animals (post-babies), inanimate objects and abstract nouns (perceived as individual)
Neuter: human and animal babies, inanimate objects and abstract nouns (not perceived as individual), mass nouns

This 'reorganization of pronominal gender assignment' (Stenroos 2008: 469) seems to have unfolded in various ways then in the various dialects; but not necessarily in random ways, with the possible influence of Latin and OF literary traditions mentioned above playing a part in and through the written register. For the SW dialects, the figures indicate that, in the corpus analysed, with the very few exceptions which have been commented upon in 2.4 above, 'it' can be considered as the default gender for all nouns denoting non-living things. It is therefore clear that the specific criterion that has predominated for these nouns is semantic: inanimateness. In view of this prevalence, and the complementary absence of 'he' anaphors, it can be safely said that no clear evidence supports the ME origin of the so-called SW masculine gender for count nouns or for 'he' as the default pronoun except for human females (Paddock 1991), at least in the geographical area of Cornwall, Devon, Dorset, Somerset and Wiltshire.

Nevalainen and Raumolin-Brunberg (1994: 183–184) list a few nouns which in their EModE data are assigned to the masculine gender; they indirectly seem to connect them with the modern SW usage in footnote 9 of their article. Nevertheless, looking for its origin in subsequent periods of the history of English falls beyond the present study's scope. Hence, what follows in section 5 below are theoretical considerations regarding prospective research into the topic.

5. Further theoretical considerations

As mentioned in section 1.2 above, the first account on the use of 'he' as the general pronoun for count nouns denoting inanimate things dates from the end of the eighteenth century: compilations of glossaries and grammars of local varieties were frequent at the time, and together with the 'imitated dialect in early literature and [. . .] self-conscious attempts to imitate dialect in poems, dialogues and the like' (Wakelin 1972: 29) used to be the most frequently (sometimes the only) source employed in dialectal studies for LModE and EModE. It is likely that an awareness of factors like those pointed out by Görlach (1999: 507) (presumed adaptation of the dialectal traits to stylistic conventions, 'sociolinguistic expectations regarding age, sex, education, etc. of the persona characterised by it' and even to prospective standard readers) has always existed; but in tracking dialectal traits, the crucial difference between the problems posed by medieval sources and those from subsequent centuries does not lie in the amount of sources, or in their accessibility. In this respect, enquiries into more recent stages of English have benefited from the same giant leap that has been granted to medieval studies by electronic corpora and digital tools.[24] As far as dialectology

---

[24] The wealth of electronic resources (corpora and other digitised texts, tools, etc.) is such that no reasonably comprehensive account is feasible within the limits of this study. For interested readers who might be nevertheless unfamiliar with certain kinds of sources, the Text Encoding Initiative site (http://www.tei-c.org/index.xml) with special attention to the Oxford Text Archive is a highly advisable starting point. For further discussion on theoretical aspects and information about particular corpora, including specifically dialectal corpora like The Online Salamanca Corpus of English Dialect Texts and The SCONE Corpus of Northern English, see Vázquez 2012.

in general and traditional dialects in particular are concerned, that difference has to do with what is the defining feature of the EModE period: the rise of Standard English (StE).

This complex unplanned process unfolded in various ways along several centuries; its essential component was writing, to the point that it was in the written language where standardisation came nearest to be completed: whereas today we can reasonably speak of a common written standard, a similar level of standardisation has never been reached in speech. Writing was related to some of the factors that received wisdom considers as having favoured the selection[25] of the East Midlands London variety of ME as the basis for the future standard (among them, the Royal Court, especially the Signet Office and the Chancery, the proximity of the two universities, and, most importantly, that most publishing houses after the introduction of the printing press were located in London); more crucial for the assessment of dialectal written sources was the role played by schools in the spread of literacy and, in consequence, in the processes of codification and stabilisation of StE.

The rise of the standard marked a crucial change in the character of the textual evidence: in the Middle Ages, writing in English meant writing in one's dialectal variety (cf. Lass 1999: 4). Hence, the difficulties in identifying and assessing ME dialectal evidence conveyed, above all, disentangling scribal layers in multiply copied texts. But from the medieval period onwards, much of the textual evidence at our disposal consists of complex clusters of texts whose regional provenance must be identified through external information (authors' biographies, publishing places, etc.), because standardisation has blurred dialectal traits to different extents: at one extreme we have published materials, including literary and non-literary works; at the other, records, personal accounts, private letters, etc.

These documentary and/or private texts have been taken as the closest type to speech before the tape-recorder era, and, hence, the sources where dialectal traits are most likely to come up. However, if a certain 'standard tinge' must have affected the literary dialects (because authors and compilers might have been native dialectal speakers, and might have cherished their dialects, but we have every reason to assume that their formal education at school was performed in StE), these other types of sources are not free from it either. Court records or personal accounts by those who could not write were transcribed by those who could. As for personal handwritten materials (such as personal letters) by people with rudimentary literacy levels, if their authors could write, they would unavoidably have been exposed to StE at some point, however brief their learning time might have been. In consequence, this 'standard fact' should be kept in mind when devising and applying tools like, say, questionnaires for dialectal LPs analogous to those employed in LALME, to any of the many electronic sources available, or to those digitised specially.

Finally, we cannot be sure of the levels of literacy of the NORM (Non-mobile, Older, Rural Male) informants for SED or Wagner's oral sources described in sections 1.2 and 2.1 above; but even in the case that they might have been very low or even non-

---

[25] For the characterisation of the English standardisation process, I follow Trudgill (2003: 24, 127–128).

existent, traditional dialects are not living fossils, despite their distinctive ME inheritance: in their long histories, many extralinguistic circumstances have affected them. Among the most influential, we can mention population movements, political issues and, in recent times, the mass media; as for education, Hughes and Trudgill write: 'In British schools great efforts are made by teachers to eradicate features of local dialect from the speech and, more particularly, the writing of their pupils', and 'the longer a child stays in school, and the more successful he is, the less regionally marked, grammatically and lexically, will be his speech' (Hughes and Trudgill 1980 [1979]: 11). It is possible, in consequence, that some dialectal traits might still be found (as it was the case in EModE legal documents from the north of the country, cf. Fernández-Cuesta & Amores-Carredano 2012: 81–82), but others may not be recoverable at all, not even from these NORM speakers.

References

An Anglo-Saxon Dictionary, based on the manuscript collections of the late Joseph Bosworth, edited and enlarged by T. Northcote Toller (available at https://www.ling.upenn.edu/~kurisuto/germanic/oe_bosworthtoller_about.html).
Aston, Guy (1997). 'Small and large corpora in language learning', in Barbara Lewandowska-Tomaszczyk and Patrick Melia (eds), *Proceedings of PALC 97*, Lodz: Lodz University Press, pp. 51–62.
Baugh, Albert C. and Thomas Cable (2005). *A History of the English Language*, 5th edition, London: Routledge.
Benskin, Michael, Margaret Laing, Vasilis Karaiskos and K. Williamson (2013–). *An Electronic Version of A Linguistic Atlas of Late Mediaeval English*, Edinburgh: The University of Edinburgh (available at http://www.lel.ed.ac.uk/ihd/elalme/elalme.html).
Bourdieu, Pierre (1990). *The Logic of Practice* [translated by R. Nice], Cambridge: Polity Press.
Burnard, Lou (2007). *Reference Guide for the British National Corpus* (XLM edition) (available at http://www.natcorp.ox.ac.uk/docs/URG/).
Clark, Cecily (1957). 'Gender in *The Peterborough Chronicle* 1070–1154', *English Studies* 38: 109–115.
Classen, E. (1919). 'On the origin of natural gender in Middle English', *Modern Language Review* 14: 97–103.
Curzan, Anne (2003). *Gender Shifts in the History of English*, Cambridge: Cambridge University Press.
Dahl, Östen (2000). 'Animacy and the notion of semantic gender', in Barbara Unterbeck and Matti Rissanen (eds), *Gender in Grammar and Cognition*, Berlin and New York: Mouton de Gruyter, pp. 99–115.
Denison, David (2007 [1998]). 'Syntax', in Suzanne Romaine (ed.), *The Cambridge History of the English Language*, vol. 4, Cambridge: Cambridge University Press, pp. 92–329.
DOE: Dictionary of Old English: A to H online (available at http://tapor.library.utoronto.ca/doe/).

Elworthy, Frederic Thomas (1886). *The West Somerset Word-book*, London: Trübner & Co.
Fernández-Cuesta, Julia and José Gabriel Amores-Carredano (2012). 'The SCONE Corpus of Northern English', in Vázquez (ed.), pp. 75–100.
Görlach, Manfred (1999). 'Regional and social variation', in Roger Lass (ed.), *The Cambridge History of the English Language*, vol. 3, Cambridge: Cambridge University Press, pp. 459–539.
Guzmán-González, Trinidad (1989). 'El Género Atribuido en Lengua Inglesa: Textos Poéticos de los Siglos XVIII, XIX y XX' ['Assigned gender in English: Poetical texts from the 18th, 19th and 20th centuries'], PhD dissertation, León: University of León.
Guzmán-González, Trinidad (2002). 'Feminine assigned gender for ships: Just a metaphor?', in Isabel Moskowich-Spiegel, Begoña Crespo-García, Emma Lezcano-González and Begoña Simal-González (eds), *Re-Interpretations of English: Essays on Language, Linguistics and Philology*, vol. 1, A Coruña: Universidade da Coruña, pp. 45–62.
Guzmán-González, Trinidad (2012a). 'Ic Ælfric wolde þas lytlan boc a-wendan to Engliscum ge-reorde . . .: A translator, a grammarian, a teacher', in Juan J. Lanero-Fernández and José L. Chamosa-González (eds), *Lengua, Traducción, Recepción. En Honor de Julio César Santoyo / Language, Translation, Reception. To Honor Julio César Santoyo*, vol. 2, León: Universidad de León, pp. 247–266.
Guzmán-González, Trinidad (2012b). 'Assigned gender in eighteenth-century prose: A corpus study', in Vázquez (ed.), pp. 269–291.
Guzmán-González, Trinidad (2013a). 'Gender assignment in present-day scientific English: A case study in the field of zoology journals', in Isabel Verdaguer, Natalia Judit Laso and Danica Salazar (eds), *Biomedical English: A Corpus-based Approach*, Amsterdam: Benjamins, pp. 145–163.
Guzmán-González, Trinidad (2013b). 'Gender, grammar, social networks and Robert Lowth', in Daniel García-Velasco, Santiago González, Francisco Martín-Miguel, Ana I. Ojea-López and Rodrigo Pérez-Lorido (eds), *A Life in Language. Estudios en Homenaje al Profesor José Luis González Escribano*, Oviedo: Ediciones de la Universidad de Oviedo, pp. 197–222.
Guzmán-González, Trinidad (2015). 'Assigned gender in a corpus of nineteenth-century correspondence among settlers of the American Great Plains', in Marina Dossena (ed.), *Transatlantic Perspectives in Late Modern English*, Amsterdam: Benjamins, pp. 199–218.
Guzmán-González, Trinidad and Santiago González (2005). '"Why Furies were made female": An approach to gender assignment in 18th-century language treatises', in Ewa Borkowska and María José Álvarez-Maurín (eds), *The Margins of Europe: Cultural and Linguistic Identities*, Silesia: University of Silesia Press, pp 81–109.
Hogg, Richard M. (1992). 'Phonology and morphology', in Richard M. Hogg (ed.), *The Cambridge History of the English Language*, vol. 1, Cambridge: Cambridge University Press, pp. 67–167.
Hogg, Richard M. (2002). *An Introduction to Old English*, Edinburgh: Edinburgh University Press.

Hughes, Arthur and Peter Trudgill (1980 [1979]). *English Accents and Dialects*, London: Edward Arnold.
Ibrahim, Muhammad Hasan (1973). *Grammatical Gender. Its Origin and Development*, The Hague and Paris: De Gruyter Mouton.
Ihalainen, Ossi (1985). 'He took the bottle and put 'n in his pocket: The object pronoun *it* in present-day Somerset', in Wolfgang Viereck (ed.), *Focus on: England and Wales*, Amsterdam: Benjamins, pp. 153–161.
Ihalainen, Ossi (1994). 'The dialects of England since 1776', in Robert Burchfield (ed.), *The Cambridge History of the English language*, vol. 5, Cambridge: Cambridge University Press, pp. 197–276.
Jones, Charles (1988). *Grammatical Gender in English: 950 to 1250*, Beckenham: Croom Helm.
Komen, Erwin R., Rosanne Hebing, Ans van Kemenade and Bettelou Los (2014). 'Quantifying information structure change in English', in Kristine Bech and Kristine G. Eide (eds), *Information Structure and Syntactic Change in Germanic and Romance Languages* [Linguistik Aktuell/Linguistics Today 213], Amsterdam/Philadelphia: Benjamins, pp. 81–110.
Laing, Margaret (2012). 'John Whittokesmede as parliamentarian and horse owner in Yale University Library, Beinecke MS 163', *SELIM. Journal of the Spanish Society for Medieval English and Literature* 17: 1–72.
Laing, Margaret (2013–). *A Linguistic Atlas of Early Middle English 1150–1325*, Edinburgh: The University of Edinburgh (available at http://www.lel.ed.ac.uk/ihd/laeme2/laeme2.html).
Laing, Margaret and Roger Lass (2013). 'Introduction. Chapter 4: Tagging', *A Linguistic Atlas of Early Middle English 1150–1325*, Edinburgh: The University of Edinburgh (available at http://www.lel.ed.ac.uk/ihd/laeme2/laeme_intro_ch4.html).
Lass, Roger (1992). 'Phonology and morphology', in Norman Blake (ed.), *The Cambridge History of the English Language*, vol. 2, Cambridge: Cambridge University Press, pp. 23–155.
Lass, Roger (1999). 'Introduction', in Roger Lass (ed.), *The Cambridge History of the English Language*, vol. 3, Cambridge: Cambridge University Press, pp. 9–12.
McIntosh, Angus, M. L. Samuels and Michael Benskin (1986). 'Introduction to linguistic profiles', *A Linguistic Atlas of Late Middle English*, vol. III, Aberdeen: Aberdeen University Press (available at http://www.lel.ed.ac.uk/ihd/elalme/intros/atlas_intro_lps.html).
MED: Middle English Dictionary (available at http://quod.lib.umich.edu/m/med/).
Moore, Samuel (1921). 'Grammatical and natural gender in Middle English', *PMLA* 36(1): 79–103.
Mustanoja, Tauno F. (1960). *A Middle English Syntax. Part I: Parts of Speech*, Helsinki: Société Néophilologique.
Nevalainen, Terttu and Helena Raumolin-Brunberg (1994). '*Its* strength and the beauty of *it*: The standardization of the third person neuter possessive in Early Modern English', in Dieter Stein and Ingrid Tieken-Boon van Ostade (eds), *Towards a Standard English 1600–1800*, Berlin: Mouton de Gruyter, pp. 171–216.

OED: *Oxford English Dictionary* (available at http://www.oed.com/).
Paddock, Harold (1991). 'The actuation problem for gender change in Wessex versus Newfoundland', in Peter Trudgill and J. K. Chambers (eds), *Dialects of English: Studies in Grammatical Variation*, London and New York: Longman, pp. 29–46.
Quirk, Randolph, Sidney Greenbaum, Geoffrey Leech and Jan Svartvik (1985). *A Comprehensive Grammar of the English Language*, London/New York: Longman.
Rissanen, Matti, Merja Kytö, Leena Kahlas-Tarkka, Matti Kilpiö, Irma Taavitsainen, Terttu Nevalainen and Helena Raumolin-Brunberg (1991). *The Helsinki Corpus of English Texts*, Helsinki: University of Helsinki (available at http://www.helsinki.fi/varieng/CoRD/corpora/HelsinkiCorpus/index.html).
Siemund, Peter (2008). *Pronominal Gender in English: A Study of English Varieties from a Cross-Linguistic Perspective*, London: Routledge.
Singer, R. (2010). 'Creativity in the use of gender agreement in Mawng', *Studies in Language* 34(2): 382–416. DOI: 10.1075/sl.34.2.06sin
Stenroos, Merja (2008). 'Order out of chaos? The English gender change in the Southwest Mildands as a process of semantically based reorganization', *English Language and Linguistics* 12(3): 445–473.
Stenroos, Merja, Martti Mäkinen, Simon Horobin and Jeremy Smith (2011). *The Middle English Grammar Corpus*, version 2011.1, Stavanger: University of Stavanger (available at http://www.uis.no/research/history-languages-and-literature/the-mest-programme/the-middle-english-grammar-corpus-meg-c/meg-c-files/).
Trudgill, Peter (1990). *The Dialects of England*, Oxford: Blackwell.
Trudgill, Peter (2003). *A Glossary of Sociolinguistics*, Edinburgh: Edinburgh University Press.
Upton, Clive, David Parry and J. D. A. Widdowson (1994). *Survey of English Dialects: The Dictionary and Grammar*, London: Routledge.
Vázquez, Nila (ed.) (2012). *Creation and Use of Historical Linguistic Corpora in Spain*, Cambridge: Cambridge Scholars Publishing.
Wagner, Susanne (2002–3). 'Gender in English pronouns. Myth and reality', PhD thesis, Freiburg: Albert-Ludwigs-Universität.
Wagner, Susanne (2005). 'Gender in English pronouns: Southwest England', in Bernd Kortmann, Tanja Herrmann, Lukas Pietsch and Susanne Wagner (eds), *A Comparative Grammar of British English Dialects: Agreement, Gender, Relative Clauses*, Berlin and New York: Mouton de Gruyter, pp. 211–367.
Wakelin, Martyn F. (1972). *English Dialects: An Introduction*, London: The Athlone Press.
Wakelin, Martyn F. (1986). *The Southwest of England*, Amsterdam and Philadelphia: Benjamins.

Appendix

{C} Oxford, Bodleian Library, Tanner 196: *Mirk's Instructions for Parish Priests*. (MEG-C L5020). 15th c.
{D1} London, British Library, Cotton Roll ii.11, language A: 3 *Documents from Crediton*. (LAEME #147). Last quarter 13th c.

{D2} London, British Library, L Cotton Roll ii.11, language B: *Document from Crediton*. (LAEME #148). Last quarter 13th c.

{D3} London, British Library, Harley 2386: Excerpts from *Mandeville's Travels*. (MEG-C L5040). 2nd quarter 15th c.

{D4} *Letters and Papers of John Shillingford, Mayor of Exeter, 1447–50*. Camden Society, NS. II Ed. S. A. Moore, New York, 1975 (1871). PP. 8.10-1732 (IV): Shillingford to his fellows, London, 2 Nov. 1447. (HC CMPRIV). 2nd quarter 15th c.

{Do1} London, British Library, Add 46487: *Sherborne Cartulary*, fols 24v–25r. (LAEME #279). 2nd quarter 13th c.

{Do2} London, British Library, Add. 11748: *Poem on the Instruments of the Passion*. (MEG-C L5340). 15th c.

{So1} Wells, Wells Cathedral Library, *Liber Albus I*, language 1, fol. 14r. (LAEME #156). c.1240.

{So2} Wells, Wells Cathedral Library, *Liber Albus I*, language 2, fols 17v–18r. (LAEME #157). c.1240.

{So3} Aberdeen, Aberdeen University Library 154, fol. 368v: *Couplet and Three Quatrains*. (LAEME #163). Last quarter 13th–1st quarter 14th c.

{So4} Oxford, Bodleian Library, Ashmole 189: *Golden Table of Pythagoras, Lunary and Religious Verse*. (MEG-C L5171a1). Late 15th c.

{W1} Cambridge, Emmanuel College 27, fols 111v, 162r–163r: *Lyrics*. (LAEME #140). 1st quarter 14th c.

{W2} Salisbury, Salisbury Cathedral Library 82, f. 271v: *Pater Noster*. (LAEME #258). 2nd half 13th c.

{W3} London, British Library, Royal 2.F.viii, fol. 1v: *Lyric* (LAEME #263). Last quarter 13th c.

{W4} London, British Library, Cotton Otho C xiii, fols 1r–146v: *Layamon B*. (LAEME #280). 3rd quarter 13th c.

{W5} London, British Library, Harley 3840, Hand A: *Agnus Castus*. (MEG-C L5311a). c.1425.

{W6} Yale University Library, Beinecke MS 163 (olim Wagstaff 9, olim Pentworth 8). c.1460–1470.

Index

A Prayer for King, Queen and People, 215;
   see also Lydgate, John
abbreviation, 45, 72, 92, 188–209
acquisition, 160, 176; *see also* affricate
acroke, 219–20
adversary, 223, 238
affricate, 94, 157–80
affrication, 157, 161–2, 169, 176, 178, 180
alliteration, 103–4, 162–3, 172–4
allophone, 119, 124, 134, 158, 164, 171
alveolar, 118, 176
American English, 125, 161
Amphytrion, 224; *see also* Plautus
anaphor, 244, 246, 248, 249, 251, 253–6, 258–9
Ancrene Riwle, 34, 166, 179
Ancrene Wisse, 28
Anglian, 73, 113, 116, 118–21; *see also* East Anglia(n)
Anglicisation, 39–42, 50–4, 57
Anglo-Norman, 157, 174–5, 254, 257
animacy, 33
   animacy hierarchy, 249, 256
Annotald, 28
apocope, 222, 231
apostrophe, 62
Asloan, MS 69
assibilation, 161–4, 169, 179–80
assummon, 219, 239
Auchinleck manuscript, 223, 229, 235
aureate, 219, 239
Australian English, 125
authorship, 46, 236

autograph, 133, 230, 238
auto-rhyme *see* rhyme
Ayenbite of Inwyt, 21, 28, 30–1, 34

back vowel *see* vowel
back-mutation, 141
back-spelling (*also* reverse spelling), 62–3, 67–8, 70, 72, 79–85, 102, 117, 133, 135–7, 151–2, 234
bas(s), 219
bedreint, 218–19
bequeath, 103
Berkshire, 129, 141–2, 149, 246
Bevis of Hampton, 229
bid, 161, 227
bloom, 236
Boece, 71
Bokenham, Osbern, 227, 233, 240
book production, 215–16
book trade, 216, 237
borrowing, 67, 72, 82–3, 157, 161, 171–2, 175–6, 180, 220, 236, 254, 257
   of orthographic traditions, 100
   see also loanword
boun, 235
breaking, 65, 67, 134
bridge, 164, 180, 219
British Library, MS Harley, 65, 79, 230
Brut Chronicle, 32–3
burgh, 39, 44, 47, 58
   court and council, 41, 43, 190–1, 199, 209
   records, 41–2, 46–7, 50, 53, 67, 199–201, 204, 209

INDEX

Cambridge, 218–19
Cambridge, Trinity College, MS R.3.19, 212–13, 215–16
Cambridge, Trinity College, MS R.3.21, 215–16
can, 227–8, 238, 240
Canterbury Tales: Reeve's Tale, 235; *see also* Chaucer, Geoffrey
Capgrave, John, 29, 223, 226, 229–30, 232–3, 240
Caroline <g>, 178–9
Caxton, William, 216, 219, 231
celsitude, 219–20, 239
centre vowel *see* vowel
chain shift, 124–6; *see also* drag-chain; push-chain; Early Vowel Shift Hypothesis; Great Vowel Shift; Northern Cities Shift
Chancery standard, 239
Charles the Bold, 217
charter, 69, 194, 198–201, 209
Chaucer, Geoffrey, 28, 34, 157, 212–13, 215–16, 218–20, 223–7, 231, 233, 235, 237, 240
    manuscripts, 215–16, 222, 226–7, 229–30
cherish, 225, 227
child, 157, 162, 172–4, 252–3, 258
Chronicle from Rolle to Edward IV, 216
Civil War, 53
clerk, 39, 46–53, 57, 236, 239
cluster h-deletion, 107–8
cluster w-deletion, 107–8
cluster x-lenition, 107–8
Cockney, 62, 125
cognate, 63, 106, 117
collocation, 244, 251
colt, 253–4, 256
community of practice, 39, 42, 44, 46, 50, 53
Complex Segment Representation, 160
CoNE (*Corpus of Narrative Etymologies*), 6, 9, 11, 91–3, 102, 106–7, 110, 161–2, 169–72, 177–80, 188
Confessio Amantis, 223; *see also* Gower, John
contact (and linguistic change), 39, 40–1, 57, 158, 175, 180, 255
contour segment, 159–60, 163–5, 170, 172, 174–80
Contour Segment Representation, 160
contraction, 44–5
Coote, Edmund, 232
Cornwall, 246–9, 251, 259
coronal, 64, 68, 77–80, 82–3, 118, 190
corpus/corpora, 1, 4–6, 21–2, 39, 41, 46, 61, 65, 70–2, 187–8, 195, 201, 206, 208, 215, 249; *see also* CoNE; Corpus of Middle English Prose and Verse; DOE Web Corpus; Dunfermline Corpus; Edinburgh Twitter Corpus; eLALME; FITS Corpus; HC; HCOS; LAEME; LAOS; ME Alliterative Corpus; MEG-C; MELD; Online Salamanca Corpus of English Dialect Texts; PCEEC; PCMEP; PLAEME; PPCEME; PPCHE; PPCMBE; PPCME; SCONE; ScotsCorr; TEAMS digital Corpus; YCOE
Corpus of Middle English Prose and Verse, 240
correspondence, 42–3; *see also* Paston Letters; Stonor Letters
court and council records *see* burgh records
Court of Love, 212–40
covert gender system *see* gender system
cuckold, 219–20
cwēman ('please'), 103–5
cweþan ('speak'), 102

dative, 21, 31
default, 205, 245–6, 248, 251, 256, 258
deformity, 219–20
degemination, 164, 167–70
deletion, 96, 105, 176; *see also* cluster h-; cluster w-
demean, 219
dental, 55, 113, 118, 137, 161, 168, 175, 177, 226
descrive, 227
descry, 227
desire, 230, 237–8
devoicing, 95
Devon, 230, 246–9, 251–2, 259
diacritic, 79–80, 82, 84, 116–17, 122; *see also* digraph
    indicating length, 67, 72, 79, 83, 116–17
    frication, 94, 110
    diphthongisation, 67, 72, 79, 83
diagnostic, 2–4, 11, 40, 53, 61, 188–9, 193, 214, 233
dialect, 1–2, 21, 98, 102, 172, 180, 214–15, 218, 230–3, 246, 259, 261; *see also* Anglian; Cornwall; Devon; Dorset; East Anglia; East Midlands; East Saxon; Glaswegian; Gloucestershire; Herefordshire; Kentish; Lincolnshire; London English; Norfolk; North; North-East Midlands; North-West

dialect (*cont.*)
    Midlands; northernism; Old English dialects; Oxfordshire; Shropshire; Somerset; South; South-East; South-Western; Staffordshire; Suffolk; Sussex; Warwickshire; West Midlands; West Saxon; Wiltshire; Worcestershire; Yorkshire
dialect atlas/survey, 3, 98, 246; *see also* LAEME; LALME; SED; SMED
  continuum, 3–4, 139
  questionnaire, 1, 4, 7, 102, 138–41, 149, 152, 249, 251, 260
  words, 235, 239
diatopic variation, 1, 43, 246
did, 232
die, 220, 224–5, 238
diffusion, 35, 39, 41–2, 50, 84, 146
Digby, MS 86, 26
digitisation, 2, 4–5, 213, 249, 259–60
digraph, 69, 94, 113, 117, 121, 139, 141, 147, 165
diphthong(al), 62, 65, 82, 84, 116–18, 124, 133–5, 157, 171, 225
Diphthong Shift, 125
diphthongisation, 63, 65–7, 72, 79, 83, 124–5
diplomatic transcription, 4–7, 23, 71, 137, 191
direct, 218–19
discourse, 22, 40, 43, 49–50, 245, 250–1, 256
distress, 231, 238
ditransitive, 21, 31–33, 35
DOE Web Corpus, 92, 99
Dorset, 123, 246, 248–9, 251, 259
drag-chain, 124–5; *see also* chain shift
Dunfermline Corpus, 39–58
duration, 161, 163, 170–1
Dutch, 2, 236

Earliest Prose Psalter, 29–31, 34
Early Modern English, 31–2, 35, 115, 248
Early Scots *see* Older Scots
Early Vowel Shift Hypothesis, 122, 124
East Anglia(n), 214–15, 221, 223, 226–7, 232–4, 237, 239
East Midlands, 102, 116, 118–19, 121, 127–9, 134, 230, 260; *see also* North-East Midlands; South-East Midlands; West Midlands
East Saxon, 113, 119, 126
edge effect, 160–1
Edh (<ð>), 23
Edinburgh Twitter Corpus, 187–8

Edmund de la Pole, 231, 233
Edward IV, 215–17
eLALME (*Electronic Linguistic Atlas of Mediæval English*), 6–7, 91–2, 99, 101, 103–4, 108, 138, 188, 214, 223–35, 237, 239, 251
epicene, 257
ere, 238–9
erst, 239–40
Estuary English, 125
etymology, 80, 92–3, 100, 106–7, 109, 115, 120, 220

fare, 225
feature rhyme *see* rhyme
fellow, 224, 226, 238
female, 244–5, 249, 256–9
feminine, 143, 166, 244, 247, 253–8
figura, 93–4, 137, 178
final *e*, 220
final *n see* nunnation
fire, 150, 231–2, 237–8
FITS (From Inglis to Scots), 6, 61–85, 136
fit-technique, 3, 7
fitting tool, 232
flawe, 218–19
forbid, 225, 238
formulaic language, 45–6
fortition, 92, 100, 102, 106–8, 179
found, 228–9, 238–9
free relative, 27
French, 20, 22, 94, 99–100, 117, 121, 149, 151, 176, 230–1, 255 *see* Old French; Borrowing
  Borrowings; l-vocalisation, 67, 82, 85
fricative, 55, 94–5, 97–98, 100, 105–8, 110, 137, 157–62, 164, 168, 176–8, 233–4, 239
  voicing, 248
friend, 138, 140, 230–1
fronting, 125

Garland of Laurell, 230; *see also* Skelton, John
gave, 213, 221, 235, 237–8
gender assignment, 244, 248, 250, 253, 258, 259
  system, 244–5, 248–9, 258
  fluid, 253–4
General Masculine Declension (GMD), 248, 256
General Neuter Declension (GND), 256
Genesis and Exodus, 27, 34, 221
genitive, 220, 222, 235–6, 252

genre, 20, 22, 39–41, 43, 50–2, 58
geographical distribution, 92, 100
Germanic, 6, 40, 67–8, 72–3, 79, 81–4, 92, 125, 133, 157–8, 174, 189; see also West Germanic
gestural overshoot/undershoot, 125
given, 213, 235
Glasgow, University of Glasgow, MS Hunter 409, 218
Glaswegian, 62, 69
Gloucestershire, 114, 118, 129, 141–2, 144, 149
Gower, John, 223, 233, 235
grammatical change, 29, 35
grammatical features, 39–41, 43
grammatical gender, 244, 248–9, 254, 257
grammatical tagging, 4–6, 20, 23–4, 46, 71, 191, 194
grammel, 23–5, 27, 191–2, 251
Great Vowel Shift (GVS), 70, 113, 114, 122–4, 126
Greek, 94, 236, 257
Grimm's Law, 92, 107

hard, 223–5, 238
Havelok, 96, 102, 118
HC (*Helsinki Corpus of English Texts*), 22, 42, 249, 257
HCOS (*Helsinki Corpus of Older Scots*), 42–3
he, 244–6, 253–9
-head, 226
heart, 107, 224–5
Henry IV, 217
Herebert, William, 133, 140, 148, 150
Herefordshire, 114, 121, 129–30, 141–4, 149, 219
Higden, Ranulf, 219
Hilton, Walter, 230
historical dialectology, 1–2, 4, 6–8, 36, 42–3, 61, 77, 161, 187–8, 195
Historical Gazetteer of English Placenames, 219
Hoccleve, Thomas, 233
horse, 249–50, 252–4, 257
hwōn ('few'), 97
hybrid form, 42; *see also* non-canonical form

iambic pentameter, 220
identity marker, 135, 152
idiolect, 39, 42, 45–6, 48, 52–5, 57, 77, 106
  idiolectal variation, 25, 44, 101
ilk, 51, 220
imperative, 115, 168

indefinite article, 51
infinitive, 115, 117, 215, 220
informant, 48–9, 51–2, 247, 260
Initial Cluster Assimilation, 107–8
Insular <ȝ>, 23, 97, 165
Insular <g>, 178
intill, 236, 238–9
into, 236, 238
-ish, 227
it (hit), 244–7, 250–6, 258–9

Kempe, Margery, 223
Kentish, 113, 116, 118, 120
Kentish Sermons, 21–2, 30
kind, 232
kite, 234, 238
kw-lenition, 102, 107, 109

La Belle Dame Sans Mercy, 222; *see also* Roos, Richard
labial, 62, 64, 68, 77–8, 80, 82, 92, 94, 96, 108
labiovelar, 92, 94
LAEME (*Linguistic Atlas of Early Middle English*), 2, 4–7, 19, 22–8, 30, 36, 43, 91–9, 101–2, 106, 108, 114–24, 126–30, 136, 167, 172, 177, 179, 187–8, 249, 251; *see also* PLAEME
LALME (*Linguistic Atlas of Late Mediæval English*), 43, 91, 98, 106, 115, 124, 135–8, 142–4, 146, 152, 190–2, 219, 249, 251, 260; *see also* eLALME
land, 228–9
LAOS (*Linguistic Atlas of Older Scots*), 2, 4–5, 6, 39, 43–6, 71, 77, 82–4, 91–2, 100, 106, 188–201, 203–4, 206, 209
Late Modern English, 248
Latin, 40, 45, 67, 82–3, 93–4, 100, 107, 149, 151, 157, 175, 188, 194, 220–1, 224, 245, 249, 254–7, 259
Layamon, 95, 172, 221, 254
legal documents *see* burgh records
legal language, 43, 53
Legend of Good Women, 222; *see also* Chaucer, Geoffrey
lemmatisation, 7, 21
lenition, 93, 98, 100, 102, 106, 108, 170, 176–9; *see also* kw-lenition; cluster x-lenition
Lewis, C. S., 213, 222, 236
lexeme, 6, 102, 105, 115–17, 122, 130
lexical leader, 123–4
Life of St Katherine, 226, 229–30; *see also* Capgrave, John

like, 230–1, 238–9
Lincolnshire, 95, 101–2, 123, 128–9, 134, 169, 223
linguistic habit, 257–8
linguistic profile (LP), 3, 7, 98, 102, 138, 191, 219, 224, 226, 237, 251, 260
Littera, 93–4, 97, 137
litteral substitution set, 136, 150
loanword, 149, 151, 158, 175–6, 178, 255
location of manuscripts, 2, 71, 73, 77, 194, 198, 202–3, 206, 208–9
London English, 224, 227, 229, 232, 237, 239
London records, 226, 235
long vowel *see* vowel
Lovelich, Henry, 233
l-vocalisation, 61–85
lowering of *i*, 122, 227, 230–1, 234, 239
Lydgate, John, 212, 215–17, 220, 223–6, 229–30, 232–3, 236–7, 239

McIntosh, Angus, 1, 3, 91, 101
macro-level variable, 41
male, 244–6, 249, 256–8, 260
Malory, Thomas, 219
man, 21, 23, 227–8, 240
Mannyng, Robert, 223
manuscript, 4–7, 20–1, 23, 28, 39, 43–6, 48, 51, 57–8, 71, 97, 104, 137, 146–7, 152, 172, 187–209; *see also* Asloan MS; Auchinleck MS; British Library; Chaucer, Geoffrey; Digby MS; Cambridge; Glasgow; New Haven; Oxford; San Marino
Margaret of York, 217, 237
masculine, 244, 246–8, 251–9
ME Alliterative Corpus, 174
MED (*Middle English Dictionary*), 92, 97, 99–100, 102–4, 106, 166, 173, 213, 219–20, 223–5, 227, 230–1, 235–6, 240, 257
MEG-C (*Middle English Grammar Corpus*), 5–7, 133, 137–9, 143–4, 149, 152, 249
MELD (*Corpus of Middle English Local Documents*), 5–7
MEOSL (Middle English Open Syllable Lengthening), 122, 125, 166, 169–71
merger, 68, 70, 82, 108, 113, 123, 125, 134–6, 141, 143, 151–2
MEST (Middle English Scribal Texts programme), 5
metadata, 5–6, 22
Metamorphoses, 223

metathesis, 220
metre, 22, 33, 163–6, 169, 172, 212–3, 215, 218, 220–2, 224, 236–7
metrician, 218–19, 239
micro-perspective, 44, 46, 50, 57
mid vowel *see* vowel
Middle Dutch, 2
Middle English, 3, 19–36, 63, 67, 83, 85, 91–110, 113–130, 133–153, 156–80, 189–90, 193, 213–15, 218, 221–2, 225, 227, 230–4, 236, 239, 244–61; *see also* corpus/corpora; MED
Middle English Dictionary *see* MED
Middle English Grammar Project, 5; *see also* MEG-C
Middle Scots, 40–1, 69–70, 189; *see also* Older Scots; Transition Scots
might, 233–4
mind, 232
mine (my), 235
Mirk, John, 216
Mischsprache, 214–15, 222, 224, 239
model, 6, 31–3, 42–3, 136, 187, 195–6, 200–1, 204–6, 208–9; *see also* statistics
generalised additive (GAM), 195–6, 200–2, 204–6, 208
linear, 195–6
mixed effect, 20, 187
Probability Multiplication, 32–3
regression, 195, 204, 208
monophthong, 117, 119, 123, 125, 134–5, 222, 225
monosyllabic, 83–4, 95, 123, 167, 170, 222
morpheme, 4, 6, 23, 45, 72–5, 77–80, 83–4, 106, 149, 188–9, 191–2

names/proper nouns, 47–9, 149, 151, 223–4, 258
narrative etymology (of *hw*), 106–10
nasal, 55, 78, 119, 122, 164, 227, 229, 239; *see also* rounding
negation, 21, 29–30, 35
neuter, 245, 249, 252–4, 256, 258
New Haven, CT, Yale University Library, Beinecke, MS 171, 219
Newburgh, Scotland, 76, 199
night, 233, 239
non erst, 239–40
non-canonical form, 42, 54
Norfolk, 100–2, 114, 117, 128, 130, 223, 225, 229–30, 233–7, 239
Norman Conquest, 63, 67, 82–3, 94–5, 113, 161, 178

North, 5, 67, 94, 99, 101–3, 108–9, 116–18, 127–8, 163, 177, 190, 226
North-East Midlands, 94, 98, 101, 108, 163, 223, 225, 229, 235, 237
North-West Midlands, 101, 103, 108, 139
Northamptonshire, 108, 118, 128
Northern Cities Shift, 125
northernism, 235
notarial protocol book, 199–201, 209
notary, 47, 50, 200
notional (gender), 249
noun, 27, 80, 115, 188–9, 192, 194, 220, 235, 244–9, 252–6, 258–9
noun phrase, 20, 248–9, 257
nunnation, 221

OED (*Oxford English Dictionary*), 104–5, 164, 175, 213, 219–20, 224, 226–7, 230, 236, 252–3, 256–7
Old English, 6, 20, 21, 28–9, 63, 67–71, 78, 80, 91–108, 113–30, 133–43, 145–7, 149–52, 157–8, 160–8, 170–2, 174–6, 178–9, 189, 226–7, 230–4, 244, 246, 248, 252, 254–8
Old English $æ^1$ and $æ^2$, 113–30
Old English dialects *see* dialect
Old French, 2, 85, 138, 157, 174, 222, 227, 257
Old Frisian, 119, 158, 178
Old Irish, 158
Old Norse (ON), 68, 117, 138, 149, 151, 166, 168, 179, 226, 234–7, 254
Old Northumbrian, 64, 99, 189
Older Scots, 2, 4, 40, 42–3, 50, 61, 63–5, 69, 78, 92, 100, 108, 116, 180, 188–95, 201, 208
Online Salamanca Corpus of English Dialect Texts, 5, 259
Open Syllable Lengthening *see* MEOSL
Optical Character Recognition (OCR), 4
Ormulum, 22, 28, 118, 120, 126, 134, 166–8
orthoepists, 115, 135
orthographic remapping of palatal c (ORPC), 172, 179
orthographic variants, 25, 39, 41, 50, 52–4, 63–5, 70, 91–130, 135–6, 138, 152, 161, 165, 168–9, 178, 188–92, 206, 229, 234; *see also* spelling
Oxford, St John's College, MS 266, 216–17, 225, 227, 237
Oxford English Dictionary see OED
Oxfordshire, 118, 129, 141–2, 149, 229

palaeography, 1, 188
palatal hardening (PH), 177–8
palatalisation, 161–3, 180
palate-alveolar, 158
Parliament of Fowls, 222; *see also* Chaucer, Geoffrey
parliamentary acts, 40, 47
parsing, 6–7, 19–21, 23, 36, 71
participle, present 40, 51–3
past participle, 51, 54, 73, 117–18, 235
part-of-speech tag *see* tagging
past inflection, 55, 235
Paston Letters, 219, 225–6, 229, 231–3, 240
paten, 218–19
PCEEC (Parsed Corpus of Early English Correspondence), 21
PCMEP (Parsed Corpus of Middle English Poetry), 21, 32–3, 35
Penn Discourse Treebank, 22
periodisation (of Scots), 41, 189
personal names *see* names/proper nouns
Peterborough Chronicle, 134, 179, 248
Petigrew of England, 215–16, 237
Philogenet, 236
phoneme, 64, 120, 134, 136, 139, 158, 160, 223
phonemic status, 119, 121, 124, 147, 153, 158, 164–5, 167, 172, 177, 179
phonemic system, 135; *see also* merger
phonemic theory, 120
phonemic variants, 64
phonemicisation, 159
phonological conditioning, 55, 70
phonological environment, 65, 67, 73, 78, 80, 83, 85, 141, 168, 171, 176
Piers Plowman, 147–8, 173
pity, 231, 238
placement uncertainty, 95, 99, 110
place-names, 62, 69, 99, 253; *see also* Historical Gazetteer of English Placenames
PLAEME (*Parsed Linguistic Atlas of Early Middle English*), 6, 19–36
plaint, 222
Plautus, 224
plural, abbreviation symbol, 190
nominal, 40, 188–9, 192, 194, 221–2, 236
verbal, 115, 215, 220, 229, 235, 238
Poema Morale, 166–9
Poetria Nova, 224; *see also* Vinsauf, Geoffrey de
post-alveolar, 176
post-vocalic, 118, 129, 166, 172

Potestas, 93, 136–7
PPCEME (*Penn-Helsinki Parsed Corpus of Early Modern English*), 19
PPCHE (*Penn Parsed Corpora of Historical English*), 6, 19, 35
PPCMBE (*Penn Parsed Corpus of Modern British English*), 20
PPCME (*Penn-Helsinki Parsed Corpus of Middle English*), 19
pragmatic unit, 250–1; *see also* UAR
Pre-cluster shortening (PCS), 168, 171
Pre-Conquest *see* Norman Conquest; Old French
present participle *see* participle
Present-Day English (PDE), 31, 84, 93, 95, 98, 108, 115, 157–61, 165, 170–73, 176, 178, 191–2, 239, 244–5
Present-Day Scots, 62, 71, 80
preterite *see* past inflection
Prick of Conscience, 147–8
principle of equal phonetic spacing, 125
printed text, 4, 41, 53
printer, 41
privy, 231, 234, 238
Promptorium Parvulorum, 223
prong, 236
pronoun, personal 24, 27, 143, 237, 244–7, 249–54, 256–7, 259
 relative, 24, 33
 R-pronoun, 34
prose, 19–22, 30, 35–6, 43, 51–2, 191, 193, 215
provenance, 3, 21, 43, 215, 222, 224, 231, 247, 257, 260
push-chain, 123–5; *see also* chain shift

quaint, 103
quake, 102
quality, 103
quarry, 102
quart, 102
quarter, 102–3
Quattor Sermones, 216; *see also* Mirk, John
quey ('heifer'), 102
(quh)ilk, 51
quick, 98, 102, 109
quilt, 102
quit, 103

raising, 96, 114, 118, 120, 122–6, 171, 230
referent, 245, 250–2, 256
referential anaphoric act, 250

referential chain, 250
regional distribution, 76–7, 214
register, 40–1, 43, 85, 206, 209, 245, 256, 259; *see also* genre
register books, 44; *see also* burgh records
regression model *see* model
relative clause, 27, 34–5, 50; *see also* free relative; *wh*-relative
relative pronoun, 24, 33–5; *see also* R-pronoun
relict, 146–7, 214–15, 224, 233, 237
require, 225, 227, 238
resolution (metrical), 163–4
retention *see* spelling
retraction, 119, 126
reversal, 92, 95, 102, 159
reverse spelling *see* back-spelling
revoicing, 94–5, 108
rhyme, 22, 27, 33, 85, 121–2, 146, 212, 214–15, 217, 222–34, 237–40; *see also rime riche*
 auto-rhyme, 223
 feature rhyme, 222
 subsequence rhyme, 222
rich, 230–1
rime riche, 223
Roland and Vernagu, 235
Romance, 68, 72–3, 82–5, 133, 178, 221, 254; *see also* French; Old French
Romaunt of the Rose, 218, 220
Roos, Richard, 222
rounding, 141, 150–1
 of *a* before nasals, 21, 96, 227–8, 239
roundness, 150, 152
R-pronoun, 34

San Marino, Huntington Library, MS HM 55, 230
sang, 228–9, 238
Scale of Perfection, 230; *see also* Hilton, Walter
SCONE (*Seville Corpus of Northern English*), 5, 259
Scottish Standard English, 40
Scottish Vowel Length Rule, 69
Scots, 1, 4, 6, 36, 39–43, 45, 51–2, 54–5, 57–8, 61–4, 67–73, 76–80, 82–5, 96, 100, 171, 180, 189, 190, 193; *see also* Scottish Standard English; Middle Scots; Older Scots; Transition Scots
Scots Gaelic, 158
ScotsCorr (*Helsinki Corpus of Scottish Correspondence*), 43–5

scribe, 3, 30, 46, 48–54, 77, 82, 95–8, 104, 115–17, 118, 120–1, 126, 135, 137, 139, 150–3, 156, 178–9, 191, 194, 201, 208–9, 213–18, 221–31, 233–40, 255
  apprenticeship, 47, 50, 53
  profile, 117, 126
  revision, 216–18
  translation, 222, 224–6, 237
  updating, 227, 237
S-curve, 153
SED (*Survey of English Dialects*), 98, 102, 246–8, 252, 260
segment or sequence problem, 156–7
sex, 244, 246, 256–7, 259; *see also* gender
she, 138–41, 143–6, 244–6, 253, 256–7
sheen, 230
shine, 230–1
short vowel *see* vowel
should, 227, 238–9
Shropshire, 121, 129–30, 141–2, 144, 147, 149
sibilant, 55–6, 160, 162
sick, 122, 230
Siege of Thebes, 216, 229–30, 233, 237; *see also* Lydgate, John
sigla, 193, 197, 222
sink, 223
Skelton, John, 230
SMED (*Survey of Middle English Dialects*), 115–16, 118–19, 122–3
social networks, 42, 49
sojour, 223, 238
sojourn, 223
Somerset, 123, 129, 246–9, 251–2, 259
sonorant, 55–6, 108, 169
sound value, 63, 93
sound-to-spelling mapping, 6, 61–2, 71
South English Legendary, 147–8
South-East Midlands, 123, 229
South-West, 116, 123, 127, 129, 244
South-West Midlands, 26, 119, 134, 136, 141, 143–4, 149, 151–3
South-West Scotland, 190
spelling, 6–7, 21, 51, 54–5, 57, 61–4, 67, 69–73, 75–85, 92–109, 114–30, 133–53, 165, 168–9, 172–3, 177–9, 188, 212, 215, 219–20, 222, 224–34, 237–9, 246, 251
  normalisation, 7
  respelling, 67
  retention of <æ>, 119
  retention of <eo>, 146, 152
  retention of <l>, 64
  retention of <n>, 221–2

reverse spelling *see* back-spelling
variation, 6, 21, 84–5, 91–3, 99, 101–2, 105–6, 117–18, 121, 237, 252; *see also* orthographic variants
sprang, 229
Staffordshire, 129, 140–1, 149
stand, 228–9, 238
Standard English (StE), 62, 70, 260
standardisation, 39, 247, 260
  of coding procedures, 6
state documents, 199–200
statistics, 1, 20, 114, 117, 120–1, 126, 143, 187–8, 195, 198, 206; *see also* model
stir, 227, 238
Stonor Letters, 229
Stow, John, 212, 215, 217
Strident Stop Representation, 160
subsequence rhyme *see* rhyme
Suffolk, 102, 117, 123, 128–30, 223, 230–3, 235–6
suspension, 190, 193–4, 197; *see also* abbreviation
Sussex, 129, 140–1, 246
syllable, 78, 82–3, 95, 115, 123, 161, 163, 166, 176, 218–9, 223; *see also* MEOSL; monosyllabic
  closed, 228
  structure, 121, 169
  unstressed, 150, 161, 220
  weight, 161–3, 166–9, 172
syllable-final /l/, 62

tagging, 4–6, 20, 23, 27–8, 46, 191–2, 250–1
TEAMS digital corpus, 229
Temple of Glas, 224; *see also* Lydgate, John
temporal distribution, 71, 75–6
text language, 26, 101
text type, 41, 43, 45, 194, 198–9, 201, 204, 209, 244; *see also* genre
that, 34
their, 237
them, 237
thenk, 231, 238
thilk, 220
thine, 234–5
think, 231, 238
Thorn (<þ>), 23, 27
Thynne, William, 218
town council *see* burgh council
town court *see* burgh court
transcription, 5, 27, 45, 72, 135, 137, 161, 188, 191–3, 196–7, 213, 216, 249
Transition Scots, 39–44, 49, 57

transitional form, 42, 54–5; *see also* non-canonical form
Transkribus, 4
Treatise of Fishing, 219
Trevisa, John, 219
Trigraph, 139
 <quh>, 40, 51
Troilus and Criseyde, 216, 224; *see also* Chaucer, Geoffrey
truncation, 193–4; *see also* abbreviation

UAR (Unit of Anaphoric Reference), 250–1, 253–4, 258
unrounding, 124
ure, 235

velar, 69, 77–8, 80–2, 94, 97, 107–8, 161–9, 172, 175, 178–9
velar palatalisation (VP), 161–2, 180
verse, 19, 21–2, 26–7, 30, 33, 35–6, 67, 93, 103, 157, 163, 166–7, 178, 214, 220, 222–3
Vinsauf, Geoffrey de, 224
visualisation, 7, 196, 200, 205
vocalisation, 61–85
vowel, 62, 64–5, 67–70, 72–3, 79–83, 95, 116–17, 119–21, 123, 133–4, 138–41, 150–1, 156, 166, 170, 194, 225, 229, 234–5
 back, 62, 64–5, 72–3, 77, 79, 82–4
 central, 150
 front, 62–3, 113, 115, 122, 134, 150–1, 166, 171, 176, 227
 harmony, 122
 high, 124, 164, 166, 171
 lengthening, 63, 171, 233; *see also* MEOSL
 long, 65, 72, 79, 82, 84, 113–14, 120, 122–5, 133–5, 139, 161, 166, 168–72, 225, 229
 low, 120, 124
 mid-to-open, 115; *see also* raising
 rounded, 96, 134–5, 139, 141, 150–2
 short, 65, 69, 72, 77, 82–4, 122–3, 133–4, 141, 161, 166, 168–9, 171
 shortening, 114–5, 120, 122–3
 system, 125, 189–90

Wales, 140–1; *see also* Welsh marches
Warwickshire, 118, 141–2, 149, 236

weak past tense *see* past inflection
well, 225–6, 238
Welsh, 158
Welsh marches, 143, 152
Wessex, 247
West Country, 246–7
West Germanic, 61, 164; *see also* Germanic
West Midlands, 102
West-Saxon, 117, 119, 121, 126, 246
what, 92, 95–6, 98
wheat, 103
wheel, 98
whelp, 99
when, 92, 95–6
where, 34, 92, 95–6, 103, 233, 237–8
wherefore, 103
whether, 95
which, 34, 63, 92, 95–6, 98, 100
whichever, 97
while, 95, 103
whirr, 103
white, 96, 99, 103–5
whither, 96, 108
whitsunday, 100
who, 92, 96–8, 100, 108
whole, 108
whom, 95–8, 108
whore, 108
whose, 96–8, 108
whoso, 98
wh-relative, 22, 33–5
why, 108
Wiltshire, 129, 141, 149, 246–9, 251, 259
Worcestershire, 95, 114, 118, 121, 123, 129–30, 141, 149
word order, 22, 28, 31
writing system, 96, 135–6; *see also* spelling
Wynn (<ƿ>), 93–7, 99, 101

yet, 225–7, 238
YCOE (York-Toronto-Helsinki Corpus of Old English Prose), 20–1, 26
Yogh (<ȝ>), 23, 93, 97–9, 213, 233
yon, 149, 235, 238–9
yonder, 235, 238
Yorkist, 217
Yorkshire, 98, 101, 117, 123, 128, 130, 137, 177

EU representative:
Easy Access System Europe
Mustamäe tee 50, 10621 Tallinn, Estonia
Gpsr.requests@easproject.com

www.ingramcontent.com/pod-product-compliance
Lightning Source LLC
Chambersburg PA
CBHW051805230426

43672CB00012B/2635